# India's Mental Healthcare Act, 2017

Richard M. Duffy · Brendan D. Kelly

# India's Mental Healthcare Act, 2017

## Building Laws, Protecting Rights

With contributions by Soumitra Pathare,
Arjun Kapoor

Springer

Richard M. Duffy
Department of Psychiatry
Trinity Centre for Health Sciences
Tallaght University Hospital
Trinity College Dublin
Dublin, Ireland

Brendan D. Kelly
Department of Psychiatry
Trinity Centre for Health Sciences
Tallaght University Hospital
Trinity College Dublin
Dublin, Ireland

ISBN 978-981-15-5008-9 ISBN 978-981-15-5009-6 (eBook)
https://doi.org/10.1007/978-981-15-5009-6



This Springer imprint is published by the registered company Springer Nature Singapore Pte Ltd.
The registered company address is: 152 Beach Road, #21-01/04 Gateway East, Singapore 189721, Singapore

*This book is dedicated to our families.*

# Acknowledgements

We are very grateful to our collaborators in this work including, but not limited to, Prof. Gautam Gulati (University of Limerick, Ireland), Dr. Valerie Murphy (University College Cork), Dr. Vasudeo Paralikar (KEM Hospital Research Centre, Pune, India), Dr. Niket Kasar (KEM Hospital Research Centre, Pune, India), Professor Choudhary L. Narayan (AN Magadh Medical College, Gaya, Bihar, India), Dr. Avinash Desousa (Lokmanya Tilak Municipal General Hospital and Medical College, Mumbai, India), Prof. Nishant Goyal (Central Institute of Psychiatry, Ranchi, India), Dr. Kaustubh Joag (The Centre for Mental Health Law and Policy, Pune, India) and Prof. Ganesan Gopalakrishnan (MVJ Medical College and Research Hospital, Bangalore, India). We also greatly appreciate the time and contributions of all the mental health professionals who attended and helped organize our focus groups in India.

We are particularly grateful to Dr. Soumitra Pathare of the Centre for Mental Health Law and Policy at the Indian Law Society, Pune, India, for his guidance in our work from the earliest stages and to Dr. Pathare and Arjun Kapoor for contributing Chap. 11 of this book.

I, Richard M. Duffy, am very grateful to everyone who supported me in writing this book. My wife Louise and son Arthur have been fantastic and very patient. June, Kevin, Nicky, Caroline, Harold and Melvin have been incredible in allowing me the time to undertake this. Professor John Sheehan and the teams in the Mater and the Rotunda have been very supportive and have allowed me the leave I have needed to get this book completed. Niamh, Isidro and Rebecca have been great for the academic pointers.

I, Brendan D. Kelly, am very grateful to everyone who assisted me as I wrote this book. I deeply appreciate the support of my wife, Regina, and children, Eoin and Isabel. I am also very grateful to my parents (Mary and Desmond), sisters (Sinéad and Niamh) and nieces (Aoife and Aisling). I owe a long-standing debt of gratitude to my teachers at Scoil Chaitríona, Renmore, Galway; St. Joseph's Patrician College, Nun's Island, Galway and the School of Medicine at NUI Galway. I am also very grateful to Dr. Larkin Feeney, Dr. John Bruzzi, Prof. Veronica O'Keane, all of my extraordinary work colleagues, my patients, their families and many, many others. Trixie deserves special mention: Hi, Trixie! Also definitely worthy of mention: Sheldon and Terry.

We are very grateful to the editors, publishers, authors and copyright holders who permitted reuse of material in this book. All reasonable efforts have been made to contact the copyright holders for all materials used. If any have been omitted, please contact the publisher.

# Contents

# Introduction


## Abstract

Mental illness is common, complex and costly. Globally, almost 800,000 people die due to suicide every year and 79% of suicides occur in low- and middle-income countries. In addition, more than 300 million people suffer from depression, but most people affected by mental illness—75% in many low-income countries—do not have access to treatment they need. Many of these people live in India, a country of 1.3 billion people, one-sixth of the planet's entire population. In light of psychiatry's long-standing relationship with mental health law, legislative reform holds particular potential for improvement of mental health services and—arguably—achieving a positive right to mental health and mental healthcare in many countries, including India. Since the late 1900s there have been significant moves in this direction with the United Nations' (UN) Principles for the Protection of Persons with Mental Illness and the Improvement of Mental Health Care in 1991, culminating in the UN Convention on the Rights of Persons with Disabilities (CRPD) which came into effect in 2008. Against this background, it was apparent that mental health and disability legislation in many countries was in need of reform. Over the following years, it also became apparent that one country—India—was taking the most dramatic steps in this direction, seeking explicitly to align its disability and mental health laws with the CRPD. This process resulted in India's Rights of Persons with Disabilities Act, 2016 and Mental Healthcare Act, 2017, which form the focus of this book.



**Keywords** Mental health • Psychiatry • Legislation • Human rights • India • Suicide

# Introduction

Mental illness is common, complex and costly. The World Health Organization (WHO) points out that almost 800,000 people die due to suicide every year, and for every completed suicide there are many more people who attempt to end their lives (WHO 2019a). Globally, suicide is the second leading cause of death among 15- to 29-year-olds, and 79% of suicides occur in low- and middle-income countries. In addition, more than 300 million people suffer from depression which is now the leading cause of ill health and disability worldwide (WHO 2019b).

Despite these figures, most of the people affected by mental illness—75% in many low-income countries—do not have access to the treatment they need (WHO 2019c). Many of these people live in India, a country with a population of 1.3 billion people. *The National Mental Health Survey of India, 2015–16* recently highlighted the magnitude of the challenges facing India in relation to mental health (Gururaj et al. 2016; Murthy 2017; Pradeep et al. 2018). This survey was a vast, invaluable joint collaborative project by nearly 500 professionals, comprising researchers, state-level administrators, data collection teams and various others from 12 states in India, coordinated and implemented by the National Institute of Mental Health and Neuro-Sciences (NIMHANS), a leading medical institution in Bangalore.

Researchers interviewed 39,532 individuals across 720 clusters in 43 districts of the 12 selected states in India, achieving a response rate of 91.9% at household level and 88.0% at individual level. Their key findings were stark:

- The overall weighted prevalence for any mental morbidity in India was 13.7% over a person's lifetime and 10.6% currently;
- Mental disorders were associated with poverty and living in urban areas;
- Depressive, neurotic and stress-related disorders were more common among women, while bipolar and alcohol use disorders were more common among men;
- The treatment gap for various mental disorders ranged between 70% and 92%, i.e. between 70% and 92% of people with various mental illnesses were not receiving the treatment they needed;
- In terms of specific mental illnesses, the treatment gap was 70.4% for bipolar affective disorder, 75.5% for psychosis, 85.0% for common mental disorders, 86.3% for alcohol use disorder and 91.8% for tobacco use.

This situation in relation to mental healthcare in India is attributable in significant part to the severe lack of resources devoted to mental health services (Duffy and Kelly 2019a). Less than 1% of India's national healthcare budget is allocated to mental health compared to 13% of the National Health Service budget in England (Campbell 2016). There are also substantial variations across different regions within India, with the highest treatment gaps generally seen in rural areas (Patel et al. 2016). Human resources are especially deficient, with just 0·3 psychiatrists per 100,000 people in India compared to 2.2 in China and 10.5 in the United States of

America (US) (WHO 2019d). There is a similar paucity of nurses working in the mental health sector in India, with just 0.8 mental health nurses per 100,000 people in India compared to 5.4 in China and 4.3 in the US.

The solution to these problems probably lies in a complex combination of overall economic progress, social change, revision of mental health policy and—the focus of this book—reform of mental health legislation. In 2017, the WHO placed particular emphasis on legal reform and rights as key ways to improve health and healthcare in a landmark report titled, *Advancing the Right to Health: The Vital Role of Law* (WHO 2017). This report paid particular attention to the problematic historical relationship between mental health and the law.

> Historically, laws have been used to structure the response to mental illness, but not always consistently with human rights. People with mental illness, like those with physical illness, require a full range of medical and social services. Instead, law has sometimes been used to incarcerate mentally ill people in sterile institutions and without the protection required under the rule of law (p. xiv).

The WHO report goes on to articulate a clear 'right' to physical and mental health.

> The right to health is a fundamental human right that is indispensable for human well-being, for well-functioning societies and economies and for the ability to exercise all other human rights. Without a basic level of health, it may be difficult or impossible for people to work, to attend school and obtain an education, to enjoy recreation, to fully participate in society and to enjoy other basic freedoms (p. 1).

The WHO presents a compelling case for the centrality of the right to health in terms of human well-being and human flourishing, but creating an explicit, legally binding right to health is not without complexity (Farmer 1999; 2003; Benatar 2013; Flood and Lemmens 2013; Kelly 2013). The right to health is, however, a concept that can evolve over time as social circumstances develop, economic conditions change and new understandings shape the contract between the individual and the state, revising expectations on both sides of the equation (Tobin 2012). Moreover, articulating rights to health, mental health, healthcare and mental healthcare *in law* can, at the very least, offer an important tool for advocacy and service improvement, especially for those who are most in need of care and, ironically, are often the least likely to receive it (Wolff 2012).

Against this background, the 2017 WHO report articulating the 'vital role of law' in 'advancing the right to health' was generally welcomed as a significant step forward of relevance not only to lawyers and the legal profession but also to policymakers and other influential actors in non-legal, health-related arenas (Lancet 2017; Gostin et al. 2019). The 2017 report held particular relevance for mental health, the branch of medicine, with—arguably—the deepest relationship to law owing to psychiatry's lengthy history of involuntary care (Shorter 1997; Harding 2000; Kelly 2016a). While most psychiatric treatments are provided on an outpatient basis, and most inpatient care is also voluntary, involuntary admission and treatment are still features of mental healthcare and both demand and require careful regulation and oversight by law (Kelly 2016b).

As such, law holds particular potential for reform in the context of psychiatry and—arguably—particular potential for articulating and achieving a positive right to mental health and mental healthcare (Dudley et al. 2012; Kelly 2015). Since the late 1900s there have been significant moves in this direction, commencing in earnest with the United Nations' (UN) *Principles for the Protection of Persons with Mental Illness and the Improvement of Mental Health Care* in 1991, which stated that 'all persons have the right to the best available mental healthcare, which shall be part of the health and social care system' (Principle 1(1)) (UN, 1991). In 1996, the WHO articulated 'ten basic principles' of mental health law, along similar lines, stating that 'everyone should benefit from the best possible measures to promote their mental well-being and to prevent mental disorders' (Principle 1) and 'everyone in need should have access to basic mental healthcare' (Principle 2) (WHO 1996).

In 2001, the WHO intensified its focus on this area by devoting its annual report to *Mental Health: New Understanding, New Hope*, and, in its recommendations, placing particular emphasis on legislation and the rights of the mentally ill (WHO 2001a; Kelly 2001). One of the WHO's ten key recommendations for action was that member states should 'establish national policies, programmes and legislation' in relation to mental healthcare, rooted in human rights.

> Mental health policy, programmes and legislation are necessary steps for significant and sustained action. These should be based on current knowledge and human rights considerations. Most countries need to increase their budgets for mental health programmes from existing low levels. Some countries that have recently developed or revised their policy and legislation have made progress in implementing their mental healthcare programmes. Mental health reforms should be part of the larger health system reforms (p. xii).

The report pointed to examples of 'human rights abuse in psychiatric hospitals' (p. 51) and recommended that 'policies should be drawn up with the involvement of all stakeholders and should be based on reliable information. Policies should ensure the respect of human rights and take account of the needs of vulnerable groups. Care should shift away from large psychiatric hospitals to community services that are integrated into general health services' (p. 76).

Seven years later, in 2008, the UN *Convention on the Rights of Persons with Disabilities* (CRPD) came into effect, aiming 'to promote, protect and ensure the full and equal enjoyment of all human rights and fundamental freedoms by all persons with disabilities, and to promote respect for their inherent dignity' (Article 1) (UN, 2006). In this context, 'persons with disabilities include those who have long-term physical, mental, intellectual or sensory impairments which in interaction with various barriers may hinder their full and effective participation in society on an equal basis with others'. The CRPD presented extensive measures designed to protect and promote rights, many of which have significant implications in the context of mental illness (Kelly, 2014).

Against this background, it was apparent that mental health and disability legislation in many countries was in need of reform (Gooding 2017). Over the following years, it also became apparent that one country—India—was taking the most dramatic steps in this direction, seeking explicitly to align its disability *and* mental health laws with the CRPD, despite the clear resource challenges it faces in these areas (Sachan 2013; Patel et al. 2016). More specifically, India's Rights of Persons with Disabilities Act, 2016 received the assent of the President of India on 27 December 2016 and was commenced in effect on 15 June 2017. The purpose of the 2016 Act is 'to give effect to the United Nations Convention on the Rights of Persons with Disabilities and for matters connected therewith or incidental thereto'. The extensive legislation presents a broad range of rights-based provisions aimed at giving effect to the CRPD and improving the rights of persons with disabilities in India. It is an ambitious piece of legislation which we examine in some detail later in this book.

Also in 2017, on 7 April, India's Mental Healthcare Act, 2017 (MHCA) received Presidential assent and it was formally commenced on 29 May 2018. Like the 2016 Act, the 2017 legislation notes that 'it is necessary to align and harmonise the existing laws with' the CRPD and goes on to present a broad range of rights-based provisions explicitly informed by the CRPD, making India's MHCA one of the most interesting and potentially progressive pieces of mental health legislation in the world (Kalmegh et al. 2018; Duffy and Kelly 2019b; 2019c). Again, we discuss this in detail throughout this book.

Perhaps the most dramatic right articulated in the 2017 Act, however, is a right to mental healthcare. The legislation states that 'every person shall have a right to access mental healthcare and treatment from mental health services run or funded by the appropriate Government' (Section 18(1)), i.e. 'services of affordable cost, of good quality, available in sufficient quantity, accessible geographically, without discrimination on the basis of gender, sex, sexual orientation, religion, culture, caste, social or political beliefs, class, disability or any other basis and provided in a manner that is acceptable to persons with mental illness and their families and care-givers' (Section 18(2)). This extraordinary and historic measure in the 2017 Act creates a justiciable right to mental healthcare for India's 1.3 billion people, one-sixth of the planet's population.

Against this background, our book aims to provide a comprehensive context to the new Indian legislation, along with a detailed description of the 2017 Act itself and a rigorous analysis of it in the context of the CRPD and WHO standards for mental health law. This analysis is aimed at mental health professionals, legal professionals, non-governmental organizations and civil servants not only in India but also in other jurisdictions that seek to revise their legislation to bring it into line with the CRPD. We examine the difficult balance held by Indian legislators in adhering to the CRPD while still delivering practical, humane and implementable legislation. We also explore how the Indian legislation was shaped by the UN and WHO standards and examine areas where the Indian legislators deviated from these guidelines. We conclude with an update on implementation kindly contributed by Dr. Soumitra Pathare and Arjun Kapoor.

Writing legislation that is concordant with the CRPD will be a necessary task for many countries over the coming years, so in this book we not only lay out the example of India but also highlight key lessons for other jurisdictions from what is essentially the largest experiment ever undertaken in the field of rights-based mental health law.

Part I of our book starts by exploring 'Mental Health Law and the Role of International Standards'. Chapter 1 sets out the 'Background to Mental Health Law', noting that mental illness and its treatments have been subjects of speculation and concern since the start of recorded history. Overall, the treatment of people with mental illness has been highly variable. While there is historical evidence that mental illness sometimes elicited compassion, treatment, support and special legal consideration, there is much greater evidence that it was generally met with stigma, neglect, marginalization and gross injustice.

In terms of mental health legislation, the nineteenth and twentieth centuries saw a relatively clear evolution from custody and containment to care and human rights (at least in theory), as legislation developed to reflect both advances in the treatment of mental illness and broader changes in politics and society. Most recently, India's MHCA was written to accord with the CRPD but does not embrace the CRPD unquestioningly. Indian legislators have, for example, included pragmatic tools for the protection and treatment of the acutely mentally ill ('supported admission'). While some of these provisions might be at odds with certain interpretations of the CPRD, they have dramatically revised Indian mental health legislation to bring it into greater accordance with core CRPD principles. India's revisions are also cognizant of the potential negative consequences of an overly literal application of the CRPD. As a result, implementation of India's MHCA will hopefully demonstrate how low- and middle-income countries can realize modern, rights-based mental health law and provide an example for the rest of the world.

Chapter 2 continues by exploring the 'United Nations and Mental Health Law', noting that, since its foundation in 1945, the UN has taken many steps to improve the well-being of people with mental illness. This has occurred through the Universal Declaration of Human Rights (1948), various other core international human rights instruments, the Principles for the Protection of Persons with Mental Illness and the Improvement of Mental Health Care (1991) and the Human Rights Council. While the Universal Declaration of Human Rights and the other initial human rights instruments related to mental illness only indirectly, the Convention on the Rights of the Child (1989) provided more detailed consideration of the topic.

In 2006, the CRPD included mental illness under the umbrella of disability and this inclusion is currently transforming mental health legislation internationally. While much of this change is positive, protecting the rights and maximizing the agency of people with mental illness, there are concerns that an excessively rigid interpretation of the CRPD could reduce access to treatment and lead to stigmatization and criminalization of the mentally ill. The 1991 UN Principles for the Protection of Persons with Mental Illness and the Improvement of Mental Health Care were, by contrast, written with more nuanced consideration of the needs of people with mental illness, but lacked the legal weight of the CRPD. Within the Human Rights Council, the Special Rapporteurs and the Working Group on Arbitrary Detention also often consider the needs of people with mental illness. Despite these measures, however, more is needed.

Chapter 3 of the book moves on to examine 'the World Health Organization and Mental Health Law' and notes that, since 1948, the WHO, too, has done much to shape the evolution of mental health law. Their initial measures were often indirect, but they have recently assertively articulated the importance of legislation in health, including mental health. The inclusion of mental disorders in the International Classification of Diseases (ICD) since 1949 has helped standardize mental health nomenclature in legislation (WHO, 1949). Later iterations of the ICD, including descriptions of conditions, further improved diagnostic reliability. In 1996, the WHO's Mental Health Care Law: Ten Basic Principles was one of the organization's earliest attempts to directly shape mental health legislation (WHO, 1996). From 2001, Project Atlas helped to identify countries without mental health legislation and countries with grossly outdated laws (WHO 2001b). The WHO has sought to address these deficits recently as part of the WHO Mental Health Action Plan 2013–2020 (WHO 2013).

The most direct attempt at influencing international mental health law came in 2005 with the WHO's Resource Book on Mental Health, Human Rights and Legislation. This provided extensive consideration of what should be addressed in mental health law and policy, and examined coercive treatments in detail. With the publication of the CRPD in 2006, the WHO Resource Book was withdrawn. Even so, the Resource Book remains the most comprehensive consideration of the legislative needs of people with mental illness. QualityRights is now the CRPD-concordant WHO publication relating to mental health, including mental health legislation, and it contains an evaluation toolkit and teaching modules, among other resources.

Part II of the book focuses on 'Mental Health Legislation in India'. Chapter 4 presents a 'History of Mental Health Legislation in India', noting that, throughout the 1900s, mental health legislation in India was significantly shaped by the British. The Lunatic Removal Act, 1851 aimed to facilitate the repatriation of British offenders with mental illness. In 1858, three additional pieces of legislation were introduced: the Lunacy (Supreme Courts) Act, the Lunacy (District Courts) Act and the Indian Lunatic Asylum Act. To these, the Military Lunatic Act was added in 1877. These pieces of legislation were consolidated in 1912 under the Indian Lunacy Act, which drew heavily on the English Lunatics Act, 1845.

Shortly after Indian independence in 1947, a modern mental health act was drafted, but this legislation took over 35 years to be adopted, finally becoming the Mental Health Act, 1987. There were concerns about the content of this legislation from the outset, as many of its provisions were over 35 years old and the delivery of mental health services had changed significantly over that time. In 2007, India's ratification of the CRPD provided further impetus for updating the legislation. The demands of the CRPD required that existing legislation be replaced rather than revised, owing to the extent of the changes needed. The passage of the Rights of Persons with Disabilities Act, 2016 also had significant implications for people with psychosocial disabilities, owing to the inclusion of mental illness in the definition of disability in the CRPD.

Chapter 5 examines India's Rights of Persons with Disabilities Act, 2016 which received the assent of the President of India on 27 December 2016 and was commenced in effect on 15 June 2017. The purpose of the Act is 'to give effect to the United Nations Convention on the Rights of Persons with Disabilities and for matters connected therewith or incidental thereto'. Key provisions cover 'rights and entitlements'; 'education'; 'skill development and employment'; 'social security, health, rehabilitation and recreation'; 'special provisions for persons with benchmark disabilities' and 'high support needs'; 'duties and responsibilities of appropriate governments'; 'registration of institutions for persons with disabilities and grants to such institutions'; 'certification of specified disabilities'; 'Central and State Advisory Boards on Disability and District Level Committee'; 'Chief Commissioner and State Commissioner for Persons with Disabilities'; 'Special Court'; 'National Fund for Persons with Disabilities'; 'State Fund for Persons with Disabilities' and 'offences and penalties'.

Overall, India's 2016 Act presents a broad range of rights-based provisions aimed at giving effect to the CRPD and improving the rights of persons with disabilities in India. It legally underpins many economic and social rights and emphasizes respect for inherent dignity; individual autonomy; full and effective inclusion and participation in society; respect for difference; acceptance of persons with disabilities; equality of opportunity; accessibility and respect for the evolving capacities of children with disabilities. Concerns centre on the 2016 Act's interactions with India's MHCA, methods of assessing and certifying disabilities, the position of families of persons with mental illness and specific concerns about neurodevelopmental disorders.

Chapter 6 of this book moves on to examine the content of India's MHCA, which received Presidential assent on 7 April 2017 and was commenced on 29 May 2018. This Act seeks explicitly to align India's mental health legislation with the CRPD (UN 2006). Key provisions of the new legislation cover 'preliminary' matters and definitions; 'mental illness and capacity to make mental healthcare and treatment decisions'; 'advance directive'; 'nominated representative'; 'rights of persons with mental illness'; 'duties of appropriate government'; 'Central Mental Health Authority'; 'State Mental Health Authority'; 'finance, accounts and audit'; 'mental health establishments'; 'Mental Health Review Boards'; 'admission, treatment and discharge' (including 'independent admission', 'admission of a minor', 'supported admission' and 'supported admission beyond 30 days'); 'responsibilities of other agencies'; 'restriction to discharge functions by professionals not covered by profession'; 'offences and penalties' and other 'miscellaneous' matters, including *de facto* decriminalization of suicide.

Overall, Chap. 6 argues that the 2017 Act presents a broad range of provisions which, if implemented, will affect virtually every element of mental health services in India. Many of the changes are clearly informed by the 2017 Act's explicit aim to meet the requirements of the CRPD. The legislation has stimulated considerable discussion in the psychiatry literature and while one line of discourse is that the new legislation was not needed in the first place, and that amendments to the Mental Health Act, 1987 would have sufficed, there is nonetheless an acceptance that the new Act will have practical and legal implications in practice and needs to be understood.

Part III of the book considers 'India's Mental Healthcare Act, 2017 and International Human Rights Standards'. Chapter 7 begins by exploring areas of concordance and non-concordance between Indian legislation (especially the MHCA) and the WHO *Checklist on Mental Health Legislation* (WHO 2005). Overall, India's MHCA and Rights of Persons with Disabilities Act, 2016 have done much to bring India's legislation in line with the WHO Checklist. As a result, India currently meets 68.0% (119/175) of the WHO standards, at least in theory (Duffy and Kelly 2017). This far surpasses many other countries whose legislation has been compared to these standards; legislation in England and Wales, for example, meets 54.2% of the standards and legislation in Ireland meets 48.2% (Kelly 2011).

Regarding the 56 WHO standards that remain unmet in India, Chap. 7 notes that eight standards relate to areas in which direct comparison is not possible and 10 relate to areas of well-justified non-concordance, with the Indian legislation embracing the principles of human rights in a more pragmatic, insightful way than the WHO in these instances. Many of the remaining standards are not addressed directly in Indian legislation but provision exists for them to be addressed in policies relating to mental healthcare, general healthcare and social care. When areas of complex comparison are excluded from the analysis and areas of justified non-concordance are considered concordant, Indian legislation meets a remarkable 77.2% (129/167) of the WHO standards, consistent with its aims to protect and promote the human rights of the mentally ill. While further work is certainly needed, India's MHCA already offers a valuable model for other countries seeking to update their mental health laws, once it is adequately resourced.

Chapter 8 moves on to consider the 'Incorporation of the United Nations' Convention on the Rights of Persons with Disabilities into Indian Law through the Rights of Persons with Disabilities Act, 2016 and the Mental Healthcare Act, 2017'. This chapter examines the extent to which Indian legislation meets CRPD requirements relating to 'equality and non-discrimination' (CRPD Article 5), 'women with disabilities' (Article 6), 'children with disabilities' (Article 7), 'awareness-raising' (Article 8), 'accessibility' (Article 9), 'right to life' (Article 10), 'risk and humanitarian emergencies' (Article 11), 'equal recognition before the law' (Article 12), 'access to justice' (Article 13), 'liberty and security of person' (Article 14), 'freedom from torture or cruel, inhuman or degrading treatment or punishment' (Article 15), 'freedom from exploitation, violence and abuse' (Article 16), 'protecting the integrity of the person' (Article 17), 'liberty of movement and nationality' (Article 18), 'living independently and being included in the community' (Article 19), 'personal mobility' (Article 20), 'freedom of expression and opinion, and access to information' (Article 21), 'respect for privacy' (Article 22), 'respect for home and the family' (Article 23), 'education' (Article 24), 'health' (Article 25), 'habilitation and rehabilitation' (Article 26), 'work and employment' (Article 27), 'adequate standard of living and social protection' (Article 28), 'participation in political and public life' (Article 29) and 'cultural life, recreation, leisure and sport' (Article 30).

Overall, Indian legislation addresses the great majority of CRPD requirements in these areas although certain areas could be improved (e.g. political rights, liberty of movement and nationality). Careful monitoring of the implementation of India's new pieces of legislation will be especially important, both for India and for other countries seeking to bring their legislation in line with the CRPD. Globally, India has taken the strongest steps to date towards legislating for social rights in this way, including, in particular, rights to free healthcare and rehabilitation.

Chapter 9 focuses more closely on the 'Compliance of India's Mental Healthcare Act, 2017 with the United Nations' Convention on the Rights of Persons with Disabilities'. More specifically, this chapter notes that the MHCA has the distinction of being the first piece of major mental health legislation explicitly written in order to comply with the CRPD and, despite various limitations and areas of non-compliance that are discussed in detail in this chapter, both the MHCA and the Rights of Persons with Disabilities Act, 2016 have done much to realize the principles of the CRPD in Indian law. Where practices outlined in the MHCA appear to contravene the CRPD, protections have usually been put in place, chiefly mediated by Mental Health Review Boards. Instances of non-concordance with the CRPD generally result from efforts to balance competing CRPD rights with each other, and this balancing act is often directly reflected in the text of the MHCA.

The two most significant areas of potential non-concordance with the CRPD relate to the role of capacity in the MHCA and the lack of sufficient protection during emergency treatment. These limitations may, however, reflect pragmatic compromises in a setting of limited resources, especially as some of the other provisions described in the MHCA might already prove too ambitious to be implemented in the first place. Overall, while India's MHCA might not be entirely in line with the interpretations of the UN Committee on the Rights of Persons with Disabilities (2014), the vast majority of its provisions are compatible with the CRPD itself.

Chapter 10, titled 'Adhering to Conventions: Intentional Grey Areas or Shirking Responsibility?', notes that mental health legislation is going through a period of transformation, driven largely by international guidelines and conventions, including the WHO *Resource Book on Mental Health, Human Rights and Legislation* (WHO 2005), the UN *Principles for the Protection of Persons with Mental Illness and the Improvement of Mental Health Care* (UN, 1991) and the CRPD (UN, 2006). As argued in previous chapters, India's Rights of Persons with Disabilities Act, 2016 and MHCA exceed the levels of concordance with international standards seen in other jurisdictions owing to their extensive inclusion of social rights and attempts to limit coercive measures.

Nevertheless, various ethical issues still arise in the Indian legislation, relating to (a) medical ethics in resource-scarce environments; (b) beneficence and definitions (e.g. the definition of disability); (c) autonomy and capacity and (d) the evidence base for care. There are, in addition, three notable and intentional deviations from the CRPD in the areas of (1) capacity and limited guardianship; (2) coercive treatments and (3) migration, citizenship and nationality. Overall, the Indian legislation seeks to balance idealism with pragmatism and to navigate six key tensions between (i) autonomy and dignity; (ii) restriction and ineffectual treatment; (iii) universal and personalized treatment options; (iv) ideal and pragmatic treatment; (v) the individual and society and (vi) involvement and privacy. Each of these tensions is explored in this chapter. Future research could usefully focus on better understanding coercion from the perspectives of all stakeholders and finding ways to avoid and reduce it, especially as India's new legislation is implemented over the coming years.

Part IV of the book, titled 'Where now?', provides an 'Implementation Update on Mental Healthcare Act, 2017' (Chap. 11), kindly contributed by Dr. Soumitra Pathare and Arjun Kapoor (Sachan 2013; Shields et al. 2013; Pathare et al. 2015; Bhugra et al. 2016a; Bhugra et al. 2016b; Bhugra et al. 2017; Kapoor and Pathare 2019; Mahomed et al. 2019). Dr. Soumitra Pathare is a Consultant Psychiatrist and Director, Centre for Mental Health Law and Policy, Indian Law Society, Pune. He was appointed by the Ministry of Health and Family Welfare, Government of India to provide technical assistance in the drafting of the MHCA. He was also appointed as a member of the policy group for drafting India's National Mental Health Policy, 2014. He currently leads the Centre's projects and is Principal Investigator of the Suicide Prevention and Implementation Research Initiative (SPIRIT).

Arjun Kapoor is a human rights lawyer and psychologist. He is currently a Research Associate and Project Manager at the Centre for Mental Health Law and Policy, Indian Law Society and is developing the Centre's law and policy unit with a specific focus on capacity building of stakeholders for implementation of the MHCA. He was previously appointed as a Law Clerk and Research Assistant to the Supreme Court of India and has experience in developing socio-legal interventions on access to justice and legal empowerment in India.

In Chap. 11, Dr. Soumitra Pathare and Arjun Kapoor point out that the MHCA has a broad mandate which places obligations on various stakeholders to ensure mental healthcare through rights-based approaches. However, this mandate is likely to be unfulfilled without effective implementation. Since its enforcement, the MHCA's implementation has progressed at a very slow pace (as of time of writing, December 2019). Many State Governments are yet to establish the State Mental Health Authority and Mental Health Review Boards which play a crucial role in the implementation of the MHCA. The legislation has also been subject to judicial scrutiny by the Supreme Court of India and High Courts in matters of public interest for adjudicating important questions of constitutional law and monitoring implementation of the MHCA at the central and state levels.

The MHCA is confronted with several challenges for its speedy and effective implementation. Mental health professionals have expressed resistance to various provisions of the MHCA including advance directives, nominated representatives and modified electroconvulsive therapy. At the bureaucratic level, there is a lack of political commitment to address mental health as a legitimate health concern on a par with physical health. Further, poor intersectoral coordination between different government departments and an inadequate trained mental health workforce are other significant barriers to the MHCA's implementation.

It is thus incumbent upon civil society to assume a proactive role in advocating for mental health as a priority on the national agenda to address systemic gaps, infrastructural deficits and human resource challenges, and to compel Governments to fulfil the MHCA's mandate.

## References


Benatar, S. R. (2013). Global health, vulnerable populations and law. *Journal of Law, Medicine and Ethics*, *41*(1), 42–47.

Bhugra, D., Pathare, S., Gosavi, C., Ventriglio, A., Torales, J., Castaldelli-Maia, J., et al. (2016a). Mental illness and the right to vote: A review of legislation across the world. *International Review of Psychiatry*, *28*(4), 395–399.

Bhugra, D., Ventriglio, A., & Pathare, S. (2016b). Freedom and equality in dignity and rights for persons with mental illness. *Lancet Psychiatry*, *3*(3), 196–197.

Bhugra, D., Tasman, A., Pathare, S., Priebe, S., Smith, S., Torous, J., et al. (2017). The WPA-*Lancet Psychiatry* Commission on the Future of Psychiatry. *Lancet Psychiatry*, *4*(10), 775–818.

Campbell, D. (2016, May 9). NHS mental health funding is still lagging behind, says report. *Guardian*. https://www.theguardian.com/society/2016/may/09/nhs-mental-health-funding-is-still-lagging-behind-says-report. Retrieved 1 June 2019.

Dudley, M., Silove, D., & Gale, F. (Eds.). (2012). *Mental health and human rights: Vision, praxis and courage*. Oxford: Oxford University Press.

Duffy, R. M., & Kelly, B. D. (2017). Concordance of the Indian Mental Healthcare Act, 2017 with the World Health Organization's Checklist on Mental Health Legislation. *International Journal of Mental Health Systems*, 11, 48.

Duffy, R. M., & Kelly, B. D. (2019a). India's mental healthcare act, 2017: Content, context, controversy. *International Journal of Law and Psychiatry*, 62, 169–178.

Duffy, R. M., & Kelly, B. D. (2019b). Global mental health. *Lancet*, *394*(10193), 118–119.

Duffy, R. M., & Kelly, B. D. (2019c). The right to mental healthcare: India moves forward. *British Journal of Psychiatry*, *214*(2), 59–60.

Farmer, P. (1999). Pathologies of power: Rethinking health and human rights. *American Journal of Public Health*, *89*(10), 1486–1496.

Farmer, P. (2003). *Pathologies of power: Health, human rights, and the new war on the poor*. Berkeley: University of California Press.

Flood, C. M., & Lemmens, T. (2013). Global health challenges and the role of law. *Journal of Law, Medicine and Ethics*, *41*(1), 9–15.

Gooding, P. (2017). *A new era for mental health law and policy: Supported decision-making and the UN convention on the rights of persons with disabilities*. Cambridge: Cambridge University Press.

Gostin, L. O., Monahan, J. T., Kaldor, J., DeBartolo, M., Friedman, E. A., Gottschalk, K., et al. (2019). The legal determinants of health: harnessing the power of law for global health and sustainable development. *Lancet*, *393*(10183), 1857–1910.

Gururaj, G., Varghese, M., Benegal, V., Rao, G. N., Pathak, K., Singh, L. K., et al. (2016). *National Mental Health Survey of India, 2015–16: Prevalence, patterns and outcomes (NIMHANS publication no. 129)*. Bengaluru: National Institute of Mental Health and Neuro Sciences.

Harding, T. W. (2000). Human rights law in the field of mental health: A critical review. *Acta Psychiatrica Scandinavica*, 399 (Suppl.), 24–30.

Kalmegh, B., Bakhshy, A., Harshe, D., & Patankar, V. (2018). *MHCA 2017: Together we can..!* Pune: SMARTT.

Kapoor, A., & Pathare, S. (2019). Section 377 and the Mental Healthcare Act, 2017: Breaking barriers. *Indian Journal of Medical Ethics, 4*(2), 1–4.

Kelly, B. D. (2001). Mental health and human rights: challenges for a new millennium. *Irish Journal of Psychological Medicine, 18*(4), 114–115.

Kelly, B. D. (2011). Mental health legislation and human rights in England, Wales and the Republic of Ireland. *International Journal of Law and Psychiatry, 34*(6), 439–454.

Kelly, B. D. (2013). Is there a human right to mental health? *Psychiatry Professional, 2*(1), 10–14.

Kelly, B. D. (2014). An end to psychiatric detention? Implications of the United Nations' convention on the rights of persons with disabilities. *British Journal of Psychiatry, 204*(3), 174–175.

Kelly, B. D. (2015). *Dignity, mental health and human rights: Coercion and the law.* Abingdon, Oxon: Routledge.

Kelly, B. D. (2016a). *Hearing voices: The history of psychiatry in Ireland.* Dublin: Irish Academic Press.

Kelly, B. D. (2016b). *Mental illness, human rights and the law.* London: RCPsych Publications.

Lancet (2017). Law: an underused tool to improve health and wellbeing for all. *Lancet, 389* (10067), 331.

Mahomed, F., Stein, M. A., Chauhan, A., & Pathare, S. (2019). 'They love me, but they don't understand me': Family support and stigmatisation of mental health service users in Gujarat, India. *International Journal of Social Psychiatry, 65*(1), 73–79.

Murthy, R. S. (2017). National mental health survey of India 2015–2016. *Indian Journal of Psychiatry, 59*(1), 21–26.

Patel, V., Xiao, S., Chen, H., Hanna, F., Jotheeswaran, A.T., Luo, D., et al. (2016). The magnitude of and health system responses to the mental health treatment gap in adults in India and China. *Lancet, 388*(10063), 3074–3084.

Pathare, S., Shields, L., Nardodkar, R., Narasimhan, L., & Bunders, J. (2015). What do service users want? A content analysis of what users may write in psychiatric advance directives in India. *Asian Journal of Psychiatry*, 14, 52–56.

Pradeep, B. S., Gururaj, G., Varghese, M., Benegal, V., Rao, G. N., Sukumar, G. M., et al. (2018). National Mental Health Survey of India, 2016: rationale, design and methods. *PLoS One, 13* (10), e0205096.

Sachan, D. (2013). Mental health bill set to revolutionise care in India. *Lancet, 382*(9889), 296.

Shields, L. S., Pathare, S., van Zelst, S. D., Dijkkamp, S., Narasimhan, L., & Bunders, J. G. (2013). Unpacking the psychiatric advance directive in low-resource settings: an exploratory qualitative study in Tamil Nadu, India. *International Journal of Mental Health Systems, 7*(1), 29.

Shorter, E. (1997). *A history of psychiatry: From the era of the asylum to the age of Prozac.* New York: John Wiley and Sons.

Tobin, J. (2012). *The right to health in international law.* Oxford: Oxford University Press.

United Nations (1991). *Principles for the protection of persons with mental illness and the improvement of mental health care.* New York: United Nations, Secretariat Centre For Human Rights. https://www.who.int/mental_health/policy/en/UN_Resolution_on_protection_of_persons_with_mental_illness.pdf. Retrieved 1 June 2019.

United Nations (2006). *Convention on the rights of persons with disabilities.* New York: United Nations. https://www.un.org/development/desa/disabilities/convention-on-the-rights-of-persons-with-disabilities/convention-on-the-rights-of-persons-with-disabilities-2.html. Retrieved 1 June 2019.

Wolff, J. (2012). *The human right to health.* New York & London: W.W. Norton and Company.

World Health Organization (1949). *Manual of the international statistical classification of diseases, injuries, and causes of death: Sixth revision of the international lists of diseases and causes of death.* Geneva: World Health Organization.

World Health Organization (1996). *Mental health care law: Ten basic principles.* Geneva: World Health Organization.

World Health Organization (2001a). *Mental health: New understanding, new hope.* Geneva: World Health Organization. https://www.who.int/whr/2001/en/. Retrieved 1 June 2019.
World Health Organization (2001b). *Mental health resources in the world. Initial results of Project Atlas.* Geneva: World Health Organization.
World Health Organization (2005). *WHO resource book on mental health, human rights and legislation.* Geneva: World Health Organization.
World Health Organization (2013). *Mental health action plan 2013-2020.* Geneva: World Health Organization.
World Health Organization (2017). *Advancing the right to health: The vital role of law.* Geneva: World Health Organization. https://www.who.int/gender-equity-rights/knowledge/advancing-the-right-to-health/en/. Retrieved 1 June 2019.
World Health Organization (2019a). *Suicide: Key facts.* Geneva: World Health Organization. https://www.who.int/news-room/fact-sheets/detail/suicide. Retrieved 1 June 2019.
World Health Organization (2019b). *Depression: Let's talk.* Geneva: World Health Organization. https://www.who.int/mental_health/management/depression/en/. Retrieved 1 June 2019.
World Health Organization (2019c). *WHO mental health gap action programme (mhGAP).* Geneva: World Health Organization. https://www.who.int/mental_health/mhgap/en/. Retrieved 1 June 2019.
World Halth Organization (2019d). *Global Health Observatory data repository: Human resources data by country.* http://apps.who.int/gho/data/node.main.MHHR?lang=en. Retrieved 1 June 2019.

# About the Authors

**Dr. Richard M. Duffy** is a Consultant, Perinatal Psychaitrists in the Rotunda Hospital, Dublin and a Liaison Psychiatrist in the Mater Misericordiae University Hospital, Dublin. He completed his medical degree at Trinity College Dublin and holds a Masters of Epidemiology from the London School of Hygiene and Tropical Medicine. Richard's current research is on the Indian Mental Healthcare Act 2017, and he has published international peer-reviewed papers on this topic. His current research into India's law is as part of a Ph.D. in Trinity College Dublin.

**Prof. Brendan D. Kelly, M.B. B.Ch. B.A.O., M.A. M.Sc. M.A., M.D. Ph.D. D. Gov. Ph.D., MCPsychI FRCPsych FRCPI FTCD** is a Professor of Psychiatry at Trinity College Dublin and Consultant Psychiatrist at Tallaght University Hospital. In addition to his medical degree (M.B. B.Ch. B.A.O.), Professor Kelly holds masters degrees in Epidemiology (M.Sc.), Healthcare Management (M.A.) and Buddhist Studies (M.A.), and doctorates in Medicine (M.D.), History (Ph.D.), Governance (D.Gov.) and Law (Ph.D.). Professor Kelly has authored and co-authored over 225 peer-reviewed publications and 450 non-peer-reviewed publications. His books include Custody, Care and Criminality: Forensic Psychiatry and Law in 19th-Century Ireland (History Press Ireland, 2014), Ada English: Patriot and Psychiatrist (Irish Academic Press, 2014), "He Lost Himself Completely": Shell Shock and its Treatment at Dublin's Richmond War Hospital (1916-19) (Liffey Press, 2014), Dignity, Mental Health and Human Rights: Coercion and the Law (Routledge, 2015), Mental Illness, Human Rights and the Law (RCPsych Publications, 2016), Hearing Voices: The History of Psychiatry in Ireland (Irish Academic Press, 2016) and Mental Health in Ireland: The Complete Guide for Patients, Families, Health Care Professionals and Everyone Who Wants To Be Well (Liffey Press, 2017). In 2017, Professor Kelly was appointed Editor-in-Chief of the International Journal of Law and Psychiatry.

# Abbreviations

| | |
|---|---|
| AD | Advance directive |
| APA | American Psychiatric Association |
| ASHA | Accredited social health activists |
| BCE | Before Common Era |
| CRPD | Convention on the Rights of Persons with Disabilities |
| DSM | Diagnostic and Statistical Manual of Mental Disorders |
| ECT | Electroconvulsive therapy |
| ESSENCE | Enabling Translation of Science to Service to Enhance Depression Care |
| EU | European Union |
| ICD | International Classification of Diseases |
| MHCA | Mental Healthcare Act, 2017 |
| NIMHANS | National Institute of Mental Health and Neuro-Sciences |
| NR | Nominated representative |
| POCSO | Protection of Children from Sexual Offences Act, 2012 |
| PTSD | Post-traumatic stress disorder |
| RPWDA | Rights of Persons with Disabilities Act, 2016 |
| SPIRIT | Suicide Prevention and Implementation Research Initiative |
| UK | United Kingdom |
| UN | United Nations |
| US | United States of America |
| WHO RB | World Health Organization's *Resource Book on Mental Health Legislation* |
| WHO | World Health Organization |

# List of Tables

# Part I
# Mental Health Law and the Role of International Standards

# Chapter 1
# Background to Mental Health Law

## 1.1 The Pre-history of Mental Health Law

There is plentiful evidence that mental illness and its treatments have been a source of speculation and concern since the start of recorded human history, ranging from early references to the use of trepanning to discussions of depression in the Ebers papyrus (c. 1550 BCE) (Bou Khalil and Richa 2014; Collado-Vázquez and Carrillo 2014; Hobert and Binello 2017; Shorter 1997; Tsermoulas et al. 2014).

According to Biblical sources, Israel's King David fled from Saul and sought refuge with Achish, King of Gath around 1000 BCE. Concerned how Achish might treat him and aware that his life may be in danger, David feigned mental illness in the belief that this would result in him being treated differently. His ruse was successful and David was able to leave Gath.

In Buddhism, it is recorded that, around 500 BCE, Buddha treated people with mental illness in a compassionate manner that contrasted starkly with how they were commonly treated in the community (Somasundaram and Murthy 2018). The Buddha's approach also contrasted with the Twelve Tables of Rome, a set of laws inscribed on bronze tablets, which adopted a much less humane approach to children with disabilities in the fifth century BCE (Berkson 2006).

For many centuries, the Islamic world leads the way in the treatment of people with mental illness. Islamic physician Abū Bakr Muhammad ibn Zakariyyā al-Rāzī set up one of the first psychiatric wards in Baghdad, Iraq in 705 CE (Sabry and Vohra 2013). Many other Islamic scholars also developed psychotherapeutic treatments (Murad and Gordon 2002) and music therapy to address mental health conditions (Haque 2004). Later, hospitals began to appear outside of the Islamic world, including the Bethlehem Royal Hospital in London, founded in 1247, and the Pitié-Salpêtrière Hospital in Paris, founded in 1656. Standards of care were, however, low, and in the late eighteenth century pioneers like Philippe Pinel in Paris and the Quakers at the York Retreat in England started advocating for more humane treatments (Kelly 2016). Their reforms had, however, little if any connection to formal legislation governing the mentally ill.



R. M. Duffy and B. D. Kelly, *India's Mental Healthcare Act, 2017*,
https://doi.org/10.1007/978-981-15-5009-6_1

From a legislative perspective, Canon Law predated civil law in Europe and often considered mental illness in a variety of different ways. It restricted access to sacraments like marriage and baptism for mentally ill (Trenery and Horden 2017) and delivered judgements in relation to suicide, which could not be followed by Christian burial. Church law also dealt with major crimes and showed some leniency to mentally ill offenders. This leniency was not, however, universal as mental illness could also be seen as punishment for sin or a spiritual affliction (Restak 2000). The best-preserved records from the Medieval period are from England and relate mostly to management of the property of the mentally ill and insanity as a defence in court (Trenery and Horden 2017).

Overall, the treatment of people with mental illness was highly variable prior to the arrival of formal legislation. While there is historical evidence that mental illness sometimes elicited compassion, treatment, support and special legal consideration, there is much greater evidence that it was generally met with stigma, neglect, marginalisation and gross injustice.

## 1.2 A Timeline of Mental Health Law

In this section, we examine the evolution of laws primarily directed at addressing societal management of people with mental illness. This evolution is summarized in Table 1.1. In England and Wales, early legislation included the Madhouses Act, 1774, the County Asylums Act, 1828 and the Criminal Lunatics Act, 1800, all of which concerned the placement or containment of people with mental illness. The Madhouses Act, 1774 demonstrates how this mass confinement was initially on a small scale, in houses, but progressed quite quickly to the industrial scale seen during the asylum era.

Later, various treatments became more common and legislation slowly recognized the need to address care as well as confinement. This is demonstrated by the Mental Treatment Act, 1930, which evolved into the Mental Health Acts, 1953 and 1983. Some countries, like India, have now taken the titles of their legislation a step further with the Mental *Healthcare* Act, 2017 (our italics), reflecting a further evolution. A growing emphasis on human rights is also apparent in both the Indian legislation and England and Wales's Mental Capacity Act, 2005 and the Mental Health (Discrimination) Act, 2013. This apparent legislative evolution from custody and containment to care and human rights is considered in more detail next.

### *1.2.1 Poor Laws and the Protection of Property*

Edward II of England's *Praerogativa Regis*, dating from 1324, is often considered the origin of modern mental health law (Somasundaram 1987). *Praerogativa Regis* gave the King wardship over the lands of 'idiots' and, later, 'lunatics'. These were

**Table 1.1** Key time periods and driving forces in mental health legislation

| Driving force behind legislation | Positive consequences of legislation | Negative consequences of legislation | Examples | Time period |
|---|---|---|---|---|
| Protection of property | Dealt with the property of people with mental illness | Made no provisions for people without money or property<br>Based on Common Law with limited safeguards | Chancery Regulation Act, 1862 (England)<br>Lunacy Regulation (Ireland) Act, 1871 | 1324–present |
| Asylum-based care | Provision of care for poor and homeless people with mental illness<br>First access to care for people with mental illness | Large-scale institutionalization<br>Often inhumane condition in asylums | The Lunatic Asylums (Ireland) Act, 1875<br>Mental Patients' Custody Act, 1900 (Japan)<br>The Law of 1838 (France) | 1800s–1960s |
| Advent of effective pharmacological treatments and the end of the asylum era | Deinstitutionalization<br>Promotion of autonomy<br>Development of community services | Insufficient bed numbers and deprivation of treatment for those needing inpatient care<br>Community-based services often underdeveloped | Mental Retardation and Community Mental Health Centers Construction Act, 1963 (USA)<br>Italian Mental Health Act, 1978 (Italy) | 1960s–1980s |
| Patient-centred, de-stigmatizing legislation pre-CRPD | Enhancing dignity and moving away from coercive treatments; enhanced protections when coercive measures are used | Patient advocacy groups felt reforms did not go far enough<br>Excessive coercive measures remain in place<br>Often works from a substitute decision-making paradigm | Mental Health Care Act, 2002 (South Africa)<br>Mental Health Ordinance, 2001 (Pakistan) | 1990s–2006 |
| CRPD-informed, rights-based mental health legislation | Affirms multiple rights especially dignity and autonomy<br>Moves away from substitute decision-making to supported decision-making | Potentially limits people with severe illness from accessing treatment<br>Criminalization of people with mental illness could occur if their capacity cannot be questioned, with resulting stigmatization | Law 29973, the General Law on People with Disabilities, 2012 (Peru)<br>Mental Healthcare Act, 2017 (India) | 2006–present |

referred to as 'Chancery' idiots or lunatics because it was the responsibility of the Lord Chancellor to take charge of their property on behalf of the monarch.

As a result, prior to the late eighteenth century, the majority of mental health legislation dealt with the estates of people with mental illness (Parry-Jones 1972). Other legislative measures that concerned the mentally ill were primarily designed to deal with criminals, the homeless and the unemployed. In the England and Wales, these were generally addressed in the Poor Law system. Overall, however, little attention was devoted to the needs of people with mental illness who did not have significant possessions. The first piece of legislation to relate to 'pauper lunatics' was the Vagrancy Act, 1744 which allowed for the incarceration of the 'furiously mad' (Hamilton 1983). Scotland had similar legislation with the Scottish Poor Law, 1845 (Farquharson 2017).

### *1.2.2 Early Residential Care*

The Poor Law system led to the expansion of 'madhouses' which had been in existence since the 1600s and which acted as precursors of the later, larger asylums. In England, these establishments were regulated in 1774 by the Madhouses Act, which attempted to ensure that people in 'madhouses' were kept in humane conditions. Private institutions for the mentally ill also existed outside the United Kingdom with a diverse array of establishments in countries ranging from India (Somasundaram 2008) to Germany (Schmideler and Steinberg 2004). Generally, these establishments were not initially regulated by legislation, although with increasing levels of detention, legislative underpinnings began to expand (e.g. the County Asylums Act, 1808 in England and Wales).

### *1.2.3 The Asylum Era*

In many ways, the rise of the asylums in the nineteenth century began in England, the first country to legislate for the large-scale building of public state asylums. These replaced and upscaled the poorly regulated 'madhouses' of the 1700s. This process began in earnest with the County Asylums Act, 1808 and France followed suit with the Law of 1838 (Shorter 1997, 2007). In 1845, England replaced the 1808 Act with the County Asylums Act, 1845 and the Lunacy Act, 1845, which provided a place of refuge for 'pauper lunatics' and mentally ill offenders. The legislation also provided for the inspection of the asylums by the Commissioners in Lunacy. Patients admitted under the Lunacy Act, 1845 did not have a right to challenge their detention in the courts. Other relevant legislation included the Lunatic Asylums Act, 1853 and the Lunacy Act, 1890.

Other countries in the British Empire developed legislation that mirrored that of England. Australia, for example, used the Dangerous Lunatics Act, 1843, which saw little change until the Mental Health Act, 1958. Ireland, Scotland, Nigeria and India all had similar pieces of legislation (Porter and Wright 2003). Canada did not incorporate the English Poor Law system when it gained independence and consequently many people with mental illness ended up in prison. In 1839, an act was passed to construct an asylum in Ontario and while it was under construction Toronto Gaol was used to care for the mentally ill (Wright et al. 2003).

Porter and Wright (2003) highlight how the asylum movement became prominent outside of the British Empire. They describe developments in South Africa, Switzerland, France, Germany, Argentina and Mexico. Norway, too, enacted its Insane Act in 1848 (Sinnssykeloven). Japan's legislation came much later, with the Mental Patients' Custody Act, 1900 and inpatient care was further embedded into law with the Mental Hospitals Act, 1919 (Suzuki 2003). Despite trailing 100 years behind other jurisdictions, the Japanese institutionalized care of individuals with mental illness had many parallels with the English system.

Generally speaking, all of these many, many asylums were built with the intention of helping people with mental illness who could not afford to pay for private care, with the result that the 'pauper insane' duly made up the vast majority of inpatients (Miller 2007). These institutions were, however, soon both overcrowded and underfunded (Piddock 2004); grounds for admission were often unclear, and if discharge occurred, it was a highly uncertain, protracted process (Luchins 1988). The asylums were also rife with medical illness and many patients died from infectious diseases such tuberculosis (Anonymous 1902). Over time, attention in the asylums inevitably shifted from the care of individual patients to the management of increasingly large, increasingly unhygienic and increasingly unmanageable institutions.

### *1.2.4 Deinstitutionalization*

The advent of effective treatments for mental illness, chiefly in the 1950s and 1960s, heralded a major shift in mental health legislation. The arrival of treatments such as chlorpromazine expanded the scope of mental health laws from simply the management of property and containment of mentally ill people, to the provision of care and treatment. This led to the dismantling of many asylums and vigorous, if variously successful, efforts to move care to outpatient settings.

The most direct approach was taken in Italy where the Mental Health Act, 1978 (the 'Basaglia Law') aimed to eliminate asylum-based care entirely (Crepet and De Plato 1983). In America, the Community Mental Health Act was passed in 1963 and resulted in a reduction in the numbers in asylums and expansion of community-based services. Reform in the UK was more gradual, following the Mental Health Act, 1959 which removed the distinction between asylums and other types of hospitals. While many psychiatric hospitals remained operational into the 1980s, the adoption of more progressive, less coercive laws to facilitate treatment undoubtedly contributed to the decline of institutional care (Rachlin 1983).

Over this period, the evolution of mental health legislation was, however, shaped by a number of disparate factors, including not only new treatments but also contemporary social and political events. For example, the libertarian and anti-establishment perspectives common in the 1960s and 1970s, combined with the rising costs of inpatient care, called into serious question the appropriateness of long-term psychiatric admissions and provided people with more protections during involuntary care (Appelbaum 1996). While this process of change was generally positive, however, it also led to the criminalisation of some people with mental illness, as the number of mentally ill people in prisons increased following the failure of the mental health system to provide a sufficient range of inpatient and outpatient treatment interventions for them (Lamb and Weinberger 2019).

### *1.2.5 Rights-Based Mental Health Law*

Following the end of the Second World War, increased emphasis was placed on human rights, as reflected in the United Nations' (UN) Universal Declaration of Human Rights, the rise of increasingly democratic forms of government, and the establishment of bodies such as the European Court of Human Rights. In psychiatry, the advent of effective treatments and the emergence of anti-psychiatry and 'survivors of psychiatry' movements further increased recognition of the rights of people with mental illness.

Against this background, many countries revised their mental health legislation in parallel with psychiatric deinstitutionalization in order to provide better mental healthcare rather than simply addressing legal matters concerning involuntary detention. For example, Western Australia introduced the Mental Health Act, 1996 which explicitly protected the rights of patients, promoted the least restrictive forms of treatment and stated that mental illness alone could not be grounds for involuntary detention. Some of the legislation of this era also removed stigmatizing terminology and provided enhanced reviews of coercive practices, as described by the World Health Organization (WHO) in its *Resource Book on Mental Health, Human Rights and Legislation* (2005).

The single-most significant force driving rights-based mental health legislation today is the UN Convention on the Rights of Persons with Disabilities (CRPD) (2006). The European Union (EU) Agency for Fundamental Rights (2015), for example, has highlighted many of the policy and legislative changes that have occurred in the EU as a result of the CRPD. The Convention has triggered a number of fundamental paradigm shifts, including replacing substitute decision-making with supported decision-making, strongly affirming capacity and autonomy, and, according to one interpretation, banning all coercive treatments (UN Committee on the Rights of Persons with Disabilities 2014).

The CRPD places patients at the centre of all mental health legislation and makes protecting rights the key driving principle. Good examples of legislation attempting to realize the CRPD include Mental Health Law 29889 in Peru (Toyama et al. 2017) and the Mental Healthcare Act, 2017 in India (Duffy and Kelly 2019). The latter is an example of legislation written explicitly to concord with the CRPD and is the chief focus of this book.

Despite all these developments, however, more than one-third of countries in the world still have no formal mental health law, and many others have highly outdated legislation that is not rights-based and primarily defines involuntary treatments rather than articulating a more positive vision of mental healthcare (WHO 2018). There is still much work to be done.

## 1.3 Political and Ideologically Driven Legislation Relating to Mental Illness

Over past decades, various laws have emerged that are not explicitly pieces of mental health legislation but that nonetheless significantly impact on people with mental illness, i.e. they do not seek comprehensively to address the needs of the mentally ill in the various countries involved, but instead address discrete areas that impact on the mentally ill in other ways. These laws are often politically or ideologically driven. Examples include legislation establishing who can be conscripted into the military, legislation concerning marriage, and laws relating to mentally ill offenders. These are often reactive pieces of legislation passed following issues that have arisen in different contexts. Indicative examples are summarised in Table 1.2 and discussed in more detail below.

### *1.3.1 Military Psychiatry*

Legislation relating to military psychiatry has had significant influence on the field of psychiatry more generally. American military psychiatry has been particularly influential. One of the key motivations behind the creation of the American Psychiatric Association's (APA) *Diagnostic and Statistical Manual of Mental Disorders* (DSM) (APA 2013) was to facilitate the treatment of veterans of World War II (Houts 2000). While the 'Medical 203' was not strictly speaking a law, it served a similar purpose, leading to the creation of the original DSM (APA 1952) and greatly influencing the inclusion of mental disorders in what would later become the WHO's *International Classification of Mental and Behavioural Disorders (Volume 10)* (WHO 1992).

Military psychiatry has also had an impact on how conditions that are common in the military are perceived when they occur in the general population. It has been suggested that the use of PTSD in American legislation impacts on how the condition is perceived more broadly, leading to the minimisation of non-combat-related PTSD and creating barriers to care for non-veterans with the condition (Purtle 2016).

**Table 1.2** Political and ideologically driven legislation that has impacted on people with mental illness

| Driving force behind legislation | Positive consequences of legislation | Negative consequences of legislation | Examples of legislation |
|---|---|---|---|
| Concerns about the mental health of soldiers | Development of psychometric testing<br>Development of treatments, especially for post-traumatic stress disorder (PTSD) and substance misuse | Interventions and legislation often not based on medical evidence but on the needs of the military<br>Over-emphasis of combat as the main cause for PTSD | Medical 203 (1943) (USA)<br>Federal Framework on Post-Traumatic Stress Disorder, 2018 (Canada) |
| Eugenics | Nil | Serialization of hundreds of thousands of people with mental illness<br>Mass euthanasia programmes<br>Propagation of racist ideology | Law for the Prevention of Genetically Diseased Offspring, 1933 (Germany)<br>Sexual Sterilization Act, 1933 (British Columbia, Canada)<br>Maternal and Infant Health Care Law, 1994 (China) |
| Events interpreted as indicating a need to protect society | Supporters of such legislation believe it reduces risk | Reduced personal autonomy, dignity and justice; increased stigma<br>Rushed legislation<br>Non-evidence-based reforms | Mental Health Act, 1973 (South Africa)<br>Proposition 63 (2004) (California)<br>Section 9.60 of New York State Mental Health Law, 1999 |
| Legislation relating to suicide | Some have argued it creates a moral and social barrier that reduces risk of suicide | Can criminalize and stigmatize people who die by suicide and their families<br>Can prevent people with suicidal ideation from seeking help<br>Obstructs the collection of data related to suicide through underreporting | Section 327 of the Criminal Code Act, 1990 (Nigeria)<br>Section 309 of Singapore Penal Code (Singapore) |

(continued)

**Table 1.2** (continued)

| Driving force behind legislation | Positive consequences of legislation | Negative consequences of legislation | Examples of legislation |
|---|---|---|---|
| Forensic psychiatry | Decriminalization of people with mental illness who engage in offending behaviour<br>Protections for people with mental illness | May be seen to limit the legal capacity of people with mental illness | Homicide Act, 1957 (England)<br>Penal Law (Article 34) (Greece) |
| Marriage laws | May provide some protections for people who do not have the mental capacity to consent to marriage but at significant cost to the rights of others | Stigmatizes people with mental illness, reducing their reproductive rights and right to a family<br>Legislation often spuriously used against women with no mental illness | The Special Marriage Act, 1954 (India)<br>Law Reform (Marriage and Divorce) Act 164, 1976 (Malaysia) |

### 1.3.2 Eugenics

In parts of North America, Poland and Germany, the evolution of psychiatry occurred in parallel with the emergence of eugenics, around the turn of the nineteenth century (Stahnisch 2014; Gawin 2007). As a result, many countries enacted legislation permitting eugenics and grossly limiting the reproductive rights of the mentally ill.

Fourteen countries explicitly legislated for involuntary sterilization (Amy and Rowlands 2018a). In 1907, the US was the first country to introduce laws allowing the forced sterilization of people with intellectual disabilities (Diekema 2003). In total, 30 US states enacted sterilization laws and over 20,000 people were sterilized on the basis of mental illness. Forced sterilization remained legal in certain states until the 1980s (Amy and Rowlands 2018a) and mental illness was the most common reason for sterilization in America for much of this time (Reilly 1987).

In 1934, the British Brock Report recommended introducing legislation that would allow for the sterilization of people who might 'transmit mental disorder or deficit' (Amy and Rowlands 2018a). In 1940, Japan introduced a National Eugenics Law that permitted the forced sterilization of people with 'inherited' mental illness. Switzerland was the first European country to introduce such laws in 1928 and they remained in force up until the 1990s (Amy and Rowlands 2018b).

The most infamous eugenics legislation was in Germany where, in 1933, the 'Law for the Prevention of Hereditarily Diseased Offspring' was passed, based heavily on the US legislation. The German law was applied to a wide range of people with mental health conditions. Germany used sterilization more frequently than other countries, sterilizing almost 400,000 people between 1933 and 1939 (Proctor 1988). After 1939, Germany adopted a 'euthanasia' programme in which it killed up to 85% of its people with severe mental illness (Wyszinski 1998). Other countries that enacted eugenics laws include Austria, Canada, Denmark, Estonia, Finland, Iceland, Japan, Mexico, Norway and Sweden. As recently as the 1990s, China introduced legislation that allowed for the sterilization of people with a history of mental illness (Pearson 1995).

While mental health law in most countries has now evolved away from explicit eugenics, some have argued that current US legislation is more inclined to fund incarceration rather than the treatment for the mentally ill and therefore facilitates a form of de facto eugenics (Appleman 2018). Either way, eugenics is a tragic episode in the history of psychiatry that must be borne in mind when considering the history of the discipline and the necessity for a clear focus on human rights in contemporary mental health legislation.

### 1.3.3 Key Events and the Protection of Society

From time to time, social and political events lead to rapid changes in legislation to address specific incidents or circumstances. This can be particularly relevant in jurisdictions that place a strong emphasis on case law, such as England and Wales. In 1843, for example, Daniel M'Naughten killed the British prime minister's secretary, believing him to be the prime minster, while suffering from paranoid delusions. This led to the M'Naughten rule which has been highly influential internationally in defining the verdict of 'not guilty by reason of insanity'. Remnants of this ruling persisted for well over a century and can still be seen in the legislation of many countries today (Arboleda-Florez 1978). In another example from the US, Anfang and Appelbaum (1996) describe how the Tarasoff case impacted legislation in the 20 years that followed the original case.

Other recent examples of laws reacting to recent events include Laura's Law (California State) and Kendra's Law (New York State), both of which provide for court ordered outpatient treatment for people with mental illness. These pieces of legislation are named in memory of two people who were killed by persons with mental illness who had refused treatment. In addition, mass shootings have prompted revisions to gun laws which have often impacted on people with mental illness (Kass 2014). Rushed legislation always runs the risk of unintended consequences and all too often these laws facilitate new limitations on the rights of the mentally ill that require careful evaluation if they are to be justified on an ongoing basis.

Contemporary politics can also influence mental health laws. One of the clearest examples of this occurred in the former Soviet Union, where mental health legislation facilitated the silencing of political opposition (Thompson 1990). Popular religious perspectives can also influence laws that pertain to mental illness, as is clear from the discussions on legislation relating mental illness with suicide and marriage (below).

### *1.3.4 Legislation Relating to Suicide*

The legal prohibition on suicide dates back to ancient Greece (Papadimitriou et al. 2007) and continued into the modern era through Church law: the Catholic Church refused to bury people who died by suicide from the sixth century onwards (Dine 2019). For this reason, establishing instances of suicide was important in medieval Europe and such cases often came before the courts (Trenery and Horden 2017). On occasion, the family of a person who had died by suicide was punished (Behere et al. 2015). This legal prohibition against suicide can also be seen in the English lexicon where people often refer to a person 'committing' suicide, a remnant of suicide's former status as a crime as well as a sin.

Germany was the first country to decriminalize suicide attempts in 1751 (Kazarian and Persad 2001). Other countries in Europe and North America began to follow suit (Behere et al. 2015). Some took a considerable period of time to make this change in legislation; Ireland, for example, passed its Criminal Law (Suicide) Act in 1993 (Osman et al. 2017). In 1983, the Roman Catholic Church revised its Canon law to permit full funeral rights for people who died by suicide.

In India, Section 309 of the Indian Penal Code makes provision for the incarceration of people who attempt suicide (Behere et al. 2015), but this has been addressed in the Mental Healthcare Act, 2017 (Section 115(1)). Section 309 of the Singapore Penal Code also prohibited suicide until this was revised in 2019. Suicide remains a criminal offence in Nigeria under Section 327 of the Criminal Code Act, 1990. A 2016 review of legislation across 192 countries identified 25 countries where suicide is currently illegal and 20 others where, under Islamic or Sharia law, suicide attempts may result in jail sentences (Mishara and Weisstub 2016). While there is a shift away from criminalizing suicide attempts, then, people who attempt suicide still receive custodial sentences in certain countries.

### *1.3.5 Forensic Psychiatry*

In its early iterations, forensic psychiatry legislation had broad powers and formed a key element of general asylum systems in many countries, such as Great Britain (through its Criminal Lunatics Act, 1800). Such legislation generally addresses the evaluation of a person's fitness to plead and the insanity defence, as well as how people with mental illness progress through the criminal justice system, how prisoners with mental illness are treated and how mental illness can lead to some degree of mitigation following offending behaviour.

Laws relating to fitness to be tried in court have been in existence for centuries (Mudathikundan et al. 2014). As early as 1583, juries had to determine if someone was 'mute of malice or by visitation of God' (Walker 1968). Legislation concerning fitness to plead was formalized during the nineteenth century with legislation like the Criminal Lunatics Act, 1800 and the Prison Act, 1865 (Mudathikundan et al. 2014). Outside of Great Britain, other countries also increasingly identified that many defendants had unmet mental health needs and these people were often diverted to forensic psychiatry hospitals (Konrad and Völlm 2014). Many countries now have formal prerequisites relating to mental health and being tried (e.g. Section 4 of Ireland's Criminal law (Insanity) Act, 2006, as amended in 2010).

As trial by jury replaced trial by ordeal in twelfth-century England, pardon started to be given to people with mental illness who had committed serious crimes (Higgins 1986). Insanity defences were heavily influenced by a number of English cases in the eighteenth and nineteenth centuries, of which the best known was the 1843 M'Naughten case (Higgins 1986). The impact of this case influenced judges and legislators across the world (Allnutt et al. 2007; Weiss and Gupta 2018). As the field of forensic psychiatry continues to evolve, future legislation will need to take account of the CRPD and its strong affirmation of legal capacity. Concerns have been raised that an overly dogmatic approach to this in the area of mental health could result in the criminalisation of people with mental illness (Freeman et al. 2015.)

### *1.3.6 Marriage Laws*

From medieval times, the ability of people with mental illness to marry has been debated in court (Trenery and Horden 2017). Positions on this issue have often been formalized in law, including, for example, Malaysia's Law Reform (Marriage and Divorce) Act 164, 1976 (Reddy 1995). In India, the Special Marriage Act, 1954 and Hindu Marriage Act, 1955 both limited the ability of people with mental illness to marry (Sharma et al. 2015). Such laws remain a major problem today and may represent a continuation of the eugenics ideology of a century earlier (see above). One 2016 analysis of 193 countries found that 37% prohibited people with mental illness from marrying and 11% stated that mental health problems were grounds for declaring a marriage void (Bhugra et al. 2016).

## 1.4 Summary

National mental health legislation has formally existed since the eighteenth century, prior to which Canon law sought to address certain issues relating to mental illness, albeit inconsistently. The British were among the first to develop dedicated mental health legislation, with their former colonies and neighbouring countries later following suit. Over this period, mental health laws have not always served people with mental illness well, often contributing to stigmatization, marginalization, separation, sterilization and even premature mortality through persistent social exclusion and de facto denial of medical and social care.

Mental health legislation has always been shaped by societal needs and contemporary ideologies as well as the needs of the mentally ill. Since the advent of effective pharmacological treatments and deinstitutionalization, such legislation has increasingly sought to pro-actively protect the rights of people with mental illness but, even so, the evolution of mental health legislation has not been free from problems.

Unintended negative consequences, such as neglect, often stem from a failure to fund the requisite paradigm shifts. In the nineteenth century, asylums were built with excellent intentions, but were underfunded, poorly managed and, later, squalid and inhumane. After the majority of asylums were closed in most countries, community treatments were, in turn, insufficiently funded; people who had been institutionalized found themselves homeless and lacking outpatient or inpatient mental healthcare owing to insufficient resourcing (Lovell 1986; Rathod et al. 2017). Paradoxically, inadequate funding of the latest rights-based iterations of mental health law could also have the inadvertent effect of worsening the realization of human rights for the mentally ill, using the idea of liberty as a cover for neglect.

Most of the recent rights-based developments are undoubtedly positive, at least in theory: they place the person at the centre of care and they make provision for mental healthcare rather than just involuntary treatment. However, psychiatry cannot be blind to the fact that many of these changes are still ideologically driven (albeit based on the contemporary ideology of rights) and could prove harmful should adequate funding not be provided to realize the new laws, resulting in a net diminution of care and support provided to the mentally ill and their families.

Developing new legislation in the absence of political will and societal change will not realize the intended benefits for the mentally ill. The goal in writing and passing mental health legislation is not the legislation itself, but improved quality and quantity of life for people with mental illness. If the CRPD is to be incorporated into national mental health law, it is important that each jurisdiction does not blindly adopt its principles, but rather strive to realize them in a manner that promotes best outcomes in their particular cultural and economic contexts. Failure to do so runs the risk of imposing an ideological dogma that might actually erode the rights of the mentally ill, rather than promote them.

### *1.4.1 India's Mental Healthcare Act, 2017*

India's new Mental Healthcare Act, 2017 (MHCA), the central focus of this book, is one of the most modern, interesting and potentially progressive pieces of mental health law in the world, but it is also acutely aware of the historical evolution of mental health legislation that is described above. As a consequence, the Indian legislation takes many steps to undo and protect against some of the older, damaging legislation that existed both in India and in other countries.

For example, the new Indian Act includes provisions prohibiting sterilisation (Section 95(1)(c)), decriminalising suicide (Section 115(1)) and promoting community-based treatment (Section 18(5)(b)). Unfortunately, other Indian laws relating to marriage are still stigmatizing for the mentally ill and limit their right to a family. Reproductive rights and the rights to a home and family are protected in the Rights of Persons with Disabilities Act, 2016 (Sections 9 and 10) but the Hindu Marriage Act, 1955 undermines many of these provisions and perpetuates outdated negative stereotypes (Narayan et al. 2015). Clearly, there is still work to be done.

Overall, India's MHCA is written to accord with the CRPD but does not embrace the CRPD unquestioningly, as some have suggested it should. Legislators have, for example, included pragmatic tools for the protection and treatment of the acutely mentally ill (e.g. 'supported admission') (Sections 89 and 90). While these provisions might be at odds with the UN Committee on the Rights of Persons with Disabilities' (2014) interpretation of the CPRD, they have dramatically revised Indian mental health legislation to bring it into greater accordance with the core principles of the CRPD itself. India's revisions also appear cognisant of the potential negative consequences of an over-literal application of the CRPD (Appelbaum 2019; Freeman et al. 2015). As a result, India's new legislation has taken large steps to protect against some of the historical errors in mental health legislation and, hopefully, demonstrate how low- and middle-income countries can realize modern, rights-based mental health law. These themes are explored in greater depth throughout the rest of this book.

## References


Allnutt, S., Samuels, A., & O'Driscoll, C. (2007). The insanity defence: From wild beasts to M'Naghten. *Australasian Psychiatry, 15*(4), 292–298.

American Psychiatric Association. (1952). *Diagnostic and statistical manual of mental disorders* (1st ed.). Washington, DC: American Psychiatric Association.

American Psychiatric Association. (2013). *Diagnostic and statistical manual of mental disorders* (5th ed.). Washington, DC: American Psychiatric Association.

Amy, J. J., & Rowlands, S. (2018a). Legalised non-consensual sterilisation—Eugenics put into practice before 1945, and the aftermath. Part 1: USA, Japan, Canada and Mexico. *European Journal of Contraception Reproductive Health Care, 23*(2), 121–129.

Amy, J. J., & Rowlands, S. (2018b). Legalised non-consensual sterilisation—Eugenics put into practice before 1945, and the aftermath. Part 2: Europe. *European Journal of Contraception Reproductive Health Care, 23*(3), 194–200.

Anfang, S. A., & Appelbaum, P. S. (1996). Twenty years after Tarasoff: Reviewing the duty to protect. *Harvard Review of Psychiatry, 4*(2), 67–76.

Anonymous. (1902). Tuberculosis in Lunatic Asylums. *British Medical Journal, 2*(2182), 1349–1351.

Appelbaum, P. (1996). Civil mental health law: Its history and its future. *Mental and Physical Disability Law Reporter, 20*(5), 599–604.

Appelbaum, P. S. (2019). Saving the UN Convention on the Rights of Persons with Disabilities—From itself. *World Psychiatry, 18*(1), 1–2.

Appleman, L. I. (2018). Deviancy, dependency, and disability: The forgotten history of eugenics and mass incarceration. *Duke Law Journal, 68*(3), 417–478.

Arboleda-Florez, J. (1978). Insanity defense in Canada. *Canadian Psychiatric Association Journal, 23*(1), 23–27.

Behere, P. B., Sathyanarayana Rao, T. S., & Mulmule, A. N. (2015). Decriminalization of attempted suicide law: Journey of fifteen decades. *Indian Journal of Psychiatry, 57*(2), 122–124.

Berkson, G. (2006). Mental disabilities in Western civilization from ancient Rome to the Prerogativa Regis. *Mental Retardation, 44*(1), 28–40.

Bhugra, D., Pathare, S., Nardodkar, R., Gosavi, C., Ng, R., Torales, J., et al. (2016). Legislative provisions related to marriage and divorce of persons with mental health problems: A global review. *International Review of Psychiatry, 28*(4), 386–392.

Bou Khalil, R., & Richa, S. (2014). When affective disorders were considered to emanate from the heart: The Ebers papyrus. *American Journal of Psychiatry, 171*(3), 275.

Collado-Vázquez, S., & Carrillo, J. M. (2014). Cranial trepanation in The Egyptian. *Neurologia, 29*(7), 433–440.

Crepet, P., & De Plato, G. (1983). Psychiatry without asylums: Origins and prospects in Italy. *International Journal of Health Services, 13*(1), 119–129.

Diekema, D. S. (2003). Involuntary sterilization of persons with mental retardation: An ethical analysis. *Mental Retardation and Developmental Disabilities Research Reviews, 9,* 21–26.

Dine, R. L. (2019). You shall bury him: Burial, suicide and the development of Catholic law and theology. *Medical Humanities*. https://doi.org/10.1136/medhum-2018-011622. [Epub ahead of print].

Duffy, R. M., & Kelly, B. D. (2019). India's Mental Healthcare Act, 2017: Content, context, controversy. *International Journal of Law and Psychiatry, 62,* 169–178.

European Union Agency for Fundamental Rights. (2015). *Implementing the United Nations Convention on the Rights of Persons with Disabilities: An overview of legal reforms in EU Member States*. Luxembourg: FRA Publications Office.

Farquharson, L. (2017). A 'Scottish poor law of lunacy'? Poor law, lunacy law and Scotland's parochial asylums. *History of Psychiatry, 28*(1), 15–28.

Freeman, M. C., Kolappa, K., de Almeida, J. M., Kleinman, A., Makhashvili, N., Phakathi, S., et al. (2015). Reversing hard won victories in the name of human rights: A critique of the General

Comment on Article 12 of the UN Convention on the Rights of Persons with Disabilities. *Lancet Psychiatry, 2*(9), 844–850.

Gawin, M. (2007). Polish psychiatrists and eugenic sterilization during the interwar period. *International Journal of Mental Health, 36*(1), 67–78.

Hamilton, J. R. (1983). Mental Health Act, 1983. *British Medical Journal, 286*(6379), 1720–1725.

Haque, A. (2004). Psychology from Islamic perspective: Contributions of early Muslim scholars and challenges to contemporary Muslim psychologists. *Journal of Religion and Health, 43*(4), 357–377.

Higgins, J. (1986). The origins of the Homicide Act 1957. *Journal of Medical Ethics, 12*(1), 8–12.

Hobert, L., & Binello, E. (2017). Trepanation in ancient China. *World Neurosurgery, 101,* 451–456.

Houts, A. C. (2000). Fifty years of psychiatric nomenclature: Reflections on the 1943 War Department Technical Bulletin, Medical 203. *Journal of Clinical Psychology, 56*(7), 935–967.

Kass, J. (2014). Gun violence and mental illness. *Lancet Psychiatry, 1*(5), 335–336.

Kazarian, S. S., & Persad, E. (2001). Cultural issues in suicidal behavior. In S. S. Kazarian & D. R. Evans (Eds.), *Handbook of cultural health psychology* (pp. 267–302). London: Elsevier.

Kelly, B. D. (2016). *Hearing voices: The history of psychiatry in Ireland.* Dublin: Irish Academic Press.

Konrad, N., & Völlm, B. (2014). Forensic psychiatric expert witnessing within the criminal justice system in Germany. *International Journal of Law and Psychiatry, 37*(2), 149–154.

Lamb, H. R., & Weinberger, L. E. (2019). Deinstitutionalization and other factors in the criminalization of persons with serious mental illness and how it is being addressed. *CNS Spectrums.* https://doi.org/10.1017/s1092852919001524. [Epub ahead of print].

Lovell, A. M. (1986). The paradoxes of reform: Re-evaluating Italy's mental health law of 1978. *Hospital & Community Psychiatry, 37*(8), 802–808.

Luchins, A. S. (1988). The rise and decline of the American asylum movement in the 19th century. *Journal of Psychology, 122*(5), 471–486.

Miller, E. (2007). Variations in the official prevalence and disposal of the insane in England under the poor law, 1850–1900. *History of Psychiatry, 18*(1), 25–38.

Mishara, B. L., & Weisstub, D. N. (2016). The legal status of suicide: A global review. *International Journal of Law and Psychiatry, 44,* 54–74.

Mudathikundan, F., Chao, O., & Forrester, A. (2014). Mental health and fitness to plead proposals in England and Wales. *International Journal of Law and Psychiatry, 37*(2), 135–141.

Murad, I., & Gordon, H. (2002). Psychiatry and the Palestinian population. *Psychiatric Bulletin, 26*(1), 28–30.

Narayan, C. L., Narayan, M., Shikha, D., & Shekhar, S. (2015). Indian marriage laws and mental disorders: Is it necessary to amend the legal provisions? *Indian Journal of Psychiatry, 57*(4), 341–344.

Osman, M., Parnell, A. C., & Haley, C. (2017). 'Suicide shall cease to be a crime': Suicide and undetermined death trends 1970–2000 before and after the decriminalization of suicide in Ireland 1993. *Irish Journal of Medical Science, 186*(1), 201–205.

Papadimitriou, J. D., Skiadas, P., Mavrantonis, C. S., Polimeropoulos, V., Papadimitriou, D. J., & Papacostas, K. J. (2007). Euthanasia and suicide in antiquity: Viewpoint of the dramatists and philosophers. *Journal of the Royal Society of Medicine, 100*(1), 25–28.

Parry-Jones, W. L. (1972). *The trade in lunacy: A study of private madhouses in England in the eighteenth and nineteenth centuries.* London: Routledge & Kegan Paul.

Pearson, V. (1995). Population policy and eugenics in China. *British Journal of Psychiatry, 167*(1), 1–4.

Piddock, S. (2004). Possibilities and realities: South Australia's asylums in the 19th century. *Australasian Psychiatry, 12*(2), 172–175.

Porter, R., & Wright, D. (Eds.). (2003). *The confinement of the insane: International perspectives, 1800–1965.* Cambridge: Cambridge University Press.

Proctor, R. N. (1988). *Racial hygiene: Medicine under the Nazis.* Cambridge, MS: Harvard University Press.

Purtle, J. (2016). 'Heroes' invisible wounds of war': Constructions of posttraumatic stress disorder in the text of US federal legislation. *Social Science and Medicine, 149*, 9–16.

Rachlin, S. (1983). The influence of law on deinstitutionalization. *New Directions for Mental Health Services, 17*, 41–54.

Reddy, R. (1995). Marriage and divorce regulation and recognition in Malaysia. *Family Law Quarterly, 29*(3), 613–625.

Reilly, P. R. (1987). Involuntary sterilization in the United States: A surgical solution. *Quarterly Review of Biology, 62*(2), 153–170.

Restak, R. (2000). *Mysteries of the mind*. Washington, DC: National Geographic Society.

Rathod, S., Pinninti, N., Irfan, M., Gorczynski, P., Rathod, P., Gega, L., et al. (2017). Mental health service provision in low- and middle-income countries. *Health Services Insights, 10*, 1178632917694350.

Sabry, W. M., & Vohra, A. (2013). Role of Islam in the management of psychiatric disorders. *Indian Journal of Psychiatry, 55*(2), S205–S214.

Schmideler, S., & Steinberg, H. (2004). Psychiatrist Johann Christian August Heinroth's (1773–1843) practical work at St George's prison, orphanage and madhouse in Leipzig. *Wurzburger Medizinhistorische Mitteilungen, 23*, 346–375.

Sharma, I., Reddy, K. R., & Kamath, R. M. (2015). Marriage, mental illness and law. *Indian Journal of Psychiatry, 57*(2), S339–S344.

Shorter, E. (1997). *A history of psychiatry: From the era of the asylum to the age of Prozac*. New York: Wiley.

Shorter, E. (2007). The historical development of mental health services in Europe. In M. Knapp, D. McDaid, E. Mossialos, & G. Thornicroft (Eds.), *Mental health policy and practice across Europe: The future direction of mental health care* (pp. 15–33). Maidenhead: Open University Press.

Somasundaram, O. (1987). The Indian Lunacy Act, 1912: The historic background. *Indian Journal of Psychiatry, 29*(1), 3–14.

Somasundaram, O. (2008). Private psychiatric care in the past, with special reference to Chennai. *Indian Journal of Psychiatry, 50*(1), 67–69.

Somasundaram, O., & Murthy, T. (2018). The Lord Buddha destigmatizes mental illness. *Indian Journal of Psychiatry, 60*(1), 135–137.

Stahnisch, F. W. (2014). The early eugenics movement and emerging professional psychiatry: Conceptual transfers and personal relationships between Germany and North America, 1880s to 1930s. *Canadian Bulletin of Medical History, 31*(1), 17–40.

Suzuki, A. (2003). The state, family, and the insane in Japan, 1900–1945. In R. Porter & D. Wright (Eds.), *The confinement of the insane: International perspectives, 1800–1965* (pp. 193–225). Cambridge: Cambridge University Press.

Thompson, L. M. (1990). Soviet straitjacket psychiatry: New legislation to end the psychiatric reign of terror in the U.S.S.R. *Syracuse Journal of International Law and Commerce, 16*(2), 271–291.

Trenery, C., & Horden, P. (2017). Madness in the middle ages. In G. Eghigian (Ed.), *The Routledge history of madness and mental health* (pp. 62–80). Abingdon: Routledge.

Toyama, M., Castillo, H., Galea, J. T., Brandt, L. R., Mendoza, M., Herrera, V., et al. (2017). Peruvian mental health reform: A framework for scaling-up mental health services. *International Journal of Health Policy and Management, 6*(9), 501–508.

Tsermoulas, G., Aidonis, A., & Flint, G. (2014). The skull of Chios: Trepanation in Hippocratic medicine. *Journal of Neurosurgery, 121*(2), 328–332.

United Nations. (2006). *Convention on the rights of persons with disabilities*. New York: United Nations. Retrieved September 23, 2019, from https://www.un.org/development/desa/disabilities/convention-on-the-rights-of-persons-with-disabilities/convention-on-the-rights-of-persons-with-disabilities-2.html.

United Nations Committee on the Rights of Persons with Disabilities. (2014). *General comment No. 1: Article 12: Equal recognition before the law*. New York: United Nations. Retrieved July 25, 2019, from http://www.ohchr.org/EN/HRBodies/CRPD/Pages/GC.aspx.

Walker, N. (1968). *Crime and insanity in England: Volume 1—The historical perspective*. Edinburgh: Edinburgh University Press.
Weiss, K. J., & Gupta, N. (2018). America's first M'Naghten defense and the origin of the black rage syndrome. *Journal of the American Academy of Psychiatry and the Law, 46*(4), 503–512.
World Health Organization. (1992). *International classification of mental and behavioural disorders* (Vol. 10). Geneva: World Health Organization.
World Health Organization. (2005). *WHO resource book on mental health, human rights and legislation*. Geneva: World Health Organization.
World Health Organization. (2018). *Mental health atlas 2017*. Geneva: World Health Organization.
Wright, D., Moran, J., & Gouglas, S. (2003). The confinement of the insane in Victorian Canada: The Hamilton and Toronto asylums c. 1861–1891. In R. Porter & D. Wright (Eds.), *The confinement of the insane: International perspectives 1800–1965* (pp. 100-128). Cambridge: Cambridge University Press.
Wyszinski, D. F. (1998). Fifty years after the Nuremberg Nazi doctors' trial: Reviewing how the laws of the Third Reich applied to individuals with oral clefts. *Plastic and Reconstructive Surgery, 101*(2), 519–527.

# Chapter 2
# The United Nations and Mental Health Law

## 2.1 The United Nations and Human Rights

Founded in 1945, with the purpose of maintaining international peace and security in the wake of the Second World War, the United Nations (UN) has done much to shape the latter half of the twentieth century. The organization currently comprises 193 member states.

In December 1948, the UN published the Universal Declaration of Human Rights, laying out a common standard of fundamental human rights (UN General Assembly 1948). Many of these rights would later be articulated in the context of people with disabilities and incorporated into the Convention on the Rights of Persons with Disabilities (CRPD) (UN 2006).

Many of the 30 articles of the Universal Declaration of Human Rights have direct relevance for people with mental illness. Article 3, for example, gives people the right to life, liberty and security of person. Article 6 protects an individual's right to recognition everywhere as a person before the law. Article 7 states that all persons are equal before the law. Article 9 prohibits arbitrary detention.

Liberty and equal status before the law were especially important to the mentally ill when the declaration was published because the asylum era was only beginning to come to an end at this point in the mid-twentieth century. Article 5 gives people protection from torture and from cruel, inhuman or degrading treatment. Special Rapporteurs within the UN have since described the use of non-consensual treatment as a form of torture (UN Human Rights Council 2013). Article 16 protects the equal right to marriage, which is still not available to many people with mental illness around the world (Bhugra et al. 2016).

The UN Human Rights Office of the High Commissioner recognizes nine core international human rights instruments, each with its own monitoring body. These are the International Convention on the Elimination of All Forms of Racial Discrimination (1965), the International Covenant on Civil and Political Rights (1966), International Covenant on Economic, Social and Cultural Rights (1966), the Convention on the Elimination of All Forms of Discrimination against Women (1979),



R. M. Duffy and B. D. Kelly, *India's Mental Healthcare Act, 2017*,
https://doi.org/10.1007/978-981-15-5009-6_2

the Convention against Torture and Other Cruel, Inhuman or Degrading Treatment or Punishment (1984), the Convention on the Rights of the Child (1989), the International Convention on the Protection of the Rights of All Migrant Workers and Members of Their Families (1990), the International Convention for the Protection of All Persons from Enforced Disappearance (2006) and the Convention on the Rights of Persons with Disabilities (2006). These fundamental documents have a much greater legal footing than other UN documents and have consequently had significant impact. While not all of them are directly relevant to mental illness, they have broad applications for people with mental health problems and attempt to eliminate practices that cause mental suffering.

Many of these conventions support the provision of healthcare in a general sense, although the International Covenant on Civil and Political Rights (UN General Assembly 1966a) repeatedly gives 'the protection of public health or morals' as grounds for *limitation* of rights. Article 12 of the International Covenant on Economic, Social and Cultural Rights addresses mental health directly, stating:

> The States Parties to the present Covenant recognize the right of everyone to the enjoyment of the highest attainable standard of physical and mental health (UN General Assembly 1966b).

Other conventions promote the delivery of healthcare, including mental healthcare, and identify the impact of psychological trauma, but the Convention on the Rights of the Child (UN General Assembly 1989) was the first of the core instruments to give detailed consideration to mental health. Article 17 gives a child a right to access media material promoting 'his or her social, spiritual and moral well-being and physical and mental health'. Article 19 protects children from 'mental violence'. Article 23 states:

> States Parties recognise that a mentally or physically disabled child should enjoy a full and decent life, in conditions which ensure dignity, promote self-reliance and facilitate the child's active participation in the community.

It continues by advocating for free assistance, training and education for carers. Article 25 gives children who have been placed in care due to their mental health a right to periodic review. Articles 27 and 29 promote the mental development of the child. Finally, Article 32 identifies the potential for economic exploitation to lead to mental harm. Following the Convention on the Rights of the Child (1989), the CRPD (2006) gave further consideration to mental health (below).

In recent years, many psychiatrists were disappointed that the UN did not include consideration of mental health in its Millennium Development Goals (Thornicroft and Votruba 2016). There were only minor improvements in the Sustainable Development Goals of the UN's 2030 Agenda for Sustainable Development (Cratsley and Mackey 2018; UN 2015). Bass and colleagues (2012) appealed to the UN to do more to address mental, neurological and substance use disorders.

In 2016, the UN General Assembly had a special session on drugs which addressed the needs of people with substance misuse disorders and will hopefully be instrumental in shifting the emphasis away from criminalisation and punishment towards rehabilitation, treatment and prevention (UN General Assembly Special Session on Drugs 2016). Encouragingly, this initiative also drew heavily on research in the area and was not defined by ideological views on substance misuse. This has been described as a positive and unprecedented step (Volkow et al. 2017).

## 2.2 The United Nations' Principles for the Protection of Persons with Mental Illness and the Improvement of Mental Health Care (1991)

The UN Principles for the Protection of Persons with Mental Illness and the Improvement of Mental Health Care (UN 1991) were initially developed by the Subcommission on the Prevention of Discrimination and Protection of Minorities in 1988, after which input was received from governments and non-governmental organizations (Moncada 1994). The completed document was adopted by the General Assembly in December of 1991 and laid out basic standards for mental healthcare. The 25 principles are not legally binding and do not articulate new rights but, rather, set existing rights from the Universal Declaration of Human Rights in the context of mental illness.

These rights include, *inter alia*, a right to life and a role in the community (Principles 3 and 7), protections from spurious, unfounded or malicious diagnoses (Principle 4), freedom from arbitrary medical examinations (Principle 5), confidentiality (Principle 6), the right to high-quality, individualised care, delivered in the least restrictive manner (Principles 8–10), and a requirement for consent to treatment, albeit with certain exceptions (Principle 11). There is also a prohibition on sterilization as a treatment for mental illness. This was an especially important step because eugenics legislation for people with mental health conditions existed into the 1990s (Amy and Rowlands 2018a, b).

The general limitation clause set out in the Preamble, however, arguably undermines impact of the entire document, stating:

> The exercise of the rights set forth in these Principles may be subject only to such limitations as are prescribed by law and are necessary to protect the health or safety of the person concerned or of others, or otherwise to protect public safety, order, health or morals or the fundamental rights and freedoms of others.

While it is both well established and logically necessary that there are certain contexts in which some rights may be limited (UN Economic and Social Council 1985), this clause is clearly too general and actively facilitates tokenistic acknowledgement of the principles. The impact of the document is further muted by the fact that the General Assembly resolutions are not legally binding but, rather, represent 'soft law' (Moncada 1994).

Despite their limitations, however, it was believed that the 1991 Principles could improve human rights monitoring, prompt legislative change and even be directly applied at a domestic and international level (Rosenthal and Rubenstein 1993). They were used to advocate for legislative change in, for example, Uruguay (Moncada 1994) and Australia (Zifcak 1996), but, overall, their effect has been incremental rather than transformative.

## 2.3 The United Nations' Convention on the Rights of Persons with Disabilities (2006)

The CRPD has been the driving force behind the latest iterations of mental health law internationally (European Union Agency for Fundamental Rights 2015). Some of the rights articulated in the CRPD are elaborations of those affirmed in 1991 Principles for the Protection of Persons with Mental Illness and the Improvement of Mental Health Care (Table 2.1). The 1991 Principles are, however, noticeably absent from the preamble to the CRPD and do not feature strongly in the history of the convention (Schulze 2010). The social rights articulated in the 1991 Principles are, however, considered in some detail in the CRPD. By contrast, the 1991 principles that relate to admission, coercive treatments and limitations of rights, and those that are ostensibly rooted in the 'biomedical model' of mental illness, are either not considered in the CRPD or have their validity called into question.

Overall, while the CRPD does not create any new rights, it contextualizes existing rights for people with disabilities (Schulze 2010). The convention was drafted between 2002 and 2006 in collaboration with non-governmental organizations representing the views of persons with disabilities. The General Assembly adopted the convention in 2006 and it came into force in 2008 (Steinert et al. 2016). The CRPD contains 50 articles; the first four address general principles, and Articles 31–50 focus on implementation of the convention, leaving 26 articles that directly address rights. While the CRPD is framed to address the needs of all people with disabilities, it explicitly includes people with long-term mental illness under its remit; Article 1 states that:

> Persons with disabilities include those who have long-term physical, mental, intellectual or sensory impairments which in interaction with various barriers may hinder their full and effective participation in society on an equal basis with others.

This inclusion of mental health under the remit of disability rights will have many positive outcomes (Morrissey 2012), although there are also likely to be unintended negative consequences. The amalgamation of all disabilities under the one umbrella has, for example, diminished focused consideration of the position of people with mental illness. The detailed discussion seen in Principle 11 of the Principles for the Protection of Persons with Mental Illness and the Improvement of Mental Health Care (UN 1991), for example, is absent in the CRPD.

As the CRPD was developed, non-governmental organizations representing people with mental illness strongly opposed any steps that might limit the legal capacity of people with mental illness (Melish 2014). Article 12 of the CRPD, which relates to legal capacity, was only agreed on in the final hours of the last meeting and, up to

**Table 2.1** The relationship between the United Nations' Principles for the Protection of Persons with Mental Illness and the Improvement of Mental Health Care and the United Nations' Convention on the Rights of Persons with Disabilities

| Principle in the Principles for the Protection of Persons with Mental Illness and the Improvement of Mental Health Care | Topic | Relevant article in the Convention on the Rights of Persons with Disabilities | Key notes |
|---|---|---|---|
| 1 | Fundamental freedoms and basic rights | Preamble, Article 3 | Specific items are considered in more detail throughout the CRPD |
| 2 | Protection of minors | Article 7 | CRDP affirms the best interests of the child |
| 3 | Life in the community | Article 19 | CRPD provides more holistic considerations and describes the supports needed |
| 4 | Determination of mental illness | Article 1 | CRPD shifts away from determination of illness, adopting a more inclusive approach; even disability is loosely defined in the CRPD |
| 5 | Medical examination | Articles 15 and 17 | CRPD protections are much more general |
| 6 | Confidentiality | Article 22 | |
| 7 | Role of community and culture | Articles 19, 23, 24, 26 and 30 | CRPD provides much broader consideration |
| 8 | Standards of care | Articles 15, 16, 17 and 25 | |
| 9 | Treatment | Article 25 | CRPD fully removed the term 'least restrictive' as it (arguably) attempts to prohibit all coercive treatment. Treatment is given less consideration in the CRPD as it moves away from a 'biomedical model' |

(continued)

**Table 2.1** (continued)

| Principle in the Principles for the Protection of Persons with Mental Illness and the Improvement of Mental Health Care | Topic | Relevant article in the Convention on the Rights of Persons with Disabilities | Key notes |
|---|---|---|---|
| 10 | Medication | Articles 15, 16, 17 and 25 | Medication is not directly considered in the CRPD as it moves away from a 'biomedical model', but is indirectly addressed in articles relating to health and autonomy |
| 11 | Consent to treatment | Articles 15 and 25 | A comprehensive consideration of contexts in which this right can be limited is absent from the CRPD |
| 12 | Notice of rights | Article 8 | CRPD gives broad consideration to this topic in practical terms and in varied contexts |
| 13 | Rights and conditions in mental health facilities | Articles 3, 12, 24, 26, 27 and 30 | CRPD strongly affirms equality in relation to recognition before the law |
| 14 | Resources for mental health facilities | Article 25 | Resources for mental health establishments are not given the same level of consideration in the CRPD |
| 15 | Admission principles | | CRPD is not working inside the 'biomedical' framework so it does not address this |
| 16 | Involuntary admission | Articles 12, 13, 14, 15, 16 and 17 | Some interpretations of Articles 12 and 14 would totally prohibit all coercive practices |

(continued)

**Table 2.1** (continued)

| Principle in the Principles for the Protection of Persons with Mental Illness and the Improvement of Mental Health Care | Topic | Relevant article in the Convention on the Rights of Persons with Disabilities | Key notes |
|---|---|---|---|
| 17 | Review body | Articles 12, 13, 14, 15, 16 and 17 | CRPD does not envisage coercive practices being used so it does not consider review on an individual level, although implementation of the CRPD, in general, is reviewed |
| 18 | Procedural safeguards | Articles 12, 13, 14, 15, 16 and 17 | Under the CRPD, safeguards should be provided in law to *prevent* involuntary admission |
| 19 | Access to information | Articles 12 and 21 | Not addressed adequately in the CRPD and is a potentially significant omission |
| 20 | Criminal offenders | Articles 12 and 13 | The equal recognition affirmed in the CRPD may actually limit the rights of people with disabilities in a forensic setting |
| 25 | Saving of existing rights | Article 4 | |

*Notes*
CRPD: United Nations' Convention on the Rights of Persons with Disabilities
Principles 21–24 of the UN Principles for the Protection of Persons with Mental Illness and the Improvement of Mental Health Care were not included in this table because they related specifically to the realization of the Principles

this point, many parties had sought provisions that would permit involuntary treatments in certain contexts (Degener and Begg 2017). This debate has continued to evolve, as the UN Committee on the Rights of Persons with Disabilities (2014), who are responsible for interpreting the CRPD, state that 'forced treatment by psychiatric and other health and medical professionals is a violation of the right to equal recognition before the law' (p. 11). This further elaboration of the CRPD is seen by some as going a step too far and has raised many concerns (below).

### *2.3.1 Innovations of the Convention on the Rights of Persons with Disabilities*

The CRPD has led to many fundamental changes in mental health legislation that are extremely positive (European Union Agency for Fundamental Rights 2015). The convention does not just address negative rights but also dedicates large sections to the affirmation of positive rights. This will hopefully advance progressive reform around the world. India provides an excellent example of what is possible, as it revises its legislation to make it concordant with the CRPD and gives its citizens a justiciable right to mental healthcare (Duffy and Kelly 2019). The CRPD's affirmation of positive rights also has helped to shift the focus of mental health legislation from the regulation of involuntary treatment to the provision of healthcare and the positive protection of various other rights.

The convention has also done much to enhance the decision-making of people with mental illness, changing the paradigm from substitute decision-making to supported decision-making. In parallel, the decision-making framework has shifted from promoting someone's perceived 'best interests' to attempting to maximize their 'rights, will and preferences'. These complementary steps empower persons receiving mental healthcare and provide them with more agency. This has led to an expansion in research relating to coercive practices and might—hopefully—contribute to a reduction in involuntary treatments (Aguilera-Serrano et al. 2018).

### *2.3.2 Criticism of the Convention on the Rights of Persons with Disabilities' Impact on People with Mental Illness*

The provisions of the CRPD have not been universally or uncritically embraced by all mental health professionals (Appelbaum 2019). Many have raised concerns about the apparently absolute prohibition on coercive treatments (Kelly 2014). Freeman and colleagues (2015) have highlighted how the Committee on the Rights of Persons with Disabilities' interpretation of the CRPD and, in particular, their General Comment on Article 12 may actually undermine the rights of people with disabilities. They argue that an absolute need for informed consent in all contexts this will deprive many people of treatments and that affirming full legal capacity at all times may result in increased incarceration of people with acute episodes of illness. They also describe how this might lead to a deprivation of the right to life and increased stigmatization.

In a similar vein, Szmukler (2019) highlights that not all UN-related bodies agree with the Committee on the Rights of Persons with Disabilities' absolute prohibition on involuntary detention. He also suggests that there is insufficient evidence that such a decisive course represents the preferences of people with major mental illness.

The CRPD was not designed to address the needs of people with acute episodes of mental illness and its preamble makes no reference to the Principles for the Protection of Persons with Mental Illness and the Improvement of Mental Health Care (UN 1991) or other documents specifically relating to mental health (Duffy and Kelly 2017). Consistent with this, it is clear that insufficient consideration has been given to how its principles will be realized in the context of acute severe mental illness (Dawson 2015).

This omission has not gone unnoticed. In England and Wales, the 2018 Independent Review of the Mental Health Act 1983 (2018) reaffirmed the use of coercive treatments both on an inpatient basis and under community treatment orders, which is at complete odds with the Committee on the Rights of Persons with Disabilities' (2014) interpretation of the CRPD. In doing this, England and Wales have essentially ignored key elements of the committee's interpretation. Some analysts have even proposed that the United Kingdom should consider withdrawing from the CRPD altogether (Gosney and Bartlett 2019).

## 2.4 The United Nations' Human Rights Council

The UN General Assembly established the UN Human Rights Council in 2006 to replace the Commission on Human Rights. This council regularly hears from Special Rapporteurs who report on a range of topics. The rapporteur on torture has identified the treatment of people with mental illness as torture, on a number of occasions. They have, for example, highlighted how mental health services have been used to facilitate discrimination and violence against lesbian, gay, bisexual, transgender and intersex persons (UN Human Rights Council 2016). They have also expressed concern about coercive treatments. For example, in 2018, they stated:

> The risk is particularly high in the context of forced institutionalization and treatment of persons with psychosocial disabilities, who are often stripped of their legal capacity and not, or only inadequately, involved in decisions taken with regard to their treatment (UN General Assembly 2018).

The inclusion of mental health treatments under the heading of torture is of particular concern because torture is a non-derogable right (UN Economic and Social Council 1985). While contexts may exist where liberty or freedom of speech may need to be limited, the UN acknowledges no context in which torture is permissible.

The UN Human Rights Council also hears from the Special Rapporteur on the right of everyone to the enjoyment of the highest attainable standard of physical and mental health. These reports have often expressed concern at current mental health practices. In 2017, the report was critical of psychiatry's reported over-reliance on the 'biomedical model' of mental illness and its treatment, questioned the objectivity of psychiatric research, opposed the continuing use of coercive measures and called for a paradigm shift in the treatment of mental health conditions (UN Human Rights Council 2017a).

The UN Human Rights Council also has a working group on arbitrary detention that has reported that people with psychosocial and intellectual disabilities are often deprived of their liberty. They have, *inter alia*, identified the difficulties experienced by elderly people, highlighted forced treatment by religious organizations (UN Human Rights Council 2017b), described the mental health consequences of detention during migration proceedings (UN Human Rights Council 2018) and drawn attention to the involuntary detention of people who are dependent on illicit drugs (UN Human Rights Council 2015). These reports have an impact on the ground. For example, through the work of the UN Human Rights Council, other UN bodies and the human rights groups, pressure is being applied to reduce the arbitrary detention of people with substance misuse problems, although much more still needs to be done to protect rights in this complex, contested area (Amon et al. 2014).

## References

Aguilera-Serrano, C., Guzman-Parra, J., Garcia-Sanchez, J. A., Moreno-Küstner, B., & Mayoral-Cleries, F. (2018). Variables associated with the subjective experience of coercive measures in psychiatric inpatients: A systematic review. *Canadian Journal of Psychiatry, 63*(2), 129–144.

Amon, J. J., Pearshouse, R., Cohen, J. E., & Schleifer, R. (2014). Compulsory drug detention in East and Southeast Asia: Evolving government, UN and donor responses. *International Journal on Drug Policy, 25*(1), 13–20.

Amy, J. J., & Rowlands, S. (2018a). Legalised non-consensual sterilisation—Eugenics put into practice before 1945, and the aftermath. Part 1: USA, Japan, Canada and Mexico. *European Journal of Contraception Reproductive Health Care, 23*(2), 121–129.

Amy, J. J., & Rowlands, S. (2018b). Legalised non-consensual sterilisation— Eugenics put into practice before 1945, and the aftermath. Part 2: Europe. *European Journal of Contraception Reproductive Health Care, 23*(3), 194–200.

Appelbaum, P. S. (2019). Saving the UN Convention on the Rights of Persons with Disabilities—From itself. *World Psychiatry, 18*(1), 1–2.

Bass, J. K., Bornemann, T. H., Burkey, M., Chehil, S., Chen, L., Copeland, J. R., et al. (2012). A United Nations General Assembly Special Session for mental, neurological, and substance use disorders: The time has come. *PLoS Medicine, 9*(1), e1001159.

Bhugra, D., Pathare, S., Nardodkar, R., Gosavi, C., Ng, R., Torales, J., et al. (2016). Legislative provisions related to marriage and divorce of persons with mental health problems: A global review. *International Review of Psychiatry, 28*(4), 386–392.

Cratsley, K., & Mackey, T. K. (2018). Health policy brief: Global mental health and the United Nations' sustainable development goals. *Family Systems and Health: The Journal of Collaborative Family Healthcare, 36*(2), 225–229.

Dawson, J. (2015). A realistic approach to assessing mental health laws' compliance with the UNCRPD. *International Journal of Law and Psychiatry, 40,* 70–79.

Degener, T., & Begg, A. (2017). From invisible citizens to agents of change: A short history of the struggle for the recognition of the rights of persons with disabilities at the United Nations. In V. D. Fina, R. Cera, & G. Palmisano (Eds.), *The United Nations Convention on the Rights of Persons with Disability: A commentary* (pp. 1–40). Cham: Springer.

Duffy, R. M., & Kelly, B. D. (2017). Rights, laws and tensions: A comparative analysis of the Convention on the Rights of Persons with Disabilities and the WHO Resource Book on Mental Health, Human Rights and Legislation. *International Journal of Law and Psychiatry, 54,* 26–35.

Duffy, R. M., & Kelly, B. D. (2019). The right to mental healthcare: India moves forward. *British Journal of Psychiatry, 214*(2), 59–60.

European Union Agency for Fundamental Rights. (2015). *Implementing the United Nations Convention on the Rights of Persons with Disabilities (CRPD): An overview of legal reforms in EU Member States*. Luxembourg: Publications Office of the European Union.

Freeman, M. C., Kolappa, K., de Almeida, J. M., Kleinman, A., Makhashvili, N., Phakathi, S., et al. (2015). Reversing hard won victories in the name of human rights: A critique of the General Comment on Article 12 of the UN Convention on the Rights of Persons with Disabilities. *Lancet Psychiatry, 2*(9), 844–850.

Gosney, P., & Bartlett, P. (2019). The UK Government should withdraw from the Convention on the Rights of Persons with Disabilities. *British Journal of Psychiatry.* https://doi.org/10.1192/bjp.2019.182. [Epub ahead of print].

Independent Review of the Mental Health Act 1983. (2018). *Modernising the Mental Health Act: Increasing choice, reducing compulsion.* London: Gov.uk. Retrieved September 23, 2019, from https://assets.publishing.service.gov.uk/government/uploads/system/uploads/attachment_data/file/778897/Modernising_the_Mental_Health_Act_-_increasing_choice__reducing_compulsion.pdf.

Kelly, B. D. (2014). An end to psychiatric detention? Implications of the United Nations Convention on the Rights of Persons with Disabilities. *British Journal of Psychiatry, 204*(3), 174–175.

Melish, T. J. (2014). An eye towards effective enforcement: Technical-comparative approach to the negotiations. In M. Sabatello & M. Schulze (Eds.), *Human rights and disability advocacy* (pp. 70–96). Philadelphia: University of Pennsylvania Press.

Moncada, A. C. (1994). Involuntary commitment and the use of seclusion and restraint in Uruguay: A comparison with the United Nations Principles for the Protection of Persons with Mental Illness. *University of Miami Inter-American Law Review, 25*(3), 589–620.

Morrissey, F. (2012). The United Nations Convention on the Rights of Persons with Disabilities: A new approach to decision-making in mental health law. *European Journal of Health Law, 19*(5), 423–440.

Rosenthal, E., & Rubenstein, L. S. (1993). International human rights advocacy under the "Principles for the Protection of Persons with Mental Illness". *International Journal of Law and Psychiatry, 16*(3–4), 257–300.

Schulze, M. (2010). *Understanding the UN Convention on the Rights of Persons with Disabilities* (3rd ed.). New York: Handicap International.

Steinert, C., Steinert, T., Flammer, E., & Jaeger, S. (2016). Impact of the UN convention on the rights of persons with disabilities (UN-CRPD) on mental health care research—A systematic review. *BMC Psychiatry, 16,* 166.

Szmukler, G. (2019). "Capacity", "best interests", "will and preferences" and the UN Convention on the Rights of Persons with Disabilities. *World Psychiatry, 18*(1), 34–41.

Thornicroft, G., & Votruba, N. (2016). Does the United Nations care about mental health? *Lancet Psychiatry, 3*(7), 599–600.

United Nations. (1991). *Principles for the protection of persons with mental illness and the improvement of mental health care.* New York: United Nations, Secretariat Centre For Human Rights. Retrieved November 19, 2019, from https://www.who.int/mental_health/policy/en/UN_Resolution_on_protection_of_persons_with_mental_illness.pdf.

United Nations (2006). *Convention on the rights of persons with disabilities*. New York: United Nations. https://www.un.org/development/desa/disabilities/convention-on-the-rights-of-persons-with-disabilities/convention-on-the-rights-of-persons-with-disabilities-2.html. Accessed 19 November 2019.

United Nations. (2015). *2030 Agenda for sustainable development*. New York: United Nations.

United Nations Committee on the Rights of Persons with Disabilities. (2014). *General comment No. 1: Article 12: Equal recognition before the law*. New York: United Nations. Retrieved November 19, 2019, from http://www.ohchr.org/EN/HRBodies/CRPD/Pages/GC.aspx.

United Nations Economic and Social Council. (1985). *Siracusa principles on the limitation and Derogation Provisions in the International Covenant on Civil and Political Rights*. Geneva: United Nations.

United Nations General Assembly. (1948). *Universal declaration of human rights (217 [III] A)*. Paris: United Nations General Assembly. Retrieved November 19, 2019, from https://www.ohchr.org/EN/UDHR/Documents/UDHR_Translations/eng.pdf.

United Nations General Assembly. (1966a). *International covenant on civil and political rights (2200A [XXI])*. New York: United Nations General Assembly. Retrieved November 19, 2019, from https://www.ohchr.org/Documents/ProfessionalInterest/ccpr.pdf.

United Nations General Assembly. (1966b). *International covenant on economic, social and cultural rights (2200A [XXI])*. New York: United Nations General Assembly. Retrieved November 19, 2019, from https://www.ohchr.org/Documents/ProfessionalInterest/cescr.pdf.

United Nations General Assembly. (1989). *Convention on the rights of the child*. New York: United Nations General Assembly. Retrieved November 19, 2019, from https://www.refworld.org/docid/3ae6b38f0.html.

United Nations General Assembly. (2018). *Interim report of the special rapporteur on torture and other cruel, inhuman or degrading treatment or punishment, 20 July*. New York: United Nations General Assembly. Retrieved November 19, 2019, from https://documents-dds-ny.un.org/doc/UNDOC/GEN/N18/232/16/PDF/N1823216.pdf.

United Nations General Assembly Special Session on Drugs. (2016). *Outcome document of the 2016 United Nations general assembly special session on the world drug problem*. Vienna: United Nations. Retrieved November 19, 2019, from https://www.unodc.org/documents/postungass2016/outcome/V1603301-E.pdf.

United Nations Human Rights Council. (2013) *Report of the special rapporteur on torture and other cruel, inhuman or degrading treatment or punishment, 1 February. A/HRC/22/53*. New York: United Nations. Retrieved November 19, 2019, from https://www.refworld.org/docid/51136ae62.html.

United Nations Human Rights Council. (2015). *Report of the working group on arbitrary detention, 10 July. A/HRC/30/36*. New York: United Nations. Retrieved November 19, 2019, from https://documents-dds-ny.un.org/doc/UNDOC/GEN/G15/154/30/PDF/G1515430.pdf.

United Nations Human Rights Council. (2016). *Report of the Special Rapporteur on torture and other cruel, inhuman or degrading treatment or punishment, 5 January. A/HRC/31/57*. New York: United Nations. Retrieved November 19, 2019, from https://documents-dds-ny.un.org/doc/UNDOC/GEN/G16/000/97/PDF/G1600097.pdf.

United Nations Human Rights Council. (2017a). *Report of the special rapporteur on the right of everyone to the enjoyment of the highest attainable standard of physical and mental health, 28 March. A/HCR/35/21*. New York: United Nations. Retrieved November 19, 2019, from https://documents-dds-ny.un.org/doc/UNDOC/GEN/G17/076/04/PDF/G1707604.pdf.

United Nations Human Rights Council. (2017b). *Report of the working group on arbitrary detention, 19 July. A/HRC/36/37*. New York: United Nations. Retrieved November 19, 2019, from https://documents-dds-ny.un.org/doc/UNDOC/GEN/G17/216/49/PDF/G1721649.pdf.

United Nations Human Rights Council. (2018). *Report of the working group on arbitrary detention, 2 July. A/HRC/39/45*. New York: United Nations. Retrieved November 19, 2019, from https://documents-dds-ny.un.org/doc/UNDOC/GEN/G18/196/69/PDF/G1819669.pdf.

Volkow, N. D., Poznyak, V., Saxena, S., Gerra, G., & UNODC-WHO Informal International Scientific Network. (2017). Drug use disorders: Impact of a public health rather than a criminal justice approach. *World Psychiatry, 16*(2), 213–214.

Zifcak, S. (1996). The United Nations principles for the protection of people with mental illness: Applications and limitations. *Psychiatry, Psychology and Law, 3*(1), 1–9.

# Chapter 3
# The World Health Organization and Mental Health Law

## 3.1 The World Health Organization and the International Classification of Diseases

The WHO is a specialized agency of the United Nations (UN). It was established in 1948 and has its headquarters in Geneva. It works with the 193 member states of the UN across 150 offices worldwide. The WHO took over responsibility for the International Classification of Diseases (ICD) shortly after its establishment. The earliest iterations of the ICD dealt only with causes of mortality. ICD 6, in 1949, was the first classification document to deal with morbidity and consequently it was also the first to consider mental illness (WHO 1949; Hirsch et al. 2016). ICD 6 included a chapter entitled 'Mental, Psychoneurotic, and Personality Disorders' which comprised three sections: 'Psychoses', 'Psychoneurotic Disorders' and 'Disorders of Character, Behavior, and Intelligence'. It presented a list of diseases and did not include descriptions or diagnostic criteria. As a result, many of the conditions described lacked objectivity. For example, ICD 6 included inadequate personality (320.3), neurocirculatory asthenia (315.0) and passive dependency (321.1). There was no change between ICD 6 and ICD 7 in the classification of mental disorders (WHO 1957).

Extensive revisions were included in ICD 8 with a large expansion in the number of conditions recognized (WHO 1965). ICD 9 (WHO 1977) produced a fundamental paradigm shift as descriptions and diagnostic features were included, greatly enhancing reliability and strengthening the use of ICD-based terminology in legislation. ICD 10 represented a significantly more detailed classification system with the number of codes increasing to over 155,000 (WHO 1994; Topaz et al. 2013). In 2018, a version of ICD 11 was released after over a decade in development, with another extensive revision of diagnostic criteria in mental health, particularly in the area or personality disorders (WHO 2018a). It is anticipated to come into operation in 2022.

While these documents may not directly shape legislation, they clarify who can be treated and how they can be treated under the law. Increasing the objectivity of



R. M. Duffy and B. D. Kelly, *India's Mental Healthcare Act, 2017*,
https://doi.org/10.1007/978-981-15-5009-6_3

diagnosis of mental health conditions helps to protect against some of the abuses seen in psychiatry in the past (Feighner et al. 1972; Telles Correia 2017).

The benefits, challenges and limitations of creating an internationally standardized diagnostic schedule, particularly in psychiatry, have been long recognized (Sartorius 1976). While debates concerning validity and content continue to this day (Schroeder et al. 2010), making diagnosis in psychiatry more objective has broad and generally positive implications for treatment and, consequently, for the consistent application of legislation in relation to mental disorder.

## 3.2 The World Health Organization's Mental Health Care Law: Ten Basic Principles (1996)

The WHO's 1996 publication Mental Health Care Law: Ten Basic Principles (WHO 1996) was developed following a detailed review of the mental health legislation in 45 countries. It was strongly informed by the Principles for the Protection of Persons with Mental Illness and the Improvement of Mental Health Care (UN 1991). These ten principles and their relations to later WHO and UN documents are summarized in Table 3.1. Their influence on the medical literature as a whole, however, has been, unfortunately, limited. Despite this, the principles were forward-thinking in seeking to promote mental healthcare and prevent mental disorders (Kelly 2013).

## 3.3 World Mental Health Atlas (2001–2017)

Since 2001, the WHO has published a World Mental Health Atlas every three to four years. Project Atlas was commenced to address the treatment gap in mental illness (WHO 2001a). This project initially only established whether or not countries had mental health law and when their legislation was last updated. It did not consider the content of the legislation in any detail. The survey was expanded in 2011 and countries were asked if there were legal provisions on mental health in 'other laws (e.g. welfare, disability, employment, anti-discrimination, general health legislation, etc.)' (WHO 2011). This provided a more comprehensive description of the international picture.

In 2011, the Atlas also gave some consideration to the content of law, e.g. it considered if legislation permitted primary healthcare nurses to diagnose and treat mental illness. The 2014 edition considered national harmonization with international human rights instruments and whether or not existing legislation was implemented. Interestingly, this identified that no Southeast Asian country was fully implementing its mental health legislation (WHO 2015a). All of these findings were self-reported by respective nations and, where possible, these data were compared to independent sources, although this was not always feasible. In addition to the general atlas, the WHO has also produced country-specific findings. Most recently, the 2017 Atlas

**Table 3.1** The World Health Organization's Mental Health Care Law: Ten Basic Principles and how they relate to the World Health Organization's Resource Book on Mental Health, Human Rights and Legislation and the United Nations' Convention on the Rights of Persons with Disabilities

| Basic principle in the World Health Organization's (WHO) Mental Health Care Law: Ten Basic Principles | Relevant sections in the WHO's Resource Book on Mental Health, Human Rights and Legislation (WHO RB) checklist | Relevant articles in the United Nations' (UN) Convention on the Rights of Persons with Disabilities (CRPD) | Notes |
|---|---|---|---|
| 1: Promotion of mental health and prevention of mental disorders | C: Access to mental healthcare<br>D: Rights of users of mental health services | 4: General obligations<br>8: Awareness<br>25: Health | The CRPD gives limited consideration to prevention as it relates to all disabilities and avoids the 'biomedical model' |
| 2: Access to basic mental health care | A: Preamble and objectives<br>C: Access to mental healthcare<br>D: Rights of users of mental health services<br>G: Voluntary treatments<br>U-X: Discrimination, housing, employment, social security | 3: General principles<br>5: Equality and non-discrimination<br>25: Health | The basic principle was very broad including dignity, maximizing autonomy and voluntary treatment. The CRPD has developed this to include the right 'to the enjoyment of the highest attainable standard of health' |
| 3: Mental health assessments in accordance with internationally accepted principles | B: Definitions<br>F: Competence, capacity and guardianship<br>N: Determinations of mental disorder | 12: Equal recognition before the law<br>25: Health | ICD codes have been central to this provision. Issues of capacity in the CRPD are at odds with the two other documents |

(continued)

**Table 3.1** (continued)

| Basic principle in the World Health Organization's (WHO) Mental Health Care Law: Ten Basic Principles | Relevant sections in the WHO's Resource Book on Mental Health, Human Rights and Legislation (WHO RB) checklist | Relevant articles in the United Nations' (UN) Convention on the Rights of Persons with Disabilities (CRPD) | Notes |
|---|---|---|---|
| 4: Provision of the least restrictive type of mental health care | C: Access to mental health care<br>F: Competence, capacity and guardianship<br>I: Involuntary admission<br>L: Involuntary treatment in community Settings<br>P. Seclusion and restraint | 3: General principles<br>12: Equal recognition before the law<br>19: Living independently and being included in the community<br>25: Health | All restrictive measures are (arguably) prohibited under the CRPD and hence not considered, but autonomy and community-based living are considered in detail |
| 5: Self-determination | F: Competence, capacity and guardianship<br>G: Voluntary admission and treatment<br>K: Proxy consent for treatment<br>O: Special treatments<br>Q. Clinical and experimental research | 12: Equal recognition before the law<br>14: Liberty and security of person<br>16: Freedom from exploitation, violence and abuse<br>17: Protecting the integrity of the person | Provisions in the CRPD affirm self-determination in all contexts and it gives limited consideration to any limitations of this right |
| 6: Right to be assisted in the exercise of self-determination | | 4: General obligations<br>9: Accessibility<br>12: Equal recognition before the law<br>16: Freedom from exploitation, violence and abuse<br>21: Freedom of expression and opinion, and access to information | This was a very progressive principle, much more in line with the CRPD than other principles. It aimed for a provision the CRPD is still striving for today. This is poorly addressed in the WHO RB |

(continued)

**Table 3.1** (continued)

| Basic principle in the World Health Organization's (WHO) Mental Health Care Law: Ten Basic Principles | Relevant sections in the WHO's Resource Book on Mental Health, Human Rights and Legislation (WHO RB) checklist | Relevant articles in the United Nations' (UN) Convention on the Rights of Persons with Disabilities (CRPD) | Notes |
|---|---|---|---|
| 7: Availability of review procedure | D: Rights of users of mental health services<br>F: Competence, capacity and guardianship<br>O: Special treatments<br>R: Oversight and review mechanisms<br>T: Mentally ill offenders | 12: Equal recognition before the law<br>14: Liberty and security of person | The CRPD's review process is contained in standard law as it does not see a justification for coercive treatments on the basis of disability |
| 8: Automatic periodical review mechanism | F: Competence, capacity and guardianship<br>I: Involuntary admission<br>J: Involuntary treatment<br>P. Seclusion and restraint<br>R: Oversight and review mechanisms<br>Z: Protection of vulnerable groups | 12: Equal recognition before the law<br>14: Liberty and security of person | |
| 9: Qualified decision-maker | B: Definitions<br>F: Competence, capacity and guardianship<br>N: Determinations of mental disorder | 25: Health | Not directly considered in the CRPD as it uses a social model of disability |
| 10: Respect of the rule of law | The WHO RB seeks to guide legislation and influence national and regional legislation | 4: General obligations<br>9: Accessibility<br>11: Situations of risk and humanitarian emergencies<br>12: Equal recognition before the law<br>14: Liberty and security of person | The CRPD has been adopted as international law in many states; it actively seeks to revise and challenge national laws; in Article 11, it appeals to international law |

*Notes*
*WHO* World Health Organization
*UN* United Nations
*CRPD* Convention of the Rights of Persons with Disabilities (UN 2006)
*WHO RB* World Health Organization's Resource Book on Mental Health Legislation (WHO 2005)

began to demonstrate progress in mental health law and an international move to harmonize national mental health law with human rights standards, which is a key theme of this book (WHO 2018b).

## 3.4 The World Health Report (2001)

The 2001 Atlas contributed to the WHO's 2001 World Health Report which was devoted to 'Mental Health: New Understanding, New Hope' (2001b). This publication aimed to 'raise the public and professional awareness of the real burden of mental disorders and their costs in human, social and economic terms' (p. xi). It also sought to reduce stigmatization and discrimination. To do this, it made ten recommendations, one of which was to establish national policies, programmes and legislation. In the relevant sections, the WHO identified that mental health legislation should not solely address involuntary treatment but should codify the 'fundamental principles, values, goals, and objectives of mental health policy' (p. 84) (Kelly 2001).

The publication highlighted previous findings that a quarter of countries had no mental health legislation in 2001 and 20% had mental health legislation that was over 40 years old (WHO 2001a). The authors emphasized the need for comprehensive mental health legislation, but besides the very general comments quoted above they did not make recommendations for the content of such legislation. This omission was, however, comprehensively addressed four years later in the WHO's Resource Book on Mental Health, Human Rights and Legislation (WHO 2005).

## 3.5 The World Health Organization Resource Book on Mental Health, Human Rights and Legislation (2005)

In 2005, the WHO released its Resource Book on Mental Health, Human Rights and Legislation (WHO RB), which provided jurisdictions with suggestions regarding what needed to be addressed in national mental health law and policy (WHO 2005). This document has three sections looking at the context of mental health law, the content of legislation and the drafting, adoption and implementation process. The WHO RB provides detailed consideration of how legislation can be aligned with the Principles for the Protection of Persons with Mental Illness and the Improvement of Mental Health Care (UN 1991) and provides examples of legislative approaches in different jurisdictions. Careful consideration is given to competing ethical principles, local resources and complex, nuanced situations. The WHO RB provides detailed exploration of the rights of people with mental illness and elaborates on numerous social and economic rights including housing, employment and social security.

Where coercive measures are legislated for, the WHO RB recommends the inclusion of extensive review processes.

The Resource Book has an appendix that includes a checklist for mental health legislation. This comprises 175 items or human rights standards, divided into 27 categories. This checklist has been previously used to evaluate national mental health legislation in Ireland, India, England and Wales (Duffy and Kelly 2017a; Kelly 2011). The WHO RB was written the year before the CRPD was drafted (UN 2006) and consequently it is not CRPD-concordant; the WHO RB retains provisions for involuntary treatment, substitutes decision-making, community treatment orders, seclusion and restraint. All of these are, arguably, prohibited under the CRPD, at least according to the UN Committee on the Rights of Persons with Disabilities (2014). The WHO RB also uses a 'best interests' paradigm, although it gives significant weight to individual preference, albeit mostly in the context of advance directives. This is at odds with the shift that occurred with the CRPD, towards 'rights, will and preference' and supported decision-making frameworks.

The WHO RB is heavily influenced by a so-called 'biomedical model' of disability, whereas the more recent CRPD uses a rights-based model which, in the context of mental healthcare, has both substantial benefits and some drawbacks (UN 2006; Duffy and Kelly 2017a). Consequently, the WHO RB is generally incompatible with the CRPD. The now outdated Resource Book considers multiple situations and contexts in which capacity can be questioned, autonomy limited and coercive practices used. It suggests protective measures and review processes for occasions when such measures are employed. The two documents, the WHO RB and CRPD, adhere to staunchly different paradigms and are significantly ideologically incompatible (Duffy and Kelly 2017b). Against this background, the advent of the CRPD prompted the WHO to develop the QualityRights initiative which seeks to promote human rights and recovery in mental health in a way that is compatible with the CRPD. This is discussed below.

## 3.6 Mental Health and Development (2010)

In 2010, the WHO published a document called Mental Health and Development: Targeting People with Mental Health Conditions as a Vulnerable Group (WHO 2010). This document sought to focus the attention of governments and civil society on mental health matters. It highlighted how people with mental illness are a vulnerable and marginalized group and argued that this merits direct interventions. From a legal perspective, the document highlighted how people with psychosocial disabilities often lose autonomy, have restricted voting rights, are impacted by restrictive marriage laws, experience legal barriers to accessing finance and need social rights to be tailored to their needs.

The WHO also called for mental health laws that affirm human rights and the repeal of laws that create barriers for people with mental illness. The document highlighted how increasing autonomy and supports to strengthen decision-making capacity can only occur alongside enhanced community-based treatments. This publication was used to advocate for improved mental healthcare in multiple low-income countries (Skeen et al. 2010; Raja et al. 2012).

## 3.7 World Health Organization Mental Health Action Plan 2013–2020 (2013)

The Mental Health Action Plan 2013–2020 was the first mental health action plan released by the WHO (WHO 2013; Saxena and Setoya 2014). It aims to support countries in developing laws 'consistent with international and regional human rights instruments' (p. 11). Published after the introduction of the CRPD, the Action Plan makes multiple references to legislation, but, in contrast to earlier WHO documents, focuses solely on a subset of rights and does not make provisions for involuntary treatment. For example:

> The action plan emphasizes the need for services, policies, legislation, plans, strategies and programmes to protect, promote and respect the rights of persons with mental disorders in line with the International Covenant on Civil and Political Rights, the International Covenant on Economic, Social and Cultural Rights, the Convention on the Rights of Persons with Disabilities, the Convention on the Rights of the Child and other relevant international and regional human rights instruments (p. 7)

Despite this paradigm shift, the Mental Health Action Plan still references the WHO-RB in its appendix of 'Selected WHO technical materials and resources on mental health', acknowledging its ongoing usefulness. In aligning with these international human rights standards, the Mental Health Action Plan omits detailed consideration of protection during use of coercive measures, review policies and capacity (all of which were addressed in the WHO's Ten Basic Principles and the WHO RB).

Despite the CRPD, many jurisdictions have retained coercive practices in psychiatry. In addition, there is significant uncertainty about a total prohibition on coercive treatments among many groups, including psychiatrists (Appelbaum 2019; Freeman et al. 2015), countries (Independent Review of the Mental Health Act 1983, 2018) and even other UN bodies (Szmukler 2019). Removing coercive practices from trained professionals with comprehensive review systems may lead to coercion by families, communities or societies, possibly through the criminal justice system (Freeman et al. 2015). While additional consideration needs to be given to how coercive measures can be minimized in mental health services, the complete cessation of meaningful discussion on this topic would do a profound disservice to the mentally ill. Even so, the Mental Health Action Plan 2013–2020, along with the QualityRights toolkit (WHO 2012), was one of the first WHO documents apparently to oppose coercive treatments.

Despite this issue, the Action Plan usefully highlights the absence of mental health legislation in many jurisdictions, especially in low- and middle-income countries. In the document, the WHO sets a global target that 50% of countries will develop or update their mental health legislation in line with contemporary human rights standards by 2020. The support of professional associations will clearly be needed to achieve this goal (Saxena et al. 2014). A collaborative approach is suggested, in which countries work together to develop effective rights-based legislation.

The Action Plan envisages legislation as a tool to facilitate access to mental healthcare and as a mechanism for addressing inequalities and deficits in service provision. In a broader sense, the WHO acknowledges that legislation is a vital tool for the realization of all healthcare goals—not just in mental health (WHO 2017). Psychiatry, with its long history of familiarity with legislation, may be especially well placed to harness legal provisions to improve the quality of life of people with mental health problems (Duffy and Kelly 2017c). Regrettably, the Mental Health Gap Action Programme Guidelines for Mental, Neurological and Substance Use Disorders, initially released in 2008 and updated in 2015 (WHO 2015b), omit any meaningful consideration of legislation.

## 3.8 World Health Organization QualityRights Initiative (2012)

One of the stated objectives of the WHO QualityRights initiative is to 'reform national policies and legislation in line with best practice, the CRPD and other international human rights standards' (WHO 2019a). QualityRights have published extensive training and advocacy resources. The training consists of five core modules: human rights, mental health, disability and human rights, legal capacity and the right to decide, recovery and the right to health and freedom from coercion, violence and abuse. In addition, there are three specialized training modules: recovery practices for mental health and well-being, strategies to end seclusion and restraint, and supported decision-making and advance planning. The steps to reduce coercive treatments are greatly to be welcomed and need to be embraced widely. The finding of abuses that have occurred in mental health facilities are highly disturbing and clearly must be addressed (Fawzy 2015).

The QualityRights Initiative is the WHO's response to the challenges of making mental healthcare concordant with the CRPD and other international human rights standards (Funk and Drew 2017). As part of this, QualityRights have developed a toolkit that can be used to evaluate mental health practice in given jurisdictions (WHO 2012). This toolkit identifies five themes that are each divided into standards, and each standard is subdivided into criteria, resulting in a total of 116 criteria. As many of these elements could be codified in law, this development is of particular relevance regarding themes three ('The right to exercise legal capacity and the right to personal liberty and the security of person') and four ('Freedom from torture or cruel, inhuman or degrading treatment or punishment and from exploitation, violence and abuse').

These standards and criteria have already been deployed in a variety of countries, particularly in Europe (WHO Regional Office for Europe 2018). The resultant reports are very thorough and highly informative, but are also problematic in a few regards. For example, they often place practices that are unjustifiable in any context alongside practices that are permitted by legislation, implicitly creating the impression that these practices are somehow equivalent. For example:

> At one group of facilities, service users felt pressured by their psychiatrist to take medications. Sexual abuse of many female service users was described in another group of facilities, which had not been formally investigated and therefore not prosecuted (WHO Regional Office for Europe 2018; p. 27).

There are other examples, e.g.

> Service users are informed of and have access to procedures to file appeals and complaints, on a confidential basis, to an outside, independent legal body on issues related to neglect, abuse, seclusion or restraint, admission or treatment without informed consent and other relevant matters (WHO 2012; p. 84).

The modules on capacity (WHO 2019b) and supported decision-making (WHO 2019c) provide numerous examples of well-thought-through, rights-based approaches to support people with mental illness and emphasize the need to allow a person with a mental health problem to direct their care as well as the importance of good and clear communication with their healthcare providers, family and carers. They also highlight many gross violations of human rights that occur for people with psychosocial disabilities.

However, these documents also present multiple scenarios that describe psychiatric treatments as ineffectual, administered in an abusive manner and resulting in major side effects; by way of contrast, psychosocial interventions and attempts to de-escalate situations by listening to the person's concerns are portrayed as universally effective. There is limited discussion of the remedies that should be employed if rights-based interventions prove ineffective.

The capacity module highlights that 'binding advance planning documents in countries have not been fully compliant with the CRPD' (p. 22), as they are non-binding when people come under mental health legislation or are invoked when someone is deemed too lose capacity rather than at a time of the person's choosing. There is a good discussion of a 'Ulysses clause', whereby people at risk of developing an acute episode of mental illness can make advance decisions that they cannot override during a period of illness (WHO 2019c; Sarin 2012).

As Freeman and colleagues (2015) highlight, however, many aspects of this kind of work that incorporate extreme interpretations of the CRPD run the risk of criminalizing people with mental illness. The module alludes to this indirectly in two places. It states that 'people with disabilities can only be detained on the same basis (or for the same reasons) as all other citizens (e.g. following a criminal sentence)' (WHO 2019b) (p. 29). This statement may prove to be the norm if people with mental illness are not able to receive treatment at times where they lack capacity and refuse treatment.

The WHO material also highlights that, with regard to detention on the basis of risk, 'other groups at higher risk of violence (e.g. gang members, persons drinking alcohol with a history of domestic violence) cannot be detained on the basis of increased violence risk'. However, these are groups that are over-represented in prison populations and, if dogmatically implemented, the CRPD may have a similar effect on people with mental illness.

In the QualityRights document that relates to seclusion and restraint (WHO 2019d), there is direct acknowledgement that there may be criminalization of people with mental illness; it states:

> When someone is acting in a way which is very dangerous to others, this person should be stopped in the same manner as you would stop anyone, with or without a disability – such as by involving a specially trained group who are equipped with the skills to manage the situation (e.g. a response team, see topic 10) or alternatively in some instances law enforcement bodies (e.g. the police force) to guarantee the security of all (p. 21).

This will invariably result in acute mental health episodes being dealt with by law enforcement staff with minimal training in mental illness who do not know the people receiving treatment (unlike mental healthcare staff). This may lead to increased levels of harm, as restraint and seclusion will still occur, albeit in a forensic rather than a therapeutic setting. This would be a backward step: prison is toxic for the mentally ill.

Overall, the QualityRights documents bring WHO policy more in line with the interpretation of the CRPD provided by the UN Committee on the Rights of Persons with Disabilities (2014). This is most starkly seen in the modules relating to Freedom from violence, coercion and abuse (WHO 2019e), supported decision-making and advance planning (WHO 2019c) and seclusion and restraint (WHO 2019d). These documents describe how legislation permitting coercive treatments may amount to torture and may violate the CRPD—and they suggest that there is 'a lack of sanctions and remedies from the courts' for this (WHO 2019e; p. 17). While there has undoubtedly been a CRPD-driven paradigm shift in recent years, this last statement seems like an excessive and very sudden departure form previous WHO publications, which until recently supported a degree of involuntary treatment under specific circumstances and with various safeguards and review processes in place (WHO 2005).

## References

Appelbaum, P. S. (2019). Saving the UN Convention on the Rights of Persons with Disabilities—From itself. *World Psychiatry, 18*(1), 1–2.

Duffy, R. M., & Kelly, B. D. (2017a). Concordance of the Indian Mental Healthcare Act, 2017 with the World Health Organization's Checklist on Mental Health Legislation. *International Journal of Mental Health Systems, 11*, 48.

Duffy, R. M., & Kelly, B. D. (2017b). Rights, laws and tensions: A comparative analysis of the Convention on the Rights of Persons with Disabilities and the WHO Resource Book on Mental Health, Human Rights and Legislation. *International Journal of Law and Psychiatry, 54*, 26–35.

Duffy, R. M., & Kelly, B. D. (2017c). Can psychiatry lead the way in legislating for health and wellbeing? *Irish Medical Journal, 110*(6), 591.

Fawzy, M. E. (2015). Quality of life and human rights conditions in a public psychiatric hospital in Cairo. *International Journal of Human Rights in Healthcare, 8*(4), 199–217.

Feighner, J., Robins, E., Guze, S., Woodruff, R., Winokur, G., & Munos, R. (1972). Diagnostic criteria for use in psychiatric research. *Archives of General Psychiatry, 26,* 57–63.

Freeman, M. C., Kolappa, K., de Almeida, J. M., Kleinman, A., Makhashvili, N., Phakathi, S., et al. (2015). Reversing hard won victories in the name of human rights: A critique of the General Comment on Article 12 of the UN Convention on the Rights of Persons with Disabilities. *Lancet Psychiatry, 2*(9), 844–850.

Funk, M., & Drew, N. (2017). WHO QualityRights: Transforming mental health services. *Lancet Psychiatry, 4*(11), 826–827.

Hirsch, J. A., Nicola, G., McGinty, G., Liu, R. W., Barr, R. M., Chittle, M. D., et al. (2016). ICD-10: History and context. *American Journal of Neuroradiology, 37*(4), 596–599.

Independent Review of the Mental Health Act 1983. (2018). *Modernising the Mental Health Act: Increasing choice, reducing compulsion.* London: Gov.uk. Retrieved December 17, 2019, from https://assets.publishing.service.gov.uk/government/uploads/system/uploads/attachment_data/file/778897/Modernising_the_Mental_Health_Act_-_increasing_choice__reducing_compulsion.pdf.

Kelly, B. D. (2001). Mental health and human rights: Challenges for a new millennium. *Irish Journal of Psychological Medicine, 18*(4), 114–115.

Kelly, B. D. (2011). Mental health legislation and human rights in England, Wales and the Republic of Ireland. *International Journal of Law and Psychiatry, 34*(6), 439–454.

Kelly, B. D. (2013). Is there a human right to mental health? *Psychiatry Professional, 2*(1), 10–14.

Raja, S., Underhill, C., Shrestha, P., Sunder, U., Mannarath, S., Wood, S. K., et al. (2012). Integrating mental health and development: A case study of the Basic Needs Model in Nepal. *PLoS medicine, 9*(7), e1001261.

Sarin, A. (2012). On psychiatric wills and the Ulysses clause: The advance directive in psychiatry. *Indian Journal of Psychiatry, 54*(3), 206–207.

Sartorius, N. (1976). Methodologic problems of common terminology, measurement, and classification. 11. Modifications and new approaches to taxonomy in long-term care: advantages and limitations of the ICD. *Medical Care, 14*(Suppl. 5), 109–115.

Saxena, S., Funk, M., & Chisholm, D. (2014). WHO's Mental Health Action Plan 2013–2020: What can psychiatrists do to facilitate its implementation? *World Psychiatry, 13*(2), 107–109.

Saxena, S., & Setoya, Y. (2014). World Health Organization's Comprehensive Mental Health Action Plan 2013–2020. *Psychiatry Clinical Neurosciences, 68*(8), 585–586.

Schroeder, K., Andresen, B., Naber, D., & Huber, C. G. (2010). Diagnostic validity of ICD-10 personality dimensions: A multitrait-multimethod analysis of two self-report questionnaires and a structured interview. *Psychopathology, 43*(2), 110–120.

Skeen, S., Lund, C., Kleintjes, S., Flisher, A., & The MHaPP Research Programme Consortium. (2010). Meeting the Millennium Development Goals in Sub-Saharan Africa: what about mental health? *International Review of Psychiatry, 22*(6), 624–631.

Szmukler, G. (2019). 'Capacity', 'best interests', 'will and preferences' and the UN Convention on the Rights of Persons with Disabilities. *World Psychiatry, 18*(1), 34–41.

Telles Correia, D. (2017). The concept of validity throughout the history of psychiatry. *Journal of Evaluation of Clinical Practice, 23*(5), 994–998.

Topaz, M., Shafran-Topaz, L., & Bowles, K. H. (2013). ICD-9 to ICD-10: Evolution, revolution, and current debates in the United States. *Perspectives in Health Information Management, 10*(Spring), 1d.

United Nations. (1991). *Principles for the protection of persons with mental illness and the improvement of mental health care.* New York: United Nations, Secretariat Centre For Human Rights. Retrieved December 17, 2019, from https://www.who.int/mental_health/policy/en/UN_Resolution_on_protection_of_persons_with_mental_illness.pdf.

United Nations. (2006). *Convention on the rights of persons with disabilities*. New York: United Nations. Retrieved November 19, 2019, from https://www.un.org/development/desa/disabilities/convention-on-the-rights-of-persons-with-disabilities/convention-on-the-rights-of-persons-with-disabilities-2.html.

United Nations Committee on the Rights of Persons with Disabilities. (2014). *General comment No. 1: Article 12: Equal recognition before the law*. New York: United Nations. Retrieved November 19, 2019, from http://www.ohchr.org/EN/HRBodies/CRPD/Pages/GC.aspx.

World Health Organization. (1949). *Manual of the international statistical classification of diseases, injuries, and causes of death: Sixth revision of the international lists of diseases and causes of death*. Geneva: World Health Organization.

World Health Organization. (1957). *Manual of the international statistical classification of diseases, injuries, and causes of death: Based on the recommendations of the seventh revision conference, 1955, and adopted by the ninth World Health Assembly under the WHO nomenclature regulations*. Geneva: World Health Organization.

World Health Organization. (1965). *Manual of the international statistical classification of disease, injuries, and causes of death. Based on the recommendations of the eighth revision conference, 1965, and adopted by the nineteenth World Health Assembly*. Geneva: World Health Organization.

World Health Organization. (1977). *Manual of the international statistical classification of disease, injuries, and causes of death. Based on the recommendations of the ninth revision conference, 1975, and adopted by the twenty-ninth World Health Assembly*. Geneva: World Health Organization.

World Health Organization. (1994). *International classification of mental and behavioural disorders 10*. Geneva: World Health Organization.

World Health Organization. (1996). *Mental health care law: Ten basic principles*. Geneva: World Health Organization.

World Health Organization. (2001a). *Mental health resources in the world. Initial results of Project Atlas*. Geneva: World Health Organization.

World Health Organization. (2001b). *The world health report 2001: Mental health, new understanding, new hope*. Geneva: World Health Organization.

World Health Organization. (2005). *WHO resource book on mental health, human rights and legislation*. Geneva: World Health Organization.

World Health Organization. (2010). *Mental health and development: Targeting people with mental health conditions as a vulnerable group*. Geneva: World Health Organization.

World Health Organization. (2011). *Mental health atlas 2011*. Geneva: World Health Organization.

World Health Organization. (2012). *WHO QualityRights tool kit to assess and improve quality and human rights in mental health and social care facilities*. Geneva: World Health Organization.

World Health Organization. (2013). *Mental health action plan 2013–2020*. Geneva: World Health Organization.

World Health Organization. (2015a). *Mental health atlas 2014*. Geneva: World Health Organization.

World Health Organization. (2015b). *Update of the Mental Health Gap Action Programme (mhGAP) guidelines for mental, neurological and substance use disorders, 2015*. Geneva: World Health Organization.

World Health Organization. (2017). *Advancing the right to health: The vital role of law*. Geneva: World Health Organization. Retrieved June 1, 2019, from https://www.who.int/gender-equity-rights/knowledge/advancing-the-right-to-health/en/.

World Health Organization. (2018a). *ICD-11: Classifying disease to map the way we live and die*. Geneva: World Health Organization. Retrieved December 2, 2019, from https://www.who.int/news-room/spotlight/international-classification-of-diseases.

World Health Organization. (2018b). *Mental health atlas 2017*. Geneva: World Health Organization.

World Health Organization. (2019a). *Transforming services and promoting human rights. WHO QualityRights training and guidance: Mental health and social services. Course guide*. Geneva: World Health Organization.

World Health Organization. (2019b). *Legal capacity and the right to decide. WHO QualityRights Core training: Mental health and social services. Course guide.* Geneva: World Health Organization.

World Health Organization. (2019c). *Supported decision-making and advance planning. WHO QualityRights specialized training. Course guide.* Geneva: World Health Organization.

World Health Organization. (2019d). *Strategies to end seclusion and restraint. WHO QualityRights specialized training. Course guide.* Geneva: World Health Organization.

World Health Organization. (2019e). *Freedom from coercion, violence and abuse. WHO QualityRights core training: Mental health and social services. Course guide.* Geneva: World Health Organization.

World Health Organization Regional Office for Europe. (2018). *Mental health, human rights and standards of care. Assessment of the quality of institutional care for adults with psychosocial and intellectual disabilities in the WHO European region.* Copenhagen: World Health Organization Regional Office for Europe.

# Part II
# Mental Health Legislation in India

# Chapter 4
# History of Mental Health Legislation in India

## 4.1 Early Mental Healthcare in India

Like all medical traditions worldwide, Indian medicine has long had an awareness of mental illness. In Unani medicine, from the thirteenth century CE, many different illnesses were described by one of its key practitioners Najabuddin Unhammad (c. 1222) (Nizamie and Goyal 2010). Ayurveda- (Somasundaram 1984) and Siddha-based medicine also presented descriptions of psychiatric symptomatology and mental illness (Somasundaram et al. 1985).

Even prior to the introduction of formal legislation, there was an increasing awareness of the European approach to treating mental illness in India from as early as the sixteenth century (Sanjeev 2003). Mental hospitals initially arrived in India from the Muslim world, but these did little for most Indians with mental illness (Sharma and Varma 1984). There were no large institutions housing people with mental illness. Prior to British rule, families cared for the mentally ill (Sharma 2006). Large-scale modern psychiatry, when it developed, mirrored the British asylum system (Mishra et al. 2018), although it is debated to what extent these 'madhouses', asylums and hospitals were used by native Indians as opposed to merchants, soldiers, travellers and affluent Indians (Verma 1995).

The first asylum in India opened in Bombay in 1745, when a ward in a Bombay hospital was set aside for 'lunatics' (Crawford 1914). This was followed by developments in Calcutta, where a hospital for the treatment of people with mental illness was opened in 1784 (Kumar and Kumar 2008). Few additional asylums were constructed until the Lunatic Asylum Act, 1858 which led to the opening of multiple facilities across India (e.g. in Agra in 1859). By 1900, 26 asylums were being run by the Indian government and the numbers resident in such institutions grew accordingly (Mills 2001).

Until the middle of the nineteenth century, the treatment of people with mental illness occurred without formal legislative provisions under Indian law. From 1851 onwards, however, legislation was gradually introduced. This process was shaped by key political events and ultimately led to what is arguably one of the most progressive



R. M. Duffy and B. D. Kelly, *India's Mental Healthcare Act, 2017*,
https://doi.org/10.1007/978-981-15-5009-6_4

**Table 4.1** Timeline of key developments in Indian mental health legislation and their context

| Year | Key events | Legislation |
|---|---|---|
| 1745 | First asylum founded in Bombay | – |
| 1757 | Beginning of 'Company Rule' in India | – |
| 1851 | – | Lunatic Removal Act |
| 1858 | Start of British rule in India | Lunacy (Supreme Courts) Act<br>Lunacy (District Courts) Act<br>Indian Lunatic Asylum Act |
| 1860 | Criminalization of suicide | Penal Code |
| 1877 | – | Military Lunatic Act |
| 1898 | – | Code of Criminal Procedure (Chapter 34) |
| 1900 | – | Prisoners Act |
| 1912 | – | Indian Lunacy Act |
| 1947 | Indian Independence | – |
| 1949 | – | Constitution of India |
| 1987 | – | Mental Health Act |
| 1995 | – | Persons with Disabilities Act |
| 1999 | – | National Trust Act |
| 2007 | Ratification of the United Nations' Convention on the Rights of Persons with Disabilities by India | – |
| 2012 | – | Protection of Children from Sexual Offences Act |
| 2014 | New mental health policy | – |
| 2016 | – | Rights of Persons with Disabilities Act |
| 2017 | – | Mental Healthcare Act |

mental health laws internationally: the Mental Healthcare Act, 2017, which is the chief focus of this book. This evolution is described in Table 4.1.

## 4.2 Early Mental Health Legislation in India

English legislation was introduced during the period of 'Company Rule' in India before 'Direct Crown Rule' came into place in 1858. The first piece of metal health legislation introduced was the Lunatic Removal Act, 1851 (Firdosi and Ahmad 2016). This facilitated the removal of mentally ill offenders from India to England at the expense of the East India Company and supported the forensic assessment of offenders with potential mental illness. The Indian climate was often blamed for mental illness and it was felt that returning people to the United Kingdom (UK) could remedy this.

The Lunatic Removal Act, 1851 was a short piece of legislation, comprising just seven sections. People of 'European birth' who committed crimes but were found to be of 'unsound mind' could be removed to 'any part of the United Kingdom' (Section 1). The Act gave the Government of India 'sufficient warrant and authority for the purpose of removal' and, on return to the UK, the person fell under the Criminal Lunacy Act, 1800 (Section 2). The cost of removal and treatment fell to the East India Company (Section 3), but this cost became a debt that the removed person then owed (Section 4).

When the English government took over in 1858, they attempted to reduce costs by limiting transfers to England (Weiss 1983). This was facilitated by increasing the number of asylums in India (Ernst 1987). Even so, this legislation had widespread use beyond India, with sections being applied in China and Korea (Hong Kong Daily Press Office 1912). The Lunatic Removal Act was repealed after India gained independence, through the British Statutes (application to India) Repeal Act, 1960.

In 1858, the year that the rule of India passed from the British East India Company to the British Crown, three mental health laws were enacted. First, the Lunacy (Supreme Courts) Act dealt with the judicial evaluation of mental health in presidency towns. These towns were the initial trading ports found by the British East India Company: Madras, Calcutta and Bombay. Second, the Lunacy (District Courts) Act, 1858 provided similar legal framework for cases outside of presidency towns. Third, the Indian Lunatic Asylum Act, 1858 governed detention in asylums (Nambi et al. 2016).

These laws primarily dealt with the detention of the mentally ill, the disposal of their estates and the management of 'pauper lunatics' (people with mental illness without the means to pay privately for treatment). These were the matters commonly dealt with in mental health legislation of that era in many other countries. The Indian legislation was heavily based on the English law of the time, including the Lunatics Act, 1845 and the County Asylums Act, 1845 (Somasundaram 1987). These Acts were used with regularity and quickly entered common parlance in the relevant communities (Bhattacharyya 2013). The Indian Lunatic Asylum Act was amended in 1886 and 1889 and a fourth act, the Military Lunatic Act, 1877, was later added to the Indian legislation (Firdosi and Ahmad 2016).

In 1860, the Indian Penal code criminalized suicide, stating that 'whoever attempts to commit suicide and does any act towards the commission of such offence, shall be punished with simple imprisonment for a term which may extend to one year or with fine, or with both' (Section 309). While this provision was rarely used, it remains in place today and has been employed from time to time, even in recent decades. There was, however, a noted shift in perceptions concerning the criminalization of suicide in the years leading up to the Mental Healthcare Act, 2017 (MHCA) (Vadlamani and Gowda 2019).

As a result, and despite Section 309 remaining in the Penal Code, the MHCA takes significant steps to decriminalize suicide, stating that 'notwithstanding anything contained in Section 309 of the Indian Penal Code any person who attempts to commit suicide shall be presumed, unless proved otherwise, to have severe stress and shall not be tried and punished under the said Code' (Section 115(1)). In addition, 'the appropriate Government shall have a duty to provide care, treatment and rehabilitation to a person, having severe stress and who attempted to commit suicide, to reduce the risk of recurrence of attempt to commit suicide' (Section 115(2)). Abetting suicide remains a crime under the Indian Penal Code.

From a historical perspective, two other Acts are also related significantly to people with mental illness: Chapter 34 the Code of Criminal Procedure, 1898 and Section 30 of the Prisoners Act, 1900 (Somasundaram 1987). The Code of Criminal Procedure made extensive provision for the management of people with mental illness accused of breaking the law. This included fitness to stand trial, acquittal on the grounds of insanity and matters relating to disposal. Section 30 of the Prisoners Act, 1900 dealt with the management of prisoners with mental illnesses, including transfer to asylums.

## 4.3 Indian Lunacy Act, 1912

The Indian Lunacy Act, 1912 amended, consolidated, revised and replaced existing mental health legislation in an attempt to bring Indian legislation in line with the English Lunacy Act, 1890 (amended in 1891) (Somasundaram 1987). The 1912 Act brought an end to the idea of the diverse asylum, where Indian and European ideas could co-exist, and so the asylums in India became archetypal colonial institutions (Bhattacharyya 2013). This revision of the legislation was motivated by a general outcry at the conditions in which people with mental illness were being kept (Narayan and Shikha 2013). The 1912 Act was a substantial document with 101 sections covering a vast array of topics. The main parts of the legislation addressed the 'Reception, care and treatment of Lunatics', 'Care and Treatment', 'Proceedings in Lunacy in Presidency-towns', 'Proceedings in Lunacy outside Presidency-towns', 'Establishment of Asylums', 'Expenses of Lunatics' and various other 'Rules'. When the 1912 Act came into force, it applied to over quarter of a billion people whose mental health needs were served by just over 7,000 beds (Overbeck-Wright 1921).

One of the central fears of the day, and an issue carefully addressed in the 1912 Act, was the improper detention of sane people for nefarious reasons. Section 18(2) prohibited reception orders being 'made upon a certificate founded only upon facts communicated by others' and required the medical officer to distinguish 'facts observed by himself from facts communicated by others'. Despite this measure, if someone was detained inappropriately, it was very difficult to get the detention order revised. While it could be done, it required the person or persons who signed the initial order to agree that the order should be revoked and two or more of the visitors of the said asylum had to sanction the revocation (Section 27). Each asylum had at least three visitors, one of whom was a doctor. These people inspected the asylum and met the patients monthly. These monthly inspections were the closest thing in the Act to a review process for detained patients.

The Act gave significant power to magistrates to make decisions regarding people who were deemed to be of unsound mind. They could, *inter alia*, appoint substitute decision-makers, have people committed to an asylum and detain people pending transfer to asylums. Some of these decisions required the agreement of a medical officer. Some limits were placed on the length of time a person could be detained pending a medical examination (Section 16). While it may be very far removed from modern rights-based legislation, there were some provisions for the rights of the mentally ill. In Section 15, Magistrates were directed to investigate any person with a mental illness who 'is cruelly treated or neglected by any relative or other person having the charge of him'. While similar protections had existed prior to the 1912 Act, they were seldom employed (Mills 2006).

Interestingly, the 1912 Act made some distinctions between capacity for making different decisions and did not treat decision-making capacity as a global concept. Sections 46 and 65(2) drew a distinction between a person having capacity to manage 'himself' (sic) and having capacity to manage their 'affairs'. While this demonstrated a degree of nuance in the concept of capacity, it still undermined the person's right to manage their financial and family matters. This loss of financial autonomy was further compounded by Sections 49–56 which gave the courts 'power to dispose of lunatic's property for certain purposes' and described a wardship process. This continued in Sections 67–80, which addressed the management of the property and affairs of people found to be of unsound mind. There was the potential for the revision of a declaration of unsoundness of mind should someone's clinical condition have changed (Section 60). Despite the focus on how care would be paid for, provisions were made for people who could not pay for their treatment and who had no assets; under Section 86, their treatment was paid for by the government.

The 1912 Act had many progressive features. It was, for example, one of the first pieces of mental health law to consider voluntary admissions (Section 4). The status of voluntary patients was not recognized in the English and Welsh law until 1930 (Somasundaram 1987) and, even today, many countries only consider involuntary patients in their mental health legislation. The 1912 Act also addressed 'wandering or dangerous lunatics', mental illness in the armed forces, and mentally ill offenders and prisoners. All of these were important issues at the time, and many remain so today.

While the Lunacy Act, 1912 was in force, people could be found to be 'criminal lunatics' under the Code of Criminal Procedure, 1973, the Prisoners Act, 1900 or the Indian Army Act, 1911. 'Wandering lunatics' and 'criminal lunatics' presented particular challenges to services over this period and greatly increased the numbers admitted to asylums. These people often proved difficult to discharge, greatly increasing the cost of running the institutions (Mills 2006). While the 1912 legislation did not change this situation drastically, its detailed consideration of such cases was a welcome addition to the rather complex legislative landscape. Section 84 began the licencing of asylums at a state level and licences could be revoked if asylums were not providing effective treatments. In addition, the Act evolved to a degree over time, e.g. in 1922, the term 'mental hospital' replaced 'lunatic asylum' (Somasundaram 1987).

## 4.4 Constitution of India, 1949 and Representation of the People Act, 1950

The Constitution of India is the largest constitution in the world, comprising almost 400 articles (Rao and Panchmukhi, undated). As India moves to embrace rights-based mental health legislation, it is clear that many of the principles of such legislation are already underpinned by the country's highly progressive Constitution. While the Constitution predates the CRPD and does not explicitly refer to disability or mental illness, it protects many civil rights and includes protections of social and economic rights, such as education.

The Constitution also gives consideration to issues that would be seen as more peripheral in other jurisdictions, e.g. Article 47 aims to prohibit alcohol (though few states have adopted this) (Khandelwal et al. 2004). The Constitution also guarantees many fundamental rights including rights to equality, freedom and protection from exploitation. Article 21 provides protection from gross violations of these fundamental rights, prohibiting deprivations of life or personal liberty unless prescribed by law.

These constitutional provisions are, however, just one part of a legal landscape that also includes other, more problematic provisions. The Representation of the People Act, 1950, for example, prohibits people of 'unsound mind' from holding public office. Similar provisions concerning people who have been found to be of 'unsound mind' exist in the Hindu Marriage Act, 1955, Indian Succession Act, 1925 and Indian Contract Act, 1872 (Narayan and Shikha 2013). Depending on how these provisions are applied, they may provide protections for people with mental illness in certain situations or may actively foster discrimination and marginalization in others.

## 4.5 India's Mental Health Act, 1987

India gained independence in 1947, but continued to use the Indian Lunacy Act, 1912 until it was replaced by the Mental Health Act, 1987. The 1987 Act is divided into 10 chapters and has 98 Sections. The Act had been drafted in 1950, but took 37 years to receive presidential assent (Trivedi 2002). It did not come into effect in all states and union territories until 1993 (Rastogi 2005).

Despite these delays with implementation, India's 1987 Act introduced many positive changes to mental healthcare in India. It adopted a more human rights-based approach to care, replaced much of the stigmatizing terminology, created the Central and State Mental Health Authorities, simplified admission and discharge policies, and facilitated proxy consent for involuntary admission and the admission of minors (Rastogi 2005; Nambi et al. 2016). It was also the first of India's mental health acts to consider outpatient treatment and thus helped shift the focus of psychiatric care from the psychiatric hospitals to the community, at least in theory. The Act also introduced separate inpatient services for people with addiction-based problems and provided children with separate mental health services.

Despite these advances, the 1987 Act was heavily criticized for a number of reasons. First, it failed to align with government policy, India's Mental Health Programme or many World Health Organization guidelines. Second, the new legislation approached mental illness from a legal perspective rather than a clinical one and consequently placed arguably excessive power in the hands of judges rather than clinicians. Third, the Act did little to address stigma or the inappropriate use of mental health legislation or to educate society as a whole about mental illness. Fourth, little consideration was given to psychiatry outside of admission to mental hospitals. Finally, the police were often the only means of transporting involuntary patients to hospital, which added to stigma, rather than reducing it (Nambi et al. 2016).

The 1987 Act also gave insufficient consideration to General Hospital Psychiatric Units, as it focused on stand-alone psychiatric hospitals and nursing homes (Math et al. 2011). Rastogi (2005) identified this as a limitation and thought that their inclusion would improve their general standard and the treatment that people with mental health problems received in such settings. A major injustice occurred where no relatives came forward to support a person in hospital, as such people could then, in theory, be detained indefinitely.

Overall, some of the innovations of the 1987 Act were steps in the rights direction, but they still fell short of the legislative standards of the time. For example, the Act simplified the admission and discharge processes (Rastogi 2005), but made no mention of rehabilitation or care after discharge. The 1987 Act also gave consideration to research (which was not present in the 1912 Act) and prohibited research without valid consent, but allowed relatives to provide consent on the patient's behalf. Even at the time, a more detailed consideration of this complex issue was required.

## 4.6 Modern Indian Legislation

While not directly relating to psychiatry, the Protection of Children from Sexual Offences Act, 2012 (POSCO) (amended in 2019) is highly relevant for clinicians, especially those working in the area of child and adolescent psychiatry or with adults who have children (Seth 2015). The legislation places a legal obligation on mental health professionals to report all occurrences of child abuse. Many professionals have questioned if current structures and resourcing levels may result in such reporting actually causing harm to the people who experienced abuse, rather than helping them or protecting others (Jain and Jain 2018). This issue has yet to be fully resolved and its implications for mental health services yet to be fully explored.

Overall, India's early ratification of the CRPD in 2007 clearly put a significant onus on India to update its mental health legislation. As the Mental Health Act, 1987 was drafted in 1950, it was felt that it would not be possible to revise it and, so, a decision was taken to replace it with the MHCA. The new legislation, which was commenced in 2018, is complemented by the Rights of Persons with Disabilities Act,

2016, which replaced the Persons with Disabilities Act, 1995. The Rights of Persons with Disabilities Act, 2016 also has significant implications for people with mental illness owing to the CRPD's definition of 'persons with disabilities' to 'include those who have long-term physical, mental, intellectual or sensory impairments which in interaction with various barriers may hinder their full and effective participation in society on an equal basis with others' (United Nations 2006; Article 1). The details of the Rights of Persons with Disabilities Act, 2016 and MHCA are discussed in detail in later chapters of this book, especially in relation to human rights.

## References

Bhattacharyya, A. (2013). *Indian insanes: Lunacy in the 'native' asylums of colonial India, 1858–1912*. Doctoral dissertation. Cambridge: Harvard University.

Crawford, D. G. (1914). *A history of the Indian medical services, 1600–1913*. London: Thacker.

Ernst, W. (1987). The rise of the European lunatic asylum in colonial India (1750–1858). *Bulletin of the Indian Institute of History of Medicine (Hyderabad), 17*(2), 94–107.

Firdosi, M. M., & Ahmad, Z. Z. (2016). Mental health law in India: Origins and proposed reforms. *BJPsych International, 13*(3), 65–67.

Hong Kong Daily Press Office. (1912). *Directory and chronicle for China, Japan, Corea, Indo-China, Siam, Netherlands India, Borneo, the Philippines for the year 1912*. London: Hong Kong Daily Press Office.

Jain, S., & Jain, H. (2018). Mandatory reporting of sexual offences in Indian legislation: An ethical dilemma for medical professionals. *Natlional Medical Journal of India, 31*(2), 125–126.

Khandelwal, S. K., Jhingan, H. P., Ramesh, S., Gupta, R. K., & Srivastava, V. K. (2004). India: Mental health country profile. *International Review of Psychiatry, 16*(1–2), 126–141.

Kumar, S., & Kumar, R. (2008). Institute of mental health and hospital, Agra: Evolution in 150 years. *Indian Journal of Psychiatry, 50*(4), 308–312.

Math, S. B., Murthy, P., & Chandrashekar, C. R. (2011). Mental Health Act (1987): Need for a paradigm shift from custodial to community care. *Indian Journal of Medical Research, 133*(3), 246–249.

Mills, J. (2001). The history of modern psychiatry in India, 1858–1947. *History of Psychiatry, 48*(4), 431–458.

Mills, J. (2006). Modern psychiatry in India: The British role in establishing an Asian system, 1858–1947. *International Review of Psychiatry, 18*(4), 333–343.

Mishra, A., Mathai, T., & Ram, D. (2018). History of psychiatry: An Indian perspective. *Indian Psychiatry Journal, 27*(1), 21–26.

Nambi, S., Ilango, S., & Prabha, L. (2016). Forensic psychiatry in India: Past, present, and future. *Indian Journal of Psychiatry, 58*(2), S175–S180.

Narayan, C. L., & Shikha, D. (2013). Indian legal system and mental health. *Indian Journal of Psychiatry, 55*(2), S177–S181.

Nizamie, S. H., & Goyal, N. (2010). History of psychiatry in India. *Indian Journal of Psychiatry, 52*(1), S7–S12.

Overbeck-Wright, A. W. (1921). *Lunacy in India*. London: Baillière Tindal and Cox.

Rao, R., & Panchmukhi, P. R. (undated). *Health and the Indian constitution*. Centre for Multidisciplinary Development Research. Retrieved December 18, 2019, from http://cmdr.ac.in/editor_v51/assets/Mono-7.pdf.

Rastogi, P. (2005). Mental Health Act, 1987—An analysis. *Journal of Indian Academy of Forensic Medicine, 27*(3), 176–179.

Sanjeev, J. (2003). Psychiatry and confinement in India. In R. Porter & D. Wright (Eds.), *The confinement of the insane: International perspectives, 1800–1965* (pp. 273–298). Cambridge: Cambridge University Press.
Seth, R. (2015). Child abuse and neglect in India. *Indian Journal of Pediatrics, 82*(8), 707–714.
Sharma, S. (2006). Psychiatry, colonialism and Indian civilization: A historical appraisal. *Indian Journal of Psychiatry, 48*(2), 109–112.
Sharma, S. D., & Varma, L. P. (1984). History of mental hospitals in Indian sub-continent. *Indian Journal of Psychiatry, 26*(4), 295–300.
Somasundaram, O. (1984). History of psychiatry in India. In A. De Souza & A. D. De Souza (Eds.), *Psychiatry in India* (pp. 13–20). Bombay: Bhalani Book Depot.
Somasundaram, O., Jayaramakrishnan, T., & Suresh Kumar, M. (1985). Psychiatry in Siddha (Tamil) system of medicine. *Indian Journal of Psychological Medicine, 9*(1), 38–45.
Somasundaram, O. (1987). The Indian Lunacy Act, 1912: The historic background. *Indian Journal of Psychiatry, 29*(1), 3–14.
Trivedi, J. K. (2002). The mental health legislation: An ongoing debate. *Indian Journal of Psychiatry, 44*(2), 95–96.
United Nations. (2006). *Convention on the rights of persons with disabilities.* New York: United Nations. Retrieved September 23, 2019, from https://www.un.org/development/desa/disabilities/convention-on-the-rights-of-persons-with-disabilities/convention-on-the-rights-of-persons-with-disabilities-2.html.
Vadlamani, L. N., & Gowda, M. (2019). Practical implications of Mental Healthcare Act 2017: Suicide and suicide attempt. *Indian Journal of Psychiatry, 61*(4), S750–S755.
Verma, L. P. (1995). Psychiatry in Unani medicine. *Indian Journal of Social Psychiatry, 11,* 10–15.
Weiss, M. G. (1983). The treatment of insane patients in India in the lunatic asylums of the nineteenth century. *Indian Journal of Psychiatry, 25*(4), 312–316.

# Chapter 5
# India's Rights of Persons with Disabilities Act, 2016

## 5.1 Background to India's Rights of Persons with Disabilities Act, 2016

India's Rights of Persons with Disabilities Act, 2016 (RPWDA) received the assent of the President of India on 27 December 2016 and was commenced in effect on 15 June 2017. The Act followed on from the Persons with Disabilities (Equal Opportunities, Protection of Rights and Full Participation) Act, 1995 (Suresh 2014), which—critically—preceded the United Nations' (UN) Convention on the Rights of Persons with Disabilities (CRPD) (UN 2006; Rao et al. 2016; Kalmegh et al. 2018; Raveesh et al. 2019).

Against this background, the purpose of India's RPWDA is 'to give effect to the United Nations Convention on the Rights of Persons with Disabilities and for matters connected therewith or incidental thereto'. The Act's Preamble notes that the UN General Assembly adopted the Convention 'on the 13th day of December, 2006'; 'India is a signatory to the said Convention'; 'India ratified the said Convention on the 1st day of October, 2007' and 'it is considered necessary to implement the Convention'.

The purpose of the CRPD itself is set out in Article 1 of the Convention:

> The purpose of the present Convention is to promote, protect and ensure the full and equal enjoyment of all human rights and fundamental freedoms by all persons with disabilities, and to promote respect for their inherent dignity. Persons with disabilities include those who have long-term physical, mental, intellectual or sensory impairments which in interaction with various barriers may hinder their full and effective participation in society on an equal basis with others.

Article 5 of the CRPD places particular emphasis on 'equality and non-discrimination':

1. States Parties recognize that all persons are equal before and under the law and are entitled without any discrimination to the equal protection and equal benefit of the law.



R. M. Duffy and B. D. Kelly, *India's Mental Healthcare Act, 2017*,
https://doi.org/10.1007/978-981-15-5009-6_5

2. States Parties shall prohibit all discrimination on the basis of disability and guarantee to persons with disabilities equal and effective legal protection against discrimination on all grounds.
3. In order to promote equality and eliminate discrimination, States Parties shall take all appropriate steps to ensure that reasonable accommodation is provided.
4. Specific measures which are necessary to accelerate or achieve de facto equality of persons with disabilities shall not be considered discrimination under the terms of the present Convention.

Against this background, India's RPWDA duly notes that the UN 'Convention lays down the following principles for empowerment of persons with disabilities: (a) respect for inherent dignity, individual autonomy including the freedom to make one's own choices, and independence of persons; (b) non-discrimination; (c) full and effective participation and inclusion in society; (d) respect for difference and acceptance of persons with disabilities as part of human diversity and humanity; (e) equality of opportunity; (f) accessibility; (g) equality between men and women; (h) respect for the evolving capacities of children with disabilities and respect for the right of children with disabilities to preserve their identities' (Preamble).

The RPWDA itself is divided into 17 chapters dealing with 'preliminary' matters and definitions (Section 5.2.1 of this chapter), 'rights and entitlements' (Section 5.2.2), 'education' (Section 5.2.3), 'skill development and employment' (Section 5.2.4), 'social security, health, rehabilitation and recreation' (Section 5.2.5), 'special provisions for persons with benchmark disabilities' (Section 5.2.6), 'special provisions for persons with disabilities with high support needs' (Section 5.2.7), 'duties and responsibilities of appropriate governments' (Section 5.2.8), 'registration of institutions for persons with disabilities and grants to such institutions' (Section 5.2.9), 'certification of specified disabilities' (Section 5.2.10), 'Central and State Advisory Boards on Disability and District Level Committee', (Section 5.2.11), 'Chief Commissioner and State Commissioner for Persons with Disabilities' (Section 5.2.12), 'Special Court' (Section 5.2.13), 'National Fund for Persons with Disabilities' (Section 5.2.14), 'State Fund for Persons with Disabilities' (Section 5.2.15), 'offences and penalties' (Section 5.2.16) and 'miscellaneous' matters (Section 5.2.17).

Each of these elements of the RPWDA is described in the remainder of this chapter, followed by a brief overall discussion of the measures in the legislation. A more detailed exploration of the human rights implications of the RPWDA and (especially) the Mental Healthcare Act, 2017 is provided in Chaps. 7, 8, 9 and 10 of this book. Both pieces of legislation need to be considered in tandem, however, in order to fully describe the relevant legislative landscape and to understand how the situation has changed significantly over the past decade.

## 5.2 Provisions of the Rights of Persons with Disabilities Act, 2016

### 5.2.1 *'Preliminary' Matters and Definitions*

The RPWDA starts by stating that the new legislation 'shall come into force on such date as the Central Government may, by notification in the Official Gazette, appoint' (Section 1(2)). In the event, the legislation received the assent of the President of India on 27 December 2016 and was commenced in effect on 15 June 2017.

In the Act, 'person with disability' means 'a person with long term physical, mental, intellectual or sensory impairment which, in interaction with barriers, hinders his full and effective participation in society equally with others' (Section 2(s)). A 'barrier' is 'any factor including communicational, cultural, economic, environmental, institutional, political, social, attitudinal or structural factors which hampers the full and effective participation of persons with disabilities in society' (Section 2(c)).

'Discrimination' means 'any distinction, exclusion, restriction on the basis of disability which [has] the purpose or effect of impairing or nullifying the recognition, enjoyment or exercise on an equal basis with others of all human rights and fundamental freedoms in the political, economic, social, cultural, civil or any other field and includes all forms of discrimination and denial of reasonable accommodation' (Section 2(h)). 'Reasonable accommodation' means 'necessary and appropriate modification and adjustments, without imposing a disproportionate or undue burden in a particular case, to ensure to persons with disabilities the enjoyment or exercise of rights equally with others' (Section 2(y)).

### 5.2.2 *'Rights and Entitlements'*

The RPWDA states that 'the appropriate Government shall ensure that the persons with disabilities enjoy the right to equality, life with dignity and respect for his or her integrity equally with others' (Section 3(1)), and 'shall take steps to utilise the capacity of persons with disabilities by providing appropriate environment' (Section 3(2)).

'No person with disability shall be discriminated on the ground of disability, unless it is shown that the impugned act or omission is a proportionate means of achieving a legitimate aim' (Section 3(3)) and 'no person shall be deprived of his or her personal liberty only on the ground of disability' (Section 3(4)). 'The appropriate Government shall take necessary steps to ensure reasonable accommodation for persons with disabilities' (Section 3(5)). This is highly consistent with the requirements of the CRPD.

In addition, 'the appropriate Government and the local authorities shall take measures to ensure that the women and children with disabilities enjoy their rights equally with others' (Section 4(1)) and 'ensure that all children with disabilities shall have right on an equal basis to freely express their views on all matters affecting them and provide them appropriate support' (Section 4(2)).

'Persons with disabilities shall have the right to live in the community' (Section 5(1)) and government 'shall endeavour' to ensure they 'are (a) not obliged to live in any particular living arrangement; and (b) given access to a range of in-house, residential and other community support services' (Section 5(2)). The government shall also 'take measures to protect persons with disabilities from being subjected to torture, cruel, inhuman or degrading treatment' (Section 6(1)).

'No person with disability shall be a subject of any research without (i) his or her free and informed consent' and '(ii) prior permission of a Committee for Research on Disability constituted in the prescribed manner for the purpose by the appropriate Government in which not less than half of the Members shall themselves be either persons with disabilities or Members of the registered organisation' (Section 6(2)). In this context, 'registered organisation' means 'an association of persons with disabilities or a disabled person organisation, association of parents of persons with disabilities, association of persons with disabilities and family members, or a voluntary or non-governmental or charitable organisation or trust, society, or non-profit company working for the welfare of the persons with disabilities, duly registered' (Section 2(z)).

In addition, 'the appropriate Government shall take measures to protect persons with disabilities from all forms of abuse, violence and exploitation and to prevent the same, shall' (a) 'provide legal remedies'; (b) 'take steps for avoiding such incidents'; (c) 'take steps to rescue, protect and rehabilitate victims'; and (d) 'create awareness and make available information among the public' (Section 7(1)). Possible 'abuse, violence or exploitation' must be notified to the local Executive Magistrate (Section 7(2)) who 'shall take immediate steps to stop or prevent its occurrence', including rescuing the victim, providing 'protective custody to the person with disability, if such person so desires', and 'maintenance' (Section 7(3)). Police officers have specific responsibilities in relation to notification, information, legal aid and rights (Section 7(4)). If indicated, the Executive Magistrate 'may forward the complaint to [the relevant] Judicial or Metropolitan Magistrate' (Section 7(5)).

'Persons with disabilities shall have equal protection and safety in situations of risk, armed conflict, humanitarian emergencies and natural disasters' (Section 8(1)). 'No child with disability shall be separated from his or her parents on the ground of disability except on an order of competent court, if required, in the best interest of the child' (Section 9(1)). In such cases, the 'court shall place such child with his or her near relations, and failing that within the community in a family setting or in exceptional cases in shelter home run by the appropriate Government or non-governmental organisation' (Section 9(2)).

Persons with disabilities shall 'have access to appropriate information regarding reproductive and family planning' (Section 10(1)); shall not 'be subject to any medical procedure which leads to infertility without his or her free and informed consent' (Section 10(2)); and shall be 'able to exercise the right to access any court' or similar body 'without discrimination on the basis of disability' (Section 12(1)), with suitable 'support for exercising legal rights' (Section 12(2)). Polling stations and related material are to be 'accessible' and 'easily understandable' (Section 11), and all public documents shall be 'in accessible formats' (Section 12(4)).

'The appropriate Government shall ensure that the persons with disabilities' (a) 'have [the] right, equally with others, to own or inherit property, movable or immovable, control their financial affairs and have access to bank loans, mortgages and other forms of financial credit' (Section 13(1)); and (b) 'enjoy legal capacity on an equal basis with others in all aspects of life and have the right to equal recognition everywhere as any other person before the law' (Section 13(2)).

'A person with disability may alter, modify or dismantle any support arrangement and seek the support of another' (Section 13(4)) and, when a conflict of interest arises with 'a person providing support', that person 'shall abstain from providing support' (Section 13(3)). 'Any person providing support to the person with disability shall not exercise undue influence and shall respect his or her autonomy, dignity and privacy' (Section 13(5)).

'Where a district court or any designated authority, as notified by the State Government, finds that a person with disability, who had been provided adequate and appropriate support but is unable to take legally binding decisions, may be provided further support of a limited guardian to take legally binding decisions on his behalf in consultation with such person [...] Provided that the [relevant authority] may grant total support to the person with disability requiring such support or where the limited guardianship is to be granted repeatedly, in which case, the decision regarding the support to be provided shall be reviewed' by the relevant authority (Section 14(1)).

In this context, 'limited guardianship' is 'a system of joint decision which operates on mutual understanding and trust between the guardian and the person with disability, which shall be limited to a specific period and for specific decision and situation and shall operate in accordance to the will of the person with disability'.

There are transitional provisions for existing guardians (Section 14(2)) and for appeal (Section 14(3)). 'Social awareness to support persons with disabilities in exercise of their legal capacity' shall be increased (Section 15(1)) and relevant authorities 'shall take measures for setting up suitable support arrangements to exercise legal capacity by persons with disabilities living in institutions and those with high support needs and any other measures as may be required' (Section 15(2)). 'Institution' means 'an institution for the reception, care, protection, education, training, rehabilitation and any other activities for persons with disabilities' (Section 2(o)). 'Rehabilitation' refers to 'a process aimed at enabling persons with disabilities to attain and maintain optimal, physical, sensory, intellectual, psychological environmental or social function levels' (Section 2(za)).

### *5.2.3 'Education'*

The RPWDA states that 'the appropriate Government and the local authorities shall endeavour that all educational institutions funded or recognised by them provide inclusive education to the children with disabilities', admitting them and providing equal opportunities; making 'facilities accessible'; providing 'reasonable accommodation' and supports 'in environments that maximise academic and social development'; using appropriate means of communication; detecting 'specific learning disabilities' in a timely way and taking appropriate action; monitoring participation and attainment; and providing transport (Section 16).

In this context, 'inclusive education' means 'a system of education wherein students with and without disability learn together and the system of teaching and learning is suitably adapted to meet the learning needs of different types of students with disabilities' (Section 2(m)).

To 'promote and facilitate inclusive education', 'the appropriate Government and the local authorities shall [conduct a] survey of school going children' every five years, 'identifying children with disabilities, ascertaining their special needs and the extent to which these are being met' (Section 17). They shall also 'establish adequate number of teacher training institutions'; 'train and employ teachers, including teachers with disability'; 'train professionals and staff to support inclusive education'; 'establish [an] adequate number of resource centres'; 'promote the use of appropriate augmentative and alternative modes' of communication; provide free learning materials to students with benchmark disabilities up to the age of 18 years; 'provide scholarships in appropriate cases'; 'make suitable modifications in the curriculum and examination system'; 'promote research to improve learning' (Section 17); and 'promote, protect and ensure participation of persons with disabilities in adult education' (Section 18).

### *5.2.4 'Skill Development and Employment'*

The RPWDA requires that 'the appropriate Government shall formulate schemes and programmes including provision of loans at concessional rates to facilitate and support employment of persons with disabilities especially for their vocational training and self-employment' (Section 19(1)). These 'schemes and programmes [...] shall provide for inclusion' in 'vocational and skill training schemes and programmes'; 'adequate support and facilities'; 'exclusive skill training programmes'; 'active links with the market'; marketing of resultant products; and 'maintenance of disaggregated data on the progress made' (Section 19(2)).

'No Government establishment shall discriminate against any person with disability in any matter relating to employment', although exceptions may be made 'having regard to the type of work' involved (Section 20(1)). 'Every Government establishment shall provide reasonable accommodation and appropriate barrier free and conducive environment[s]' (Section 20(2)). 'No promotion shall be denied to a person merely on the ground of disability' (Section 20(3)). Neither can a Government establishment 'dispense with or reduce in rank, an employee who acquires a disability' (Section 20(4)). Every establishment must have a policy on these matters (Section 21) and maintain appropriate records (Section 22); in this context, the term 'establishment' includes 'a Government establishment and private establishment' (Section 2(i)). A grievance procedure is outlined (Section 23).

### *5.2.5 'Social Security, Health, Rehabilitation and Recreation'*

In relation to 'social security, health, rehabilitation and recreation', 'the appropriate Government shall within the limit of its economic capacity and development formulate necessary schemes and programmes to safeguard and promote the right of persons with disabilities for adequate standard of living to enable them to live independently or in the community' (Section 24(1)). The 'quantum of assistance to the persons with disabilities under such schemes and programmes shall be at least 25% higher than the similar schemes applicable to others' (Section 24(1)), with due regard for diversity (Section 24(2)).

These schemes 'shall provide for community centres'; 'facilities for persons including children with disabilities who have no family or have been abandoned'; support during disasters or conflict; 'support to women with disability for livelihood and for upbringing of their children'; 'access to safe drinking water and appropriate and accessible sanitation'; 'aids and appliances, medicine and diagnostic services and corrective surgery free of cost'; 'disability pension'; 'unemployment allowance'; 'care-giver allowance'; 'comprehensive insurance scheme'; and 'any other matter which the appropriate Government may think fit', subject to various conditions (Section 24(3)). In this context, a 'caregiver' is 'any person including parents and other family members who with or without payment provides care, support or assistance to a person with disability' (Section 2(d)).

In addition, 'the appropriate Government and the local authorities shall take necessary measures for the persons with disabilities to provide [...] free healthcare' locally, with 'barrier-free access' and 'priority in attendance and treatment' (Section 25(1)). They shall also 'take measures and make schemes or programmes to promote healthcare and prevent the occurrence of disabilities' through surveys; preventive measures; screening; training staff; sponsoring awareness; promoting 'pre-natal, perinatal and post-natal care of mother and child'; public education; providing healthcare during 'natural disasters and other situations of risk'; providing 'essential medical facilities for life saving emergency treatment and procedures'; and promoting 'sexual and reproductive healthcare' (Section 25(2)).

Government shall also provide 'insurance schemes for their employees with disabilities' (Section 26) and, with the local authorities, 'within their economic capacity and development, undertake or cause to be undertaken services and programmes of rehabilitation, particularly in the areas of health, education and employment for all persons with disabilities' (Section 27(1)), possibly through 'non-governmental organisations' (Section 27(2)). There are also requirements for government to support 'research and development' (Section 28); 'the rights of all persons with disabilities to have a cultural life and to participate in recreational activities equally with others' (e.g. sponsorship, 'a disability history museum', 'making art accessible', 'promoting recreation centres', 'facilitating participation' 'redesigning courses' and 'developing technology') (Section 29); and 'effective participation in sporting activities' (Section 30).

### 5.2.6 *'Special Provisions for Persons with Benchmark Disabilities'*

The RPWDA specifies that 'person with benchmark disability' means 'a person with not less than 40% of a specified disability where specified disability has not been defined in measurable terms and includes a person with disability where specified disability has been defined in measurable terms, as certified by the certifying authority' (Section 2(r)). 'Every child with benchmark disability between the age of six to 18 years shall have the right to free education in a neighbourhood school, or in a special school, of his choice' (Section 31(1)). 'The appropriate Government and local authorities shall ensure' that this right is fulfilled (Section 31(2)).

In addition, 'all Government institutions of higher education and other higher education institutions receiving aid from the Government shall reserve not less than 5% [of] seats for persons with benchmark disabilities' (Section 32(1)). 'Persons with benchmark disabilities shall be given an upper age relaxation of five years for admission in institutions of higher education' (Section 32(2)).

There is a 'reservation' whereby 'every appropriate Government shall appoint in every Government establishment, not less than 4% of the total number of vacancies in the cadre strength in each group of posts meant to be filled with persons with benchmark disabilities of which 1% each shall be reserved for persons with benchmark disabilities under clauses (a), (b) and (c) and 1% for persons with benchmark disabilities under clauses (d) and (e), namely: (a) blindness and low vision; (b) deaf and hard of hearing; (c) locomotor disability including cerebral palsy, leprosy cured, dwarfism, acid attack victims and muscular dystrophy; (d) autism, intellectual disability, specific learning disability and mental illness; (e) multiple disabilities', although there may be exemptions (Section 34).

'The appropriate Government and the local authorities shall, within the limit of their economic capacity and development, provide incentives to employer in private sector to ensure that at least 5% of their work force is composed of persons with benchmark disability' (Section 35).

There shall also be 5% reservations in (a) 'allotment of agricultural land and housing in all relevant schemes and development programmes, with appropriate priority to women with benchmark disabilities'; (b) 'all poverty alleviation and various developmental schemes with appropriate priority to women with benchmark disabilities'; and (c) 'allotment of land on concessional rate, where such land is to be used for the purpose of promoting housing, shelter, setting up of occupation, business, enterprise, recreation centres and production centres' (Section 37).

### 5.2.7 *'Special Provisions for Persons with Disabilities with High Support Needs'*

The RPWDA provides that 'any person with benchmark disability, who considers himself to be in need of high support, or any person or organisation on his or her behalf, may apply to an authority, to be notified by the appropriate Government, requesting to provide high support' (Section 38(1)). 'High support' means 'an intensive support, physical, psychological and otherwise, which may be required by a person with benchmark disability for daily activities, to take independent and informed decision to access facilities and participating in all areas of life including education, employment, family and community life and treatment and therapy' (Section 2(l)). An assessment shall occur (Sections 38(2) and (3)) and, on receipt of that report, 'the authority shall take steps to provide support' (Section 38(4)).

### 5.2.8 *'Duties and Responsibilities of Appropriate Governments'*

The Government, with appropriate consultation, 'shall conduct, encourage, support or promote awareness campaigns and sensitisation programmes to ensure that the rights of the persons with disabilities provided under this Act are protected' (Section 39(1)). These 'programmes and campaigns' shall:

- 'Promote values of inclusion, tolerance, empathy and respect for diversity';
- 'Advance recognition of the skills, merits and abilities of persons with disabilities and of their contributions to the workforce [and] labour market';
- 'Foster respect for the decisions made by persons with disabilities on all matters related to family life, relationships, bearing and raising children';
- 'Provide orientation and sensitisation at the school, college, university and professional training level';
- 'Provide orientation and sensitisation on disabling conditions and rights of persons with disabilities to employers, administrators and co-workers'; and
- 'Ensure that the rights of persons with disabilities are included in the curriculum in universities, colleges and schools' (Section 39(2)).

There shall be rules 'laying down the standards of accessibility for the physical environment, transportation, information and communications, including appropriate technologies and systems, and other facilities and services provided to the public in urban and rural areas' (Section 40).

Specific provisions are outlined relating to 'access to transport' (Section 41); 'access to information and communication technology' (Section 42); 'universally designed consumer products' (Section 43); 'mandatory observance of accessibility norms' for buildings (Section 44); a 'time limit for making existing [public] infrastructure and premises accessible' (normally 5 years) (Section 45); 'time limit for accessibility by service providers' (normally 2 years) (Section 46); and 'social audit' of all schemes (Section 48). In this context, 'universal design' means 'the design of products, environments, programmes and services to be usable by all people to the greatest extent possible, without the need for adaptation or specialised design and shall apply to assistive devices including advanced technologies for particular group of persons with disabilities' (Section 2(ze)).

With respect to 'human resource development', 'all universities shall promote teaching and research in disability studies including establishment of study centres for such studies' (Section 47(2)). In addition, 'the appropriate government' shall:

- 'Mandate training on disability rights in all courses for the training of Panchayati Raj members [local administrators], legislators, administrators, police officials, judges and lawyers';
- 'Induct disability as a component for all education courses for schools, colleges and university teachers, doctors, nurses, para-medical personnel, social welfare officers, rural development officers, ASHA workers [accredited social health activists], *anganwadi* workers [at rural child care centres], engineers, architects, other professionals and community workers';
- 'Initiate capacity building programmes including training in independent living and community relationships for families, members of community and other stakeholders and care providers on care giving and support';
- 'Ensure independence training for persons with disabilities to build community relationships on mutual contribution and respect';
- 'Conduct training programmes for sports teachers with focus on sports, games, adventure activities'; and
- 'Any other capacity development measures as may be required' (Section 47(1)).

### *5.2.9 'Registration of Institutions for Persons with Disabilities and Grants to Such Institutions'*

In relation to the registration of institutions, the RPWDA states that 'no person shall establish or maintain any institution for persons with disabilities except in accordance with a certificate of registration issued in this behalf by the competent authority', although 'an institution for care of mentally ill persons, which holds a valid licence under Section 8 of the Mental Health Act, 1987 or any other Act for the time being in force, shall not be required to be registered under this Act' (Section 50).

There are procedures for 'application and grant of certificate of registration' (Section 51), 'revocation of registration' (e.g. for breach of rules or conditions) (Section 52) and appeal (Section 53), although 'nothing contained in this Chapter shall apply to an institution for persons with disabilities established or maintained by the Central Government or a State Government' (Section 54). In addition, 'the appropriate Government may within the limits of their economic capacity and development, grant financial assistance to registered institutions to provide services and to implement the schemes and programmes in pursuance of the provisions of this Act' (Section 55).

### *5.2.10 'Certification of Specified Disabilities'*

'The Central Government shall notify guidelines for the purpose of assessing the extent of specified disability in a person' (Section 56) and designate 'certifying authorities' (Section 57). A 'specified disability' is a disability in one of the five categories of disabilities as specified in the Schedule to the Act (Section 2(zc)): 'physical', 'intellectual', 'mental behaviour', other specific disabilities, and 'multiple disabilities'.

In the Schedule, 'physical disability' includes 'locomotor disability' ('leprosy cured person', 'cerebral palsy', 'dwarfism', 'muscular dystrophy' and 'acid attack victims'), 'visual impairment' (blindness and 'low vision'), 'hearing impairment' (deaf and 'hard of hearing'), and 'speech and language disability' (such as aphasia), with further details provided for each sub-category (Schedule, Section 1).

'Intellectual disability' is 'a condition characterised by significant limitation both in intellectual functioning (reasoning, learning, problem solving) and in adaptive behaviour which covers a range of every day, social and practical skills'; this includes 'specific learning disabilities' and 'autism spectrum disorder' (Schedule, Section 2).

'Mental illness' means 'a substantial disorder of thinking, mood, perception, orientation or memory that grossly impairs judgment, behaviour, capacity to recognise reality or ability to meet the ordinary demands of life, but does not include retardation which is a condition of arrested or incomplete development of mind of a person, specially characterised by subnormality of intelligence' (Schedule, Section 3).

Other specific disabilities can be due to 'chronic neurological conditions' (such as multiple sclerosis and Parkinson's disease) and 'blood disorder' (such as haemophilia, thalassemia and sickle cell disease).

'Any person with specified disability may apply' for 'a certificate of disability' (Section 58(1)) and, following assessment, the 'certifying authority' shall '(a) issue a certificate of disability to such person' or '(b) inform him in writing that he has no specified disability' (Section 58(2)). There is provision for appeal (Section 59).

### *5.2.11 'Central and State Advisory Boards on Disability and District Level Committee'*

The RPWDA states that 'the Central Government shall, by notification, constitute a body to be known as the Central Advisory Board on Disability to exercise the powers conferred on, and to perform the functions assigned to it, under this Act' (Section 60(1)). The Board shall include 'the Minister in charge of Department of Disability Affairs in the Central Government, Chairperson'; 'the Minister of State in charge dealing with Department of Disability Affairs in the Ministry in the Central Government, Vice Chairperson'; 'three Members of Parliament'; various public officials; the chairpersons and directors of a range of organisations; 'five members who are experts in the field of disability and rehabilitation'; 'ten members, as far as practicable, being persons with disabilities, to represent non-governmental organisations concerned with disabilities or disabled persons organisations'; and various others (Section 60(2)).

There are provisions relating to 'terms and conditions of service of members' (Section 61), 'disqualifications' (Section 62), 'vacation of seats by members' (Section 63) and meetings (Section 64). The Board 'shall be the national-level consultative and advisory body on disability matters, and shall facilitate the continuous evolution of a comprehensive policy for the empowerment of persons with disabilities and the full enjoyment of rights' (Section 65(1)). More specifically, the Board shall:

- 'Advise the Central Government and the State Governments on policies, programmes, legislation and projects with respect to disability';
- 'Develop a national policy to address issues concerning persons with disabilities';
- 'Review and coordinate the activities of all departments of the government and other governmental and non-governmental organisations';
- 'Take up the cause of persons with disabilities with the concerned authorities and the international organisations with a view to provide for schemes and projects for the persons with disabilities in the national plans';
- 'Recommend steps to ensure accessibility, reasonable accommodation, non-discrimination for persons with disabilities vis-à-vis information, services and the built environment and their participation in social life';
- 'Monitor and evaluate the impact of laws, policies and programmes to achieve full participation of persons with disabilities'; and
- 'Such other functions as may be assigned from time to time by the Central Government' (Section 65(2)).

In addition to the 'Central Advisory Board on Disability', every State Government shall 'constitute a body to be known as the State Advisory Board on Disability' comprising 'the Minister in charge of the Department in the State Government dealing with disability matters, Chairperson'; 'the Minister of State or the Deputy Minister in charge of the Department in the State Government dealing with disability matters, if any, Vice-Chairperson'; various secretaries to the State Government in relevant departments; 'three Members of the State Legislature'; 'five members who are experts in the field of disability and rehabilitation'; 'five members to be nominated by the State Government by rotation to represent the districts'; 'ten persons as far as practicable, being persons with disabilities, to represent non-governmental organisations or associations'; 'not more than three representatives of the State Chamber of Commerce and Industry'; and an 'officer not below the rank of Joint Secretary in the Department dealing with disability matters in the State Government', as 'member-secretary' (Section 66(2)).

There are provisions relating to 'terms and conditions of service of members' (Section 67), 'disqualification' (Section 68), 'vacation of seats' (Section 69) and meetings (Section 70). 'The State Advisory Board shall be the State-level consultative and advisory body on disability matters, and shall facilitate the continuous evolution of a comprehensive policy for the empowerment of persons with disabilities and the full enjoyment of rights' (Section 71(1)). Its functions are the same at those of the Central Advisory Board, but at State level (Section 71(2)).

### *5.2.12 'Chief Commissioner and State Commissioner for Persons with Disabilities'*

The Central Government may 'appoint a Chief Commissioner for Persons with Disabilities' (Section 74(1)) and 'two Commissioners to assist the Chief Commissioner, of which one Commissioner shall be a person with disability' (Section 74(2)). All must have 'special knowledge or practical experience in respect of matters relating to rehabilitation' (Section 74(3)). 'The Chief Commissioner shall be assisted by an advisory committee comprising of not more than eleven members drawn from the experts from different disabilities' (Section 74(8)). 'The Chief Commissioner shall':

- 'Identify, *suo motu* [on their own motion] or otherwise, the provisions of any law or policy, programme and procedures, which are inconsistent with this Act and recommend necessary corrective steps';
- 'Inquire, *suo motu* or otherwise, [into] deprivation of rights of persons with disabilities and safeguards available to them in respect of matters for which the Central Government is the appropriate Government and take up the matter with appropriate authorities for corrective action';
- 'Review the safeguards provided by or under this Act or any other law for the time being in force for the protection of rights of persons with disabilities and recommend measures for their effective implementation';
- 'Review the factors that inhibit the enjoyment of rights of persons with disabilities and recommend appropriate remedial measures';
- 'Study treaties and other international instruments on the rights of persons with disabilities and make recommendations for their effective implementation';
- 'Undertake and promote research in the field of the rights of persons with disabilities';
- 'Promote awareness of the rights of persons with disabilities and the safeguards available for their protection';
- 'Monitor implementation of the provisions of this Act and schemes, programmes meant for persons with disabilities';

- 'Monitor utilisation of funds disbursed by the Central Government for the benefit of persons with disabilities'; and
- 'Perform such other functions as the Central Government may assign' (Section 75(1)).

'Whenever the Chief Commissioner makes a recommendation to an authority [in respect of matters for which the Central Government is the appropriate Government], that authority shall take necessary action on it, and inform the Chief Commissioner of the action taken within three months', and 'where an authority does not accept a recommendation, it shall convey reasons for non-acceptance to the Chief Commissioner within a period of three months, and shall also inform the aggrieved person' (Section 76). The 'powers of [the] Chief Commissioner' are outlined (Section 77) and an annual report is required, 'along with a memorandum of action taken or proposed' by the Central Government (Section 78).

In addition to the Central Government appointing a Chief Commissioner, 'the State Government may, by notification, appoint a State Commissioner for Persons with Disabilities' (Section 79(1)) with 'special knowledge or practical experience in respect of matters relating to rehabilitation' (Section 79(2)). 'The State Commissioner shall be assisted by an advisory committee comprising of not more than five members drawn from the experts in the disability sector' (Section 79(7)).

The functions of the State Commissioner are the same at those of the Chief Commissioner, but at State level, apart from the requirement to 'study treaties and other international instruments on the rights of persons with disabilities and make recommendations for their effective implementation' (Section 75(1)(e)); that role is reserved for the Chief Commissioner (Section 80). The effect of a recommendation by the State Commissioner is the same as that of the Chief Commissioner, but at State level (Section 81). The 'powers of [the] State Commissioner' are outlined (Section 82) and an annual report is required, 'along with a memorandum of action taken or proposed' by the State Government (Section 83).

### *5.2.13 'Special Court'*

The RPWDA provides that, 'for the purpose of providing speedy trial, the State Government shall, with the concurrence of the Chief Justice of the High Court, by notification, specify for each district, a Court of Session to be a Special Court to try the offences under this Act' (Section 84). The State Government may appoint 'a Special Public Prosecutor for the purpose of conducting cases' (Section 85(1)).

### *5.2.14 'National Fund for Persons with Disabilities'*

With regard to funding, 'there shall be constituted a Fund to be called the National Fund for persons with disabilities' which shall be credited with all sums (a) from other specified funds; (b) 'payable by banks, corporations, financial institutions in pursuance of judgment dated the 16th April, 2004 of the Hon'ble Supreme Court in Civil Appeal Nos. 4655 and 5218 of 2000'; (c) 'received by way of grant, gifts, donations, benefactions, bequests or transfers'; (d) 'received from the Central Government including grants-in-aid'; and (e) 'from such other sources as may be decided by the Central Government' (Section 86). Provisions are made for 'accounts and audit' (Section 87).

### *5.2.15 'State Fund for Persons with Disabilities'*

Also regarding funding, 'there shall be constituted a Fund to be called the State Fund for persons with disabilities by a State Government' (Section 88(1)) which 'shall be utilised and managed in such manner as may be prescribed by the State Government' (Section 88(2)). Provisions are made for accounts, audit and related matters (Sections 88(3)–(6)).

### *5.2.16 'Offences and Penalties'*

With regard to 'offences and penalties', 'any person who contravenes any of the provisions of this Act, or of any rule made thereunder shall for first contravention be punishable with fine which may extend to 10,000 rupees and for any subsequent contravention with fine which shall not be less than 50,000 rupees but which may extend to 500,000 rupees' (Section 89). Companies and those working in them are also liable unless the offence was committed without their knowledge or if they 'had exercised all due diligence' (Section 90(1)).

'Whoever fraudulently avails or attempts to avail any benefit meant for persons with benchmark disabilities, shall be punishable with imprisonment for a term which may extend to two years or with fine which may extend to 100,000 rupees or with both' (Section 91). Punishment of imprisonment for six months to five years and a fine can result if a person:

- 'Intentionally insults or intimidates with intent to humiliate a person with disability in any place within public view';
- 'Assaults or uses force to any person with disability with intent to dishonour him or outrage the modesty of a woman with disability';
- 'Having the actual charge or control over a person with disability voluntarily or knowingly denies food or fluids to him or her';

- 'Being in a position to dominate the will of a child or woman with disability and uses that position to exploit her sexually';
- 'Voluntarily injures, damages or interferes with the use of any limb or sense or any supporting device of a person with disability'; or
- 'Performs, conducts or directs any medical procedure to be performed on a woman with disability which leads to or is likely to lead to termination of pregnancy without her express consent except in cases where medical procedure for termination of pregnancy is done in severe cases of disability and with the opinion of a registered medical practitioner and also with the consent of the guardian of the woman with disability' (Section 92).

Failure to produce relevant books, accounts, documents or other information required under the Act is punishable with a 'fine which may extend to 25,000 rupees in respect of each offence, and in case of continued failure or refusal, with further fine which may extend to 1,000 rupees for each day' (Section 93). However, 'no Court shall take cognizance of an offence alleged to have been committed by an employee of the appropriate Government under this Chapter, except with the previous sanction of the appropriate Government or a complaint is filed by an officer authorised by it in this behalf' (Section 94).

### 5.2.17 *'Miscellaneous'*

Finally, 'miscellaneous' provisions in the RPWDA cover the 'application of other laws' (which is 'not barred') (Section 96); 'protection of action taken in good faith' for certain government officials (Section 97); 'power to remove difficulties' encountered in implementation (Section 98); 'power to amend Schedule' of 'specified disability' (Section 99); and the 'power of Central Government' (Section 100) and 'State Government' (Section 101) to make rules about various matters. Finally, the Persons with Disabilities (Equal Opportunity Protection of Rights and Full Participation) Act, 1995 is repealed (Section 102(1)).

## 5.3 Rights, Needs and Opportunities

Overall, the RPWDA presents a broad range of rights-based provisions aimed at giving effect to the CRPD and improving the rights of persons with disabilities in India. With regard to mental illness, in particular, the legislation complements India's Mental Healthcare Act, 2017 to a certain extent and legally underpins many of the economic and social rights of persons with mental illness: it emphasizes respect for inherent dignity, individual autonomy (including the freedom to make one's own choices) and independence of persons; non-discrimination; full and effective inclusion and participation in society; respect for difference and acceptance of persons with disabilities as part of human diversity and humanity; equality of opportunity; accessibility; equality between women and men; respect for the evolving capacities of children with disabilities and respect for the right of children with disabilities to preserve their identities (Duffy and Kelly 2017).

The RPWDA also provides improved definitions of key constructs in disability care, an enhanced focus on rights, and guidelines for assessment and certification of disabilities, although there are concerns about a lack of emphasis on mental illness, centralization of disability certification and insufficient clarity about screening instruments, resource allocation and guidelines for inclusive education (Balakrishnan et al. 2019).

Overall, however, many of the measures in the RPWDA are highly consistent with the 'general obligations' of states parties outlined in the CRPD 'to ensure and promote the full realization of all human rights and fundamental freedoms for all persons with disabilities without discrimination of any kind on the basis of disability' (Article 4). These include, *inter alia*, obligations to 'adopt all appropriate legislative, administrative and other measures for the implementation of the rights recognized in the present Convention'; 'take all appropriate measures, including legislation, to modify or abolish existing laws, regulations, customs and practices that constitute discrimination against persons with disabilities'; 'take into account the protection and promotion of the human rights of persons with disabilities in all policies and programmes'; 'take all appropriate measures to eliminate discrimination on the basis of disability by any person, organization or private enterprise' and 'provide accessible information to persons with disabilities about mobility aids, devices and assistive technologies, including new technologies, as well as other forms of assistance, support services and facilities'.

More specifically, the right to healthcare outlined in Section 25 of the RPWDA appears broadly consistent with Article 25 of the CRPD which requires states to 'recognize that persons with disabilities have the right to the enjoyment of the highest attainable standard of health without discrimination on the basis of disability' and 'take all appropriate measures to ensure access for persons with disabilities to health services that are gender-sensitive, including health-related rehabilitation'. States must also 'provide persons with disabilities with the same range, quality and standard of free or affordable health care and programmes as provided to other persons'; 'provide those health services needed by persons with disabilities specifically because of their disabilities, including early identification and intervention as appropriate, and services designed to minimize and prevent further disabilities, including among children and older persons' and 'provide these health services as close as possible to people's own communities, including in rural areas'.

The RPWDA also presents a range of specific provisions apparently aimed at fulfilling Article 9 of the CRPD which requires states 'to enable persons with disabilities to live independently and participate fully in all aspects of life' and'take appropriate measures to ensure to persons with disabilities access, on an equal basis with others, to the physical environment, to transportation, to information and communications, including information and communications technologies and systems, and to other facilities and services open or provided to the public, both in urban and in rural areas'.

Access to justice is addressed in Section 12 of the RPWDA and this, too, appears broadly consistent with Article 13 of the CRPD which requires states to 'ensure effective access to justice for persons with disabilities on an equal basis with others, including through the provision of procedural and age-appropriate accommodations, in order to facilitate their effective role as direct and indirect participants, including as witnesses, in all legal proceedings, including at investigative and other preliminary stages'. In addition, 'to help to ensure effective access to justice for persons with disabilities, States Parties shall promote appropriate training for those working in the field of administration of justice, including police and prison staff'.

While the RPWDA goes a considerable distance to meeting many of these (and other) requirements of the CRPD, at least in theory, certain concerns have emerged over the past few years, especially in relation to mental illness (a key focus of this book). In the first instance, certain aspects of the RPWDA appear non-synchronous with the Mental Healthcare Act, 2017 (e.g. how guardianship and nominated representatives will relate to each other) and these apparent discontinuities require greater examination and resolution. This might only occur as the Mental Healthcare Act, 2017 is being implemented over the coming years (Duffy and Kelly 2019a, b).

In addition, it is not entirely clear how the rather general nature of the RPWDA will allow it to address some of the specific challenges presented by mental illness (Kelly 2014; Narayan and John 2017). This issue is underlined by the fact that the Mental Healthcare Act, 2017 does not directly address certain key areas of discrimination or social rights highlighted in the CRPD or the World Health Organization (WHO) *Resource Book on Mental Health, Human Rights and Legislation* (WHO 2005; Duffy and Kelly 2017), although the RPWDA does address at least some of these areas, at least to a certain extent.

Other concerns relate to the observations that the RPWDA relies excessively on non-governmental organizations and does not sufficiently address the needs of families of persons with mental illness, especially when resource limitations in mental health services in India (Isaac 2015; Jiloha 2015; Patel et al. 2016) mean that family members often need to be deeply involved in mental healthcare (Narayan and John 2017; Pavitra et al. 2019). It has also been recommended that there should have been special emphasis and dedicated social welfare measures to bring people with mental illness into the mainstream, and support them to overcome the environmental and attitudinal barriers that they face (Rao et al. 2016).

There are, in addition, ongoing concerns regarding scales for assessing mental disability; challenges in psychiatric disability certification; issues concerning certifying temporary versus permanent disability; quantification of disability; certifying autism, mental illness and learning disability (and combinations); challenges in providing reservation in higher educational institutions and employment (Math et al. 2019) and specific concerns related to persons with neurodevelopmental disorders (John et al. 2018).

Overall, however, the RPWDA provided a clear articulation of the rights of persons with disabilities, placed renewed emphasis on the CRPD in relation to disability and mental illness, and re-articulated useful principles of relevance to specific issues that arise in relation to these topics from time to time (Singh 2019). The legislation also provided the backdrop to the emergence of India's Mental Healthcare Act, 2017, which is considered in detail in the next chapter (Chap. 6) and explored in the context of the WHO Checklist on Mental Health Legislation (WHO 2005) in Chap. 7. Chapter 8 then examines relevant Indian legislation in the context of the CRPD and Chap. 9 focuses on the Mental Healthcare Act, 2017 in this context. Chapter 10 looks more generally at issues raised by adherence or non-adherence with international standards and conventions. Chapter 11 concludes the book with an update on implementation of the Mental Healthcare Act, 2017 on the ground in India, kindly contributed by Dr. Soumitra Pathare and Arjun Kapoor.

## References

Balakrishnan, A., Kulkarni, K., Moirangthem, S., Kumar, C. N., Math, S. B., & Murthy, P. (2019). The Rights of Persons with Disabilities Act 2016: Mental health implications. *Indian Journal of Psychological Medicine, 41*(2), 119–125.

Duffy, R. M., & Kelly, B. D. (2017). Concordance of the Indian Mental Healthcare Act, 2017 with the World Health Organization's Checklist on Mental Health Legislation. *International Journal of Mental Health Systems, 11,* 48.

Duffy, R. M., & Kelly, B. D. (2019a). India's Mental Healthcare Act, 2017: Content, context, controversy. *International Journal of Law and Psychiatry, 62,* 169–178.

Duffy, R. M., & Kelly, B. D. (2019b). The right to mental healthcare: India moves forward. *British Journal of Psychiatry, 214*(2), 59–60.

Isaac, M. (2015). Mental health legislation in South Asian countries: Shortcomings and possible solutions. In J. K. Trivedi & A. Tripathi (Eds.), *Mental health in South Asia: Ethics, resources, programs and legislation* (pp. 319–332). Dordrecht: Springer.

Jiloha, R. C. (2015). The Mental Health Act of India. In S. Malhotra & S. Chakrabarti (Eds.), *Developments in psychiatry in India: Clinical, research and policy perspectives* (pp. 611–622). New Delhi: Springer.

John, T., Subramanyam, A. A., & Sagar, R. (2018). Strength and weakness of the guidelines of Rights of Persons with Disabilities Act, 2016 (dated January 5, 2018): With respect to the persons with neurodevelopmental disorders. *Indian Journal of Psychiatry, 60*(3), 261–264.

Kalmegh, B., Bakhshy, A., Harshe, D., & Patankar, V. (2018). *MHCA 2017: Together we can..!* Pune: SMARTT.

Kelly, B. D. (2014). An end to psychiatric detention? Implications of the United Nations' convention on the rights of persons with disabilities. *British Journal of Psychiatry, 204*(3), 174–175.

Math, S. B., Gowda, G. S., Basavaraju, V., Manjunatha, N., Kumar, C. N., Philip, S., et al. (2019). The Rights of Persons with Disabilities Act, 2016: Challenges and opportunities. *Indian Journal of Psychiatry, 61*(10), S809–S815.

Narayan, C. L., & John, T. (2017). The Rights of Persons with Disabilities Act, 2016: Does it address the needs of the persons with mental illness and their families. *Indian Journal of Psychiatry, 59*(1), 17–20.

Patel, V., Xiao, S., Chen, H., Hanna, F., Jotheeswaran, A. T., Luo, D., et al. (2016). The magnitude of and health system responses to the mental health treatment gap in adults in India and China. *Lancet, 388*(10063), 3074–3084.

Pavitra, K. S., Kalmane, S., Kumar, A., & Gowda, M. (2019). Family matters! The caregivers' perspective of Mental Healthcare Act 2017. *Indian Journal of Psychiatry, 61*(10), S832–S837.

Rao, G. P., Ramya, V. S., & Bada, M. S. (2016). The Rights of Persons with Disability Bill, 2014: How 'enabling' is it for persons with mental illness? *Indian Journal of Psychiatry, 58*(2), 121–128.

Raveesh, B. N., Gowda, G. S., & Gowda, M. (2019). How right is right-based mental health law? *Indian Journal of Psychiatry, 61*(10), S640–S644.
Singh, S. (2019). Medical Council of India's new guidelines on admission of persons with specified disabilities: Unfair, discriminatory and unlawful. *Indian Journal of Medical Ethics, 4*(1), 29–34.
Suresh, B. M. (2014). *Revisiting mental health legislation of India*. Thesis submitted to the National Law School of India University, Bangalore for the award of the degree of Doctor of Philosophy, Ph.D. Bangalore: National Law School of India University.
United Nations. (2006). *Convention on the rights of persons with disabilities*. New York: United Nations. Retrieved June 1, 2019, from https://www.un.org/development/desa/disabilities/convention-on-the-rights-of-persons-with-disabilities/convention-on-the-rights-of-persons-with-disabilities-2.html.
World Health Organization. (2005). *WHO resource book on mental health, human rights and legislation*. Geneva: World Health Organization.

# Chapter 6
# India's Mental Healthcare Act, 2017

## 6.1 Background to India's Mental Healthcare Act 2017

Following on from India's early mental health legislation and, most recently, its Mental Health Act, 1987 (Chapter 4) and Rights of Persons with Disabilities Act, 2016 (Chapter 5), and in light of relevant World Health Organization (WHO) standards (Chapter 3) and, especially, the United Nations' (UN) Convention on the Rights of Persons with Disabilities (CRPD) (UN 2006) (Chapter 2), India's new Mental Healthcare Act, 2017 (MHCA) received the assent of the President of India on 7 April 2017.

The new legislation aims to 'to provide for mental healthcare and services for persons with mental illness and to protect, promote and fulfil the rights of such persons during delivery of mental healthcare and services and for matters connected therewith or incidental thereto' (Preamble). This chapter presents a *descriptive* outline of the MHCA, summarizing its contents and providing the basis for the *analysis* presented in subsequent chapters (Duffy and Kelly 2019a).

It is important, at the outset, to emphasize that the preamble to the MHCA notes that 'the Convention on Rights of Persons with Disabilities and its Optional Protocol was adopted on the 13th December, 2006 at United Nations Headquarters in New York and came into force on the 3rd May, 2008'; that 'India has signed and ratified the said Convention on the 1st day of October, 2007' and that 'it is necessary to align and harmonise the existing laws with the said Convention'. The fundamental aim of the new Indian legislation, then, is to align India's mental health laws with the CRPD, making India's new Act one of the most interesting and potentially progressive in the world (Kalmegh et al. 2018; Duffy and Kelly 2019b).

The MHCA itself is divided into 16 chapters covering 'preliminary' matters and definitions (Section 6.2.1 of this chapter), 'mental illness and capacity to make mental healthcare and treatment decisions' (Section 6.2.2), 'advance directive' (Section 6.2.3), 'nominated representative' (Section 6.2.4), 'rights of persons with mental illness' (Section 6.2.5), 'duties of appropriate government' (Section 6.2.6),



R. M. Duffy and B. D. Kelly, *India's Mental Healthcare Act, 2017*,
https://doi.org/10.1007/978-981-15-5009-6_6

'Central Mental Health Authority' (Section 6.2.7), 'State Mental Health Authority' (Section 6.2.8), 'finance, accounts and audit' (Section 6.2.9), 'mental health establishments' (Section 6.2.10), 'Mental Health Review Boards' (Section 6.2.11), 'admission, treatment and discharge' (Section 6.2.12) (including 'independent admission', 'admission of a minor', 'supported admission' and 'supported admission beyond 30 days'), 'responsibilities of other agencies' (Section 6.2.13), 'restriction to discharge functions by professionals not covered by profession' (Section 6.2.14), 'offences and penalties' (Section 6.2.15) and 'miscellaneous' (including provisions relating to the de facto decriminalisation of suicide) (Section 6.2.16).

Each of these elements of the MHCA is described in the remainder of this chapter, followed by a brief overall discussion of the measures and reactions to them in a special supplement to the *Indian Journal of Psychiatry* published in April 2019. This is followed by the more detailed exploration of the Act's implications in terms of human rights in Chaps. 7, 8, 9 and 10 of this book. Chapter 11 presents an update on implementation kindly contributed by Dr. Soumitra Pathare and Arjun Kapoor.

## 6.2 Provisions of the Mental Healthcare Act 2017

### *6.2.1 'Preliminary' Matters and Definitions*

The 'Mental Healthcare Act, 2017' (Section 1(1)) (MHCA) 'shall extend to the whole of India' (Section 1(2)) and 'come into force on such date as the Central Government may…appoint'; or 'nine months from the date' of presidential assent (Section 1(3)). Presidential assent was provided on 7 April 2017 and the legislation commenced on 29 May 2018.

Chapter 1 of the MHCA defines key terms including 'caregiver', who is 'a person who resides with a person with mental illness and is responsible for providing care to that person and includes a relative or any other person who performs this function' (Section 2(1)(e)); 'family', which is 'a group of persons related by blood, adoption or marriage' (Section 2(1)(h)); 'relative', which is 'any person related to the person with mental illness by blood, marriage or adoption' (Section 2(1)(za)); and 'minor', which is 'a person who has not completed the age of 18 years' (Section 2(1)(t)).

'Mental illness' is 'a substantial disorder of thinking, mood, perception, orientation or memory that grossly impairs judgment, behaviour, capacity to recognise reality or ability to meet the ordinary demands of life, mental conditions associated with the abuse of alcohol and drugs, but does not include mental retardation which is a condition of arrested or incomplete development of mind of a person, specially characterised by subnormality of intelligence' (Section 2(1)(s)). 'Mental healthcare' includes 'analysis and diagnosis of a person's mental condition and treatment as well as care and rehabilitation of such person for his mental illness or suspected mental illness' (Section 2(1)(o)). This is a notably broad definition of 'mental healthcare', consistent with the legislation's generally broad remit and considerable ambition.

'Mental health establishment' means 'any health establishment, including Ayurveda, Yoga and Naturopathy, Unani, Siddha and Homoeopathy establishment, by whatever name called, either wholly or partly, meant for the care of persons with mental illness' where 'persons with mental illness are admitted and reside at, or kept in, for care, treatment, convalescence and rehabilitation', including 'any general hospital or general nursing home' but not family homes (Section 2(1)(p)).

'Informed consent' is 'consent given for a specific intervention, without any force, undue influence, fraud, threat, mistake or misrepresentation, and obtained after disclosing to a person adequate information including risks and benefits of, and alternatives to, the specific intervention in a language and manner understood by the person' (Section 2(1)(i)).

'Medical officer in charge' means 'the psychiatrist or medical practitioner [in] charge of that mental health establishment' (Section 2(1)(m)). A 'medical practitioner' is 'a person who possesses a recognised medical qualification' as defined in (i) 'the Indian Medical Council Act, 1956'; (ii) 'the Indian Medicine Central Council Act, 1970'; or (iii) 'the Homoeopathy Central Council Act, 1973', and who is registered (Section 2(1)(n)).

Definitions are provided for 'clinical psychologist' (Section 2(1)(g)) and 'psychiatric social worker', focusing on qualifications required (Section 2(1)(x)); 'mental health nurse', which 'means a person with a diploma or degree in general nursing or diploma or degree in psychiatric nursing recognised by the Nursing Council of India' and with appropriate registration (Section 2(1)(q)); and 'mental health professional', which is a psychiatrist or a 'professional registered with the concerned State Authority under Section 55' ('Functions of State Authority') or 'a professional having a post-graduate degree (Ayurveda) in Mano Vigyan Avum Manas Roga or a post-graduate degree (Homoeopathy) in Psychiatry or a post-graduate degree (Unani) in Moalijat (Nafasiyatt) or a post-graduate degree (Siddha) in Sirappu Maruthuvam' (Section 2(1)(r)).

A 'psychiatrist' is 'a medical practitioner possessing a post-graduate degree or diploma in psychiatry awarded by an university recognized by the University Grants Commission established under the University Grants Commission Act, 1956, or awarded or recognized by the National Board of Examinations and included in the First Schedule to the Indian Medical Council Act, 1956, or recognized by the Medical Council of India, constituted under the Indian Medical Council Act, 1956, and includes, in relation to any State, any medical officer who having regard to his knowledge and experience in psychiatry, has been declared by the Government of that State to be a psychiatrist for the purposes of this Act' (Section 2(1)(y)).

### 6.2.2 'Mental Illness and Capacity to Make Mental Healthcare and Treatment Decisions'

According to the MHCA, 'mental illness shall be determined in accordance with such nationally or internationally accepted medical standards (including the latest edition of the *International Classification of Disease* of the World Health Organization) as may be notified by the Central Government' (Section 3(1)) (WHO 1992). In addition, the following provisions also apply:

- 'No person or authority shall classify a person as a person with mental illness, except for purposes directly relating to the treatment of the mental illness or in other matters as covered' in relevant legislation (Section 3(2));
- The 'mental illness of a person shall not be determined on the basis of (a) political, economic or social status or membership of a cultural, racial or religious group, or for any other reason not directly relevant to mental health status of the person; (b) non-conformity with moral, social, cultural, work or political values or religious beliefs prevailing in a person's community' (Section 3(3));
- 'Past treatment or hospitalisation in a mental health establishment though relevant, shall not by itself justify any present or future determination of the person's mental illness' (Section 3(4));
- 'The determination of a person's mental illness shall alone not imply or be taken to mean that the person is of unsound mind unless he has been declared as such by a competent court' (Section 3(5)).

The MHCA also provides a clear definition of mental capacity, which is to be judged without reference to any pre-existing diagnoses: 'Every person, including a person with mental illness shall be deemed to have capacity to make decisions regarding his mental healthcare or treatment if such person has ability to (a) understand the information that is relevant to take a decision on the treatment or admission or personal assistance; or ['or' is an error and should read 'and'] (b) appreciate any reasonably foreseeable consequence of a decision or lack of decision on the treatment or admission or personal assistance; or ['or' is an error and should read 'and'] (c) communicate the decision under sub-clause (a) by means of speech, expression, gesture or any other means' (Section 4(1)) (Duffy and Kelly 2019a). Information 'shall be given to a person using simple language, which such person understands or in sign language or visual aids or any other means to enable him to understand the information' (Section 4(2)). This is an important and helpful provision.

In addition, 'where a person makes a decision regarding his mental healthcare or treatment which is perceived by others as inappropriate or wrong, that by itself, shall not mean that the person does not have the capacity to make mental healthcare or treatment decision' (Section 4(3)).

### 6.2.3 'Advance Directive'

Every adult 'shall have a right to make an advance directive in writing', specifying 'the way the person wishes to be cared for and treated for a mental illness'; 'the way the person wishes not to be cared for and treated' and 'the individual or individuals, in order of precedence' they want to appoint as their 'nominated representative' (Section 5(1)). This—importantly—can be done 'irrespective of [the person's] past mental illness or treatment for the same' (Section 5(2)).

The person's advance directive 'shall be invoked only when [the] person ceases to have capacity to make mental healthcare or treatment decisions and shall remain effective until such person regains capacity' (Section 5(3)). It can be over-ruled if the person has capacity (Section 5(4)); 'may be revoked, amended or cancelled by the person who made it at any time' (Section 8(1)); and is 'ab initio void' if it is 'contrary to any law' (Section 5(5)). The directive must 'be made in the manner as may be specified' in regulations (Section 6); shall be kept in 'an online register' which is 'available to the concerned mental health professionals as and when required' (Section 7); but does not apply to 'emergency treatment' (Section 9).

Regarding the effect of an advance directive, the MHCA specifies that 'it shall be the duty of every medical officer in charge of a mental health establishment and the psychiatrist in charge of a person's treatment to propose or give treatment to a person with mental illness, in accordance with his valid advance directive' (Section 10).

'Where a mental health professional or a relative or a care-giver of a person desires not to follow an advance directive' they 'shall make an application to the concerned [Mental Health Review] Board to review, alter, modify or cancel the advance directive' (Section 11(1)). 'After giving an opportunity of hearing to all concerned parties (including the person whose advance directive is in question)' the Board shall 'either uphold, modify, alter or cancel the advance directive after taking into consideration the following, namely (a) whether the advance directive was made by the person out of his own free will and free from force, undue influence or coercion; or (b) whether the person intended the advance directive to apply to the present circumstances, which may be different from those anticipated; or (c) whether the person was sufficiently well informed to make the decision; or (d) whether the person had capacity to make decisions relating to his mental healthcare or treatment when such advanced directive was made; or (e) whether the content of the advance directive is contrary to other laws or constitutional provisions' (Section 11(2)).

At a practical, day-to-day level, 'the person writing the advance directive and his nominated representative' must ensure treating practitioners have 'access to the advance directive' (Section 11(3)) and 'the legal guardian shall have right to make an advance directive in writing in respect of a minor' (Section 11(4)). 'A medical practitioner or a mental health professional shall not be held liable' for (a) 'any unforeseen consequences on following a valid advance directive' (Section 13(1)) or (b) 'not following a valid advance directive, if he has not been given a copy' (Section 13(2)). These are reasonable pragmatic measures, likely to foster confidence among health professionals dealing with advance directives.

### 6.2.4 'Nominated Representative'

The Act states that every adult 'shall have a right to appoint a nominated representative' (Section 14(1)) who must be a competent, consenting adult (Section 14(3)) who is nominated in writing (Section 14(2)). 'Where no nominated representative is appointed', the following persons, 'in the order of precedence, shall be deemed to be the nominated representative of a person with mental illness, namely (a) the individual appointed as the nominated representative in the advance directive'; (b) 'a relative'; (c) 'a care-giver'; (d) 'a suitable person appointed as such by the concerned [Mental Health Review] Board; or (e) if no such person is available to be appointed as a nominated representative, the Board shall appoint the Director, Department of Social Welfare, or his designated representative, as the nominated representative' (Section 14(4)).

In the interim, 'a person representing [a registered] organisation [...] working for persons with mental illness, may temporarily be engaged by the mental health professional' as a nominated representative (Section 14(4)).

A person who has appointed a nominated representative 'may revoke or alter such appointment at any time' (Section 14(6)) and a Board may replace the representative 'if it is of the opinion that it is in the interest of the person with mental illness to do so' (Section 14(7)). 'The appointment of a nominated representative, or the inability of a person with mental illness to appoint a nominated representative, shall not be construed as the lack of capacity' to make mental healthcare decisions (Section 14(8)).

'All persons with mental illness shall have capacity to make mental healthcare or treatment decisions but may require varying levels of support from their nominated representative to make decisions' (Section 14(9)). 'In case of minors, the legal guardian shall be their nominated representative, unless the concerned [Mental Health Review] Board orders otherwise' (Section 15(1)); for example, if 'a mental health professional or any other person acting in the best interest of the minor' presents evidence that 'the legal guardian is not acting in the best interests of the minor' or is 'not fit' for the role, the Board 'may appoint any suitable individual' as nominated representative (Section 15(2)).

'While fulfilling [their] duties under this Act, the nominated representative shall' have a considerable range of duties and responsibilities, many of which are notably complex, including the following:

(a) 'Consider the current and past wishes, the life history, values, cultural background and the best interests of the person with mental illness';
(b) 'Give particular credence to the views of the person with mental illness to the extent that the person understands the nature of the decisions under consideration';
(c) 'Provide support to the person with mental illness in making treatment decisions';
(d) 'Have right to seek information on diagnosis and treatment to provide adequate support to the person with mental illness';

(e) 'Have access to the family or home based rehabilitation services as provided';
(f) 'Be involved in discharge planning';
(g) 'Apply to the mental health establishment for admission' (under Sections 87, 89 or 90);
(h) 'Apply to the concerned Board on behalf of the person with mental illness for discharge' (under Sections 87, 89 or 90);
(i) 'Apply to the concerned Board against violation of rights of the person with mental illness in a mental health establishment';
(j) 'Appoint a suitable attendant' (under Section 87);
(k) 'Have the right to give or withhold consent for research' (Section 17).

### *6.2.5 'Rights of Persons with Mental Illness'*

Chapter 5 of the MHCA outlines a series of 'rights of persons with mental illness' under 11 headings, including rights to 'access mental health care' (Section 18), 'community living' (Section 19), 'protection from cruel, inhuman and degrading treatment' (Section 20), 'equality and non-discrimination' (Section 21), 'information' (Section 22), 'confidentiality' (Section 23), 'restriction on release of information in respect of mental illness' (Section 24), 'access medical records' (Section 25), 'personal contacts and communication' (Section 26), 'legal aid' (Section 27) and 'make complaints about deficiencies' in services (Section 28).

Most dramatically, perhaps, 'every person shall have a right to access mental healthcare and treatment from mental health services run or funded by the appropriate Government' (Section 18(1)), 'services of affordable cost, of good quality, available in sufficient quantity, accessible geographically, without discrimination on the basis of gender, sex, sexual orientation, religion, culture, caste, social or political beliefs, class, disability or any other basis and provided in a manner that is acceptable to persons with mental illness and their families and care-givers' (Section 18(2)). This is an extraordinary and hugely important part of the legislation, granting a justiciable right to mental healthcare to India's population of some 1.3 billion people, one-sixth of the planet's entire population.

To achieve this, the government 'shall make sufficient provision as may be necessary' (Section 18(3)), including 'acute mental healthcare services' (outpatient and inpatient); 'half-way homes, sheltered accommodation, supported accommodation'; 'services to support family of person with mental illness or home based rehabilitation'; 'hospital and community based rehabilitation establishments and services'; 'child mental health services and old age mental health services' (Section 18(4)).

In addition, the government shall 'integrate mental health services into general healthcare services'; 'provide treatment in a manner, which supports persons with mental illness to live in the community and with their families'; ensure that 'long term care' is 'used only in exceptional circumstances, for as short a duration as possible, and only as a last resort when appropriate community based treatment' has failed;

ensure services are available locally insofar as possible; and pay for access elsewhere if needed for children and the elderly (Section 18(5)).

'Persons with mental illness living below the poverty line [or] who are destitute or homeless shall be entitled to mental health treatment and services free of any charge' (Section 18(7)). The government 'shall ensure that the mental health services shall be of equal quality to other general health services and no discrimination be made in quality of services provided to persons with mental illness' (Section 18(8)). All 'medicines on the Essential Drug List shall be made available free of cost to all persons with mental illness at all times at health establishments run or funded' by the government, as shall 'essential medicines from any similar list relating to the appropriate ayurvada, yoga, unani, siddha, homoeopathy or naturopathy systems' (Section 18(10)). The government 'shall take measures to ensure that necessary budgetary provisions in terms of adequacy, priority, progress and equity are made for effective implementation' of these provisions (Section 18(11)).

Social inclusion is also addressed in the legislation: 'Every person with mental illness shall (a) have a right to live in, be part of and not be segregated from society; and (b) not continue to remain in a mental health establishment merely because he does not have a family or is not accepted by his family or is homeless or due to absence of community based facilities' (Section 19(1)). 'Where it is not possible for a mentally ill person to live with his family or relatives, or where a mentally ill person has been abandoned by his family or relatives, the appropriate Government shall provide support as appropriate including legal aid and to facilitate exercising his right to family home and living in the family home' (Section 19(2)) and access to 'half-way homes, group homes and the like' (Section 19(3)).

Looking at rights more broadly, the MHCA also states that 'every person with mental illness shall have a right to live with dignity' (Section 20(1)); 'be protected from cruel, inhuman or degrading treatment in any mental health establishment' and shall have rights to (a) 'live in safe and hygienic environment'; (b) 'adequate sanitary conditions'; (c) 'reasonable facilities for leisure, recreation, education and religious practices'; (d) 'privacy'; (e) 'proper clothing'; (f) 'not be forced to undertake work in a mental health establishment and to receive appropriate remuneration for work'; (g) 'have adequate provision for preparing for living in the community'; (h) 'adequate provision for wholesome food, sanitation, space and access to articles of personal hygiene, in particular, women's personal hygiene'; (i) 'not be subject to compulsory tonsuring (shaving of head hair)'; (j) 'wear own personal clothes' and 'not be forced to wear uniforms'; and (k) 'be protected from all forms of physical, verbal, emotional and sexual abuse' (Section 20(2)).

'Every person with mental illness shall be treated as equal to persons with physical illness in the provision of all healthcare' (Section 21(1)). 'A child under the age of three years of a woman receiving care, treatment or rehabilitation at a mental health establishment shall ordinarily not be separated from her during her stay in such establishment' except if there is risk to the child or temporary separation 'is in the interest and safety of the child' (when supervised access may be appropriate) (Section 21(2)). In terms of health insurance, 'every insurer shall make provision for medical insurance for treatment of mental illness on the same basis as is available for treatment of physical illness' (Section 21(4)).

'A person with mental illness and his nominated representative shall have the rights' to information about relevant legislative provisions and 'criteria for admission'; the 'right to make an application to the concerned Board for a review of the admission'; 'the nature of the person's mental illness and the proposed treatment plan' (Section 22(1)). The patient shall have the right to confidentiality in respect of health and care (Section 23(1)) except when 'release of information to the nominated representative' is necessary for healthcare professionals to fulfil statutory duties; it is necessary to release information to other health professionals providing care; when release 'is necessary to protect any other person from harm or violence'; by order of a statutory authority; or 'release of information in the interests of public safety and security' (Section 23(2)). The right to confidentiality applies to photographs and 'all information stored in electronic or digital format in real or virtual space' (Section 24).

'All persons with mental illness shall have the right to access their basic medical records' (Section 25(1)) unless 'disclosure would result in (a) serious mental harm to the person with mental illness; or (b) likelihood of harm to other persons' (Section 25(2)), in which case the mental health professional shall inform the patient 'of his right to apply to the concerned Board for an order to release such information' (Section 25(3)).

Inpatients 'shall have the right to refuse or receive visitors and to refuse or receive and make telephone or mobile phone calls at reasonable times subject to the norms of such mental health establishment' (Section 26(1)), and the right to access email (Section 26(2)). Exceptions to these restrictions include communications or visits from various statutory and legal actors, and the person's medical practitioner (Section 26(4)). There are rights to free 'legal aid' (Section 27) and to 'make complaints about deficiencies' in services (Section 28).

### *6.2.6 'Duties of Appropriate Government'*

Chapter 6 of the MHCA gives the government extensive duties 'to plan, design and implement programmes for the promotion of mental health and prevention of mental illness' (Section 29(1)) and 'plan, design and implement public health programmes to reduce suicides and attempted suicides' (Section 29(2)). The government must also 'take all measures to ensure that (a) 'the provisions of this Act are given wide publicity'; (b) 'programmes to reduce stigma associated with mental illness' are implemented effectively; and (c) 'appropriate government officials [including police officers] are given periodic sensitisation and awareness training on the issues under this Act' (Section 30). These are broad, population-level responsibilities that will likely prove essential for effective implementation of the legislation across India's vast population and terrain.

The government also has responsibilities under the Act in relation to human resources, education, training (Section 31) and 'effective co-ordination between services provided by concerned Ministries and Departments such as those dealing with health, law, home affairs, human resources, social justice, employment, education, women and child development, medical education to address issues of mental health care' (Section 32). The government shall also 'make efforts to meet internationally accepted guidelines for number of mental health professionals on the basis of population, within ten years from the commencement of this Act' (Section 31(3)). This is, arguably, one of the most important provisions of the entire Act and will prove vital for successful realization of the Act's considerable potential.

### 6.2.7 'Central Mental Health Authority'

The Central Government shall establish a 'Central Mental Health Authority' (Section 33). Membership is set out to include various public officials and health professionals as well as 'two persons representing persons who have or have had mental illness', 'two persons representing care-givers of persons with mental illness or organisations representing care-givers' and 'two persons representing non-governmental organisations which provide services to persons with mental illness' (Section 34(1)). Members with conflicts of interest cannot participate in relevant deliberations or decisions (Sections 39 and 44(5)).

Once the new Authority is established, 'all the assets and liabilities of the Central Authority for Mental Health Services constituted under [the Mental Health Act, 1987] shall stand transferred to, and vested in, the Central Authority' (Section 42(a)). The Central Authority will meet at least twice yearly (Section 44(1)) and its functions will be to:

(a) 'Register all mental health establishments under the control of the Central Government and maintain a register of all mental health establishments in the country';
(b) 'Develop quality and service provision norms for different types of mental health establishments under the Central Government';
(c) 'Supervise all mental health establishments under the Central Government and receive complaints about deficiencies' in services;
(d) 'Maintain a national register of clinical psychologists, mental health nurses and psychiatric social workers';
(e) 'Train all persons including law enforcement officials, mental health professionals and other health professionals about the provisions and implementation of this Act';
(f) 'Advise the Central Government on all matters relating to mental healthcare and services';
(g) 'Discharge such other functions with respect to matters relating to mental health as the Central Government may decide' (Section 43(1)).

### 6.2.8 'State Mental Health Authority'

Every State Government shall establish a 'State Mental Health Authority' (Section 45). Membership is set out to include various public officials and health professionals (including 'one eminent psychiatrist') as well as 'two persons representing persons who have or have had mental illness', 'two persons representing care-givers of persons with mental illness or organisations representing care-givers' and 'two persons representing non-governmental organisations which provide services to persons with mental illness' (Section 46(1)). Members with conflicts of interest cannot participate in relevant deliberations or decisions (Sections 51 and 56(5)).

Once each State Authority has been established, 'all the assets and liabilities of the State Authority for Mental Health Services constituted under [the Mental Health Act, 1987] shall stand transferred to, and vested in, the State Authority' (Section 54(a)). The State Authority will meet at least four times yearly (Section 56(1)) and its functions will be to:

(a) 'Register all mental health establishments in the State [except those registered with the Central Authority] and maintain and publish (including online on the internet) a register of such establishments';
(b) 'Develop quality and service provision norms for different types of mental health establishments in the State';
(c) 'Supervise all mental health establishments in the State and receive complaints about deficiencies' in services;
(d) 'Register clinical psychologists, mental health nurses and psychiatric social workers in the State';
(e) 'Train all relevant persons including law enforcement officials, mental health professionals and other health professionals about the provisions and implementation of this Act';
(f) 'Discharge such other functions with respect to matters relating to mental health as the State Government may decide' (Section 55(1)).

### 6.2.9 'Finance, Accounts and Audit'

The Central Government may 'make to the Central Authority grants of such sums of money as the Central Government may think fit for being utilised for the purposes of this Act' (Section 57) and the State Government may do likewise for the State Authority (Section 61). Various rules and regulations apply, along with various forms of oversight (e.g. annual reports) (Sections 57–64).

### 6.2.10 'Mental Health Establishments'

All mental health establishments must be registered under the Act (Section 65(1)). For registration, each establishment must fulfil (a) 'the minimum standards of facilities and services as may be specified by regulations made by the [Central or State] Authority'; (b) 'the minimum qualifications for the personnel engaged'; (c) 'provisions for maintenance of records and reporting'; and (d) 'any other conditions as may be specified by regulations' (Section 65(4)). 'While specifying the minimum standards for mental health establishments [the Authority may] have regard to local conditions' (Section 65(5)(c)).

Section 66 outlines a detailed 'procedure for registration, inspection and inquiry of mental health establishments' and the 'Authority shall cause to be conducted an audit of all registered mental health establishments by such person or persons (including representatives of the local community) as may be prescribed, every three years, so as to ensure that such mental health establishments comply with the requirements of minimum standards' (Section 67(1)). The establishment may be charged for this audit (Section 67(2)).

'The Authority may, *suo motu* [on its own motion] or on a complaint received from any person with respect to non-adherence of minimum standards specified by or under this Act or contravention of any provision thereof, order an inspection or inquiry of any mental health establishment' (Section 68(1)). 'Any mental health establishment aggrieved by an order of the Authority refusing to grant registration or renewal of registration or cancellation of registration, may, within a period of 30 days from such order, prefer an appeal to the High Court' (Section 69).

The Central or State 'Authority shall maintain in digital format a register of mental health establishments' (Section 71). In addition, 'every mental health establishment shall display [its] certificate of registration' (Section 70(1)) and 'the contact details including address and telephone numbers of the concerned [Mental Health Review] Board' (Section 72(1)), and facilitate access to the Board for review (Section 72(2)).

### 6.2.11 'Mental Health Review Boards'

The MHCA states that 'the State Authority shall, by notification, constitute Boards to be called the Mental Health Review Boards' (Section 73(1)) with each Board comprising (a) 'a District Judge, or an officer of the State judicial services who is qualified to be appointed as District Judge or a retired District Judge' (who shall chair the Board); (b) a 'representative of the District Collector or District Magistrate or Deputy Commissioner'; (c) 'two members of whom one shall be a psychiatrist and the other shall be a medical practitioner'; and (d) 'two members who shall be persons with mental illness or care-givers or persons representing organisations of persons with mental illness or care-givers or non-governmental organisations working in the field' (Section 74(1)). Various disqualifications apply (including 'an offence which involves moral turpitude') (Section 74(2)) and the term of office is five years (Section 75(1)). A quorum is three members (Section 76(2)) and decisions will be made by consensus, majority vote, or the president or chairperson's 'casting vote' (Section 76(1)).

'Any person with mental illness or his nominated representative or a representative of a registered non-governmental organisation, with the consent of such a person, being aggrieved by the decision of any of the mental health establishment or whose rights under this Act have been violated, may make an application to the Board seeking redressal or appropriate relief' (Section 77(1)).

'The Board, on receipt of an application [relating to 'admission of person with mental illness as independent patient in mental health establishment' (Section 85(1))] shall, subject to the provisions of this section, endeavour to hear and dispose of the same within a period of 90 days' (Section 80(1)). Applications 'for appointment of nominated representative' (Section 14(4)(d)), 'challenging admission of a minor' (Section 87) and 'challenging supported admission' (Section 89(10) and (11)) shall be dealt with within seven days (Section 80(2)). 'The Board shall dispose of an application challenging supported admission under Section 90 ['supported admission beyond 30 days'] within a period of 21 days' (Section 80(3)) and all other applications within 90 days (Section 80(4)).

'The proceeding of the Board shall be held *in camera*' (Section 80(5)) and, 'in respect of any application concerning a person with mental illness, [at] the mental health establishment' (Section 80(8)). Parties 'may appear in person or be represented by a counsel or a representative of their choice' (Section 80(7)); others may attend under certain circumstances (Section 80(9)); and the patient 'shall have the right to give oral evidence' (Section 80(10)). The Board can require witnesses to attend (Section 80(11)) and shall, within five days, 'communicate its decision to the parties in writing' (Section 80(13)).

'The Central Authority shall appoint an Expert Committee to prepare a [binding] guidance document for medical practitioners and mental health professionals, containing procedures for assessing, when necessary [...] the capacity of persons to make mental health care or treatment decisions' (Sections 81(1) and (2)).

'The powers and functions of the Board shall, include all or any of the following':

(a) 'To register, review, alter, modify or cancel an advance directive';
(b) 'To appoint a nominated representative';
(c) 'To receive and decide application from a person with mental illness or his nominated representative or any other interested person against the decision of medical officer or mental health professional in charge of mental health establishment' under Sections 87 ('admission of minor'), 89 ('supported admission') or 90 ('supported admission beyond 30 days').
(d) 'To receive and decide applications in respect non-disclosure of information' (Section 25(3));
(e) 'To adjudicate complaints regarding deficiencies in care and services' (Section 28);

(f) 'To visit and inspect prison or jails and seek clarifications from the medical officer in-charge of health services in such prison or jail' (Section 82(1)).

'Where it is brought to the notice of a Board or the Central Authority or State Authority, that a mental health establishment violates the rights of persons with mental illness, the Board or the Authority may conduct an inspection and inquiry and take action to protect their rights' (Section 82(2)). 'The Board, in consultation with the Authority, may take measures to protect the rights of persons with mental illness as it considers appropriate' (Section 82(3)). There are penalties for noncompliance with 'orders or directions of the Authority or the Board' including fines of up to 500,000 rupees and cancelling 'the registration of such mental health establishment after giving an opportunity of being heard' (Section 82(4)). Appeal is 'to the High Court' (Section 83).

## *6.2.12 'Admission, Treatment and Discharge'*

Chapter 12 of the MHCA outlines four different kinds of admission: 'independent admission' (Sections 85, 86 and 88), 'admission of minor' (Section 87), 'supported admission' (Section 89) and 'supported admission beyond 30 days' (Section 90). Each will be considered here in turn.

### 6.2.12.1 'Independent Admission'

'Independent patient or an independent admission' refers 'to the admission of [a] person with mental illness, to a mental health establishment, who has the capacity to make mental healthcare and treatment decisions or requires minimal in making decisions' (Section 85(1)). The MHCA specifies that 'all admissions in the mental health establishment shall, as far as possible, be independent admissions except when such conditions exist as make supported admission unavoidable' (Section 85(2)).

'Independent admission' occurs at the request of the patient (Section 86(1)) once 'the medical officer or mental health professional in charge of the establishment [...] is satisfied that (a) the person has a mental illness of a severity requiring admission'; (b) 'is likely to benefit from admission and treatment'; and (c) 'has understood the nature and purpose of admission'; 'has made the request for admission of his own free will, without any duress or undue influence'; and possesses mental capacity (Section 86(2)).

An 'independent patient' 'shall be bound to abide by order and instructions or bye-laws of the mental health establishment' (Section 86(4)) but 'shall not be given treatment without his informed consent' (Section 86(5)). Discharge must occur 'immediately on request made by such person or if the person disagrees with his admission' (Sections 88(1) and 86(7)) unless 'the mental health professional is of the opinion that':

(a) 'Such person is unable to understand the nature and purpose of his decisions and requires substantial or very high support from his nominated representative'; or
(b) 'Has recently threatened or attempted or is threatening or attempting to cause bodily harm to himself'; or
(c) 'Has recently behaved or is behaving violently towards another person or has caused or is causing another person to fear bodily harm from him'; or
(d) 'Has recently shown or is showing an inability to care for himself to a degree that places the individual at risk of harm to himself' (Section 88(3)).

In these situations, 'a mental health professional may prevent discharge of [an independent patient] for a period of 24 h so as to allow his assessment necessary' for 'supported admission' (Section 88(3)). The person shall then 'be either admitted as a supported patient' or discharged within 24 h (Section 88(4)). This is the equivalent of 'voluntary admission' in many other jurisdictions.

#### 6.2.12.2 'Admission of a Minor'

For the admission of a minor (i.e. a person not yet 18 years of age) (Section 2(1)(t)), 'the nominated representative of the minor shall apply to the medical officer in charge of a mental health establishment for admission' (Section 87(2)). Admission may occur 'if two psychiatrists, or one psychiatrist and one mental health professional or one psychiatrist and one medical practitioner, have independently examined the minor on the day of admission or in the preceding seven days and both independently conclude based on the examination and, if appropriate, on information provided by others,' that:

(a) 'The minor has a mental illness of a severity requiring admission';
(b) 'Admission shall be in the best interests of the minor, with regard to his health, well-being or safety, taking into account the wishes of the minor if ascertainable and the reasons for reaching this decision';
(c) 'The mental healthcare needs of the minor cannot be fulfilled unless he is admitted'; and
(d) 'All community based alternatives to admission have been shown to have failed or are demonstrably unsuitable for the needs of the minor' (Section 87(3)).

'A minor so admitted shall be accommodated separately from adults, in an environment that takes into account his age and developmental needs' (Section 87(4)). In addition, the Act states that:

- 'The nominated representative or an attendant appointed by the nominated representative shall under all circumstances stay with the minor in the mental health establishment for the entire duration of the admission' (Section 87(5));
- 'A minor shall be given treatment with the informed consent of his nominated representative' (Section 87(7));
- 'If the nominated representative no longer supports admission' or requests discharge, 'the minor shall be discharged' (Section 87(8));

- Admissions of minors are to be notified to the Mental Health Review Board within 72 h (Section 87(9)) and, if continued beyond 30 days, reviewed by the Board (Section 87(12)).

#### 6.2.12.3 'Supported Admission'

This section of the MHCA covers admission and treatment without patient consent. The legislation states that a person 'shall' be admitted as a 'supported admission' 'upon application by the nominated representative of the person' if:

(a) 'The person has been independently examined on the day of admission or in the preceding seven days, by one psychiatrist and the other being a mental health professional or a medical practitioner, and both independently conclude based on the examination and, if appropriate, on information provided by others, that the person has a mental illness of such severity that the person (i) has recently threatened or attempted or is threatening or attempting to cause bodily harm to himself; or (ii) has recently behaved or is behaving violently towards another person or has caused or is causing another person to fear bodily harm from him; or (iii) has recently shown or is showing an inability to care for himself to a degree that places the individual at risk of harm to himself';
(b) 'The psychiatrist or the mental health professionals or the medical practitioner, as the case may be, certify, after taking into account an advance directive, if any, that admission to the mental health establishment is the least restrictive care option possible in the circumstances'; and
(c) 'The person is ineligible to receive care and treatment as an independent patient because the person is unable to make mental healthcare and treatment decisions independently and needs very high support from his nominated representative in making decisions' (Section 89(1)).

The 'supported admission' must, in the first instance, end when the person no longer meets these criteria (Sections 89(3) and 89(13)) or after 30 days (Section 89(2)). At this point, the person is discharged; the person can remain as an 'independent patient' (Section 89(5)); or the 'supported admission' can continue (Section 89(4)) under certain circumstances (Section 90).

The patient 'shall be provided treatment after taking into account (a) an advance directive if any; or (b) informed consent of the patient with the support of his nominated representative' (Section 89(6)). If the person 'requires nearly 100% support from his nominated representative in making a decision in respect of his treatment, the nominated representative may temporarily consent to the treatment plan of such person on his behalf' (Section 89(7)). The medical officer must 'review the capacity of the patient to give consent every seven days' (Section 89(8)).

All 'supported admissions' must be notified to the Mental Health Review Board within three days (for 'a woman or a minor') or seven days (others) (Section 89(9)).

'A person admitted under this section or his nominated representative or a representative of a registered non-governmental organisation with the consent of the person, may apply to the concerned Board for review of the decision' to admit the person (Section 89(10)). The Board will perform a binding review within seven days (Section 89(11)).

#### 6.2.12.4 'Supported Admission Beyond 30 Days'

In the event that a 'supported' patient 'requires continuous admission and treatment beyond 30 days' (or readmission within seven days of discharge) (Section 90(1)), the MHCA states that 'the medical officer or mental health professional in charge of a mental health establishment, upon application by the nominated representative of a person with mental illness, shall continue admission of such person with mental illness' if:

(a) 'Two psychiatrists have independently examined the person with mental illness in the preceding seven days and both independently conclude based on the examination and, on information provided by others that the person has a mental illness of a severity that the person (i) has consistently over time threatened or attempted to cause bodily harm to himself; or (ii) has consistently over time behaved violently towards another person or has consistently over time caused another person to fear bodily harm from him; or (iii) has consistently over time shown an inability to care for himself to a degree that places the individual at risk of harm to himself';
(b) 'Both psychiatrists, after taking into account an advance directive, if any, certify that admission to a mental health establishment is the least restrictive care option possible under the circumstances'; and
(c) 'The person continues to remain ineligible to receive care and treatment as a independent patient as the person cannot make mental healthcare and treatment decisions independently and needs very high support from his nominated representative, in making decisions' (Section 90(2)).

These admissions must be reported to the Mental Health Review Board within seven days (Section 90(3)) and 'the Board shall, within a period of 21 days from the date of last admission or readmission [...] permit such admission or readmission or order discharge of such person' (Section 90(4)), bearing in mind '(a) the need for institutional care to such person; (b) whether such care cannot be provided in less restrictive settings based in the community' (Section 90(5)).

'The Board may require the medical officer or psychiatrist in charge of treatment of such person with mental illness to submit a plan for community based treatment and the progress made, or likely to be made, towards realising this plan' (Section 90(6)). In addition, the 'non-existence of community based services' cannot justify such an admission (Section 90(7)), which is, in the first instance, limited to 90 days (Section 90(8)) but can be extended for 120 days and periods of 180 days thereafter, if relevant criteria are met (Section 90(9)).

The patient 'shall be provided treatment, after taking into account (a) an advance directive; or (b) informed consent of the person with the support from his nominated representative' (Section 90(11)). If the patient 'requires nearly 100% support from his nominated representative, in making decision in respect of his treatment, the nominated representative may temporarily consent to the treatment plan of such person on his behalf' (Section 90(12)). The medical officer must 'review on the expiry of every fortnight, the capacity of such person to give consent' (Section 90(13)).

The patient 'or his nominated representative or a representative of a registered non-governmental organisation with the consent of the person, may apply to the concerned Board for review of the decision of the medical officer or mental health professional in charge of medical health establishment to admit such person in such establishment and the decision of the Board thereon shall be binding on all parties' (Section 90(14)).

Discharge occurs 'if the Board refuses to permit admission or continuation thereof or readmission', 'on the expiry of the periods' defined, or 'earlier if such person no longer falls within the criteria' (Sections 90(10) and 90(15)). The person may then remain as an independent patient (Section 90(16)).

'An independent' or 'supported' patient may be granted leave 'subject to such conditions, if any, and for such duration as such medical officer or psychiatrist may consider necessary' (Section 91). Patients who are absent without leave can be returned by the police (Section 92). Patients can be moved between mental health establishments by order of the Mental Health Review Board provided 'intimation and reasons for the transfer have been given to the person with mental illness and his nominated representative' (Section 93(1)).

'Emergency treatment' 'may be provided by any registered medical practitioner to a person with mental illness either at a health establishment or in the community, subject to the informed consent of the nominated representative, where the nominated representative is available, and where it is immediately necessary to prevent (a) death or irreversible harm to the health of the person; or (b) the person inflicting serious harm to himself or to others; or (c) the person causing serious damage to property belonging to himself or to others where such behaviour is believed to flow directly from the person's mental illness' (Section 94(1)). This provision 'includes transportation of the person with mental illness to a nearest mental health establishment for assessment' (Section 94(1)) but not electroconvulsive therapy (Section 94(3)). This is limited to 72 h, increasing to seven days 'during a disaster or emergency' (Section 94(4)).

The following treatments cannot be provided: '(a) electroconvulsive therapy without the use of muscle relaxants and anaesthesia; (b) electroconvulsive therapy for minors; (c) sterilization of men or women, when such sterilization is intended as a treatment for mental illness; (d) chained in any manner or form whatsoever' (Section 95(1)). However, 'if, in the opinion of psychiatrist in charge of a minor's treatment, electroconvulsive therapy is required, then, such treatment shall be done with the informed consent of the guardian and prior permission of the concerned Board' (Section 95(2)).

Psychosurgery shall require informed consent from the patient and approval from the Mental Health Review Board (Section 96(1)). A patient 'shall not be subjected to seclusion or solitary confinement, and, where necessary, physical restraint may only be used when (a) it is the only means available to prevent imminent and immediate harm to person concerned or to others; (b) it is authorised by the psychiatrist' (Section 97(1)). 'Physical restraint shall not be used for a period longer than it is absolutely necessary to prevent the immediate risk of significant harm' (Section 97(2)); must be recorded and justified (Section 97(3)); 'shall not be used as a form of punishment or deterrent' or 'on the ground of shortage of staff' (Section 97(4)); and must be notified to the relevant Board (Sections 97(7) and 97(9)). The patient's nominated representative must be informed within 24 h (Section 97(5)).

During transitions of care (e.g. discharge, transfer, or change of psychiatrist), the psychiatrist 'shall consult with' the patient, 'the nominated representative, the family member or care-giver with whom the person with mental illness shall reside on discharge from the hospital, the psychiatrist expected to be responsible for the person's care and treatment in the future, and such other persons as may be appropriate, as to what treatment or services would be appropriate for the person' (Section 98(1)).

Researchers 'shall obtain free and informed consent from all persons with mental illness for participation in any research involving interviewing the person or psychological, physical, chemical or medicinal interventions' (Section 99(1)). If the person 'is unable to give free and informed consent but does not resist participation', permission 'shall be obtained from concerned State Authority' (Section 99(2)). The State Authority may allow the research 'based on informed consent being obtained from the nominated representative' if:

(a) 'The proposed research cannot be performed on persons who are capable of giving free and informed consent';
(b) 'The proposed research is necessary to promote the mental health of the population represented by the person';
(c) 'The purpose of the proposed research is to obtain knowledge relevant to the particular mental health needs of persons with mental illness';
(d) 'A full disclosure of the interests of persons and organisations conducting the proposed research is made and there is no conflict of interest involved'; and
(e) 'The proposed research follows all the national and international guidelines and regulations concerning the conduct of such research and ethical approval has been obtained' (Section 99(3)).

Consent may be withdrawn at any time (Section 99(5)) and the Act does 'not restrict research based study of the case notes of a person who is unable to give informed consent, so long as the anonymity of the persons is secured' (Section 99(4)).

### 6.2.13 *'Responsibilities of Other Agencies'*

Chapter 13 of the MHCA outlines 'responsibilities of other agencies' including police officers, magistrates and custodial institutions.

Regarding police officers, 'every officer in-charge of a police station shall have a duty' to 'take under protection any person' (a) 'found wandering at large within the limits of the police station whom the officer has reason to believe has mental illness and is incapable of taking care of himself'; or (b) 'within the limits of the police station whom the officer has reason to believe to be a risk to himself or others by reason of mental illness' (Section 100(1)). The officer must inform the person of 'the grounds for taking him into such protection' or else inform his nominated representative 'if in the opinion of the officer such person has difficulty in understanding' (Section 100(2)).

The person 'shall be taken to the nearest public health establishment as soon as possible but not later than 24 h from the time of being taken into protection, for assessment of the person's healthcare needs' (Section 100(3)); they must not 'be detained in the police lock up or prison in any circumstances' (Section 100(4)). If, following assessment (Section 100(5)), the 'medical officer or mental health professional in-charge [...] finds that such person does not have a mental illness of a nature or degree requiring admission to the mental health establishment, he shall inform his assessment to the police officer [who] shall take the person to the person's residence or in case of homeless persons, to a Government establishment for homeless persons' (Section 100(6)).

The police must try to trace and inform the family of 'a person with mental illness who is homeless or found wandering in the community' (Section 100(7)) and inform the 'Magistrate' if a 'person residing within the limits of the police station has a mental illness and is being ill-treated or neglected' (Section 101(1)). Any person who believes 'that a person has mental illness and is being ill-treated or neglected' must report this to the police (Section 101(2)). Following such a report, 'the Magistrate may cause the person with mental illness to be produced before him' (Section 101(3)) and 'may, order in writing (a) that the person is conveyed to a public mental health establishment for assessment and treatment', or (b) authorise admission for up to 10 days to enable assessment and 'plan for necessary treatment, if any' (Section 102(1)). After this period, 'the medical officer or mental health professional in charge of the mental health establishment shall submit a report to the Magistrate and the person shall be dealt with in accordance with the provisions of this Act' (Section 102(2)).

Section 103 outlines specific provisions for the transfer of 'prisoners with mental illness' to mental health establishments and a requirement that 'the medical officer of a prison or jail shall send a quarterly report to the concerned Board certifying therein that there are no prisoners with mental illness in the prison or jail' (Section 103(3)). The Board may visit the prison to enquire about prisoners with mental illness (Section 103(4)). In addition, 'the appropriate Government shall [set up a] mental health establishment in the medical wing of at least one prison in each State and Union territory' (Section 103(6)).

'If it appears to the person in-charge of a State run custodial institution (including beggars homes, orphanages, women's protection homes and children homes) that any resident of the institution has, or is likely to have, a mental illness, then, he shall take such resident of the institution to the nearest mental health establishment run or funded by the appropriate Government for assessment and treatment' (Sections 104(1) and 104(2)). Finally, the Mental Health Review Board can advise the courts 'if during any judicial process before any competent court, proof of mental illness is produced and is challenged' (Section 105).

### *6.2.14 'Restriction to Discharge Functions by Professionals Not Covered by Profession'*

The MHCA states that 'no mental health professional or medical practitioner shall discharge any duty or perform any function not authorised by this Act or specify or recommend any medicine or treatment not authorised by the field of his profession' (Section 106).

### *6.2.15 'Offences and Penalties'*

Specific penalties are outlined in the MHCA for operating 'a mental health establishment without registration' (5,000–50,000 rupees for a first contravention; 50,000–200,000 rupees for a second; and 200,000–500,000 rupees for subsequent contraventions) (Section 107(1)); serving as a mental health professional in an unregistered establishment (up to 25,000 rupees) (Section 107(2)); and contravening 'any of the provisions of this Act' or 'any rule or regulation made thereunder' (imprisonment for up to six months and/or a fine of up to 10,000 rupees for a first contravention; imprisonment for up to two years and/or a fine between 50,000 and 500,000 rupees for subsequent contraventions) (Section 108). Companies, too, are responsible if they knew of the offence or neglected their roles (Section 109(2)).

### *6.2.16 'Miscellaneous'*

The MHCA states that the 'Central Government may, by a general or special order, call upon the Authority or [Mental Health Review] Board to furnish, periodically or as and when required any information concerning' their activities (Section 110(1)). The State Government is granted similar powers in relation to the State Authority and the Board (Section 110(2)). The Authority is 'bound by such directions on questions of policy, other than those relating to technical and administrative matters, as the Central Government may give in writing to it', provided the Authority is, 'as far as practicable', 'given an opportunity to express its views' (Section 111(1)), although 'the decision of the Central Government [is] final' (Section 111(2)).

If necessary, the Central Government can 'supersede the Central Authority for such period, not exceeding six months, as may be specified', under certain conditions (Section 112(1)); perform the Authority's roles itself (Section 112(2)); and appoint a fresh Authority (Section 112(3)). The State Government is granted similar powers in relation to the State Authority (Section 113). There are 'special provisions for states in north-east and hill states' owing to 'communication, travel and transportation difficulties', relating to the functioning of [Mental Health Review] Boards and timelines within the Act (Section 114).

With regard to suicide, Section 309 of the Indian Penal Code states that 'whoever attempts to commit suicide and does any act towards the commission of such offence, shall be punished with simple imprisonment for a term which may extend to one year or with fine, or with both'. Section 115 of the MHCA, however, now specifies that 'notwithstanding anything contained in Section 309 of the Indian Penal Code any person who attempts to commit suicide shall be presumed, unless proved otherwise, to have severe stress and shall not be tried and punished under the said Code' (Section 115(1)). 'The appropriate Government shall have a duty to provide care, treatment and rehabilitation to a person, having severe stress and who attempted to commit suicide, to reduce the risk of recurrence of attempt to commit suicide' (Section 115(2)). This is a de facto decriminalisation of suicide and an explicit commitment to provide care to those affected.

Further provisions govern a 'bar of jurisdiction' for 'any suit or proceeding in respect of any matter which the Authority or the Board is empowered by or under this Act to determine' (Section 116); 'transitory provisions' (Section 117); legal protection for Government and members of the Authority or Board (Section 119); the 'overriding effect' of the Act on 'other law' and related measures (Section 120); the 'power of Central Government and State Governments to make rules' (Section 121); the 'power of Central Authority to make regulations' (Section 122); the 'power of State Authority to make regulations' (Section 123); the laying of Central Government rules and Central Authority regulations 'before each House of Parliament' (Section 124(1)); and the laying of State Government rules and State Authority regulations 'before each House of the State Legislature' (Section 124(2)).

'If any difficulty arises in giving effect to the provisions of this Act [within two years of commencement], the Central Government may, by order, published in the Official Gazette, make such provisions, not inconsistent with the provisions of this Act, as may appear to be necessary or expedient for removing the difficulty' (Section 125(1)). Finally, the Mental Health Act, 1987 is repealed, subject to transitional arrangements (Section 126).

## 6.3 A Vision for Change?

Overall, India's MHCA presents a very broad range of provisions which, if implemented, will affect virtually every element of mental health services in India. Many of the changes are clearly informed by the Act's explicit aim to meet the requirements of the CRPD.

The new Indian legislation has stimulated considerable discussion in the psychiatry literature. In April 2019, on the second anniversary of the MHCA receiving Presidential assent (7 April 2017), the *Indian Journal of Psychiatry*, official publication of the Indian Psychiatric Society, published a dedicated supplement with no fewer than 33 articles relating to the legislation in various ways (Dalal 2019; Vaishnav 2019). While one line of discourse was that the new legislation was not needed in the first place, and that amendments to the Mental Health Act, 1987 would have sufficed, there was nonetheless an acceptance of the facts that the new Act would have practical and legal implications in practice and needed to be understood (Kumar 2019).

The themes of the papers in the supplement reflected many of the themes that had emerged over the previous two years and, indeed, during the development of the legislation itself (Suresh 2014; Isaac 2015; Jiloha 2015): the role of the CRPD and human rights standards in shaping the legislation (Ameen et al. 2019; Raveesh et al. 2019a); the need for specific amendments to facilitate implementation (Math et al. 2019a; Singh 2019); issues relating to consent and research (Ali et al. 2019a); assessments of capacity for mental healthcare decisions (Namboodiri 2019); advance directives and nominated representatives (Philip et al. 2019); alternatives to restraint (Raveesh et al. 2019b; Raveesh and Lepping 2019); suicide and attempted suicide (Vadlamani and Gowda 2019); child and adolescent psychiatry (Sharma and Kommu 2019); old age psychiatry (Sivakumar et al. 2019); the homeless mentally ill (Swaminath et al. 2019); community treatment orders (Gowda et al. 2019a); civil commitment (Mannekote et al. 2019); the development of rules and regulations (Narayan and Shekhar 2015; Hongally et al. 2019a); the perspectives of caregivers (Pavitra et al. 2019) and liabilities and penalties (Hongally et al. 2019b). Many of these themes feature throughout the remaining chapters in this book, especially in relation to their implications in terms of human rights.

The April 2019 supplement to the *Indian Journal of Psychiatry* also included many welcome papers looking at the practical challenges of implementation (Singh 2019); the needs for appropriate training (Harbishettar and Murthy 2019), peer-group support (Harbishettar et al. 2019a) and a 'code of practice' (Nallur 2019); documentation under the new legislation (Gajera et al. 2019; Hongally et al. 2019b); its impact on addiction and addiction services (Mohan and Math 2019); issuing of certificates (Ali et al. 2019b); discharge planning (Gowda et al. 2019b); dealing with statutory bodies (Prashanth et al. 2019); the potential role of technology (Kumar et al. 2019); the Rights of Persons with Disabilities Act, 2016 (Math et al. 2019b); the implications of the MHCA in relation to founding and managing a mental health establishment (Gowda et al. 2019c) and health insurance for mental illness (Bijal et al. 2019).

Other papers covered issues relating to ethics (Indla and Radhika 2019); the doctor–patient relationship (Harbishettar et al. 2019b); violence against doctors (Reddy et al. 2019); and ethical and legal issues relating to the sale of medicines by registered medical practitioners at their clinics (Math et al. 2019c). One of the most interesting papers concerned the cost of implementing the new legislation, which the authors estimated at 940,730 million rupees (€12 billion or £11 billion) annually (Math et al. 2019d). The authors also pointed out, however, that the annual cost to the government of *non-investment* in mental health services was 6.5 times more than that.

The background to many of these issues and the implications of the MHCA itself in terms of human rights are explored in detail in the remaining chapters of this book. More specifically, Chap. 7 provides a point-by-point comparison of the MHCA with the WHO Checklist on Mental Health Legislation (WHO 2005) and Chaps. 8 and 9 examine the legislation in the context of the CRPD. Chapter 10 looks more generally at issues raised by adherence or non-adherence with international standards and conventions, while Chap. 11 provides an update on implementation on the ground in India, kindly contributed by Dr. Soumitra Pathare and Arjun Kapoor.

## References

Ali, F., Gajera, G., Gowda, G. S., Srinivasa, P., & Gowda, M. (2019a). Consent in current psychiatric practice and research: An Indian perspective. *Indian Journal of Psychiatry, 61*(10), S667–S675.

Ali, F., Gowda, G. S., & Gowda, M. (2019b). Approach to and practical challenges in certification in Psychiatry. *Indian Journal of Psychiatry, 61*(10), S710–S716.

Ameen, S., Gowda, M., & Ramkumar, G. S. (2019). Mental Healthcare Act 2017: Preface to the supplement. *Indian Journal of Psychiatry, 61*(10), S637–S639.

Bijal, A. S., Kumar, C. N., Manjunatha, N., Gowda, M., Basavaraju, V., & Math, S. B. (2019). Health insurance and mental illness. *Indian Journal of Psychiatry, 61*(10), S791–S797.

Dalal, P. K. (2019). Message from Vice President, Indian Psychiatric Society. *Indian Journal of Psychiatry, 61*(10), S634.

Duffy, R. M., & Kelly, B. D. (2019a). India's Mental Healthcare Act, 2017: Content, context, controversy. *International Journal of Law and Psychiatry, 62,* 169–178.

Duffy, R. M., & Kelly, B. D. (2019b). The right to mental healthcare: India moves forward. *British Journal of Psychiatry, 214*(2), 59–60.

Gajera, G., Srinivasa, P., Ameen, S., & Gowda, M. (2019). Newer documentary practices as per Mental Healthcare Act 2017. *Indian Journal of Psychiatry, 61*(10), S686–S692.

Gowda, G. S., Enara, A., Raveesh, B. N., & Gowda, M. (2019a). Is it the right time to implement community treatment order in India? *Indian Journal of Psychiatry, 61*(10), S816–S820.

Gowda, M., Gajera, G., Srinivasa, P., & Ameen, S. (2019b). Discharge planning and Mental Healthcare Act 2017. *Indian Journal of Psychiatry, 61*(10), S706–S709.

Gowda, M. R., Das, K., Gowda, G. S., Karthik, K. N., Srinivasa, P., & Muthalayapapa, C. (2019c). Founding and managing a mental health establishment under the Mental Healthcare Act 2017. *Indian Journal of Psychiatry, 61*(10), S735–S743.

Harbishettar, V., Enara, A., & Gowda, M. (2019a). Making the most of Mental Healthcare Act 2017: Practitioners' perspective. *Indian Journal of Psychiatry, 61*(10), S645–S649.

Harbishettar, V., Krishna, K. R., Srinivasa, P., & Gowda, M. (2019b). The enigma of doctor-patient relationship. *Indian Journal of Psychiatry, 61*(10), S776–S781.

Harbishettar, V., & Murthy, P. (2019). Reorientation of postgraduate training in the background of the Mental Healthcare Act 2017. *Indian Journal of Psychiatry, 61*(10), S804–S808.

Hongally, C., Sneha, V., & Archana, G. (2019a). How to make rules and regulations for the states in accordance with the Mental Healthcare Act 2017. *Indian Journal of Psychiatry, 61*(10), S827–S831.

Hongally, C., Sripad, M. N., Nadakuru, R., Meenakshisundaram, M., & Jayaprakasan, K. P. (2019b). Liabilities and penalties under Mental Healthcare Act 2017. *Indian Journal of Psychiatry, 61*(10), S724–S729.

Indla, V., & Radhika, M. S. (2019). Hippocratic oath: Losing relevance in today's world? *Indian Journal of Psychiatry, 61*(10), S773–S775.

Isaac, M. (2015). Mental health legislation in South Asian countries: Shortcomings and possible solutions. In J. K. Trivedi & A. Tripathi (Eds.), *Mental health in South Asia: Ethics, resources, programs and legislation* (pp. 319–332). Dordrecht: Springer.

Jiloha, R. C. (2015). The Mental Health Act of India. In S. Malhotra & S. Chakrabarti (Eds.), *Developments in psychiatry in India: Clinical, research and policy perspectives* (pp. 611–622). New Delhi: Springer.

Kalmegh, B., Bakhshy, A., Harshe, D., & Patankar, V. (2018). *MHCA 2017: Together we can..!* Pune: SMARTT.

Kumar, V. (2019). Message from Hon. General Secretary, Indian Psychiatric Society. *Indian Journal of Psychiatry, 61*(10), S635.

Kumar, M. S., Krishnamurthy, S., Gowda, M. R., & Dhruve, N. (2019). The dawn of eMental health professional. *Indian Journal of Psychiatry, 61*(10), S730–S734.

Mannekote, S., Pillai, A., & Harbishettar, V. (2019). Civil commitment of persons with mental illness: Comparison of the Mental Healthcare Act 2017 with corresponding legislations of the USA. *Indian Journal of Psychiatry, 61*(10), S821–S826.

Math, S. B., Basavaraju, V., Harihara, S. N., Gowda, G. S., Manjunatha, N., Kumar, C. N., et al. (2019a). Mental Healthcare Act 2017—Aspiration to action. *Indian Journal of Psychiatry, 61*(10), S660–S666.

Math, S. B., Gowda, G. S., Basavaraju, V., Manjunatha, N., Kumar, C. N., Philip, S., et al. (2019b). The Rights of Persons with Disabilities Act, 2016: Challenges and opportunities. *Indian Journal of Psychiatry, 61*(10), S809–S815.

Math, S. B., Manjunatha, N., Kumar, C. N., Gowda, G. S., Philip, S., Enara, A., et al. (2019c). Sale of medicines by Registered Medical Practitioners at their clinics: Legal and ethical issues. *Indian Journal of Psychiatry, 61*(10), S786–S790.

Math, S. B., Gowda, G. S., Basavaraju, V., Manjunatha, N., Kumar, C. N., Enara, A., et al. (2019d). Cost estimation for the implementation of the Mental Healthcare Act 2017. *Indian Journal of Psychiatry, 61*(10), S650–S659.

Mohan, A., & Math, S. B. (2019). Mental Healthcare Act 2017: Impact on addiction and addiction services. *Indian Journal of Psychiatry, 61*(10), S744–S749.

Nallur, D. G. (2019). The need for 'code of practice' as a supplement to Mental Healthcare Act 2017. *Indian Journal of Psychiatry, 61*(10), S798–S803.

Namboodiri, V. (2019). Capacity for mental healthcare decisions under the Mental Healthcare Act. *Indian Journal of Psychiatry, 61*(10), S676–S679.

Narayan, C. L., & Shekhar, S. (2015). The Mental Health Care Bill 2013: A critical appraisal. *Indian Journal of Psychological Medicine, 37*(2), 215–219.

Pavitra, K. S., Kalmane, S., Kumar, A., & Gowda, M. (2019). Family matters! The caregivers' perspective of Mental Healthcare Act 2017. *Indian Journal of Psychiatry, 61*(10), S832–S837.

Philip, S., Rangarajan, S. K., Moirangthem, S., Kumar, C. N., Gowda, M. R., Gowda, G. S., et al. (2019). Advance directives and nominated representatives: A critique. *Indian Journal of Psychiatry, 61*(10), S680–S685.

Prashanth, N. R., Abraham, S. E., Hongally, C., & Madhusudan, S. (2019). Dealing with statutory bodies under the Mental Healthcare Act 2017. *Indian Journal of Psychiatry, 61*(10), S717–S723.
Raveesh, B. N., Gowda, G. S., & Gowda, M. (2019a). How right is right-based mental health law? *Indian Journal of Psychiatry, 61*(10), S640–S644.
Raveesh, B. N., Gowda, G. S., & Gowda, M. (2019b). Alternatives to use of restraint: A path toward humanistic care. *Indian Journal of Psychiatry, 61*(10), S693–S697.
Raveesh, B. N., & Lepping, P. (2019). Restraint guidelines for mental health services in India. *Indian Journal of Psychiatry, 61*(10), S698–S705.
Reddy, I. R., Ukrani, J., Indla, V., & Ukrani, V. (2019). Violence against doctors: A viral epidemic? *Indian Journal of Psychiatry, 61*(10), S782–S785.
Sharma, E., & Kommu, J. V. S. (2019). Mental Healthcare Act 2017, India: Child and adolescent perspectives. *Indian Journal of Psychiatry, 61*(10), S756–S762.
Singh, O. P. (2019). Mental Healthcare Act (MHCA 2017): Is a relook necessary for effective implementation? *Indian Journal of Psychiatry, 61*(10), S636.
Sivakumar, P. T., Mukku, S. S., Antony, S., Harbishettar, V., Kumar, C. N., & Math, S. B. (2019). Implications of Mental Healthcare Act 2017 for geriatric mental health care delivery: A critical appraisal. *Indian Journal of Psychiatry, 61*(10), S763–S767.
Suresh, B.M. (2014). *Revisiting mental health legislation of India.* Thesis submitted to the National Law School of India University, Bangalore for the award of the degree of Doctor of Philosophy, Ph.D. Bangalore: National Law School of India University.
Swaminath, G., Enara, A., Rao, R., Kumar, K. V., & Kumar, C. N. (2019). Mental Healthcare Act, 2017 and homeless persons with mental illness in India. *Indian Journal of Psychiatry, 61*(10), S768–S772.
United Nations. (2006). *Convention on the rights of persons with disabilities.* New York: United Nations. Retrieved June 1, 2019, from https://www.un.org/development/desa/disabilities/convention-on-the-rights-of-persons-with-disabilities/convention-on-the-rights-of-persons-with-disabilities-2.html.
Vadlamani, L. N., & Gowda, M. (2019). Practical implications of Mental Healthcare Act 2017: Suicide and suicide attempt. *Indian Journal of Psychiatry, 61*(10), S750–S755.
Vaishnav, M. (2019). Message from President, Indian Psychiatric Society. *Indian Journal of Psychiatry, 61*(10), S633.
World Health Organization. (1992). *International classification of mental and behavioural disorders.* Geneva: World Health Organization.
World Health Organization. (2005). *WHO resource book on mental health, human rights and legislation.* Geneva: World Health Organization.

# Part III
# India's Mental Healthcare Act, 2017 and International Human Rights Standards

# Chapter 7
# India's Mental Healthcare Act, 2017 and the World Health Organization's Checklist on Mental Health Legislation

## 7.1 Introduction

India's Mental Healthcare Act, 2017 (MHCA) addresses many of the items listed in the 'Checklist on Mental Health Legislation' published in the World Health Organization's (WHO) *Resource Book on Mental Health Legislation* (WHO RB) (WHO 2005) including many social and economic rights that are often omitted from mental health legislation in other countries (Duffy and Kelly 2017a).

Writing legislation concordant with the standards of the WHO RB can present many challenges and often requires a highly nuanced understanding of the relevant ethical issues (Kelly 2011). In addition, the WHO recently withdrew the WHO RB as it was composed prior to the United Nations' (UN) Convention on the Rights of Persons with Disabilities (CRPD) (UN 2006) and appears to conflict with it in a number of key areas (Duffy and Kelly 2017b). Despite this fact, the WHO RB still has much in common with the CRPD and remains the most comprehensive human rights tool available for the analysis of mental health legislation in relation to human rights standards.

This chapter focuses on the WHO RB which aims to guide governments and legislators in developing legislation that affirms and protects the rights of the mentally ill, as was the case in India. The WHO RB is not a legally binding document, and there are no formal inspection bodies that monitor jurisdictions' adherence to it. The Indian legislation was drawn up to address the CRPD and not the WHO RB, but it still addresses many key areas of the WHO RB. This chapter explores areas of high and low concordance, key omissions and other relevant deviations from WHO standards in the new Indian legislation.

For each of the standards in the WHO RB checklist, the Indian legislation is classified in a binary manner as either concordant or not. In the text of this chapter, more nuanced interactions between the Indian legislation and WHO checklist are explored in greater depth in relation to specific areas, along with potential justifications for, and implications of, deviations, where appropriate. Alphanumeric designations for



R. M. Duffy and B. D. Kelly, *India's Mental Healthcare Act, 2017*,
https://doi.org/10.1007/978-981-15-5009-6_7

each human rights standard are provided to assist with clarity and cross-referencing with the WHO RB (to which the capital letters in this chapter's text and tables refer).

The WHO RB is clear that the WHO does not expect all of these matters to be addressed in specific mental health legislation. Consequently, where a standard is not addressed in the MHCA, other relevant legislation is considered, but all references to sections of Indian legislation in this chapter relate to the MHCA unless stated otherwise.

Apart from the MHCA, the primary piece of legislation that contributes to meeting the standards of the WHO RB in India is the Rights of Persons with Disabilities Act, 2016. Other acts reviewed include relevant sections of the Indian Penal Code, 1860, the Code of Criminal Procedure, 1973, the Medical Termination of Pregnancy Act, 1971, and the Narcotic Drugs and Psychotropic Substances Act, 1985.

There are advantages and disadvantages to dealing with a broad range of issues (housing, social welfare, etc.) in dedicated mental health legislation rather than more general legislation. One of the key benefits of the latter option (dealing with such issues through general rather than dedicated mental health legislation) is that any consequent limitations of rights do not occur on the basis of a diagnosis or having a mental health problem. This is—broadly—the system being implemented in Northern Ireland, for example, in its new mental capacity legislation which focuses on decision-making capacity, largely regardless of diagnosis (Kelly 2016).

The need for dedicated legislation is, however, highlighted by the existence of the CRPD, which is explicit in stating that it does not create any new rights but rather identifies a need for specific disability legislation. For the purpose of the present analysis, it is also relevant that, while the WHO RB says that its human rights standards might be met through mental health policy as well as law, it still presents a detailed checklist for mental health *legislation*, rather than other forms of legislation or policy. Against this background, it is useful to examine in greater depth areas of limited or non-concordance between the MHCA and the WHO RB, as we do in this chapter.

## 7.2 Areas of Concordance

Areas of full concordance between the MHCA and the WHO RB include standards relating to clinical and experimental research, discrimination, housing, various civil issues, and offences and penalties.

Three WHO RB standards relate to clinical and experimental research, and all are addressed in MHCA (Table 7.1). Section 17(k) gives a nominated representative the 'the right to give or withhold consent for research'. This is expanded upon in Section 99(3). The rest of Section 99 addresses research and consent to research in a more comprehensive manner: Section 99(1) articulates the need for free and informed consent for participation in research and Section 99(2) addresses consent for people who can assent but not consent; in such cases, permission to conduct research can be obtained from the State Mental Health Authority.

**Table 7.1** Concordance of Indian legislation with the World Health Organization Checklist on Mental Health Legislation's standards relating to clinical and experimental research

| Legislative issue | | Is Indian legislation concordant? |
|---|---|---|
| Q1 | Does the law state that informed consent must be obtained for participation in clinical or experimental research from both voluntary and involuntary patients who have the ability to consent? | Yes |
| Q2a | Where a person is unable to give informed consent (and where a decision has been made that research can be conducted): Does the law ensure that proxy consent is obtained from either the legally appointed guardian or family member, or from an independent authority constituted for this purpose? | Yes |
| Q2b | Where a person is unable to give informed consent (and where a decision has been made that research can be conducted): Does the law state that the research cannot be conducted if the same research could be conducted on people capable of consenting, and that the research is necessary to promote the health of the individual and that of the population represented? | Yes |

WHO RB standard Q1 is addressed in a much more useful way in the MHCA than it is presented in the WHO RB. Q1 in the WHO RB divides individuals into 'voluntary and involuntary patients' but as the MHCA is attempting to remove such language (in order to align with the CRPD), the Indian legislation identifies much more accurately individuals who can give free and informed consent and individuals who are unable to give free and informed consent but do not resist participation.

Section 99(3) appears to introduce the possibility of a third group who are not assenting but whose nominated representatives permit participation. Q2a is, hence, addressed in Section 99(3) where the nominated representative provides proxy consent in certain contexts. The relationship between Sub-sections 2 and 3 here is important, especially if the State Mental Health Authority can grant permission to conduct research without using Section 99(3) for assenting patients. In addition, the Rights of Persons with Disabilities Act, 2016 states that such research could need to get the permission of a Committee for Research on Disability, which would be an independent body (Section 6(2)(ii)).

WHO RB item Q2b is well addressed in Section 99(3)(a) of the MHCA which states that proxy consent can only be used if 'the proposed research cannot be performed on persons who are capable of giving free and informed consent' and Section 99(3)(b) which requires that 'the proposed research is necessary to promote the mental health of the population represented by the person'. The Rights of Persons with Disabilities Act, 2016 also affirms the need for free and informed consent under its 'Protection from cruelty and inhuman treatment' provisions (Section 6(2)).

Overall, India's MHCA comprehensively covers most standards relating to clinical and experimental research; one area of potential weakness is the relationship between Sections 99(2) and 99(3). In addition to addressing these important standards, both the MHCA and the Rights of Persons with Disabilities Act, 2016 do much else to pro-actively promote research in individuals impacted by mental illness (e.g. Sections 19(j), 25(2)(a), 28, 47(2), 75(1)(f) and 80(e) of the Rights of Persons with Disabilities Act, 2016).

The issue of discrimination is addressed by one standard in the WHO RB which requires that law includes provisions aimed at stopping discrimination against people with mental illness (U1). Section 18(2) of the MHCA prohibits discrimination in accessing mental healthcare 'on the basis of gender, sex, sexual orientation, religion, culture, caste, social or political beliefs, class, disability or any other basis'. Section 18(8) prohibits any discrimination in the provision of mental healthcare compared to physical healthcare.

In addition, Section 21(1) provides that 'every person with mental illness shall be treated as equal to persons with physical illness in the provision of all healthcare which shall include the following, namely: (a) there shall be no discrimination on any basis including gender, sex, sexual orientation, religion, culture, caste, social or political beliefs, class or disability; (b) emergency facilities and emergency services for mental illness shall be of the same quality and availability as those provided to persons with physical illness; (c) persons with mental illness shall be entitled to the use of ambulance services in the same manner, extent and quality as provided to persons with physical illness; (d) living conditions in health establishments shall be of the same manner, extent and quality as provided to persons with physical illness; and (e) any other health services provided to persons with physical illness shall be provided in same manner, extent and quality to persons with mental illness'.

With regard to housing, the WHO RB requires that legislation ensures non-discrimination in the allocation of housing (V1), provides housing for the mentally ill through subsidized housing or state housing schemes (V2) and provides halfway homes and long-stay, supported homes where needed (V3). All of these standards are met in the MHCA (Sections 18(4)(b), 19(3) and 121(4)(b)) and the Rights of Persons with Disabilities Act, 2016 (Sections 12(3), 65(2)(e) and 71(2)(e)), which also meets WHO RB requirements relating to employment (W) (Chapter IV), social security (X) (Section 24) and civil and other rights (Y) (Sections 12(1), 16(i) and 20). Provisions relating to offences and penalties (AZ) are included in both the Rights of Persons with Disabilities Act, 2016 (Chapter XVI) and MHCA (Chapter XV), consistent with WHO RB requirements.

## 7.3 Areas of Non-concordance, Omissions and Deviations

### *7.3.1 Key Areas of Non-concordance*

Indian legislation, including the MHCA, falls short of the standards set by the WHO RB checklist in three key areas: involuntary treatment in community settings, determinations of mental disorder and protection of vulnerable groups (Table 7.2). It is useful to consider each of these areas in turn.

#### 7.3.1.1 Involuntary Treatment in Community Settings

Looking first at involuntary treatment in community settings, it is worth noting that there is a lack of compelling evidence to support involuntary treatment in the community (i.e. outside hospital settings) (Rugkåsa 2016) and while treatment in the community can initially appear to be a less restrictive option than inpatient care, the availability of less restrictive means of coercion could possibly result in a lower threshold for use.

Against this background, India's MHCA does not provide for means for involuntary treatment in the community (Table 7.3). Advance directives and nominated representatives may exercise some influence in the community but the person with mental capacity is still free to decline treatment or change their advance directive or nominated representative if they wish. Involuntary treatment in the community can occur in the context of an emergency (Section 94(1)).

**Table 7.2** Legislative issues in the World Health Organization Checklist on Mental Health Legislation that are not adequately addressed in Indian legislation

| Legislative issue | | Standards met (%) |
|---|---|---|
| L | Involuntary treatment in community settings | 0/2 (0%) |
| N | Determinations of mental disorder | 1/3 (33%) |
| Z | Protection of vulnerable groups (Women) (Minorities) | 3/7 (43%) |

**Table 7.3** Concordance of Indian legislation with the World Health Organization Checklist on Mental Health Legislation's standards relating involuntary treatment in community settings

| Legislative issue | | Is Indian legislation concordant? |
|---|---|---|
| L1 | Does the law provide for involuntary treatment in the community as a 'less restrictive' alternative to an inpatient mental health facility? | No |
| L2 | Are all the criteria and safeguards required for involuntary inpatient treatment also included for involuntary community-based treatment? | No |

**Table 7.4** Concordance of Indian legislation with the World Health Organization Checklist on Mental Health Legislation's standards relating to determinations of mental disorder

| Legislative issue | | Is Indian legislation concordant? |
|---|---|---|
| N1a | Does the legislation define the level of skills required to determine mental disorder? | No |
| N1b | Does the legislation specify the categories of professionals who may assess a person to determine the existence of a mental disorder? | No |
| N2 | Is the accreditation of practitioners codified in law and does this ensure that accreditation is operated by an independent body? | Yes |

#### 7.3.1.2 Determinations of Mental Disorder

There is no health without mental health, and there can be no sustained understanding of mental illness without reliable diagnosis. Accurate diagnosis is essential in order to deliver evidence-based treatments, conduct high-quality research and provide patients and carers with vital information concerning mental illness. The WHO RB checklist suggests three standards that are required in relation to determination of mental disorder; Indian legislation meets just one of these standards (Table 7.4).

Indian legislation is concordant with only one of the suggested three standards, i.e. that the accreditation of practitioners is codified in law and accreditation is by an independent body (N2) (Section 2). The legislation does not, however, define the level of skill required to determine mental disorder (N1a) or specify the categories of professions who assess for mental disorders (N1b). This is despite an entire section of the MHCA being dedicated to the determination of mental illness (Section 3). The failure of the Indian Act to legislate for these standards may relate to the human resource limitations in Indian psychiatry, with just 0.30 psychiatrists per 100,000 population in India, compared to 1.7 in China (Patel et al. 2016). With such small numbers of psychiatrists, overly restrictive guidelines concerning diagnosis could—paradoxically—restrict access to treatment.

#### 7.3.1.3 Protection of Vulnerable Groups

Vulnerable groups with mental illness are at particular risk of neglect and exploitation, and therefore require special consideration. The WHO RB identifies three groups that it suggests require specific protection: minors, women and minorities. In this section, we consider the positions of women and minorities, as the deficiencies are particularly significant with respect to these cohorts. The non-concordance with the WHO RB concerning minors is discussed in the section on key omissions in areas of generally good concordance (below). Of the seven WHO RB standards that pertain to women and minorities, Indian legislation addresses only three (Table 7.5). This is

**Table 7.5** Concordance of Indian legislation with the World Health Organization Checklist on Mental Health Legislation's standards relating to protection of vulnerable groups (women and minorities)

| Legislative issue | | Is Indian legislation concordant? |
|---|---|---|
| Z1 (Women) | Does legislation allow women with mental disorders equal rights with men in all matters relating to civil, political, economic, social and cultural rights? | Yes |
| Z2a (Women) | Does the law ensure that women in mental health facilities have adequate privacy? | No |
| Z2b (Women) | Does the law ensure that women in mental health facilities are provided with separate sleeping facilities from men? | No |
| Z3 (Women) | Does legislation state that women with mental disorders should receive equal mental health treatment and care as men, including access to mental health services and care in the community, and in relation to voluntary and involuntary admission and treatment? | Yes |
| Z1 (Minorities) | Does legislation specifically state that persons with mental disorders should not be discriminated against on the grounds of race, colour, language, religion, political or other opinions, national, ethnic or social origin, legal or social status? | Yes |
| Z2 (Minorities) | Does the legislation provide for a review body to monitor involuntary admission and treatment of minorities and ensure non-discrimination on all matters? | No |
| Z3 (Minorities) | Does the law stipulate that refugees and asylum seekers are entitled to the same mental health treatment as other citizens of the host country? | No |

a failing that the Indian legislation shares with mental health legislation in England, Wales and Ireland (Kelly 2011).

Both the MHCA (Sections 18(2) and 21(1)(a)) and Rights of Persons with Disabilities Act, 2016 (Preamble (g) and Section 4(1)) guarantee women equal rights (Z1 Women). The MHCA does so in relation to healthcare, while the Rights of Persons with Disabilities Act, 2016 provides broader protections in all domains of life. Women's privacy is not, however, given special consideration (Z2a Women) and, in general, the consideration of privacy in the MHCA is superficial at best (Duffy and

Kelly 2017c). This has added importance in relation to women because women are also not guaranteed separate sleeping facilities from men, as suggested by the WHO (Z2b Women).

Regarding minorities (Z Minorities), the MHCA affirms non-discrimination concerning healthcare (Sections 18(2) and 21(1)(a)) and the Rights of Persons with Disabilities Act, 2016 affirms non-discrimination in general (Preamble (b) and (d)). While the Rights of Persons with Disabilities Act, 2016 is concerned about discrimination against people with disabilities, however, it makes no specific reference to minorities with disabilities. No review body monitors the involuntary admission of minorities or ensures non-discrimination (Z2 Minorities). No special consideration is given to asylum seekers and refugees (Z3 Minorities), despite the fact that this is a particularly vulnerable group with substantial mental health needs who commonly experience discrimination and therefore require particular consideration (Duffy and Kelly 2015).

### 7.3.2 *Key Omissions in Areas of Generally Good Concordance*

Many areas of the MHCA align well with the WHO RB but even some areas of generally good concordance have notable omissions. This situation pertains to nine of the 27 sub-sections of the WHO RB, and these will be addressed systematically in this section (Table 7.6).

#### 7.3.2.1 Preamble and Objectives

The WHO RB provides comprehensive guidance on what should be included in the, preamble to and objectives of mental health legislation (A). The MHCA is concordant with five out of the six objectives (Table 7.7). A clearly articulated preamble and objectives setting the context are especially important for the MHCA, as the Mental Health Act, 1987 was in place for over 30 years and the new legislation represents a paradigm shift for Indian law.

Throughout the MHCA, there is a failure to emphasize and address discrimination outside of the context of healthcare (A2a). While non-discrimination is promoted in the Rights of Persons with Disabilities Act, 2016 (Table 7.7), these references pertain to disability rather than all mental illness and fail to address needs specific to mental illness. Due to the severity, prevalence and impact of discrimination relating to mental illness, a more comprehensive statement is warranted in the MHCA itself.

**Table 7.6** Key omissions from Indian legislation in areas of generally good concordance with the World Health Organization Checklist on Mental Health Legislation

| Legislative issue | | Specific omission | |
|---|---|---|---|
| A | Preamble and objectives | A2a | Non-discrimination not discussed outside of healthcare |
| B | Definitions | B3 | No mention of personality disorder or clear definition of substance misuse |
| C | Access to mental healthcare | C1 | No clear method of funding |
| D | Rights of users of mental health services | D5 | No minimum conditions for mental health facilities |
| | | D6a | Limited consideration of privacy |
| F | Competence, capacity and guardianship | F4 | No regular review of limited guardianship |
| | | F5 | Duties, duration of limited guardian not laid out in law |
| | | F6 | No process for establishing guardians remit |
| | | F7 | No systematic review of limited guardians |
| M | Emergency situations | M5 | No imperative to seek admission as soon as possible when emergency treatment is needed |
| | | M7 | No means to appeal emergency treatment outside of the nominated representative |
| P | Seclusion and restraint | P3 | No maximum period for seclusion or restraint |
| | | P4 | Periods or seclusion and restraint can follow immediately after one another |
| | | P5 | No human resource initiatives to minimize seclusion and restraint |
| R | Oversight and review mechanisms | R1ai | Supported admissions can last 51 days before review |
| | | R1aiii | No review of long-term independent patients. |
| | | R1aiv | No guidance to minimize intrusive treatments |
| | | R2aiii<br>R2aiv | No routine collection or publication of statistics on supported admission and treatments. |
| | | R3biv | No right to an interpreter during appeals |
| Z | Protection of vulnerable groups (Minors) | Z4 | Wishes of minors not adequately considered |
| | | Z5 | No explicit prohibition of psychosurgery |

**Table 7.7** Concordance of India's Mental Healthcare Act, 2017 with World Health Organization Checklist on Mental Health Legislation's standards relating to preamble and objectives

| Legislative issue | | Is the MHCA concordant? | Relevant MHCA section |
|---|---|---|---|
| A1a | Does the legislation have a preamble which emphasizes the human rights of people with mental disorders? | Yes | Preamble |
| A1b | Does the legislation have a preamble which emphasizes the importance of accessible mental health services for all? | Yes | Preamble, Section 18 |
| A2a | Does the legislation specify that the purpose and objectives to be achieved include non-discrimination against people with mental disorders? | No | Sections 18(1), 18(8) and 21(1)(a), [Also: Rights of Persons with Disabilities Act, 2016, Preamble (b) and Section 3] |
| A2b | Does the legislation specify that the purpose and objectives to be achieved include promotion and protection of the rights of people with mental disorders? | Yes | Preamble, Sections 2(1)(j)(ii), 89(1)(b), 90(2)(b) |
| A2c | Does the legislation specify that the purpose and objectives to be achieved include improved access to mental health services? | Yes | Section 18 |
| A2d | Does the legislation specify that the purpose and objectives to be achieved include a community-based approach? | Yes | Sections 18(5)(b), 18(5)(c), 19, 87(3)(d), 90(5)(b), 90(6), 90(7) |

#### 7.3.2.2 Definitions

Clear definitions are an essential component of any legislation. This is especially true in circumstances where definitions may influence limitations of rights; the CRPD, for example, requires that 'any deprivation of liberty is in conformity with the law' (Article 14). In this context, the MHCA has provisions for 'supported' admission, questioning the capacity of an individual, and challenging advance directives, so robust definitions are essential in all of these areas. The MHCA, however, meets just three of the six standards suggested in the WHO RB (Table 7.8).

**Table 7.8** Concordance of India's Mental Healthcare Act, 2017 with the World Health Organization Checklist on Mental Health Legislation's standards relating to definitions

| Legislative issue | | Is the MHCA concordant? | Relevant MHCA section |
|---|---|---|---|
| B1 | Is there a clear definition of mental disorder/mental illness/mental disability/mental incapacity? | Yes | Section 2(1)(s) |
| B2 | Is it evident from the legislation why the particular term (above) has been chosen? | No | Section 3(1) |
| B3 | Is the legislation clear on whether or not mental retardation/intellectual disability, personality disorders and substance abuse are being covered in the legislation? | No | Section 2(1)(s) |
| B4 | Are all key terms in the legislation clearly defined? | No | Section 2, Section 4(1) |
| B5 | Are all the key terms used consistently throughout the legislation (i.e. not interchanged with other terms with similar meanings)? | Yes | Throughout |
| B6 | Are all 'interpretable' terms (i.e. terms that may have several possible interpretations or meanings or may be ambiguous in terms of their meaning) in the legislation defined? | Yes | Throughout |

It is not clear from the legislation why the term 'mental illness' is used instead of mental disorder, mental disability or mental incapacity (B2). The Indian legislation generally aligns itself with the WHO *International classification of mental and behavioural disorders* (1992) (Section 3(1)). This would suggest the use of 'mental disorder', although 'mental illness' may well be a more commonly understood term and may also be the least stigmatizing of the four terms.

The most concerning deviation from the WHO RB guidelines on definitions, however, relates to the *boundaries* of the term 'mental illness' (B3). While mental illness itself is well defined, and the exclusion of 'mental retardation' explicit, there is only superficial mention of substance misuse and no reference to personality disorder (Section 2(1)(s)). In strict terms, it appears that the provisions of the MHCA could apply to people with personality disorder.

It is particularly important to address this issue because the MHCA states that anyone who attempts suicide is to be presumed to have severe stress and is entitled to treatment (Section 115). This section of the MHCA functions as a de facto decriminalization of suicide but may have unintended consequences if personality disorder is not given adequate consideration. For example, individuals with emotionally unstable personality disorder commonly experience suicidality as a key feature of their disorder but there are widely varying therapeutic approaches to this in different centres.

The definition of substance misuse in the MHCA is also ambiguous and this, too, might lead to significant problems in practice following implementation. As presently written, all the provision of the MHCA could, in theory, apply to acute intoxication, harmful substance use, dependence or substance-induced psychosis.

While other key terms are generally well defined (B4) in the legislation (Section 2), the final version of the MHCA that received presidential assent on 7 April 2017 included a very significant error concerning the definition of mental capacity: subclauses (a) and (b) of Section 4(1) ended with 'or' instead of 'and'. This drastically altered the definition of capacity and is, presumably, an error. Correction is needed.

#### 7.3.2.3 Access to Mental Healthcare

Access to mental healthcare is the single greatest bioethical issue in healthcare today. Globally, a strong majority of people affected by mental illness—75% in many low-income countries—do not have access to the treatment they need (WHO 2019). India's treatment gap is 85% for common mental disorders and as high as 92% for some disorders (Gururaj et al. 2016). This makes access to mental healthcare a key issue in any attempt to improve the human rights of individuals with mental illness in India.

Six of the eight WHO RB standards pertaining to 'access to mental healthcare' (C) are met by the Indian legislation. More specifically, the WHO RB suggests that 'legislation state that mental health services should be provided on an equal basis with physical health care' (C2) and this is far surpassed by the MHCA which provides a legally binding right to mental healthcare (Section 18(1)). This represents substantial progress in a country which, like most countries, has no legally enforceable right to general healthcare.

The MHCA also promotes mental health within primary health care (C4) (Section 18(5)(a)), access to psychotropic drugs (C5) (Section 18(10)), a psychosocial, rehabilitative approach (C6) (Sections 2(1)(o) and 18(4)), access to health insurance (C7) (Section 21(4) and Rights of People with Disabilities Act, 2016, Sections 2(x) and 24(3)(j)) and community care (C8) (Sections 18(5)(c), 20(2)(g), 87(3)(d), 90(5)(b), 90(6) and 90(7)).

Clear guidelines for funding, required by the WHO RB (C1), are absent from the legislation (Section 57). This may well prove to be the most concerning omission from the MHCA given its ambitious articulation of a right to mental healthcare. Currently, Indian mental health services are significantly under resourced with less than 1% of India's health budget going to mental health (Patel et al. 2016). The right to mental healthcare in the MHCA gives legal footing to demands for additional resources and places an onus on the government to provide appropriate services (Section 18(10)). Underfunding may inhibit the feasibility of MHCA and potentially lead to sections of the legislation being ignored or dismissed as impractical, which would be regrettable.

The MHCA grants equality in mental health care (Section 21(1)), prohibits discrimination (including discrimination due to culture) (Sections 18(2) and 21(1)(a)) and ensures that individuals receive information in a language or form they can understand (Section 22(1)(d)). These steps fall short, however, of the WHO RB requirement to allocate culturally appropriate resources to underserved populations (C3).

Overall, in terms of providing for rights, the MHCA represents a sea change for Indian legislation and will hopefully prove transformative in reducing stigma and closing the treatment gap. Realizing this potential will, however, depend on funding, and the MHCA's failure to follow through on its articulation of a right to mental healthcare with robust legislative provisions for funding might well prove its undoing (see Chap. 11).

#### 7.3.2.4 Rights of Users of Mental Health Services

Mental health legislation is increasingly defined and shaped by rights. This is a welcome and necessary progression away from legislation exclusively centred on involuntary treatment and forensic matters. Sixteen standards are set out in the WHO RB relating to the rights of users of mental health services (D) and Indian legislation comprehensively addresses 14 of these. Many of these rights are addressed in both the MHCA and the Rights of Persons with Disabilities Act, 2016.

Indian legislation affirms the rights to respect, dignity and humane treatment (D1) in both the MHCA (Section 20) and Rights of Persons with Disabilities Act, 2016 (Sections 3(1) and 13(5)). The individual's right to confidentiality (D2) is outlined (Section 23 and 24), along with circumstances in which such confidentiality can be breached (D2b) (Section 23 (2)). In these circumstances, individuals may challenge the release of information (D2c), initially to the relevant Mental Health Review Board (Section 77) and subsequently to the State High Court (Section 83). The initial appeal to the Mental Health Review Board, however, can take up to 90 days (Section 80(4)). No direct sanctions are laid out for breaches of confidentiality (D2a) but sanctions for any breach of the MHCA by individuals (Section 108) or companies (Section 109) are described.

Free and full access to medical records by an individual and their representative (D3) is affirmed (Section 25(1)). Circumstances in which this access can be denied (D3a) are also laid out (Section 25(2)), as are processes for appealing such decisions (D3b) (Sections 25(3), 28 and 69).

The MHCA (Section 20(2)) and Rights of Persons with Disabilities Act, 2016 (Section 6(1)) both protect persons from cruel, inhuman and degrading treatment

(D4). Some, however, might see this as internally inconsistent as the MHCA also makes provision for electroconvulsive therapy, seclusion and restraint (Sections 95 and 97).

Privacy (D6) is a fundamental human right, but in-depth discussion of the subtleties of privacy is often absent from the medical literature and from legislation (Duffy and Kelly 2017c). As privacy is considered in the MHCA under the section relating to cruel, inhuman and degrading treatment (Section 20(2)(d)), it must be seen as a non-derogable right in this context (UN Economic and Social Council 1985). Such rights cannot be limited in any circumstances and, as such, the MHCA's failure to consider different domains of privacy or stipulate minimum levels of privacy (D6a) is of concern. The WHO RB provides a rare and highly useful examination of the varying elements of privacy in a variety of contexts (WHO 2005).

In addition to privacy, the second human rights standard with which the MHCA fails to concord concerns the minimal conditions to be maintained in mental health facilities for a safe, therapeutic and hygienic environment (D5). The MHCA refers to minimum standards but allows them to be decided outside the legislation (Sections 18(9), 65(3), 65(4)(a), 66(9), 67(1), 68(1), 122(2)(e) and 123(2)(a)). These minimum standards also apply to general hospital psychiatric units that were not subject to licensing under the Mental Health Act, 1987. This deviation from the WHO RB guidelines allows the relevant authority to have regard to local service infrastructure (Section 65(5)(c). While this is a pragmatic provision, it will be important that clear and effective policy is promptly implemented at local level.

The Indian legislation adequately addresses the final four standards concerning the rights of users of mental health services. It forbids inadequately remunerated or forced labour (D7) (Section 20(2)(f)). It makes provision for educational activities, vocational training, leisure and recreational activities, and meeting the religious or cultural needs of people with mental disorders (D8) (Section 20(1)(c) and Rights of Persons with Disabilities Act, 2016, Sections 16, 18, 19 and 27). It instructs authorities to inform patients of their rights (D9) (Section 22(1)), and it involves service users in policy and legislation development (D10) (Sections 34(1), 46(1) and 74(1)).

It is very reasonable that the two areas of non-concordance with the WHO RB may be dealt with in policy; in the case of the minimum standards for mental health establishments, this is even suggested in the law. This manner of providing for rights allows a state to give careful consideration to its financial situation and mental health infrastructure but this must remain under careful review to mitigate the risk of non-observance of rights.

#### 7.3.2.5 Competence, Capacity and Guardianship

Historically, professionals' judgements about mental competency and capacity have done much to limit and violate the rights of individuals with mental illness (Shorter 1997). Too often, formal and informal guardianship arrangements have been used excessively. Some jurisdictions, including Northern Ireland, have shifted their legislation away from mental illness (however, defined) and centred it on mental capacity (Kelly 2016). The CRPD strongly affirms the legal capacity of individuals with disability (Article 12), and there is growing research about the mental capacity of people receiving treatment for physical and mental health conditions (Lepping et al. 2015; Murphy et al. 2018; Curley et al. 2019a, b).

'Capacity' is clearly defined in the MHCA (Section 4) and while 'competency' is not (F2), the legislation is nonetheless sufficient to meet the relevant WHO RB standard (F2). The MHCA also lays down criteria for determining mental capacity (Section 4) and proposes the development of a guidance document for assistance (Section 81(1)). In the legislation, however, advance directives, nominated representatives and the definition of 'capacity' pertain only to decisions concerning healthcare; no reference is made to financial decisions. This was previously covered in India's Mental Health Act, 1987 (Sections 52–54). Guardianship, which may cover financial and other decisions, is addressed in the Rights of Persons with Disabilities Act, 2016 (Section 14) and runs in parallel with the nominated representative in the MHCA.

The Rights of Persons with Disabilities Act, 2016 describes the provision of a 'limited guardian' who may take legally binding decisions for 'a person with disability who has been provided with adequate and appropriate support but is unable to take legally binding decisions' (Section 14(1)). The procedure for the appointment of a limited guardian is clearly described, but the duties, duration (F5) and areas of responsibility (F6) are to be determined by the state governments. In the Rights of Persons with Disabilities Act, 2016, there is no provision for systematic reviews of limited guardianship (F7), although state governments may prescribe this, and there is a right to appeal the decision (F8) (Section 14(3)).

With regard to 'nominated representatives', the MHCA is very clear regarding appointment (Section 14), duties and responsibilities (Section 17), although it should be noted that these people do not act on behalf of the individual in the manner described in the WHO RB (F5), but rather support the decision-making of the individual. The MHCA, however, offers no guidelines about the duration of the nominated representative's activities, and this may have important consequences in the future.

Finally, while the MHCA and the Rights of Persons with Disabilities Act, 2016 meet only four of the eight standards suggested by the WHO RB in relation to competence, capacity and guardianship, there is scope for many of the deficiencies to be addressed in policy (Table 7.9). It will be important that such policy is pragmatic, comprehensive and timely.

#### 7.3.2.6 Emergency Situations

In emergency situations, interventions often occur without the supervision of a qualified psychiatrist and, as a result, it is important that sufficient protections are provided

**Table 7.9** Concordance of Indian legislation with the World Health Organization Checklist on Mental Health Legislation's standards regarding competence, capacity and guardianship

| Legislative issue | | Is Indian legislation concordant? |
|---|---|---|
| F1 | Does legislation make provision for the management of the affairs of people with mental disorders if they are unable to do so? | Yes |
| F2 | Does the law define 'competence' and 'capacity'? | Yes |
| F3 | Does the law lay down a procedure and criteria for determining a person's incapacity/incompetence with respect to issues such as treatment decisions, selection of a substitute decision-maker, making financial decisions? | Yes |
| F4 | Are procedures laid down for appeals against decisions of incapacity/incompetence, and for periodic reviews of decisions? | No |
| F5 | Does the law lay down procedures for the appointment, duration, duties and responsibilities of a guardian to act on behalf of a patient? | No |
| F6 | Does the law determine a process for establishing in which areas a guardian may take decisions on behalf of a patient? | No |
| F7 | Does the law make provision for a systematic review of the need for a guardian? | No |
| F8 | Does the law make provision for a patient to appeal against the appointment of a guardian? | Yes |

to minimize any limitations of rights. Generally, the WHO RB's suggestions for emergency situations (M) are well addressed in the MHCA, with five of the seven WHO RB standards met directly in the legislation.

The criteria (M1) and procedures (M2) for emergency treatment are clearly laid out in the MHCA (Section 94). The MHCA adds a third criterion to justify emergency treatment—serious damage to property—in addition to serious risk of harm to self or to others (Section 94(1)). Emergency treatment must be delivered by qualified and accredited practitioners (M3) (Section 94(1)), i.e. a registered medical practitioner, which is defined in Section 2(n). These treatments are limited to three days (M4) (Section 94(4)). There are two exceptions to this time limit: in emergency situations, it can be extended to seven days (Section 94(4)) and in North-East and Hill States it is extended to five days due to local infrastructure (Section 114(1)).

Electroconvulsive therapy (ECT) (Section 94(3)), psychosurgery (Section 96 (1)) and sterilization (Section 95(1)(c)) are forbidden in emergency situations (M6). Research can be permitted in emergencies (M6) once it has ethical approval and complies with all national and international guidelines (Section 99). This is an important and highly necessary deviation from the WHO RB: if safe, effective treatment is to be delivered in emergency situations; it is vital there is an evidence base to support it. Ideally, this would be gathered in non-emergency situations but research questions may arise for which this is not possible, and the MHCA allows for research in emergency situations under such circumstances.

The first and most important omission in relation to emergencies is that Indian legislation does not specify the need to initiate procedures for involuntary admission and treatment, if needed, as soon as possible after the emergency situation has ended (M5), although there is provision for transportation to a mental health establishment as part of emergency treatment (Section 94(1)). Emergency treatment is terminated by either the passing of 72 h or assessment at a mental health establishment (Section 94(4)). The concern is that it is possible under the MHCA for treatment to be given in the community, while delaying assessment at a mental health establishment.

The second omission in relation to emergencies is that there are no guidelines for timely appeal against emergency treatment. In the MHCA, there is no concept of emergency 'admission' (M7). In place of an emergency admission, there is an emergency assessment (Section 94), which may then lead to a supported admission, in which all the normal rights to appeal would apply (Section 89(10)). Regarding emergency *treatment*, the nominated representative's consent is required if they are present (Section 94(1)). Outside of the role of the nominated representative, however, the individual or the family can only appeal to the Mental Health Review Board which can take up to 90 days to resolve such an appeal (Section 80(4)). This makes preventing emergency treatment highly unlikely in practice. Once the MHCA is implemented, it will be important to ensure that emergency treatment is not used inappropriately. National- or state-level policy will likely play an important role in regulating its use.

#### 7.3.2.7 Seclusion and Restraint

Seclusion and restraint are areas of increasing concern in psychiatry and, even if it is accepted that they are necessary in certain contexts, geographical and temporal variations in use clearly require explanation and regulation. India's MHCA is concordant with three of the WHO RB's six suggested standards in regard to seclusion and restraint (P). The MHCA clearly states that these measures can be used only 'to prevent imminent and immediate harm to the person concerned or to others' (P1) (Section 97(1)(a)) and that they should never be used for punishment or convenience (P2) (Section 97(4)). Clear procedures are described for use of seclusion and restraint (P6), including provisions governing who authorizes these practices (Section 97(1)(b)), recording of details and justification (Section 97(3)), that they must occur at a mental health establishment (Section 97(6)), notification of the nominated representative (Section 97(5)) and notification to the Mental Health Review Board (Section 97(7)).

The three areas of omission are all addressed in part in the legislation but not to a degree sufficient to meet the WHO RB's standards. The MHCA states that physical restraint shall not be used for a period longer than is absolutely necessary to prevent the immediate risk of significant harm (Section 97(2)), but, despite this provision, there is no maximum time that seclusion can last (P3) and no prohibition on consecutive periods of seclusion (P4). The MHCA's position may, however, be safer for patients, because an inflexible rule on duration of seclusion or physical restraint may result in chemical restraint or potential risk to the individual or others.

The MHCA also states that mental health establishments shall not use restraint merely on the grounds of 'staff shortage' (Section 97(4)) and proposes measures to address these shortages (Section (31)). It stops short, however, of encouraging 'the development of appropriate structural and human resource requirements that minimize the need for seclusion and restraint' (P5). This particular provision could be justifiably addressed in policy rather than legislation. Human resource limitations present major challenges for Indian mental health services (Patel et al. 2016).

Overall, while the MHCA does much to address the WHO RB standards for seclusion and restraint, coercive practices, if they occur at all, need to occur within very clearly described legal parameters and careful consideration must to be given to all factors that may contribute to such practices. Hence, it is important that definitive and robust guidelines are provided and enforced as part of implementation of the MHCA.

#### 7.3.2.8 Oversight and Review Mechanisms

Oversight and review (R) are essential components of mental health legislation. They are of particular importance for a piece of mental health legislation that will apply to 1.3 billion people spread across 27 state jurisdictions, governing the delivery of mental healthcare through a combination of state facilities, centrally run hospitals, charity organizations and private enterprises (Duffy and Kelly 2019). The WHO RB describes 24 standards in relation to oversight and review mechanisms; the MHCA is concordant with 17 of them (Table 7.10).

In order to understand the Indian oversight and review mechanisms, it is important to discuss the role of three bodies created and/or re-defined by the MHCA: Mental Health Review Boards, State Mental Health Authorities and the Central Mental Health Authority. Each will be considered in turn.

Mental Health Review Boards (Chapter XI) are judicial bodies (R1) (Section 74(1)(a)), each comprising a judge, a civil servant, two doctors (one of who is a psychiatrist) and two people with personal experience of mental illness (R1b) (Section 71(1)). Their roles include reviewing supported admissions and all admissions of minors, adjudicating appeals against such admissions (R1aii), dealing with advance directives, appointing nominated representatives and deciding on non-disclosure of information (Section 82(1)).

All supported admissions are not, however, automatically reviewed by the relevant Mental Health Review Board (R1ai). Review is not mandatory during the first 30 days of supported admission, although the Mental Health Review Board must be informed within seven days of a supported admission occurring (Section 89(9)(b))

**Table 7.10** Concordance of Indian legislation with the World Health Organization Checklist on Mental Health Legislation's standards regarding oversight and review mechanisms

| Legislative issue | | Is Indian legislation concordant? |
|---|---|---|
| R1 | Does the law set up a judicial or quasi-judicial body to review processes related to involuntary admission or treatment and other restrictions of rights? | Yes |
| R1a(i) | Does the above body assess each involuntary admission/treatment? | No |
| R1a(ii) | Does the above body entertain appeals against involuntary admission and/or involuntary treatment? | Yes |
| R1a(iii) | Does the above body review the cases of patients admitted on an involuntary basis (and long-term voluntary patients)? | No |
| R1a(iv) | Does the above body regularly monitor patients receiving treatment against their will? | Yes |
| R1a(v) | Does the above body authorize or prohibit intrusive and irreversible treatments (such as psychosurgery and ECT)? | Yes |
| R1b | Does the composition of this body include an experienced legal practitioner and an experienced health care practitioner, and a 'wise person' reflecting the 'community' perspective? | Yes |
| R1c | Does the law allow for appeal of this body's decisions to a higher court? | Yes |
| R2 | Does the law set up a regulatory and oversight body to protect the rights of people with mental disorders within and outside mental health facilities? | Yes |
| R2a(i) | Does the above body conduct regular inspections of mental health facilities? | Yes |
| R2a(ii) | Does the above body provide guidance on minimizing intrusive treatments? | No |
| R2a(iii) | Does the above body maintain statistics; on, for example, the use of intrusive and irreversible treatments, seclusion and restraints? | No |
| R2a(iv) | Does the above body maintain registers of accredited facilities and professionals? | Yes |
| R2a(v) | Does the above body report and make recommendations directly to the appropriate government minister? | Yes |
| R2a(vi) | Does the above body publish findings on a regular basis? | No |

(continued)

**Table 7.10** (continued)

| Legislative issue | | Is Indian legislation concordant? |
|---|---|---|
| R2b | Does the composition of the body include professionals (in mental health, legal, social work), representatives of users of mental health facilities, members representing families of people with mental disorders, advocates and laypersons? | Yes |
| R2c | Is this body's authority clearly stated in the legislation? | Yes |
| R3a | Does the legislation outline procedures for submissions, investigations and resolutions of complaints? | Yes |
| R3b(i) | Does the law stipulate the time period from the occurrence of the incident within which the complaint should be made? | No[a] |
| R3b(ii) | Does the law stipulate a maximum time period within which the complaint should be responded to, by whom and how? | Yes |
| R3b(iii) | Does the law stipulate the right of patients to choose and appoint a personal representative and/or legal counsel to represent them in any appeals or complaints procedures? | Yes |
| R3b(iv) | Does the law stipulate the right of patients to an interpreter during the proceedings, if necessary? | No |
| R3b(v) | Does the law stipulate the right of patients and their counsel to access copies of their medical records and any other relevant reports and documents during the complaints or appeals procedures? | Yes |
| R3b(vi) | Does the law stipulate the right of patients and their counsel to attend and participate in complaints and appeals procedures? | Yes |

[a]Indicates an area of well-justified non-concordance with the WHO RB

(three days in the case of a minor or female) (Section 89(9)(a)). During these initial 30 days, the admitted individual, their nominated representative or a representative of a registered non-governmental organization with the consent of the person, may appeal to the Mental Health Review Board to review the decision concerning the supported admission (Section 89(10)).

After 30 days, the admission moves from a Section 89 admission to a Section 90 admission. The Mental Health Review Board is informed within seven days (Section 90(3)) and then has 21 days in which to determine if the supported admission is permitted (Section 90(4)). Consequently, an individual could be admitted for up to 51 days without automatic review. No provision is made for the review of long-term independent patients (R1aiii).

In addition to challenging a supported admission, patients or involved parties can challenge their treatment (R1aii) (Section 77(1)). While Mental Health Review Boards do not review people receiving treatment against their will (R1aiv), they do review supported patients under the MHCA and treatment without informed consent can only occur in this context. Mental Health Review Boards also regulate intrusive and irreversible treatments (R1av) (Sections 95(2) and 96(b)). Should an individual wish to challenge the decision of a Mental Health Review Board, they can appeal to the state's High Court (R1c) (Section 83).

The Central Mental Health Authority and State Mental Health Authorities provide regulation and oversight in many areas of mental health, not just inpatient admissions (R2). Members of the two authorities include a wide range of mental health professionals, service users, advocates (R2b) and representatives of the Department of Health and Family Welfare (Sections 34(1) and 46(1)). This Central Mental Health Authority also advises government (R2av) (Section 43(1)(f)). The roles of these bodies also include inspecting mental health establishments (R2ai) (Section 68(1)) and maintaining a list of registered clinical psychologists, mental health nurses and psychiatric social workers (R2aiv) (Sections 43(1)(d) and 55(1)(d)). Guidelines relating to psychiatrists are addressed in the Indian Medical Council Act, 1956 (Section 2(1)(y)). No register is defined in the MHCA for occupational therapists, counsellors, psychotherapists or other specialties.

The most important omission in the MHCA regarding oversight and review is that no reference is made to the maintenance of statistics on supported admission, seclusion, restraint, psychosurgery or ECT (R2aiii), although the legislation does give the Central Mental Health Authority powers to address this in policy (Sections 96(2) and 97(8)). Most of this information will, in theory, be available through Mental Health Review Boards (Sections 89(9), 90(3), 95(2), 96(1)(b) and 97(7)) so a national register should be established. Without such a register, there can be no publication of regular statistics (R2avi).

The MHCA and the Rights of Persons with Disabilities Act, 2016 both make provisions to create bodies or policies to reduce intrusive treatments, but neither piece of legislation lays out comprehensive steps to minimize such treatments (R2aii). Under the MHCA, the Central Mental Health Authority and the State Mental Health Authorities can specify quality and service provision norms (Sections 43(1)(b) and 55(1)(b)) and provide guidance on capacity assessment (Section 81(2)). The Mental Health

Review Boards in collaboration with the State Mental Health Authorities may take appropriate steps to protect the rights of persons with mental illness (Section 82(3)). The Central Authority may regulate the use of seclusion, restraint (Section 97(8)) and psychosurgery (Section 96(2)).

In addition, the Rights of Persons with Disabilities Act, 2016 sets up two bodies, which may also reduce intrusive treatments: the State and Central Advisory Boards on Disability (Chapter XI). Their roles include advising government, developing policy, monitoring the impact of laws and taking up the cause of persons with disability. All these steps may well result in the reduction of intrusive treatments but this is not an explicit aim of these boards (Rights of Persons with Disabilities Act, 2016, Sections 65 and 71)) or in the MHCA (Sections 43 and 55), as required by the WHO RB (R2ii).

The WHO RB describes procedural requirements for the submission, investigation and resolution of complaints (R3a), and these are generally well addressed in the Indian legislation (Sections 28, 43(1)(c), 55(1)(c), 77(1) and 82(1)(e)) and the Rights of Persons with Disabilities Act, 2016 (Sections 4(c) and 23(2)). The MHCA provisions include a time frame for response (Section 80(1–4)) and the manner of such response (Section 80 (5–14)) (R3bii), at least in relation to certain areas (e.g. supported admission).

The MHCA also provides a patient and their counsel with access to their medical records during the appeal process (R3bv) (Section 25(1)). An individual and their nominated representative have a right to participate in the appeals process (R3bvi) (Sections 80(7) and (10)). During appeals, an individual has a right to choose their nominated representative (Section 14) and can be represented by a counsel or a representative of their choice (R3biii) (Section 80(7)); if needed, this counsel can be provided free of charge (Section 27).

The complainant does not have the right to an interpreter (R3biv) although they and their nominated representative have a right to receive the information in a language and form that can be understood (Section 22(1)(d)). The WHO RB suggests a time period from the occurrence of the incident within which the complaint should be made (R3bi) but this is not present in the Indian legislation. This may result in appeals occurring long after an event and will place an additional burden on the Mental Health Review Boards, but it enhances the patient's rights and is another example of a well-justified deviation from the WHO RB.

All these oversight and review mechanisms will, of course, be of little use if they are not integrated into regular, day-to-day practice. Close monitoring will be needed in the early stages of implementation of the MHCA to ensure that this occurs.

#### 7.3.2.9 Protection of Vulnerable Groups (Minors)

The MHCA itself is an acknowledgement that certain groups need to be singled out for protection or affirmative action; its provision of a right to mental healthcare in a country that does not have a right to general healthcare is a striking demonstration of this fact (Duffy and Kelly 2019). And while the Act offers limited protections that

**Table 7.11** Concordance of Indian legislation with the World Health Organization Checklist on Mental Health Legislation's standards regarding protection of minors

| Legislative issue | | Is Indian legislation concordant? |
|---|---|---|
| Z1 (Minors) | Does the law limit the involuntary placement of minors in mental health facilities to instances where all feasible community alternatives have been tried? | Yes |
| Z2a (Minors) | If minors are placed in mental health facilities, does the legislation stipulate that they should have a separate living area from adults? | Yes |
| Z2b (Minors) | If minors are placed in mental health facilities, does the legislation stipulate that the environment is age-appropriate and takes into consideration the developmental needs of minors? | Yes |
| Z3 (Minors) | Does the law ensure that all minors have an adult to represent them in all matters affecting them, including consenting to treatment? | Yes |
| Z4 (Minors) | Does the law stipulate the need to take the opinions of minors into consideration on all issues affecting them (including consent to treatment), depending on their age and maturity? | No |
| Z5 (Minors) | Does legislation ban all irreversible treatments for children? | No |

are specific to women and minorities (Tables 7.5 and 7.6), it makes good provision for the protection of minors (Z) (Table 7.11).

The protection afforded to minors under the Indian legislation is generally good. It ensures that the admission of minors in mental health facilities can only occur after all community-based options have been exhausted (Z1 Minors) (Section 87(3)(d)). Such facilities must be age-appropriate (Z2b Minors) (Section 87(4)) and not adult wards (Z2a Minors) (Section 87(4)). During admission, the nominated representative or an appointed attendant accompanies the minor at all times (Section 87(5)) and the nominated representative must consent to all treatment (Section 87(7)) and support ongoing admission (Section 87 (8)) (Z3 Minors).

There are, however, two standards on which the MHCA fails to fully align with the WHO RB in relation to protection of minors. First, the MHCA does not give sufficient weight to the opinion of the minor (Z4 Minors), although their view is to be considered in relation to admission (Section 87(3)(b)) and the nominated representative should give consideration to their wishes (Sections 17(a) and (b)). In light of the vulnerable situation such minors are in, however, a more explicit affirmation of the need to take their opinion into consideration is warranted. Second, psychosurgery is not explicitly prohibited in minors (Z5 Minors) although psychosurgery would have to be approved by a Mental Health Review Board (Section 96(1)(b)).

### 7.3.3 *Well-Justified, Progressive Deviations*

There are two general areas where the Indian legislation deviates from the WHO RB and where the rationale for divergence demonstrates a nuanced and progressive expression and even expansion of WHO RB standards. These relate to the rights of family and other carers (E) and special treatments (O). While much of the non-concordance between the WHO RB checklist and the Indian legislation is for clear, practical reasons, these areas stand out as reflecting decisive positions taken by Indian legislators consistent with the most modern iterations of human rights legislation. In addition to these two general areas, there are also numerous other well-justified areas of non-concordance in relation to other, single standards (Table 7.12 and above).

#### 7.3.3.1 The Rights of Families and Other Carers

The role of families and carers can present significant challenges even to experienced mental health professionals. The path between confidentiality and collaboration can become a tightrope with both families and patients sometimes feeling aggrieved. The WHO RB checklist has five standards relating to the rights of family and carers (E), only one of which the Indian law concords with (Table 7.13).

The rights of family and carers are neither explicit nor automatic in the new Indian legislation: their rights to information (E1) (Sections 17(d) and 22(1)), to be involved in treatment planning (E2) (Sections 17 and 22(1)(c)) and to appeal involuntary admission (E3) (Sections 17(h), 77(1), 82(1)(c), 87(8)) are mediated through the role of nominated representative for the most part. Even so, while the MHCA arguably allows for families to be sidelined from an individual's treatment, many provisions exist which give them protected rights (below). In addition, the possible indirect acquisition of additional rights through the construct of the nominated representative is coupled with provisions giving the individual receiving treatment discretionary privacy, confidentiality and the ability to exclude family involvement should he or she desire this.

In specific circumstances, the MHCA gives special consideration to families and caregivers outside of the role of the nominated representative. If an individual is being discharged to live with a family member or caregiver, the treating psychiatrist may consult with them prior to discharge (Section 98(1)). When an individual with mental illness is homeless or found wandering in the community, the police have a duty to trace and inform their family (Section 100(7)).

Relatives and carers are also given special consideration when the individual with mental illness has not nominated a representative; in these cases, they become the nominated representative (Section 14(4)). In situations where a family does not agree

**Table 7.12** Potentially well-justified, progressive deviations of India's Mental Healthcare Act, 2017 from the World Health Organization Checklist on Mental Health Legislation

| Legislative issue | | Justification for non-adherence |
|---|---|---|
| E1 | Does the law entitle families or other primary carers to information about the person with a mental disorder (unless the patient refuses the divulging of such information)? | The role of the nominated representative in the MHCA gives the individual receiving treatment a degree of privacy and protection from their family should that be necessary, as well as support |
| E2 | Are family members or other primary carers encouraged to become involved in the formulation and implementation of the patient's individualized treatment plan? | |
| E3 | Do families or other primary carers have the right to appeal involuntary admission and treatment decisions? | |
| E4 | Do families or other primary carers have the right to apply for the discharge of mentally ill offenders? | |
| L1 | Does the law provide for involuntary treatment in the community as a 'less restrictive' alternative to an inpatient mental health facility? | Community treatment orders lack an evidence base and do not feature in the Indian legislation |
| L2 | Are all the criteria and safeguards required for involuntary inpatient treatment also included for involuntary community-based treatment? | |
| O3 | Are psychosurgery and other irreversible treatments outlawed on involuntary patients? | Indian legislation does not outlaw such treatments for involuntary patients, acknowledging that certain involuntary patients have the mental capacity to consent |
| O4 | Does the law specify the need for informed consent when using ECT? | The Indian legislation permits access to this potentially life-saving treatment for patients who lack mental capacity to consent to them |
| O6 | Does the law prohibit the use of ECT in minors? | Cases may arise where ECT is warranted and justified in those under 18 and this is permitted in the Indian legislation |
| R3b(i) | Does the law stipulate the time period from the occurrence of the incident within which the complaint should be made? | The Indian legislation does not do this and thus provides individuals with a longer time to report incidents |

**Table 7.13** Concordance of Indian legislation with the World Health Organization Checklist on Mental Health Legislation's standards regarding the rights of families and other carers

| Legislative issue | | Is Indian legislation concordant? |
|---|---|---|
| E1 | Does the law entitle families or other primary carers to information about the person with a mental disorder (unless the patient refuses the divulging of such information)? | No |
| E2 | Are family members or other primary carers encouraged to become involved in the formulation and implementation of the patient's individualized treatment plan? | No |
| E3 | Do families or other primary carers have the right to appeal involuntary admission and treatment decisions? | No |
| E4 | Do families or other primary carers have the right to apply for the discharge of mentally ill offenders? | No |
| E5 | Does legislation ensure that family members or other carers are involved in the development of mental health policy, legislation and service planning? | Yes |

with a person's choice of nominated representative, they can appeal to the Mental Health Review Board (Section 16). Relatives and caregivers can apply to alter or cancel advance directives (Section 11(1)). Family and carers are also to be involved in the development of mental health policy, legislation and service planning (E5) (Sections 34(1) and 46(1)).

No special provision is made for appealing for the discharge of mentally ill offenders (E5), and judges have the right to divert such people away from the criminal justice system; should they be detained under Section 89 or 90 of the MHCA, the relevant rights would apply.

These limitations on family rights could prove substantial (Duffy and Kelly 2017a). They proved controversial as the new legislation evolved and concern was expressed that they were incompatible with Indian culture (Asokan 2014). Indian mental health professionals may well desire legislation more in line with the WHO RB standards, although it remains to be seen how widely the role of the nominated representative will be utilized and how often it will involve exclusion of the family in practice. It appears likely that most nominated representatives will be family members.

#### 7.3.3.2 Special Treatments

The WHO RB proposes ten standards concerning special treatments (O). This is a diverse area of the checklist; it covers sterilization, abortion, medical and surgical procedures, psychosurgery and ECT. These are highly controversial topics that have been associated with significant human rights violations around the world in the past (Shorter 1997). While substantial steps forward have been taken to reduce violations in these areas in many countries, further progress is required. Consequently, standards such as these in the WHO RB are extremely important. In general, Indian legislation comprehensively addresses the WHO RB's standards concerning special treatments (Table 7.14). While it fails to be concordant with four of the standards, in three of those instances the deviation is well justified.

**Table 7.14** Concordance of Indian legislation with the World Health Organization Checklist on Mental Health Legislation's standards relating to special treatments

| Legislative issue | | Is Indian legislation concordant? |
|---|---|---|
| O1 | Does the law prohibit sterilization as a treatment for mental disorder? | Yes |
| O1a | Does the law specify that the mere fact of having a mental disorder should not be a reason for sterilization or abortion without informed consent? | No |
| O2 | Does the law require informed consent for major medical and surgical procedures on persons with a mental disorder? | Yes |
| O2a | Does the law allow medical and surgical procedures without informed consent, if waiting for informed consent would put the patient's life at risk? | Yes |
| O2b | In cases where inability to consent is likely to be long term, does the law allow authorization for medical and surgical procedures from an independent review body or by proxy consent of a guardian? | Yes |
| O3 | Are psychosurgery and other irreversible treatments outlawed on involuntary patients? | No[a] |
| O3a | Is there an independent body that makes sure there is indeed informed consent for psychosurgery or other irreversible treatments on involuntary patients? | Yes |
| O4 | Does the law specify the need for informed consent when using ECT? | No[a] |
| O5 | Does the law prohibit the use of unmodified ECT? | Yes |
| O6 | Does the law prohibit the use of ECT in minors? | No[a] |

[a]Areas of well-justified non-concordance

The MHCA prohibits sterilization as a treatment for mental illness (O1, O1a) (Section 95(1)(c)), and the Rights of Persons with Disabilities Act, 2016 protects reproductive rights (Section 10). No mention is made of abortion in the MHCA. Terminations of pregnancy are permitted in certain contexts in India (Medical Termination of Pregnancy Act, 1971, Section 3(2)) with the woman's consent (Section 3(4)(b)); provision is also made for women lacking mental capacity (Section 3(4)(a)) and this is clarified in the Rights of Persons with Disabilities Act, 2016, which states that termination of pregnancy may be allowed in cases of severe disability where the opinion of the medical practitioner and the guardian of the woman with disability are considered (Section 92(f)). The MHCA, Rights of Persons with Disabilities Act, 2016 and Medical Termination of Pregnancy Act, 1971 all fail, however, to explicitly state that 'the mere fact of having a mental disorder should not be a reason for sterilization or abortion without informed consent' (O1a).

The MHCA makes only one reference to medical treatments and none to surgical treatments (except psychosurgery) (O2). In an emergency, 'any medical treatment' can be given if it directly relates to the emergency (Section 94(1)). While this may cover an episode of delirium, this provision does not appear to apply inside a mental health establishment or to a supported patient.

No direct reference is made in the MHCA or Rights of Persons with Disabilities Act, 2016 to the need for informed consent prior to medical and surgical procedures, though these are addressed in the Indian Contract Act, 1872 and the Indian Penal Code, 1860. However, the government must ensure that persons with disabilities enjoy legal capacity on an equal basis with others (Rights of Persons with Disabilities Act, 2016, Section 13(2)) and, on this basis, consent would be required from all individuals capable of giving it (O2). Where that capacity to give informed consent is absent either in an emergency situation (O2a) or in the long term (O2b), a limited guardian may make legally binding decisions on behalf of the individual who lacks mental capacity (Rights of Persons with Disabilities Act, 2016, Section 14).

Psychosurgery is not forbidden in involuntary patients as suggested by the WHO RB (O3) but is permitted only with the consent of the individual and Mental Health Review Board approval (Section 96(1)) (O3a). Regarding ECT, unmodified procedures are prohibited (O5) (Section 95(1)(a)), and this has proved controversial among Indian psychiatrists (Andrade et al. 2012, 2017; Ray 2016; Duffy et al. 2019). Informed consent is, however, not necessarily required (O4), although consent can be obtained from the nominated representative (Sections 89(7) and 90(12)). With the permission of a guardian and the Mental Health Review Board, ECT can be delivered to a minor (O6) (Section 95(2)), and this is seen as a well-justified departure from the WHO RB as by some Indian psychiatrists (Balhara and Mathur 2012; Grover et al. 2017).

The MHCA makes a small but important, progressive deviation from the WHO RB in the area of psychosurgery. The WHO RB suggests that psychosurgery should not be permitted for involuntary patients (O3). This could potentially prevent a supported patient from receiving a beneficial treatment. The MHCA correctly identifies decision-making capacity rather than status of admission as the key issue here. This is important: Mandarelli and colleagues (2018) demonstrate high levels of decision-making capacity in many patients receiving non-consensual psychiatric treatment. The MHCA affirms that certain supported patients may retain their capacity to make treatment decisions. To have a blanket rule banning all involuntary patients from receiving such treatment, even in cases where they can consent, would discriminate against involuntary patients.

Similarly, in the area of ECT, the WHO RB would deprive individuals with limited capacity of potentially life-saving treatment (O4); the MHCA's deviation from this WHO RB standard is, again, well merited, once appropriate safeguards are observed.

Clearly, the Indian legislation has demonstrated a willingness to challenge the WHO RB standards and to give individuals increased treatment options. Careful monitoring will be needed to ensure that this works out well in practice, although it is clear that the ban on unmodified ECT will continue to be controversial among Indian psychiatrists (Duffy et al. 2019).

## 7.4 Overall Assessment

### *7.4.1 Strengths and Limitations of This Analysis*

This chapter's analysis of Indian legislation in the context of the WHO RB has two chief strengths. First, the authors are experienced in the systematic analysis of mental health legislation using the WHO RB and its Checklist for Mental Health Legislation (Kelly 2011; Duffy and Kelly 2017a). Second, the authors have an external vantage point on the Indian legislation. Both authors work primarily outside of India and were not involved in the development or drafting of the Indian legislation. Within India, the new legislation is a controversial and much discussed topic, so the authors' positions bring an external perspective to the analysis.

This chapter's analysis also has several limitations. The authors' external vantage point is also a limitation because not working inside the Indian system limits the ability to understand fully the context of the legislation. To mitigate this, Indian psychiatrists were consulted regularly throughout our programme of work and we travelled to India on multiple occasions during this analysis. In addition, Chap. 11 of this book presents an update on implementation of the Mental Healthcare Act, 2017 on the ground in India, kindly contributed by Dr. Soumitra Pathare and Arjun Kapoor.

The WHO RB recommends that a diverse committee from a variety of disciplines undertake reviews of legislation. This analysis, however, was conducted by two psychiatrists. As a result, our examination of the legislation is, in part, an attempt to stimulate further debate and research by others on this important topic. The input of allied health professionals will be an important component of future analyses and revisions of the Indian legislation.

It is also important to note the limitations inherent in any 'black-letter' analysis of pieces of legislation (as presented in this chapter). The focus of 'black-letter' analysis is to look at the theory of the law rather than its realization. Ultimately, however, the realization of legislation is more important than its theoretical value (Sen 2009). This may prove particularly relevant in the context of the MHCA owing to the great ambition inherent in the legislation and especially its provision of a legally binding right to mental healthcare (Chapter V).

Well-written law that is excessively idealistic and poorly implemented may well do more harm than poorly written legislation that is pragmatic and well implemented. The new Indian legislation is still in the early days of implementation, and it will take a number of years to see how it is fully realized. The transition period between presidential assent and implementing the MHCA was initially estimated at nine months (Section 1(3)) but true implementation and (hopefully) full realization of its considerable potential will undoubtedly take much longer.

### 7.4.2 Summary and Conclusions

India's MHCA and Rights of Persons with Disabilities Act, 2016 have done much to bring India's legislation in line with the WHO RB. Owing in large part to these two ambitious pieces of legislation, Indian legislation currently meets 68.0% (119/175) of the WHO RB's criteria. This far surpasses other countries whose legislation has been compared to the WHO RB, e.g. legislation in England and Wales meets 54.2% of the standards, while Irish legislation meets just 48.2% (Kelly 2011).

Regarding the standards that remain unmet in India, eight relate to areas where direct comparison is essentially impossible and 10 are in areas of well-justified non-concordance, with the Indian legislation delivering nuanced positions that embrace the principles of human rights in a more insightful way than the WHO RB does. Many of the remaining unmet standards are not addressed directly in the legislation but provision exists for them to be addressed in policy. When areas of complex comparison are excluded from the analysis and areas of justified non-concordance are considered concordant, an impressive 77.2% (129/167) of the WHO RB standards are met in Indian legislation.

The WHO RB (2005) requires revision and needs to be brought into line with the CRPD (2006). In that process, consideration could be given to limiting the remit of any successor to the WHO RB to issues that need to be included in legislation specifically, rather than issues that might be best addressed in policy. Nevertheless, for the moment, the WHO RB remains the most comprehensive guideline available for assessing mental health legislation and, for the most part, India has composed legislation that rises to its considerable challenges.

## References


Andrade, C., Shah, N., Tharyan, P., Reddy, M. S., Thirunavukarasu, M., Kallivayalil, R. A., et al. (2012). Position statement and guidelines on unmodified electroconvulsive therapy. *Indian Journal of Psychiatry, 54*(2), 119–133.

Andrade, C., Praharaj, S. K., Desai, N., Harshe, D., & Karia, S. (2017). Unmodified electroconvulsive therapy: Concerns about reporting in a retrospective study. *Indian Journal of Psychiatry, 59*(1), 125–126.

Asokan, T. V. (2014). Forensic psychiatry in India: The road ahead. *Indian Journal of Psychiatry, 56*(2), 121–127.

Balhara, Y. P., & Mathur, S. (2012). ECT prohibition for children and adolescents in Mental Health Care Act of India: A step in the right direction??? *Journal of ECT, 28*(1), 1–2.

Curley, A., Murphy, R., Plunkett, R., & Kelly, B. D. (2019a). Categorical mental capacity for treatment decisions among psychiatry inpatients in Ireland. *International Journal of Law and Psychiatry, 64,* 43–59.

Curley, A., Murphy, R., Plunkett, R., & Kelly, B. D. (2019b). Concordance of mental capacity assessments based on legal and clinical criteria: A cross-sectional study of psychiatry inpatients. *Psychiatry Research, 276,* 160–166.

Duffy, R. M., & Kelly, B. D. (2015). Psychiatric assessment and treatment of survivors of torture. *Advances in Psychiatric Treatment, 21*(2), 106–115.

Duffy, R. M., & Kelly, B. D. (2017a). Concordance of the Indian Mental Healthcare Act, 2017 with the World Health Organization's Checklist on Mental Health Legislation. *International Journal of Mental Health Systems, 11,* 48.

Duffy, R. M., & Kelly, B. D. (2017b). Rights, laws and tensions: A comparative analysis of the Convention on the Rights of Persons with Disabilities and the WHO Resource Book on Mental Health, Human Rights and Legislation. *International Journal of Law and Psychiatry, 54,* 26–35.

Duffy, R. M., & Kelly, B. D. (2017c). Privacy, confidentiality and carers: India's harmonization of national guidelines and international mental health law. *Ethics, Medicine and Public Health, 3*(1), 98–106.

Duffy, R. M., & Kelly, B. D. (2019). The right to mental healthcare: India moves forward. *British Journal of Psychiatry, 214*(2), 59–60.

Duffy, R. M., Gulati, G., Paralikar, V., Kasar, N., Goyal, N., Desousa, A., et al. (2019). A focus group study of Indian psychiatrists' views on electroconvulsive therapy under India's Mental Healthcare Act 2017: 'the ground reality is different'. *Indian Journal of Psychological Medicine, 41,* 507–515.

Grover, S., Varadharajan, N., & Avasthi, A. (2017). A qualitative study of experience of parents of adolescents who received ECT. *Asian Journal of Psychiatry, 30,* 109–113.

Gururaj, G., Varghese, M., Benegal, V., Rao, G. N., Pathak, K., Singh, L. K., et al. (2016). *National Mental Health Survey of India, 2015–16: Prevalence, patterns and outcomes (NIMHANS publication no. 129).* Bengaluru: National Institute of Mental Health and Neuro Sciences.

Kelly, B. D. (2011). Mental health legislation and human rights in England, Wales and the Republic of Ireland. *International Journal of Law and Psychiatry, 34*(6), 439–454.

Kelly, B. D. (2016). *Mental illness, human rights and the law.* London: RCPsych Publications.

Lepping, P., Stanly, T., & Turner, J. (2015). Systematic review on the prevalence of lack of capacity in medical and psychiatric settings. *Clinical Medicine, 15*(4), 337–343.

Mandarelli, G., Carabellese, F., Parmigiani, G., Bernardini, F., Pauselli, L., Quartesan, R., et al. (2018). Treatment decision-making capacity in non-consensual psychiatric treatment: A multicentre study. *Epidemiology and Psychiatric Sciences, 27*(5), 492–499.

Murphy, R., Fleming, S., Curley, A., Duffy, R. M., & Kelly, B. D. (2018). Who can decide? Prevalence of mental incapacity for treatment decisions in medical and surgical hospital inpatients in Ireland. *QJM, 111*(12), 881–885.

Patel, V., Xiao, S., Chen, H., Hanna, F., Jotheeswaran, A. T., Luo, D., et al. (2016). The magnitude of and health system responses to the mental health treatment gap in adults in India and China. *Lancet, 388*(10063), 3074–3084.
Ray, A. K. (2016). How bad was unmodified electroconvulsive therapy? A retrospective study. *Indian Journal of Psychiatry, 58*(2), 212–215.
Rugkåsa, J. (2016). Effectiveness of community treatment orders: The international evidence. *Canadian Journal of Psychiatry, 61*(1), 15–24.
Sen, A. (2009). *The idea of justice*. London: Allen Lane.
Shorter, E. (1997). *A history of psychiatry: From the era of the asylum to the age of Prozac*. New York: Wiley.
United Nations. (2006). *Convention on the rights of persons with disabilities*. New York: United Nations. Retrieved June 1, 2019, from https://www.un.org/development/desa/disabilities/convention-on-the-rights-of-persons-with-disabilities/convention-on-the-rights-of-persons-with-disabilities-2.html.
United Nations Economic and Social Council. (1985). *Siracusa principles on the limitation and Derogation Provisions in the International Covenant on Civil and Political Rights*. Geneva: United Nations.
World Health Organization. (1992). *International classification of mental and behavioural disorders*. Geneva: World Health Organization.
World Health Organization. (2005). *WHO resource book on mental health, human rights and legislation*. Geneva: World Health Organization.
World Health Organization. (2019). WHO Mental Health Gap Action Programme (mhGAP). Retrieved May 12, 2019, from https://www.who.int/mental_health/mhgap/en/.

# Chapter 8
# Incorporation of the United Nations' Convention on the Rights of Persons with Disabilities into Indian Law Through the Rights of Persons with Disabilities Act, 2016 and the Mental Healthcare Act, 2017

## 8.1 Introduction

The United Nations' (UN) *Convention on the Rights of Persons with Disabilities* (CRPD) (UN 2006) was drafted between 2002 and 2006 and opened for signature in 2007. The convention seeks to drive change in disability and mental health legislation globally (Harpur 2012), shifting emphasis towards person-centred, rights-based law (Duffy and Kelly 2017a). The CRPD applies existing human rights in the context of people with disabilities, with the goal of facilitating equal inclusion and minimizing stigma.

Many factors contribute to the potential impact of the CRPD. First, extensive input was received from organizations which represent the interests of people with disabilities in developing the CRPD (Schulze 2010). Second, as of 2019, there are over 160 signatories to the convention. Third, the CRPD's broad definition of disability has provided many parties with motivation to back the CRPD:

> Persons with disabilities include those who have long-term physical, mental, intellectual or sensory impairments which in interaction with various barriers may hinder their full and effective participation in society on an equal basis with others (Article 1).

The CRPD comprises a Preamble and 50 articles. Articles 1–4 address definitions, purpose and principles. Articles 5–30 describe specific civil and social rights which the CRPD aims to protect. Articles 31–50 describe the practicalities of implementations, reporting and the role of the Committee on the Rights of Persons with Disabilities. Articles 5–18 primarily focus on civil rights, whereas Articles 19–30 affirm social rights.

Few countries have embraced the CRPD with the enthusiasm of India—at least in theory. India's Rights of Persons with Disabilities Act, 2016 (RPWDA) and Mental Healthcare Act, 2017 (MHCA) are pioneering in that they are explicitly written to comply with the CRPD. The incorporation of International law into domestic law can be a very complex procedure, however, and different countries have used a variety of methods to realize this. These can be broadly categorized as direct and indirect methods (Mullan 2012).



R. M. Duffy and B. D. Kelly, *India's Mental Healthcare Act, 2017*,
https://doi.org/10.1007/978-981-15-5009-6_8

Using a direct method, international legislation is given the force of law at a domestic level, whereas indirect incorporation uses the international legislation as an interpretive lens for domestic legislation. One of the complications with direct incorporation centres on clarifying what, precisely, is being incorporated into domestic law. In the case of the CRPD, the role of the UN Committee on the Rights of Persons with Disabilities is one such consideration. This Committee plays a key role in interpreting the CRPD, so a direct incorporation of the entire CRPD could potentially lead to an external agency determining, or at least substantially shaping, domestic legislation.

The Preambles of both the RPWDA and MHCA suggest indirect incorporation of the CRPD into both pieces of legislation. This stops short of giving the CRPD full legal effect in India but still accords considerable weight to the convention. Much of the content of these two Acts is therefore written to give direct effect to many of the individual components of the CRPD. Section 96 of the RPWDA makes it clear that the CRPD-informed RPWDA sits on a par with other Indian legislation, whereas the MHCA is more robust and accords itself over-riding priority in respect of other Indian laws (Section 120).

This chapter examines how the RPWDA and the MHCA give effect to the specific components of the CRPD in Indian legislation. Policy and other legislation are also mentioned where relevant, but their examination has not been exhaustive. For each article and sub-article of the CRPD, we identify and examine relevant sections of the RPWDA and MHCA. This chapter focuses on Articles 5–30 of the CRPD which provide rights to people with disabilities. Articles 1–4 are more general in nature, and Articles 31–50 relate primarily administrative and procedural issues, so these are not examined in the same fashion here.

Assessment of concordance with the CRPD can be complex. Some of the articles of the CRPD can appear mutually inconsistent, especially where there is internal conflict and a balancing or weighting of rights is required (Duffy and Kelly 2017b). Consequently, we have not made a simplistic or binary judgement on whether or not each CRPD article is adequately addressed in the Indian legislation, but we have, rather, highlighted and discussed key issues relating to each statement. This analysis adopts a black-letter approach (i.e. it is concerned with the legislation as it is written) as matters concerning funding, policy, resources and realization are not the primary focus of this chapter (although these are discussed to a certain extent here and elsewhere).

While just and progressive laws do not necessarily produce a just and progressive society, it is essential that any attempt a creating such a society is underpinned by well-formed legislation. It should be noted that there are numerous examples of legislation not being followed in relation to people with disabilities (Delhi Commission for Protection of Child Rights 2010), and these matters, too, necessitate examination in their own right, but they are outside the scope of this chapter.

## 8.2 Concordance with the United Nations' Convention on the Rights of Persons with Disabilities

### *8.2.1 Article 5: Equality and Non-discrimination*

Sections of the RPWDA and the MHCA that relate to Article 5 of the CRPD are summarized in Table 8.1. Both the MHCA and the RPWDA do much to promote equality. The Preamble of the RPWDA, in line with the CRPD, makes non-discrimination one of the core principles for the empowerment of persons with disabilities. Discrimination is given a very broad definition in the RPWDA:

> 'Discrimination' in relation to disability, means any distinction, exclusion, restriction on the basis of disability which [has] the purpose or effect of impairing or nullifying the recognition, enjoyment or exercise on an equal basis with others of all human rights and fundamental freedoms in the political, economic, social, cultural, civil or any other field and includes all forms of discrimination and denial of reasonable accommodation (Section 2(h)).

'Barrier' is also defined in very broad terms:

> 'Barrier' means any factor including communicational, cultural, economic, environmental, institutional, political, social, attitudinal or structural factors which hampers the full and effective participation of persons with disabilities in society (Section 2(c)).

The RPWDA then prohibits discrimination on the basis of disability, albeit with a caveat:

> No person with disability shall be discriminated on the ground of disability, unless it is shown that the impugned act or omission is a proportionate means of achieving a legitimate aim (Section 3(3)).

The term 'legitimate aim' is not defined, and this leaves a large margin for potentially legal discrimination, although the legislation goes on to articulate specific prohibitions on discrimination in access to justice (Section 12(1)); property ownership, finance and control of financial affairs (Section 13(1)); educational institutions (Section 16(i)); and employment in government institutions (Section 20(1)). The government also has a broad duty to ensure 'reasonable accommodation for persons with disabilities' (Section 3(5)):

> 'Reasonable accommodation' means necessary and appropriate modification and adjustments, without imposing a disproportionate or undue burden in a particular case, to ensure to persons with disabilities the enjoyment or exercise of rights equally with others (Section 2(y)).

Again, the caveat ('without imposing a disproportionate or undue burden') is not defined and thus creates a potentially significant loophole. Even so, both the Central and State Advisory Boards on Disability have clear roles in ensuring accessibility and reasonable accommodation (Sections 65(1)) and 71(2)(e)), and hopefully this will facilitate realization of Article 5.3 of the CRPD ('reasonable accommodation'), further supported by the RPWDA's inclusion of 'denial of reasonable accommodation' in its definition of 'discrimination' (Section 2(h)). Additional legal protections

**Table 8.1** Incorporation of Article 5 of the Convention on the Rights of Persons with Disabilities ('Equality and non-discrimination') into Indian law through the Rights of Persons with Disabilities Act, 2016 and Mental Healthcare Act, 2017

| Article of the CRPD | Abridged description of CRPD article and sub-articles | Key sections in the RPWDA | Key sections in the MHCA | Notes |
|---|---|---|---|---|
| 5 | Equality and non-discrimination | 2(h), 3, 13 | 18(2, 8), 21 | – |
| 5.1 | Equality before and under the law and non-discriminatory entitlement to the equal protection and benefit of the law | 13(2) | 4, 14(9) | Potential for loss of capacity under the MHCA |
| 5.2 | Prohibition of all discrimination on the basis of disability and guarantee of legal protection against discrimination | Preamble, 3, 84, 85, 89–95 | 18(2, 8), 21, 27, 107–109 | |
| 5.3 | The state's role to ensure that reasonable accommodation is provided to eliminate discrimination | 2(h, y), 3(5), 65(2)(e), 71(2)(e) | 4(2), 18(2), 22(1)(d) | Large exemptions relating to accommodations |
| 5.4 | Measures to accelerate equality shall not be considered discrimination. | Not addressed | Not addressed | The existence of the MHCA and the RPWDA are an acknowledgment of this |

*Notes*
*CRPD* Convention on the Rights of Persons with Disabilities
*RPWDA* Rights of Persons with Disabilities Act, 2016
*MHCA* Mental Healthcare Act, 2017

are provided by the establishment of a 'Special Court' and 'Special Public Prosecutor' (Chapter XIII) (although their scope and admissibility criteria will need careful evaluation) and the Act's specification of offences and penalties (Chapter XVI).

The MHCA directly addresses equality for people with mental illness in comparison to people with physical illness, prohibiting discrimination in mental healthcare on the basis of 'gender, sex, sexual orientation, religion, culture, caste, social or political beliefs, class or disability' (Section 21(a)). Section 18(2) affirms the 'right to access mental healthcare and treatment' without discrimination in a fashion similar to Section 21, but with the additional prohibition of discrimination on 'any other basis'. The MHCA, however, addresses equality *only* in terms of healthcare provision. Addressing discrimination and equality more broadly is left to the RPWDA.

Sections 4 and 14(9) of the MHCA discuss capacity, which has strong implications for equality before the law, but the MHCA considers *only* capacity to make 'mental healthcare decisions'. Additional legal protection against discrimination in relation to mental healthcare is provided in Section 27, which entitles a person with mental illness to free legal services to exercise their rights under the Act. Further protection from discrimination could be realized through Sections 107–109 which deal with offences and penalties. The MHCA does not, however, mention 'reasonable accommodation', although Sections 4(2) and 22(1)(d) promote the use of appropriate language and aids to enhance understanding, while Section 18(2) states that 'mental healthcare and treatment' shall be 'accessible'.

Despite these significant measures to increase equality, it is arguable that the very existence of law that applies to certain people (e.g. those with mental health problems or disabilities) but not to others is intrinsically discriminatory (Szmukler and Bach 2015). The same rationale could, however, be used to call the entire CRPD into question as it sets existing human rights standards in the very specific context of people with disabilities (Duffy and Kelly 2017a). This issue is, however, addressed in Article 5.4 of the CRPD which states that 'specific measures which are necessary to accelerate or achieve de facto equality of persons with disabilities shall not be considered discrimination under the terms of the present Convention'. The very existence of the RPWDA and the MHCA indicate that Indian legislators agree that steps to accelerate equality do not amount to discrimination.

### *8.2.2 Article 6: Women with Disabilities*

Sections of the RPWDA and the MHCA that relate to Article 6 of the CRPD are summarized in Table 8.2. The RPWDA specifies 'equality between men and women' as a principle in its Preamble (g). Section 4(1) states that 'Government and the local authorities shall take measures to ensure that the women and children with disabilities enjoy their rights equally with others'; this aligns closely with Article 6.1 of the CRPD.

This is very positive, although the implications of Section 4(1) are so broad that more specific additional legislation or comprehensive policy would also be of great assistance. Such measures are mostly absent from the RPWDA itself, although Section 24(2) gives consideration to gender in the creation of schemes to promote an adequate standard of living for people with disabilities; Section 24(3)(d) gives women with disabilities support to raise children; Section 25(2)(f) gives women with disabilities a right to perinatal care; Section 25(2)(k) provides for sexual and reproductive healthcare 'especially for women with disability'; Sections 37(a) and

**Table 8.2** Incorporation of Article 6 of the Convention on the Rights of Persons with Disabilities ('Women with disabilities') into Indian law through the Rights of Persons with Disabilities Act, 2016 and the Mental Healthcare Act, 2017

| Article of the CRPD | Abridged description of CRPD article and sub-articles | Key sections in the RPWDA | Key sections in the MHCA | Notes |
|---|---|---|---|---|
| 6 | Women with disabilities | Preamble, 4 | 18(2), 20(2)(h), 21(1)(a), 21(2–3), | General lack of specific provisions |
| 6.1 | States Parties will take measures to ensure that women and girls with disabilities have full and equal enjoyment of all human rights and fundamental freedoms | 4(1), 24(2), 24(3)(d), 25(2)(f, k), 37(a–b), 92(d) | 87(6), 89(9)(a) | – |
| 6.2 | States Parties shall take measures to ensure development, advancement and empowerment of women, to guarantee the human rights and fundamental freedoms | Not addressed | Not addressed | Absent from these two pieces of legislation |

*Notes*
*CRPD* Convention on the Rights of Persons with Disabilities
*RPWDA* Rights of Persons with Disabilities Act, 2016
*MHCA* Mental Healthcare Act, 2017

37(b) give women priority in land, housing and property schemes for people with disabilities; and Section 92(d) makes the sexual exploitation of a woman with disability an offence.

The MHCA explicitly protects women from discrimination in accessing (Section 18(2)) and receiving (Section 21(1)(a)) mental healthcare. However, it remains to be seen if advance directives and nominated representatives will do more to empower women or if issues relating to literacy and education will result in increased coercion. This potential limitation of rights through the adoption of rights-based legislation may be compounded if the legislation is applied in a system that can be patriarchal (Batra and Reio 2016).

Some provisions in the MHCA aim specifically to protect women and girls. For example, female minors with male nominated representatives require a female attendant (Section 87(6)); the supported admission of a female has to be reported to the local Mental Health Review Board in three days rather than the seven for adult males (Section 89(9)(a)); and women with children under the age of three years have a right to not be separated from their child during admission, as far as is possible and safe (Section 21(2–3)). However, the MHCA fails to comply with many important practical steps suggested by the *WHO Resource Book on Mental Health, Human Rights and Legislation* (WHO RB) (WHO 2005; Duffy and Kelly 2017c) including, for example, rights concerning privacy and guaranteeing single-sex sleeping facilities.

Overall, positive steps are taken in both the RPWDA and MHCA to protect women and girls, but more needs to be done to enhance the general development, advancement and empowerment of women with disabilities, as is called for in Article 6.2 of the CRPD. In 2018, India ranked 108 out of 149 countries in terms of gender equality and also had a high level of 'missing women' owing, in part, to gendered lack of access to healthcare (World Economic Forum 2018). In addition, failure to protect women with disabilities from discrimination in India leads to under reporting of sexual violence (Dawn 2014), exploitation and poverty (Poreddi et al. 2015), and impaired sexual and reproductive health (Dean et al. 2017). Specific legislation protecting women in institutions and protecting women with disabilities from domestic violence could do much more to further the rights of women with disabilities (National CRPD Coalition-India 2019).

In light of these considerations, a robust governmental response is merited. Improved data collection would also greatly enhance our understanding of the current situation; all state and national routine data relating to women could usefully be stratified based on whether they have a disability or not; and—likewise—all data relating to disability could be linked to data on gender. This is not always the case at present (National Disability Network & National Committee on the Rights of Persons with Disabilities 2017).

### *8.2.3 Article 7: Children with Disabilities*

Sections of the RPWDA and the MHCA that relate to Article 7 of the CRPD are summarized in Table 8.3. The RPWDA takes many steps to support the rights of children with disabilities. The Act's Preamble states one of the key principles of the RPWDA is 'respect for the evolving capacities of children with disabilities and respect for the right of children with disabilities to preserve their identities' (h). This statement, in combination with the provisions of Section 4 ('Women and children with disabilities'), addresses, at least in part, Article 7.3 of the CRPD, which states that:

> States Parties shall ensure that children with disabilities have the right to express their views freely on all matters affecting them, their views being given due weight in accordance with their age and maturity, on an equal basis with other children, and to be provided with disability and age-appropriate assistance to realize that right.

Article 7.1 of the CRPD requires states to 'take all necessary measures to ensure the full enjoyment by children with disabilities of all human rights and fundamental freedoms on an equal basis with other children'. This is reflected in the RPWDA which states that 'the appropriate Government and the local authorities shall take measures to ensure that the women and children with disabilities enjoy their rights equally with others' (Section 4(1)). In addition, the RPWDA provides specific protections for living with family in a home environment (Section 9), inclusive education (Sections 16–17, and 31(1)) and abandoned or orphaned children (Section 24(3)(b)), and also provides protection from sexual exploitation (Section 92(2)). These measures complement the extensive protections that exist elsewhere in both the Constitution of India and various policy documents (National CRPD Coalition-India 2019).

The RPWDA does not, however, adequately address Article 7.2 of the CRPD, which requires that 'in all actions concerning children with disabilities, the best interests of the child shall be a primary consideration'. The RPWDA mentions the 'best interest of the child' only once, and in a very specific context:

> No child with disability shall be separated from his or her parents on the ground of disability except on an order of competent court, if required, in the best interest of the child (Section 9(1)).

By contrast, in the MHCA 'the best interests of the child' is the underpinning principle for how a nominated representative to a minor should act (Section 15(2)(a)) and 'best interest' is a necessary motivation for the admission of a minor (Section 87(3)(b)).

The MHCA also takes many other steps to incorporate CRPD-based rights in relation to children (Sharma and Kommu 2019). It is, for example, necessary to exhaust community-based treatment options prior to the admission of a child (Section 87(3)(c–d)); this measure partly protects children's 'human rights and fundamental freedoms' in line with Article 7.1 of the CRPD. Section 87(8) of the RPWDA allows admissions of children to continue only with the permission of the nominated representative, and Section 87(4) ensures that children are accommodated separately from adults. Section 87(5) states that:

> The nominated representative or an attendant appointed by the nominated representative shall under all circumstances stay with the minor in the mental health establishment for the entire duration of the admission.

Section 95(1) of the RPWDA states that 'electroconvulsive therapy for minors' shall not be used, but Section 95(2) adds that 'if, in the opinion of psychiatrist in charge of a minor's treatment, electroconvulsive therapy is required, then, such treatment shall be done with the informed consent of the guardian and prior permission of the concerned [Mental Health Review] Board'.

Overall, while many of these measures clearly seek to protect the rights of minors with mental health needs, it is possible that they might also act as additional barriers to accessing healthcare under certain circumstances (Sharma and Kommu 2019). This has been raised in particular in relation to electroconvulsive therapy (Duffy et al. 2018, 2019). Access to all forms of mental healthcare is especially important issue for children and adolescents as they experience a significant treatment gap in India (Sharan and Kumar 2016; Siddeswara et al. 2018).

Section 87(3)(b) of the MHCA gives some weight to the views of the minor but stops short of the rights described in Article 7.3 of the CRPD, which recommends comprehensive evaluation of the views of the minor with consideration being given to their age and maturity and the provision of age-appropriate material to aid them. This relative lack of acknowledgement of the evolving capacity of the child is also seen in India's Juvenile Justice (Care and Protection of Children) Act, 2015 (National Disability Network and National Committee on the Rights of Persons with Disabilities 2017). Sharma and Kommu (2019) highlight how this is out of step with both international norms and modern understandings of adolescent development. They have also highlighted the difficult transition from the nominated representative holding all the power to individuals being able to make autonomous decisions upon turning 18.

As there are over eight million children with disabilities in India (Office of the Registrar General and Census Commissioner, India 2019), it is vital that they are given specific consideration in legislation. The definition of mental illness in Section 2(s) of the MHCA specifically excludes 'mental retardation' and, while these individuals' needs are somewhat addressed in the RPWDA, their exclusion from the MHCA may leave people with 'mental retardation', autism spectrum disorders and specific learning disabilities in a legal lacuna during times of acute need. This is particularly problematic in light of the uncertain relationship between limited guardianship in the RPWDA and the nominated representative in the MHCA (Sharma and Kommu 2019; Duffy and Kelly 2017c).

Other problems include the MHCA's failure to prescribe minimum standards for facilities to which children can be admitted (Sharma and Kommu 2019), which may allow violations of Article 7.1 of the CRPD (i.e. the requirement to 'ensure the full enjoyment by children with disabilities of all human rights and fundamental freedoms on an equal basis'). Sharma and Kommu (2019) also highlight the missed opportunity to advocate for and protect orphans with mental illnesses, children of people with mental illnesses and children in custodial institutions; these issues could be addressed outside of the MHCA, but—wherever they are addressed—they are vitally important in accordance with Article 7 of the CRPD.

Overall, both the RPWDA and the MHCA make many specific provisions for the protection of the rights of children with disabilities, but more could be done to enshrine 'best interests' as the guiding principle; greater consideration could be given to a transitional phase between ages 16 and 18, when additional rights and responsibilities are transferred from the guardian to the child; and more could be done to give the minor a voice in the decision-making process. With such high levels of deprivation among children in India (National Disability Network and National Committee on the Rights of Persons with Disabilities 2017), it is vitally important that

**Table 8.3** Incorporation of Article 7 of the Convention on the Rights of Persons with Disabilities ('Children with disabilities') into Indian law through the Rights of Persons with Disabilities Act, 2016, and the Mental Healthcare Act, 2017

| Article of the CRPD | Abridged description of CRPD article and sub-articles | Key sections in the RPWDA | Key sections in the MHCA | Notes |
|---|---|---|---|---|
| 7 | Children with disabilities | 4 | – | – |
| 7.1 | States Parties shall take all measures to ensure children with disabilities enjoy human rights and fundamental freedoms on an equal basis with other children | 4(1), 5(2)(b), 9, 16, 17, 24(3)(b), 31(1), 92(d) | – | Discrimination on the basis of age not explicitly prohibited |
| 7.2 | Concerning children with disabilities, the best interests of the child shall be a primary consideration | 9(1) | 15(2)(a), 87(3)(b) | Could be addressed in broader terms in the RPWDA |
| 7.3 | Children with disabilities have the right to express their views, their views being given due weight on an equal basis with other children, and to be provided assistance to realize that right | Preamble, 4(2) | 87(3)(b) | Not fully addressed in either the RPWDA or MHCA |

*Notes*
*CRPD* Convention on the Rights of Persons with Disabilities
*RPWDA* Rights of Persons with Disabilities Act, 2016
*MHCA* Mental Healthcare Act, 2017

children with disabilities are protected, and that relevant policies and programmes are inclusive in accommodating children with disabilities. Finally, it should be noted that age is not explicitly included as one of the grounds under which discrimination is prohibited in Section 21(1)(a) of the MHCA.

### 8.2.4 *Article 8: Awareness-Raising*

Sections of the RPWDA and the MHCA that relate to Article 8 of the CRPD are summarized in Table 8.4. Section 39 of the RPWDA addresses many of the elements of Article 8. Section 39(2) comprehensively addresses awareness relating to rights, dignity and the capabilities of persons with disabilities. These are very well covered, and careful consideration is given to practical steps that will aid realization of these provisions. Section 39(2)(d), for example, mandates the provision of 'orientation and sensitisation at the school, college, university and professional training level on the human condition of disability and the rights of persons with disabilities'.

All sections of Article 8.2 of the CRPD (which presents specific measures for awareness-raising) are well addressed in Section 39(2) of the RPWDA with the exception of the CRPD requirement for media to 'portray persons with disabilities in a manner consistent with the purpose of the present Convention'. The National CRPD Coalition-India (2019) highlights how the lack of legislation in this area effectively leaves private media companies unregulated in their stereotypical depiction of people with disabilities. A similar omission occurs in relation to the CRPD requirement to combat 'stereotypes, prejudices and harmful practices'. While the RPWDA promotes non-discrimination and inclusion in a general sense, it does not present explicit steps to tackle stigma, prejudice or stereotypes.

The MHCA by contrast directly addresses stigma in relation to mental illness (Section 30(b)). The MHCA also gives more general consideration to raising awareness of mental health issues and reducing stigma, although this is not considered in great detail in the legislation (Section 30).

The RPWDA gives special consideration to awareness campaigns for persons with disabilities above and beyond those considered in the CRPD. It proposes campaigns to 'protect persons with disabilities from all forms of abuse, violence and exploitation' (Section 7(1)) and promotes awareness about legal capacity (Section 15(1)). However, a broad interpretation of what constitutes harmful practice (addressed in Article 8.1 of the CRPD) may result in many of the provisions of the MHCA being perceived as in violation of the CRPD. These may include electroconvulsive therapy, supported admissions and treatments in emergency settings, all of which can occur under the MHCA. These are discussed in detail in Chap. 9 of this book.

Notwithstanding many of these generally positive measures, concerns have been raised about decreasing funding for awareness programmes in India (National CRPD Coalition-India 2019), translation of human rights information into state languages and provision of training in all 21 state languages (Disability Rights India Foundation, National Centre for Promotion of Employment for Disabled People & National Committee on the Rights of Persons with Disabilities 2018). The relevant programmes that are being rolled out, as directed by the legislation, are reported as being limited, often inadequate and highly heterogeneous (National Disability Network and National Committee on the Rights of Persons with Disabilities 2017). Clearly, while many strong measures exist in legislation, effective and equitable realization in practice is vital (see Chap. 11 of this book).

**Table 8.4** Incorporation of Article 8 of the Convention on the Rights of Persons with Disabilities ('Awareness-raising') into Indian law through the Rights of Persons with Disabilities Act, 2016 and the Mental Healthcare Act, 2017

| Article of the CRPD | Abridged description of CRPD article and sub-articles | Key sections in the RPWDA | Key sections in the MHCA | Notes |
|---|---|---|---|---|
| 8 | Awareness-raising | 39 | 30 | – |
| 8.1.a | States parties take measures to raise awareness throughout society, regarding persons with disabilities, to foster respect for rights and dignity | 39(2)(a) | 30(a) | – |
| 8.1.b | States parties take measures to combat stereotypes, prejudices and harmful practices relating to persons with disabilities | 39(2)(a) | 30(b) | Limited consideration in the RPWDA |
| 8.1.c | States parties take measures to promote awareness of the capabilities and contributions of persons with disabilities | 39(2)(b) | – | – |
| 8.2.a.i | Public awareness campaigns to nurture receptiveness to the rights of persons with disabilities | 7(1)(d), 15(1), 39 | – | – |
| 8.2.a.ii | Public awareness campaigns to promote positive perceptions and greater social awareness | 39 | – | – |

(continued)

**Table 8.4** (continued)

| Article of the CRPD | Abridged description of CRPD article and sub-articles | Key sections in the RPWDA | Key sections in the MHCA | Notes |
|---|---|---|---|---|
| 8.2.a.iii | Public awareness campaigns to promote recognition of skills, merits and abilities including in the workplace | 39(2)(b, e) | – | – |
| 8.2.b | Fostering an attitude of respect for the rights of persons with disabilities in the education system | 39(2)(c, f) | – | – |
| 8.2.c | Encouraging the media to portray persons with disabilities in a manner consistent with the Convention | 92(a) | 30(a) | Very limited |
| 8.2.d | Promoting awareness-training programmes regarding persons with disabilities and their rights | 7(1)(d), 15(1), 39 | 30 | – |

*Notes*
*CRPD* Convention on the Rights of Persons with Disabilities
*RPWDA* Rights of Persons with Disabilities Act, 2016
*MHCA* Mental Healthcare Act, 2017

### 8.2.5 *Article 9: Accessibility*

Sections of the RPWDA and the MHCA that relate to Article 9 of the CRPD are summarized in Table 8.5. In Article 9, accessibility refers 'to the physical environment, to transportation, to information and communications, including information and communications technologies and systems, and to other facilities and services open or provided to the public'. The RPWDA duly incorporates accessibility as a core principle in its Preamble (f). Many of the specifics of Article 9 are not included in the RPWDA, although Section 40 addresses this topic in a more general way:

> The Central Government shall, in consultation with the Chief Commissioner, formulate rules for persons with disabilities laying down the standards of accessibility for the physical

environment, transportation, information and communications, including appropriate technologies and systems, and other facilities and services provided to the public in urban and rural areas.

Infrastructural and physical entities are addressed in Sections 41, 44 and 46 of the RPWDA and, although many of these provisions are rather general, they do not include exemptions based on economic feasibility as many of the other parts of the RPWDA do. Sections 65(2)(e) and 71(2)(e) give the Central and State Advisory Boards on Disability a role in recommending steps to maximize accessibility. They also have a general role in monitoring the impacts of laws, policies and programmes (Sections 65(2)(f) and 71(2)(f)). This, however, does not relate directly to monitoring accessibility; additional provisions will be needed to ensure that this monitoring of accessibility aligns with necessary standards and guidelines.

The MHCA ensures access to mental health care and treatment (Chapter V) including making information easily understandable to people with disabilities (Section 4(2)). Notwithstanding these commitments, however, little has been achieved in these areas in recent years, and existing legislation is commonly ignored (National CRPD Coalition-India 2019). Even simple day-to-day tasks such as using public transport are greatly impacted by the failure to realize the provisions of the RPWDA (Alagappan et al. 2018). Significant budgetary provisions are required if existing legislative and policy commitments are to come to fruition (National Disability Network and National Committee on the Rights of Persons with Disabilities 2017). If both policy and legislation remain under-powered, other methods for implementing large-scale societal change will have to be explored.

**Table 8.5** Incorporation of Article 9 of the Convention on the Rights of Persons with Disabilities ('Accessibility') into Indian law through the Rights of Persons with Disabilities Act, 2016 and the Mental Healthcare Act, 2017

| Article of the CRPD | Abridged description of CRPD article and sub-articles | Key sections in the RPWDA | Key sections in the MHCA | Notes |
|---|---|---|---|---|
| 9 | Accessibility | Preamble, 40, 41, 42 | 18(2) | – |
| 9.1.a | The identification and elimination of barriers to accessibility regarding buildings, transportation and other facilities, including schools, housing, medical facilities and workplaces | 2(c, s), 20(2), 25(1)(b), 40, 41 | – | – |

(continued)

**Table 8.5** (continued)

| Article of the CRPD | Abridged description of CRPD article and sub-articles | Key sections in the RPWDA | Key sections in the MHCA | Notes |
|---|---|---|---|---|
| 9.1.b | The identification and elimination of barriers to accessibility regarding Information and communications | 2(c, s), 20(2) 42 | – | – |
| 9.2.a | States parties take measures to develop and monitor standards and guidelines for the accessibility of public services | 65(2)(f), 71(2)(f) | – | General provision |
| 9.2.b | States parties take measures to ensure private entities that offer public services take into account accessibility for persons with disabilities | 2(i), 40, 41(2), 44, 46 | – | – |
| 9.2.c | States parties take measures to provide training for stakeholders on accessibility issues | 47(1)(a, b) | – | General provision |
| 9.2.d | States parties take measures to provide signage in Braille and in easy-to-read forms in public buildings and facilities | 40, 41(1), 42, 44, 45, 46 | – | Hinges on what is developed by Section 40 |

(continued)

**Table 8.5** (continued)

| Article of the CRPD | Abridged description of CRPD article and sub-articles | Key sections in the RPWDA | Key sections in the MHCA | Notes |
|---|---|---|---|---|
| 9.2.e | States parties take measures to provide live assistance and intermediaries, to facilitate accessibility to public buildings and facilities | 40, 41(1)(a), 44, 45, 46 | – | – |
| 9.2.f | States parties take measures to promote assistance and support to persons with disabilities to access information | 2(f, n), 4(c), 40, 42, 65(2)(e), | 2(1)(i), 4(2), 22(1)(d) | – |
| 9.2.g | States parties take measures to promote access for persons with disabilities to new information and communications technologies | 2(f, n), 17(f), 29(g) | – | Multiple incentives to research but not specific to accessibility |
| 9.2.h | States parties take measures to promote the design, development, production and distribution of accessible information and communication technologies | 29(g), 43 | | |

*Notes*
*CRPD* Convention on the Rights of Persons with Disabilities
*RPWDA* Rights of Persons with Disabilities Act, 2016
*MHCA* Mental Healthcare Act, 2017

### 8.2.6 Article 10: Right to Life

Sections of the RPWDA and the MHCA that relate to Article 10 of the CRPD are summarized in Table 8.6. Article 10 requires States Parties to 'reaffirm that every human being has the inherent right to life and shall take all necessary measures to ensure its effective enjoyment by persons with disabilities on an equal basis with others'. The right to life is explicitly affirmed in Section 3(1) of the RPWDA but is not directly mentioned in the MHCA. The MHCA does permit legal provisions to protect life in emergency circumstances; this gives the right to life priority in emergency circumstances (Section 94(1)(a)). This balancing of rights in the MHCA will be discussed in Chap. 9.

The right to life is also affirmed in the Constitution of India which states that 'no person shall be deprived of his life or personal liberty except according to procedure established by law' (Article 21). Case law has demonstrated that the definition of 'life' in the Constitution is in line with what is intended in the CRPD; it does not just relate to life as the opposite to death but encompasses a right to a healthy life (Sunil Batra v. Delhi Administration, 1978 AIR 1675) and to enjoy human dignity (Maneka Gandhi v. Union of India, 1978 AIR 597, 1978 SCR (2) 621). As described in Francis Coralie v. Union Territory of Delhi (1981 AIR 746, 1981 SCR (2) 516):

> The right to live includes the right to live with human dignity and all that goes along with it, viz., the bare necessities of life such as adequate nutrition, clothing and shelter over the head and facilities for reading, writing and expressing oneself in diverse forms, freely moving about and mixing and mingling with fellow human beings and must include the right to basic necessities the basic necessities of life and also the right to carry on functions and activities as constitute the bare minimum expression of human self.

Despite the contents of Article 3(1) of the RPWDA, some commentators do not feel that the right to life is protected in the MHCA or the RPWDA (National Disability

**Table 8.6** Incorporation of Article 10 of the Convention on the Rights of Persons with Disabilities ('Right to life') into Indian law through the Rights of Persons with Disabilities Act, 2016 and the Mental Healthcare Act, 2017

| Article of the CRPD | Abridged description of CRPD article and sub-articles | Key sections in the RPWDA | Key sections in the MHCA | Notes |
|---|---|---|---|---|
| 10 | The right to life | 3(1) | 94(1)(a) | Article 21 of the Constitution of India also provides protection for the right to life |

*Notes*
*CRPD* Convention on the Rights of Persons with Disabilities
*RPWDA* Rights of Persons with Disabilities Act, 2016
*MHCA* Mental Healthcare Act, 2017

Network and National Committee on the Rights of Persons with Disabilities 2017; National CRPD Coalition-India 2019).

Affirming the right to life in the context of disability is important as there are many factors that reduce life expectancy in people with disabilities (Thomas and Barnes 2010). Affirming the right to life in the context of mental illness is also vital as the treatment gap for people with mental illness in India can be as high as 95% (Patel et al. 2016; Sagar et al. 2017). Even in countries with smaller treatment gaps, the life expectancy of people with mental illness is reduced by over ten years (Walker et al. 2015; Chang et al. 2011). While India's delay in large-scale deinstitutionalization may be negatively impacting the right to life (National CRPD Coalition-India 2019), Indian psychiatrists have expressed concerns that the provisions of the MHCA could create barriers in accessing mental healthcare and this, too, could limit the right to life (Duffy et al. 2018).

### *8.2.7 Article 11: Situations of Risk and Humanitarian Emergencies*

Sections of the RPWDA and the MHCA that relate to Article 11 of the CRPD are summarized in Table 8.7. Article 11 obliges states to take 'all necessary measures to ensure the protection and safety of persons with disabilities in situations of risk, including situations of armed conflict, humanitarian emergencies and the occurrence of natural disasters'.

**Table 8.7** Incorporation of Article 11 of the Convention on the Rights of Persons with Disabilities ('Situations of risk and humanitarian emergencies') into Indian law through the Rights of Persons with Disabilities Act, 2016 and the Mental Healthcare Act, 2017

| Article of the CRPD | Abridged description of CRPD article and sub-articles | Key sections in the RPWDA | Key sections in the MHCA | Notes |
|---|---|---|---|---|
| 11 | States party obliged to protect persons with disabilities in situations of risk, humanitarian emergencies and natural disasters | 8 | 94(4) | Additional consideration of psychosocial disability would be useful |

*Notes*
*CRPD* Convention on the Rights of Persons with Disabilities
*RPWDA* Rights of Persons with Disabilities Act, 2016
*MHCA* Mental Healthcare Act, 2017

This right is comprehensively addressed in Section 8 of the RPWDA. Section 8(1) affirms the general principles of Article 11, while Sections 8(2–4) consider practical implementation and the relationship of these measures to the Disaster Management Act, 2005. Section 8(4) even considers accessibility requirements during reconstruction following an armed conflict or natural disaster.

The MHCA, on the other hand, contains very limited consideration of disasters or humanitarian emergencies, just pointing out, for example, that these situations can lengthen the period of emergency treatment (Section 94(4)). This limited consideration is regrettable: psychosocial disabilities need particular consideration in the context of disasters and emergency situations because these conditions can limit access to treatment and precipitate new-onset illness (Amaddeo and Tansella 2012).

Finally, the consideration of disasters and humanitarian emergencies in the RPWDA is both complicated and compromised by the definition of disaster in the Disaster Management Act, 2005 which, some argue, refers to only natural disasters and excludes human conflicts (National CRPD Coalition-India 2019). Regrettably, routine data collected by India's National Disaster Management Authority is not stratified by disability status, so the magnitude of this issue is not clear (National Disability Network and National Committee on the Rights of Persons with Disabilities 2017). It is clear, however, that extensive additional training and planning will be needed to incorporate the needs of people with disabilities into disaster management plans in the future (Kett and van Ommeren 2009). Failure to support people with disabilities in emergency and disaster situations especially compromises their right to life because they experience higher rates of mortality in these circumstances compared to people without disabilities (Mace and Doyle 2017).

### 8.2.8 Article 12: Equal Recognition Before the Law

Sections of the RPWDA and the MHCA that relate to Article 12 of the CRPD are summarized in Table 8.8. Equal recognition before the law is a key component of the CRPD, and it is a major driving force for the reform of disability and mental health legislation. An exhaustive evaluation of the adherence of Indian legislation to Article 12 is a mammoth task and would require substantial input from multiple different specialities (Byrne et al. 2018). Here, we describe key pertinent issues that arise in relation to this right in the MHCA and the RPWDA.

The RPWDA affirms equal legal capacity for people with disabilities (Section 12(2)) and includes sub-sections on property, financial affairs and the nature of informal support arrangements (Section 13). Formalized support arrangements, in the form of limited guardianship, are addressed in Section 14. Some parties argue that limited guardianship is a violation of the CRPD (National CRPD Coalition-India 2019), but it could be in line with Article 12.4 of the CRPD if limits, protections and review mechanisms are described. This is the chief area of possible non-concordance with Article 12, although State Governments may provide further rules on this matter to remedy this (Section 101(2)(b)).

**Table 8.8** Incorporation of Article 12 of the Convention on the Rights of Persons with Disabilities ('Equal recognition before the law') into Indian law through the Rights of Persons with Disabilities Act, 2016 and the Mental Healthcare Act, 2017

| Article of the CRPD | Abridged description of CRPD article and sub-articles | Key sections in the RPWDA | Key sections in the MHCA | Notes |
|---|---|---|---|---|
| 12 | Equal recognition before the law | 13(2) | 4, 5, 14(9), 81 | – |
| 12.1 | Persons with disabilities have the right to recognition as persons before the law | 13(2) | 4(1) | Limitation in the MHCA |
| 12.2 | Persons with disabilities enjoy legal capacity on an equal basis with others | 13(2), 62(1)(b), 68(1)(b) | 4, 5(4) | Limiting the input of people found to be of 'unsound mind' |
| 12.3 | Access to support in exercising legal capacity | 14(1), 101(2)(b) | 4(2), 5–17 | Limited guardianship is poorly defined |
| 12.4 | Governmental provisions of safeguards to prevent abuse that relates to the exercise of legal capacity | 13(3), 13(5), 14(1) | 11(2)(a), 17(a), 22(1)(b), 89(1)(b), 89(8), 89(10), 90(13) | RPWDA has less provision for protections and review |
| 12.5 | The equal right of persons with disabilities to own or inherit property, to control their own financial affairs | 13(1, 3) | – | – |

*Notes*
*CRPD* Convention on the Rights of Persons with Disabilities
*RPWDA* Rights of Persons with Disabilities Act, 2016
*MHCA* Mental Healthcare Act, 2017

Another area in which the RPWDA deviates from the CRPD concerns membership of the State and Central Advisory Boards on Disability, as the RPWDA states that people declared by a court to be 'of unsound mind' are prohibited from being members of these boards (Sections 62(1)(b) and 68(1)(b)). These provisions actively call into question the capacity of people with psychosocial disability and appear quite inconsistent with the CRPD.

Turning to the MHCA, greater consideration is given to capacity in this piece of legislation compared to the RPWDA, possibly based on the idea that mental capacity can fluctuate substantially in people with psychosocial disabilities. This topic is often poorly addressed in mental health legislation. In its 'General Comment' on Article 12, the UN Committee on the Rights of Persons with Disabilities (2014) affirms that legal and mental capacity are distinct concepts. The MHCA, however, makes no overt distinction between these two forms of capacity. The MHCA protects an individual's 'capacity' once they can '(a) understand the information that is relevant to take a decision on the treatment'; '(b) appreciate any reasonably foreseeable consequence of a decision or lack of decision'; *and* (in its current draft the Act states 'or' but this is clearly a typographical error (Duffy and Kelly 2019a)); (c) 'communicate the decision' (Section 4(1)).

The MHCA affirms individuals' right to make healthcare choices 'perceived by others as inappropriate or wrong' (Section 4(3)) providing they have capacity. When people cease to have capacity, advance directives can come into force (Section 5(3)). A decision that a person lacks capacity needs to be reviewed every one to two weeks (Sections 89(8) and 90(13)), although this is not as rigorous as described by the CRPD (Article 12.4).

For the most part, these provisions seem to refer to *mental* capacity because they assume 'capacity' is dynamic and can be lost. *Legal* capacity appears to be addressed in Section 14(9), which states that 'all persons with mental illness shall have capacity to make mental health care or treatment decisions but may require varying levels of support'.

The MHCA does not provide any further detail on assessment of capacity but makes provision for an Expert Committee to prepare guidance (Section 81). The Draft Mental Healthcare Rules 2017 (Ministry of Health and Family Welfare 2017) also make reference to this Expert Group but add no additional information yet.

In the MHCA, two constructs support decision-making for people who require support in making decisions that relate to mental healthcare: the nominated representative (Chapter IV) and advance directive (Chapter III). The parallel construct of the nominated representative in the RPWDA is the limited guardian (Section 14). There is no mirror legislation providing advance directives in the RPWDA, and it is unclear how the limited guardian and the nominated representative relate to each other.

Several other provisions of the MHCA uphold Article 12.4 of the CRPD which requires states parties to 'ensure that all measures that relate to the exercise of legal capacity provide for appropriate and effective safeguards to prevent abuse in accordance with international human rights law'. A nominated representative must consider the 'current and past wishes, the life history, values, cultural background and the best interests of the person with mental illness' when fulfilling their duties (Section 17(a)), and a Mental Health Review Board can alter or cancel an advance directive if they feel coercion was used (Section 11(2)(a)). The MHCA principle of the least restrictive care option (Section 89(1)(b)) aligns with the CRPD's concept of proportionality. Overall, the provisions relating to nominated representatives in the MHCA are much more robust than those concerning limited guardianship in the RPWDA.

There is, however, a broader issue about the tension between legal capacity and *any* form of treatment without consent in the first place. The UN Committee on the Rights of Persons with Disabilities (2014) has been clear on this point:

> Forced treatment by psychiatric and other health and medical professionals is a violation of the right to equal recognition before the law and an infringement of the rights to personal integrity (Article 17); freedom from torture (Article 15); and freedom from violence, exploitation and abuse (Article 16). This practice denies the legal capacity of a person to choose medical treatment and is therefore a violation of Article 12 of the Convention (Paragraph 42).

In response to this position, some countries, such as the UK, are explicitly *not* attempting to adhere to the interpretation of the Committee (Independent Review of the Mental Health Act 1983 2018). India appears to be aligned with the UK rather than the Committee on this point.

Finally, taking an even broader view of the position of the mentally ill and disabled in India, it is worth noting that there are many discriminatory laws that do not provide equal recognition before the law (Cherian et al. 2013). Most of these laws are *not* in the process of being reformed and neither the MHCA nor the RPWDA will counteract them. Even so, while broader, multi-level reform of such other laws is awaited, many improvements could be expedited by robust, pragmatic applications of the MHCA and RPWDA.

### *8.2.9 Article 13: Access to Justice*

Sections of the RPWDA and the MHCA that relate to Article 13 of the CRPD are summarized in Table 8.9. These rights are primarily and comprehensively addressed in the RPWDA. The relevant protections are strengthened by the inclusion of 'access to justice' in the definition of 'public facilities and services' (Section 2(x)). The provisions described in Section 12 of the RPWDA ('Access to justice') appear to use key requirements of Article 13 of the CRPD, translate them into an Indian context and provide additional protections and supports for access. Section 27 of the MHCA provides people with mental illness with free legal services to exercise their rights under the MHCA.

Section 47(1)(a) of the RPWDA addresses training for those working in key fields, although prison staff are a notable omission. This is an important group in light of limited resources in prisons and high rates of incarceration among people with disabilities (Kallivayalil et al. 2009; Goyal et al. 2011). The MHCA also makes brief

**Table 8.9** Incorporation of Article 13 of the Convention on the Rights of Persons with Disabilities ('Access to justice') into Indian law through the Rights of Persons with Disabilities Act, 2016 and the Mental Healthcare Act, 2017

| Article of the CRPD | Abridged description of CRPD article and sub-articles | Key sections in the RPWDA | Key sections in the MHCA | Notes |
|---|---|---|---|---|
| 13 | Access to Justice | 2(x), 12 | 27 | – |
| 13.1 | Effective access to justice for persons with disabilities on an equal basis with others | 12 | 19(2), 27 | – |
| 13.2 | Appropriate training for those working in the field of administration of justice, including police and prison staff | 47(1)(a) | 30(c) | Prison staff omitted and police training could be expanded |

*Notes*
*CRPD* Convention on the Rights of Persons with Disabilities
*RPWDA* Rights of Persons with Disabilities Act, 2016
*MHCA* Mental Healthcare Act, 2017

mention of 'periodic sensitisation and awareness training on the issues under this Act' for 'appropriate Government officials including police officers and other officers of the appropriate Government' (Section 30(c)). Considering the significant role that such officers play in the MHCA (Sections 100 and 101), specific mental health training may be needed to promote meaningful access to justice for people with mental illnesses, especially as the accessibility of Indian courts for this group has been repeatedly called into question (National CRPD Coalition-India 2019; National Disability Network and National Committee on the Rights of Persons with Disabilities 2017).

### 8.2.10 Article 14: Liberty and Security of Person

Sections of the RPWDA and the MHCA that relate to Article 14 of the CRPD are summarized in Table 8.10. The Preamble (a) of the RPWDA states that the 'respect for inherent dignity, individual autonomy including the freedom to make one's own choices, and independence of persons' is a core principle of the Act. Section 3(4) states that 'no person shall be deprived of his or her personal liberty only on the

**Table 8.10** Incorporation of Article 14 of the Convention on the Rights of Persons with Disabilities ('Liberty and security of person') into Indian law through the Rights of Persons with Disabilities Act, 2016 and the Mental Healthcare Act, 2017

| Article of the CRPD | Abridged description of CRPD article and sub-articles | Key sections in the RPWDA | Key sections in the MHCA | Notes |
|---|---|---|---|---|
| 14 | Liberty and security of person | Preamble, 3(4) | 19(1) | – |
| 14.1.a | States Parties shall ensure persons with disabilities enjoy the right to liberty and security of person | Preamble, 3(4), 5 | 19, 89, 90, 94 | Possible violation in MHCA |
| 14.1.b | States Parties shall ensure persons with disabilities are not deprived of their liberty unlawfully; the existence of a disability shall not justify a deprivation of liberty | 3(4) | 3(4&5), 4, 19, 89, 90, 94 | Potential inconsistency as mental illness is part of the reason for treatment without consent |
| 14.2 | State parties shall ensure that if a person with disabilities is deprived of their liberty it is on an equal basis with others and that they receive reasonable accommodation | – | 4, 19, 89, 90, 94 | RPWDA gives no consideration to people deprived of their liberty; MHCA appears inconsistent with this |

*Notes*
*CRPD* Convention on the Rights of Persons with Disabilities
*RPWDA* Rights of Persons with Disabilities Act, 2016
*MHCA* Mental Healthcare Act, 2017

ground of disability'. Section 5 affirms the right to live in the community, which also supports liberty. The RPWDA, however, gives no particular consideration to people who are deprived of their liberty, despite this occurring in practice.

In the MHCA, Sections 89, 90 and 94 provide a legal framework for the treatment of people who lack capacity. Even so, Article 14 of the CRPD remains problematic for lawmakers writing mental health legislation because it addresses the right to liberty and security—a right that is curtailed or suspended during treatment without consent under mental health legislation. Article 14.1 of the CRPD states that 'the existence of a disability shall in no case justify a deprivation of liberty'. Consequently, the involuntary admission or treatment of a person on the grounds of mental illness can be seen as incompatible with the CRPD (Kelly 2014a). In India, Sections 3(4) and 3(5) of the MHCA prohibit deprivation of liberty *solely* on the grounds of a diagnosis or prior treatments; other requirements must be met. This, however, is *still* declared discriminatory by the Office of the UN High Commissioner for Human Rights (2009):

> Unlawful detention encompasses situations where the deprivation of liberty is grounded in the combination between a mental or intellectual disability and other elements such as dangerousness, or care and treatment. Since such measures are partly justified by the person's disability, they are to be considered discriminatory and in violation of the prohibition of deprivation of liberty on the grounds of disability, and the right to liberty on an equal basis with others prescribed by Article 14 (pp. 15–16).

The tensions inherent in this situation will be discussed in detail in Chap. 9.

### 8.2.11 Article 15: Freedom from Torture or Cruel, Inhuman or Degrading Treatment or Punishment

Sections of the RPWDA and the MHCA that relate to Article 15 of the CRPD are summarized in Table 8.11. Section 6 of the RPWDA provides protection from cruelty and inhuman treatment, including protection from research without 'free and informed consent'. General penalties and offences to deter people from maltreating people with disabilities are included in Chapters XVI of the RPWDA and XV of the MHCA.

Precisely what constitutes cruel and inhuman treatment is given greater consideration in the MHCA (Section 20). This provides explicit protections from cruel, inhuman and degrading treatment in mental health establishments. It provides rights to, *inter alia*, a safe and hygienic environment, adequate sanitary conditions, privacy, proper clothing and protection from physical, verbal, emotional and sexual abuse. Steps are taken to address some of the major human rights infringements often considered to be torture, including prohibition of unmodified electroconvulsive therapy (i.e. without anaesthetic) (Section 95(1)(a)), prohibition of seclusion or solitary confinement (Section 97(1)), and regulation and substantial limitation of physical restraint (Section 97), including banning restraint as a form of punishment or

**Table 8.11** Incorporation of Article 15 of the Convention on the Rights of Persons with Disabilities ('Freedom from torture or cruel, inhuman or degrading treatment or punishment') into Indian law through the Rights of Persons with Disabilities Act, 2016 and the Mental Healthcare Act, 2017

| Article of the CRPD | Abridged description of CRPD article and sub-articles | Key sections in the RPWDA | Key sections in the MHCA | Notes |
|---|---|---|---|---|
| 15 | Freedom from torture or cruel, inhuman or degrading treatment or punishment | 6 | 20 | – |
| 15.1 | No one shall be subjected to torture or to cruel, inhuman or degrading treatment or punishment, or non-consensual experimentation | 6 | 2(i), 17(k), 20, 89(7), 90(12), 95(2), 96, 97, | Treatment can be given without consent; modified electroconvulsive therapy is allowed |
| 15.2 | States Parties shall take all effective measures to prevent persons with disabilities from being subjected to torture or cruel, inhuman or degrading treatment or punishment | 89, 92, | 107–109 | Nothing directly penalizes torture or cruel, inhuman treatment |

*Notes*
*CRPD* Convention on the Rights of Persons with Disabilities
*RPWDA* Rights of Persons with Disabilities Act, 2016
*MHCA* Mental Healthcare Act, 2017

deterrent in any circumstance (Section 97(4)). The Act, however, permits modified electroconvulsive therapy (i.e. with anaesthetic), and the admission and treatment of persons without capacity—and these could be seen cruel or inhuman treatments owing to lack of consent in certain cases.

The MHCA addresses medical research in Section 99(1), which requires 'free and informed consent from all persons with mental illness for participating in any research involving interviewing the person or psychological, physical, chemical or medicinal interventions'. Section 99 legislates for research in non-protesting patients who lack capacity and provides for protection for people involved in such research. This may be seen as a deviation from a very literal reading of Article 15.1 of the CRPD which states that 'no one shall be subjected without his or her free consent to medical or scientific experimentation'.

If, however, people with impaired mental capacity are to receive treatment, it is vital that such treatments are based on evidence. Some of the necessary research cannot be performed on people with capacity (e.g. research into the conditions that cause the lack of mental capacity in the first place). Even so, the MHCA's facilitation of research might also be at odds with the RPWDA which states that 'no person with disability shall be a subject of any research' without 'his or her free and informed consent' (Section 6(2)). In addition, where a person lacks mental capacity in the context of a mental illness, and they have a nominated representative, that nominated representative can 'give or withhold consent for research' under the MHCA (Section 17(k)). Overall, however, and despite the inconsistencies between the MHCA, RPWDA and CRPD, it is important that there is provision to include people who cannot consent in medical research, although it is also vital that adequate protections are in place for this.

Finally, in relation to Article 15 of the CRPD, the monitoring of institutions is of particular relevance given the low standards seen in many reports, poor levels of record-keeping and increased numbers of deaths in institutions (National CRPD Coalition-India 2019). More comprehensive guidelines need to be developed and implemented in mental health establishments, some of which have been found to have inhuman and degrading conditions (Human Rights Watch 2014). In addition, while India is a signatory to the UN Convention against Torture and Other Cruel Inhuman or Degrading Treatment or Punishment ('Convention against Torture'), it has yet to ratify it; ratification would, hopefully, add urgency to addressing many of these matters in practice.

### *8.2.12 Article 16: Freedom from Exploitation, Violence and Abuse*

Sections of the RPWDA and the MHCA that relate to Article 16 of the CRPD are summarized in Table 8.12. The right to freedom from exploitation, violence and abuse is addressed in Section 7 of the RPWDA which outlines legal remedies, prevention, rehabilitation and the role of police. No mention is made of gender-based violence, as suggested in Article 16.1 of the CRPD. This is a significant omission in light of the high rates of intimate partner violence seen among people with disabilities (Brownridge 2006; Hughes et al. 2012).

Article 16.3 of the CRPD requires that all programmes that serve people with disabilities are monitored by independent authorities. Multiple bodies monitor services for people with disabilities under the RPWDA, including the Central Advisory Board on Disability (Section 65(2)(f)), State Advisory Board on Disability (Section 71(2)(f), the Chief Commissioner (Section 75(1)(h)) and the State Commissioner (Section 80(g)). This monitoring is not, however, independent and does not explicitly refer to protection from exploitation, violence and abuse.

Section 7(3) of the RPWDA outlines provisions for promoting the recovery of a person who has been the victim of such abuse, as required by Article 16.4 of the CRPD; these provisions include the rescue of the victim, rehabilitation, protection, financial support and free legal aid. In line with Article 16.5 of the CRPD,

**Table 8.12** Incorporation of Article 16 of the Convention on the Rights of Persons with Disabilities ('Freedom from exploitation, violence and abuse') into Indian law through the Rights of Persons with Disabilities Act, 2016 and the Mental Healthcare Act, 2017

| Article of the CRPD | Abridged description of CRPD article and sub-articles | Key sections in the RPWDA | Key sections in the MHCA | Notes |
|---|---|---|---|---|
| 16 | Freedom from exploitation, violence and abuse | 7 | 20(2)(k) | – |
| 16.1 | States Parties shall take all appropriate measures to protect persons with disabilities from exploitation, violence and abuse, including gender-based aspects | 7 | 20(2)(f, k) | No mention is made of gender-based violence |
| 16.2 | States Parties shall take all appropriate measures to prevent all forms of exploitation, violence and abuse | 7 | 20(2)(f, k) | – |
| 16.3 | To prevent exploitation, violence and abuse, States Parties shall ensure that facilities and programmes designed to serve persons with disabilities are independently monitored | 65(2)(f), 71(2)(f), 80(g) | 68 | Not regularly monitored and not independent |

(continued)

**Table 8.12** (continued)

| Article of the CRPD | Abridged description of CRPD article and sub-articles | Key sections in the RPWDA | Key sections in the MHCA | Notes |
|---|---|---|---|---|
| 16.4 | The provision of physical, cognitive and psychological recovery, rehabilitation and social reintegration of persons with disabilities who become victims of any form of exploitation, violence or abuse | 7(1)(c) | – | Not as comprehensive as suggested |
| 16.5 | Legislation and policies to ensure that exploitation, violence and abuse against persons with disabilities are identified, investigated and prosecuted | 7(2–5), 89, 92 | – | Extensively developed |

*Notes*
*CRPD* Convention on the Rights of Persons with Disabilities
*RPWDA* Rights of Persons with Disabilities Act, 2016
*MHCA* Mental Healthcare Act, 2017

Sections 7(2)–7(5) of the RPWDA address the identification, investigation and prosecution of abuse. The MHCA presents protections from 'all forms of physical, verbal, emotional and sexual abuse', while the person is in a mental health establishment (Section 20(2)(k)).

Overall, the RPWDA and the MHCA cover many of the key requirements of Article 16 of the CRPD but could be improved by specific consideration of vulnerable groups such as children, women and the elderly, in greater accordance with the convention.

### 8.2.13 *Article 17: Protecting the Integrity of the Person*

Sections of the RPWDA and the MHCA that relate to Article 17 of the CPRD are summarized in Table 8.13. The right to integrity of the person is directly affirmed in Section 3(1) of the RPWDA which states that 'the appropriate Government shall ensure that the persons with disabilities enjoy the right to equality, life with dignity and respect for his or her integrity equally with others'. The Preamble (a) also states that a core principle of the Act is 'respect for inherent dignity, individual autonomy including the freedom to make one's own choices, and independence of persons'.

The MHCA makes no direct mention of physical or mental integrity, but it is hoped that the Act's paradigm shift from substitute decision-making to supported decision-making, through nominated representatives and advance directives, will help preserve integrity. The attempted shift from involuntary to 'supported' treatments may also help. Despite this change in terminology, however, treatment can still occur without consent. This may be seen to violate personal integrity, especially if integrity is conceptualized as something that is primarily realized or violated in the short term rather than the medium or long term.

This issue highlights the importance of defining 'integrity' clearly. Moving from India to Europe for the purpose of this discussion, Article 3 of the European Union's (EU) *Charter of Fundamental Rights* (2000) defines integrity in more detail, outlining, *inter alia*, three key principles (aside from issues relating to cloning, which do not arise here). First, free and informed consent of the person concerned is required, according to procedures laid down in law; in India, this is addressed in relation to research in Section 6(2)(i) of the RPWDA. While there are circumstances in which treatments can be administered without the person's consent under the MHCA, these are laid down in law and are thus concordant with the EU's definition of integrity. Second, the EU highlights prohibition of eugenic practices as another key principle of integrity; sterilization is prohibited in both the MHCA (Section 95(1)(c)) and

**Table 8.13** Incorporation of Article 17 of the Convention on the Rights of Persons with Disabilities ('Protecting the integrity of the person') into Indian law through the Rights of Persons with Disabilities Act, 2016 and the Mental Healthcare Act, 2017

| Article of the CRPD | Abridged description of CRPD article and sub-articles | Key sections in the RPWDA | Key sections in the MHCA | Notes |
|---|---|---|---|---|
| 17 | Protecting the integrity of the person | Preamble, 3(1) | 20(1) | Coercive practices in the MHCA may be inconsistent with this Article |

*Notes*
*CRPD* Convention on the Rights of Persons with Disabilities
*RPWDA* Rights of Persons with Disabilities Act, 2016
*MHCA* Mental Healthcare Act, 2017

RPWDA (Section 10(2)). Third, the EU lists prohibition on making the human body a source of financial gain as another principle of integrity; commercial surrogacy is banned in India's Surrogacy (Regulation) Bill, 2018 (Parry and Ghoshal 2018).

Finally, however, treatment without consent and coercive treatment practices permitted under the MHCA may call into question the concordance of the MHCA with this article of the CRPD. These issues will be discussed further in Chap. 9.

### *8.2.14 Article 18: Liberty of Movement and Nationality*

Sections of the RPWDA and the MHCA that relate to Article 18 of the CRPD are summarized in Table 8.14. The right to liberty of movement and nationality has been strikingly omitted from both the RPWDA and MHCA. The Preamble (a) of the RPWDA acknowledges 'inherent dignity, individual autonomy including the freedom to make one's own choices' and Section 2(h) defines discrimination in very broad terms. General rights relating to legal capacity (Section 13) and equality and non-discrimination (Section 3) might also go some way towards supporting liberty of movement and nationality. Outside of these very general provisions, however, there are no specific protections of the right to movement or nationality in either the RPWDA or MHCA.

Looking at other pieces of legislation, India's Registration of Births and Deaths Act, 1969 makes the registration of births and deaths compulsory across the country (Section 8) but makes no specific reference to disability. The national rate of birth registration is only 58% and is even lower among people with disabilities; 80% to 90% of children with disabilities do not have birth certificates, according to some reports (National Disability Network and National Committee on the Rights of Persons with Disabilities 2017).

The Passports Act of 1967 also makes no reference to disability or illness. Article 21 of the Constitution of India ('Protection of life and personal liberty') has been established to include the right to a passport (Satwant Singh Sawhney v. D. Ramarathnam, Assistant Passport Officer, 1967 AIR 1836, 1967 SCR (2) 52), but there is still remarkably little discussion of rights to travel, emigration or passports in the critical or academic literature relating to the RPWDA and MHCA. This is consistent with the broader fact that travel for disabled people is a very poorly researched field in general (Bauer 2018). Crossing international boarders, accessing passports and migration are much more complex than standard travel, and this makes the requirements for research and greater supports for rights in this area more urgent.

**Table 8.14** Incorporation of Article 18 of the Convention on the Rights of Persons with Disabilities ('Liberty of movement and nationality') into Indian law through the Rights of Persons with Disabilities Act, 2016 and the Mental Healthcare Act, 2017

| Article of the CRPD | Abridged description of CRPD article and sub-articles | Key sections in the RPWDA | Key sections in the MHCA | Notes |
|---|---|---|---|---|
| 18 | Liberty of movement and nationality | Preamble, 2(h), 3, 13 | – | Only the most general references that could be interpreted to apply to this area |
| 18.1.a | The right to acquire and change a nationality and not be deprived of nationality arbitrarily or on the basis of disability | – | – | |
| 18.1.b | The right to obtain, possess and utilize documentation of their nationality | – | – | |
| 18.1.c | The freedom to leave any country | – | – | |
| 18.1.d | The right to enter one's own country | – | – | |
| 18.2 | Children with disabilities shall be registered immediately after birth and have the right to a name, a nationality and to know and be cared for by their parents | – | – | |

*Notes*
*CRPD* Convention on the Rights of Persons with Disabilities
*RPWDA* Rights of Persons with Disabilities Act, 2016
*MHCA* Mental Healthcare Act, 2017

### 8.2.15 *Article 19: Living Independently and Being Included in the Community*

Sections of the RPWDA and the MHCA that relate to Article 19 of the CRPD are summarized in Table 8.15. The right to live independently and be included in the community is explicitly affirmed in the RPWDA which grants people with disabilities 'the right to live in the community' (Section 5). In addition, 'the appropriate Government

**Table 8.15** Incorporation of Article 19 of the Convention on the Rights of Persons with Disabilities ('Living independently and being included in the community') Article 19 Living independently and being included in the community into Indian law through the Rights of Persons with Disabilities Act, 2016 and the Mental Healthcare Act, 2017

| Article of the CRPD | Abridged description of CRPD article and sub-articles | Key sections in the RPWDA | Key sections in the MHCA | Notes |
|---|---|---|---|---|
| 19 | Living independently and being included in the community | 2(n, x), 5 | 19 | – |
| 19.a | The opportunity to choose the place of residence and where and with whom one lives | 5(2)(a) | 19 | MHCA is very general and implies people live with families |
| 19.b | Persons with disabilities have access to a range of in-home, residential and other community support services | 5(2)(b) | 19(2, 3) | – |
| 19.c | Community services and facilities for the general population are available on an equal basis to persons with disabilities | 3, 40, 45(2), 46 | – | General provisions only |

*Notes*
*CRPD* Convention on the Rights of Persons with Disabilities
*RPWDA* Rights of Persons with Disabilities Act, 2016
*MHCA* Mental Healthcare Act, 2017

shall endeavour that the persons with disabilities are (a) not obliged to live in any particular living arrangement; and (b) given access to a range of in-house, residential and other community support services, including personal assistance necessary to support living with due regard to age and gender' (Section 5(2)).

The CRPD requirement for community services and facilities to be available on an equal basis to persons with disabilities is partly addressed. Some clarity is provided by the RPWDA's definitions of 'information and communication technology' (Section 2(n)) and 'public facilities and services' (Section 2(x)), but, despite these helpful definitions, the term 'public facilities and services' is not used elsewhere in the Act. Nonetheless, the RPWDA promotes equality, non-discrimination (Section 3) and accessibility, including access to 'facilities and services provided to the public in urban and rural areas' (Section 40) and public service buildings (Sections 45 and 46).

Community-based independent living is explicitly affirmed for people with mental illness in the MHCA (Section 19). Some of these provisions provide less flexibility than suggested in Article 19 of the CRPD, as the normative emphasis of the MHCA is on living with the family:

> Where it is not possible for a mentally ill person to live with his family or relatives, or where a mentally ill person has been abandoned by his family or relatives, the appropriate Government shall provide support as appropriate including legal aid and to facilitate exercising his right to family home and living in the family home (Section 19(2)).

This section of the MHCA implies that the family home is the primary or default option for accommodation outside of hospital, and this could be perceived as a forced living arrangement.

Community treatment of mental illness has a limited history in India as large-scale psychiatric hospitals have traditionally received most funding and the majority of patients. Community-based interventions remain underfunded and poorly developed in many areas (Gururaj et al. 2016; Murthy et al. 2017). Community-based rehabilitation for disabilities has been in place since the late 1970s, but services are often sparse and face significant challenges (Kumar et al. 2012). They are hampered by a lack of statistical information and a paucity of resources, and their impact is further limited by isolation from other related governmental departments (e.g. education, employment). The National Disability Network and National Committee on the Rights of Persons with Disabilities (2017) acknowledge that services to support independent living are almost non-existent. For these reasons, additional protections promoting community-based living would be welcome; neither the RPWDA nor MHCA is sufficient in this regard.

### *8.2.16 Article 20: Personal Mobility*

Sections of the RPWDA and the MHCA that relate to Article 20 of the CRPD are summarized in Table 8.16. Personal mobility gives people with disabilities substantial

**Table 8.16** Incorporation of Article 20 of the Convention on the Rights of Persons with Disabilities ('Personal mobility') into Indian law through the Rights of Persons with Disabilities Act, 2016 and the Mental Healthcare Act, 2017

| Article of the CRPD | Abridged description of CRPD article and sub-articles | Key sections in the RPWDA | Key sections in the MHCA | Notes |
|---|---|---|---|---|
| 20 | Personal mobility | 40, 41 | – | – |
| 20.a | Facilitating the personal mobility of persons with disabilities | 41 | – | Only relates to public transport |
| 20.b | Facilitating access by persons with disabilities to quality mobility aids, devices, assistive technologies and forms of live assistance and intermediaries | 41(2) | – | No mention of live assistance; limited consideration of other forms of assistance |
| 20.c | Providing training in mobility skills to persons with disabilities and to specialist staff | – | – | Only general comments |
| 20.d | Encouraging entities that produce mobility aids, devices and assistive technologies | 29(g), 30(3)(c), 41(2) | – | – |

*Notes*
*CRPD* Convention on the Rights of Persons with Disabilities
*RPWDA* Rights of Persons with Disabilities Act, 2016
*MHCA* Mental Healthcare Act, 2017

independence. This right is partly addressed in the RPWDA which provides access to transport for persons with disabilities (Sections 40 and 41). This includes providing facilities and enhancing accessibility at transport hubs and on public transport, retrofitting existing transport and improving the accessibility of roads. Section 41(2) directs the government to develop schemes to promote mobility at an affordable cost, consistent with Article 20 of the CRPD which requires states parties to encourage 'entities that produce mobility aids, devices and assistive technologies to take into account all aspects of mobility for persons with disabilities'.

These provisions in the RPWDA do not provide the degree of freedom envisaged in Article 20 but appear pragmatic and realistic. Some of the provisions come, however, with the caveat that they are to be implemented 'wherever technically feasible and safe for persons with disabilities, economically viable and without entailing major structural changes in design' (Section 41(1)(b)); this clause may limit impact. In addition, little consideration is given to personal mobility outside of *public* transport and the very general overall protections relating to accessibility discussed above. Nor does Section 41 overtly address 'assistive technologies and forms of live assistance and Intermediaries' or 'training in mobility skills', both of which are required by Article 20 of the CRPD.

Article 20 is a critically important article of the CRPD. The provision of mobility technology is often very limited in low- and middle-income countries, but when it is delivered it greatly enhances community participation (Jefferds et al. 2010). Additional research and services are especially needed to address hearing, communication and cognition-based difficulties, many of which impact substantially on mobility (Matter et al. 2017). Tangcharoensathien and colleagues (2018) describe many pervasive barriers to accessing assistive technologies in low- and middle-income countries, which need to be addressed. Increasing uptake of mobility assistance will require greater availability of relevant programmes, raising awareness, consultation with device users and substantially increased funding and research. Additional consideration of this area in both policy and legislation could greatly promote the personal mobility of people with disabilities and—in many cases—transform their lives.

### *8.2.17 Article 21: Freedom of Expression and Opinion, and Access to Information*

Sections of the RPWDA and the MHCA that relate to Article 21 of the CRPD are summarized in Table 8.17. The right to 'freedom of expression and opinion, including the freedom to seek, receive and impart information and ideas on an equal basis with others and through all forms of communication' is not comprehensively addressed in the RPWDA. There is limited mention of freedom of expression and opinion. Section 4(2) provides children with disabilities protection to express their views on all matters affecting them. For adults, no such specific protection is provided in the RPWDA, although provisions to ensure equality and non-discrimination

**Table 8.17** Incorporation of Article 21 of the Convention on the Rights of Persons with Disabilities ('Freedom of expression and opinion, and access to information') into Indian law through the Rights of Persons with Disabilities Act, 2016 and the Mental Healthcare Act, 2017

| Article of the CRPD | Abridged description of CRPD article and sub-articles | Key sections in the RPWDA | Key sections in the MHCA | Notes |
|---|---|---|---|---|
| 21 | Freedom of expression and opinion, and access to information | 2(c, f, n, x), 3(1), 4(2), 12(4)(a), 40, 42 | 4(2), 22(d) | Freedom of expression only discussed in relation to children |
| 21.a | Provision of information intended for the general public to persons with disabilities in accessible formats and technologies | 12(4)(a), 42 | – | – |
| 21.b | Accepting and facilitating the use of sign languages, Braille, augmentative and alternative communication | 2(c, f), 16(v), 17(c, f), 40 | – | – |
| 21.c | Urging private entities to provide information and services in accessible and usable formats for persons with disabilities | 25(1)(b), 44, 46 | – | Limited provisions outside of buildings and healthcare |
| 21.d | Encouraging the mass media to make their services accessible to persons with disabilities | 29(h), 42 | – | Limited provisions |
| 21.e | Recognizing and promoting the use of sign languages | 29(h), 42(ii), 60(2)(q)(ix), | 4(2) | – |

*Notes*
*CRPD* Convention on the Rights of Persons with Disabilities
*RPWDA* Rights of Persons with Disabilities Act, 2016
*MHCA* Mental Healthcare Act, 2017

might grant protection in this area (Section 3(1)). In addition, definitions of 'barrier' (Section 2(c)), 'communication' (Section 2(f)), 'information and communication technology' (Section 2(n)) and 'public facilities and services' (Section 2(x)) implicitly and explicitly place effective communication at the centre of the RPWDA.

The right to *access* information is primarily addressed in Section 42 which directs that 'all contents available in audio, print and electronic media are in accessible format' and that all 'persons with disabilities have access to electronic media by providing audio description, sign language interpretation and close captioning'. The Internet is not directly mentioned in the RPWDA, but India's National Informatics Centre (2018) has released guidelines for Indian government websites that aim to make websites citizen-centred and improve accessibility for people with disabilities. Section 12(4)(a) of the RPWDA also places responsibility on government to ensure that all their public documents are in accessible formats, but there is no explicit time frame provided for this and nor is it clear if this will be cost-free for citizens (as required by Article 21 of the CRPD). Section 12(4)(c) addresses augmentative and alternative communication.

It remains to be seen if these provisions will be successful in encouraging private entities to provide information and services in an accessible manner. For example, Section 25(1) requires 'the appropriate Government and the local authorities' to 'take necessary measures for the persons with disabilities to provide...barrier-free access in all parts of Government and private hospitals and other healthcare institutions and centres'. Sections 44, 45 and 46 address this in relation to building work, consistent with Section 40 ('Accessibility'), but the effects of these measures also remain to be seen.

The broad definition of communication in Section 2(f) gives alternative modes of communication an important place in the legislation, and Section 2(c) highlights communicational factors as potential barriers for people with disabilities. Sections 16(v) and 17 facilitate the use of sign languages, Braille, and augmentative and alternative communication in educational settings. Similar protection is present outside of educational settings through Section 40 which includes 'communications' as part of 'accessibility'. The realization of this section is dependent on the Chief Commissioner's rules concerning accessibility for persons with disabilities.

In the MHCA, people with mental illness have a right to receive information in 'simple language, which such person understands or in sign language or visual aids or any other means to enable him to understand the information' (Section 4(2)). This right to information 'in a language and form that such person receiving the information can understand' is further emphasized in Section 22(d).

Sign language is well recognized in the RPWDA and the MHCA. The Indian Sign Language Research and Training Centre is represented on the Central Advisory Board (Section 60(2)(q)(ix) of the RPWDA). Consideration is given to the training of teachers who are qualified in sign language (Section 17(c)), which is also promoted in television programmes (Section 29(h)) and government information (Section 42(ii)). The role of sign language is also acknowledged in the MHCA (Section 4(2)).

### 8.2.18 Article 22: Respect for Privacy

Sections of the RPWDA and the MHCA that relate to Article 22 of the CRPD are summarized in Table 8.18. Limited consideration is given to the right to privacy in the RPWDA and MHCA. The RPWDA states that 'any person providing support to the person with disability shall not exercise undue influence and shall respect his or her autonomy, dignity and privacy' (Section 13(5)). There is no other mention of privacy in the RPWDA. The MHCA mentions privacy just once, where it grants people a right to privacy while in mental health establishments (Section 20(2)(d)).

The MHCA also considers confidentiality, although this is absent from the RPWDA and CRPD. The distinction between confidentiality and privacy is helpful and important in considering the rights of people with disabilities (Duffy and Kelly 2017d). The nominated representative system allows for confidentiality to be maintained concerning family if a person so desires. This protection is important in cultures with strong and powerful family structures, although it has proven unpopular

**Table 8.18** Incorporation of Article 22 of the Convention on the Rights of Persons with Disabilities ('Respect for privacy') into Indian law through the Rights of Persons with Disabilities Act, 2016 and the Mental Healthcare Act, 2017

<table>
<tr><th>Article of the CRPD</th><th>Abridged description of CRPD article and sub-articles</th><th>Key sections in the RPWDA</th><th>Key sections in the MHCA</th><th>Notes</th></tr>
<tr><td>22</td><td>Respect for privacy</td><td>13(1, 5)</td><td>20(2)(d), 23(1)</td><td rowspan="2">Only considered very generally in the RPWDA and only relates to while an inpatient in the MHCA</td></tr>
<tr><td>22.1</td><td>The right to freedom from interference with privacy, family, home or correspondence or other types of communication for people with disabilities</td><td>13(1, 5)</td><td>23(1), 24(2)</td></tr>
<tr><td>22.2</td><td>State protection of the privacy of personal, health and rehabilitation information of persons with disabilities</td><td></td><td>23(1), 24(2)</td><td>No mention of medical records in the RPWDA</td></tr>
</table>

*Notes*
*CRPD* Convention on the Rights of Persons with Disabilities
*RPWDA* Rights of Persons with Disabilities Act, 2016
*MHCA* Mental Healthcare Act, 2017

with some who are concerned that families might be excluded from care decisions (Duffy et al. 2018).

The slow pace of deinstitutionalisation is a concern for the realization of the right to privacy (Murthy et al. 2017). The development of community-based living and the supports suggested in the RPWDA and the MHCA would greatly benefit privacy. The RPWDA includes provisions regarding information-gathering, but clear data protection policies are also required. The RPWDA could be more explicit in its support of privacy and give specific consideration to confidentiality.

### *8.2.19 Article 23: Respect for Home and the Family*

Sections of the RPWDA and the MHCA that relate to Article 23 of the CRPD are summarized in Table 8.19. Many of the rights relating to respect for the home and family are addressed in the RPWDA and some receive specific consideration in the context of mental illness. There is general consideration of family life in both the RPWDA (Sections 9 and 10) and MHCA (Section 19). Both Acts directly address the protection of fertility (Section 10(2) of the RPWDA and Section 95(1)(c) of the MHCA) and community-based family life (Section 9 of the RPWDA and Section 19 of the MHCA), and both give consideration to the separation of children from parents (Section 9(1) of the RPWDA and Section 21(2) of the MHCA). The MHCA's consideration of separation relates only to periods of admission to mental health establishments and only to children under the age of three years.

The RPWDA presents no specific right to marry or found a family and, although this issue could be addressed under the broad heading of 'discrimination' (Section 2(h)), specific provisions might also need to be provided. Some consideration is given to the topic in Section 39(2)(c) which mandates awareness campaigns that 'foster respect for the decisions made by persons with disabilities on all matters related to family life, relationships, bearing and raising children'. Section 10(1) also gives rights to 'information regarding reproductive and family planning'. But neither of these measures meet the requirements of the CRPD in this regard.

Neither the RPWDA nor the MHCA gives parents with disabilities adequate entitlement to supports in parenting as suggested in Article 23.2 of the CRPD. The RPWDA hints at something that may, in time, provide some help in this area when it suggests that the government should develop schemes to provide caregivers with an allowance for assisting persons with disabilities with high support needs (Section 24(3)(i)). While this does not directly address parenting, it is a step in that direction, provided funding is adequate and definitions are clear. The RPWDA outlines children's rights to 'home and family' (Section 9) and 'community life' (Section 5), and 'to freely express their views on all matters affecting them' (Section 4(2)).

Many concerns have been raised about the role and rights of the broader family under the MHCA (Duffy et al. 2018) because, outside the role of the 'nominated representative', family now has more limited rights (Duffy and Kelly 2019a). The

**Table 8.19** Incorporation of Article 23 of the Convention on the Rights of Persons with Disabilities ('Respect for home and the family') into Indian law through the Rights of Persons with Disabilities Act, 2016 and the Mental Healthcare Act, 2017

| Article of the CRPD | Abridged description of CRPD article and sub-articles | Key sections in the RPWDA | Key sections in the MHCA | Notes |
|---|---|---|---|---|
| 23 | Respect for home and the family | 9, 10 | 19 | – |
| 23.1.a | The right of all persons with disabilities to marry and to found a family | 2(h), 39(2)(c) | – | The right to marry not explicitly included |
| 23.1.b | The rights of persons with disabilities to decide the number and spacing of their children | 10(1) | – | – |
| 23.1.c | The right to retain fertility | 10(2) | 95(1)(c) | – |
| 23.2 | Appropriate assistance to persons with disabilities in the performance of their child-rearing responsibilities | 24(3)(i) | – | No meaningful provisions |
| 23.3 | Children with disabilities have equal rights with respect to family life. | 4(1), 5, 9 | – | – |
| 23.4 | A child shall not be separated from his or her parents against their will, except in accordance with applicable law, and not on the basis of a disability | 9(1) | 21(2) | The MHCA considers separation during admission |

(continued)

**Table 8.19** (continued)

| Article of the CRPD | Abridged description of CRPD article and sub-articles | Key sections in the RPWDA | Key sections in the MHCA | Notes |
|---|---|---|---|---|
| 23.5 | Where necessary, provision of alternative care within the wider family or within the community in a family setting | 9(2) | 19 | – |

*Notes*
*CRPD* Convention on the Rights of Persons with Disabilities
*RPWDA* Rights of Persons with Disabilities Act, 2016
*MHCA* Mental Healthcare Act, 2017

lack of clear definitions in the area of limited guardianship (discussed above) could further diminish these rights and will need to be comprehensively addressed.

### *8.2.20 Article 24: Education*

Sections of the RPWDA and the MHCA that relate to Article 24 of the CRPD are summarized in Table 8.20. As in the case with most social rights, the right to education is primarily addressed in the RPWDA rather than the MHCA. The RPWDA supports an inclusive education system (Sections 2(m) and 16). The underpinning aims of education suggested in Article 24 of the CRPD (to develop human potential, dignity and self-worth) are not directly affirmed in the context of education in the RPWDA, but are addressed in general terms in its Preamble and Section 3 ('Equality and non-discrimination'). The aim of fostering personality, talents, creativity, and mental and physical abilities through the education system is generally not considered, although limited consideration is given to this in the context of culture and recreation (Section 29(a)) and sporting activities (Sections 30(2) and 30(3)). While effective participation in a free society does not directly underpin the provision on education, it is central to the RPWDA in an overall sense (Preamble and Sections 2(c) and 17(f)).

Free education is provided to all children from age six to 14 years under the Constitution of India (Article 21A) and the Rights of Children to Free and Compulsory Education Act, 2009. The RPDWA extends this to the age of 18 for people with benchmark disabilities (Sections 2(r) and 31) and gives schools a duty to provide reasonable accommodation (Sections 2(y), 3(5) and 16(iii)). General and individualized supports for effective education are elaborated in detail (Sections 16 and 17) and include teaching augmentative and alternative modes of communication

**Table 8.20** Incorporation of Article 24 of the Convention on the Rights of Persons with Disabilities ('Education') into Indian law through the Rights of Persons with Disabilities Act, 2016 and the Mental Healthcare Act, 2017

| Article of the CRPD | Abridged description of CRPD article and sub-articles | Key sections in the RPWDA | Key sections in the MHCA | Notes |
|---|---|---|---|---|
| 24 | Education | 2 (l, m, x), 16–23 | 20(2)(c) | – |
| 24.1.a | An inclusive education system directed to development of human potential and a sense of dignity and self-worth, and the strengthening of respect for human rights | Preamble, 2(m), 3, 16, 17(d) | – | – |
| 24.1.b | An inclusive education system directed to the development by persons with disabilities of their personality, talents, creativity, and mental and physical abilities | 29(a), 30(2), 30(3)(c) | – | Very limited and not in the context of education |
| 24.1.c | An inclusive education system directed at enabling persons with disabilities to participate effectively in a free society | Preamble, 2(c), 17(f) | – | A goal of the RPWDA in general (not just education) |
| 24.2.a | Persons with disabilities are not excluded from the general education system on the basis of disability | 2(m), 16, 17(d) | – | – |

(continued)

**Table 8.20** (continued)

| Article of the CRPD | Abridged description of CRPD article and sub-articles | Key sections in the RPWDA | Key sections in the MHCA | Notes |
|---|---|---|---|---|
| 24.2.b | Access to an inclusive, quality and free primary education and secondary education on an equal basis with others | 2(r), 31 | – | From age 15 to 18, only persons with benchmark disabilities are entitled to free education |
| 24.2.c | Reasonable accommodation of the individual's requirements | 2(y), 3(5), 16(iii) | – | – |
| 24.2.d | Support required, within the general education system, to facilitate their effective education | 16, 17 | – | Considerable detail present |
| 24.2.e | Individualized support measures provided in environments that maximize academic and social development | 16(iv) | – | – |
| 24.3.a | The state to facilitate the learning of augmentative and alternative modes of communication and orientation and mobility skills | 17(f), 41(2) | – | Only considers communication, not orientation or mobility |
| 24.3.b | The state to facilitate learning of sign language and the linguistic identity of the deaf community | 2(f), 17(c, f), 29(h), 42(ii), 60(2)(q)(ix) | – | – |
| 24.3.c | The state to ensure that the education of persons who are blind, deaf or deaf–blind, is delivered in the most appropriate modes for the individual | 16(v) | – | – |

(continued)

**Table 8.20** (continued)

| Article of the CRPD | Abridged description of CRPD article and sub-articles | Key sections in the RPWDA | Key sections in the MHCA | Notes |
|---|---|---|---|---|
| 24.4 | Employment of teachers who are qualified in sign language and/or Braille, and to train professionals and staff who work at all levels of education | 17(c) | – | – |
| 24.5 | The state to ensure that persons with disabilities are able to access tertiary education, vocational training and adult education, with reasonable accommodation | 18, 19 | – | – |

*Notes*
*CRPD* Convention on the Rights of Persons with Disabilities
*RPWDA* Rights of Persons with Disabilities Act, 2016
*MHCA* Mental Healthcare Act, 2017

(Section 17(f)), although insufficient consideration is given to orientation or mobility skills; Section 41(2) gives limited consideration to personal mobility but falls short of the requirements of Article 24 of the CRPD. Adult education is considered in Sections 18 and 19.

The RPWDA gives significant consideration to sign language; it facilitates the learning of sign language through training of teachers (Section 17(c)) and promotion of its use (Section 17(f)). The RPWDA also supports the linguistic identity of the deaf community through the promotion of sign language interpretation or sub-titles on television (Section 29(h)) and in media (Section 42(ii)), and by the inclusion of a member of the Indian Sign Language Research and Training Centre on the Central Advisory Board on Disability (Section 60(2)(q)(ix)).

Overall, while many of the CRPD requirements relating to education are addressed in the RPWDA, it is notable that people with disabilities in India, as is often the case elsewhere, have generally low levels of education (Mathias et al. 2018) and very limited employment options (Awasthi et al. 2017). The RPWDA represents a very progressive step in this area but its implementation will require close monitoring as the scale of the issue it seeks to address is enormous.

### *8.2.21 Article 25: Health*

Sections of the RPWDA and the MHCA that relate to Article 25 of the CRPD are summarized in Table 8.21. The RPWDA partly considers both the right to healthcare (Section 25) and the right to health rehabilitation (Section 27). The consideration of gender required by the CRPD is addressed in Section 24(2). In general terms, healthcare is included in 'public facilities and services' in the RPWDA (Section 2(x)), although this phrase is not directly mentioned in the rest of the Act.

The RPWDA defines buildings used for health services as public buildings (Section 2(w)) and defines 'discrimination' to include discrimination 'in the political, economic, social, cultural, civil or any other field' (Section 2(h)); although this does not explicitly mention health, health is, presumably, included. Sexual and reproductive healths are addressed in Section 25(2)(k). Taken together, these measures appear to prohibit discrimination in the area of healthcare on the grounds of disability. It would, however, be useful if this was stated more clearly in the legislation, owing not least to the already substantial barriers faced by people with disabilities accessing many public services, including healthcare.

The provision of the same quality of healthcare to persons with disabilities as to others is partly addressed in the RPWDA, and people with disabilities are given priority in attendance and treatment (Section 25). Consent in relation to research (Section 6(2)(i)), sterilization (Section 10(2)) and termination of pregnancy (Section 92(f)) receive particular attention. Consent to medical procedures in general is not discussed in the RPWDA, and this is of particular importance owing to the role of limited guardianship under the legislation (Section 14) (see above).

**Table 8.21** Incorporation of Article 25 of the Convention on the Rights of Persons with Disabilities ('Health') into Indian law through the Rights of Persons with Disabilities Act, 2016 and the Mental Healthcare Act, 2017

| Article of the CRPD | Abridged description of CRPD article and sub-articles | Key sections in the RPWDA | Key sections in the MHCA | Notes |
|---|---|---|---|---|
| 25 | Health | 2(h, w, x), 24(2–3), 25(1), 26, 27 | 18, 21(1) | – |
| 25.a | Provision of the same range, quality and standard of free or affordable health care to people with disabilities | 2(h, w, x), 25(1), | 18, 21(1) | MHCA relates only to access to *mental* healthcare |
| 25.b | Provision of health services needed by persons with disabilities specifically because of their disabilities | – | 18(1) | Not explicitly considered in the RPWDA |
| 25.c | Provision of health services as close as possible to people's own communities | 25(1)(a) | 18(4)(d) | – |
| 25.d | Require health professionals to provide care of the same quality to persons with disabilities as to others, including consent | 6(2)(i), 10(2), 25(1), 92(f) | 2(i), 14(3), 21, 24(1), 77(1), 86(5), 96(1)(a), 99(1) | Consent for medical procedures not addressed in RPWDA. The role of the limited guardian needs to be clarified here also |
| 25.e | Prohibit discrimination against persons with disabilities in the provision of health insurance and life insurance | 2(x), 24(3)(j), 26 | 21(4) | – |

(continued)

**Table 8.21** (continued)

| Article of the CRPD | Abridged description of CRPD article and sub-articles | Key sections in the RPWDA | Key sections in the MHCA | Notes |
|---|---|---|---|---|
| 25.f | Prevent discriminatory denial of health care or health services or food and fluids on the basis of disability | 2(h, x), 25, 92 | 21(1) | The right to healthcare is affirmed but the prohibition of deprivation is less robust |

*Notes*
*CRPD* Convention on the Rights of Persons with Disabilities
*RPWDA* of Persons with Disabilities Act, 2016
*MHCA* Mental Healthcare Act, 2017

The issue of consent among people with mental illness is dealt with in some detail in the MHCA. 'Informed consent' is defined in Section 2(i) and is required for appointing a nominated representative (Section 14(3)), release of information to the media (Section 24(1)), making application to Mental Health Review Boards (Section 77(1)), treatment of an independent patient (Section 86(5)), psychosurgery (Section 96(1)(a)) and research (Section 99(1)).

The right to receive healthcare as close as possible to one's own community (required in the CRPD) is addressed in both the RPWDA (Section 25(1)(a)) and MHCA (Section 18(5)(d)). The RPWDA does not, however, articulate an unambiguous right to health services needed by persons with disabilities specifically because of their disabilities. It could be argued that this is implicit in the text, but the level of healthcare currently received by people with disabilities in India would imply the need for explicit and emphatic legislative provisions (Gudlavalleti et al. 2014).

By way of contrast, the MHCA articulates an explicit right to mental healthcare: 'Every person shall have a right to access mental healthcare and treatment from mental health services run or funded by the appropriate Government' (Section 18(1)). Government must 'ensure that as a minimum, mental health services run or funded by Government shall be available in each district' (Section 18(5)). These are highly detailed and ambitious provisions, providing a justiciable right to mental healthcare in a country of over 1.3 billion people for whom there is no equivalent right to general healthcare (Duffy and Kelly 2019b). While this commitment would undoubtedly present a gargantuan resource and logistical challenge in any country, the issues it seeks to address exact enormous personal and economic costs (Gururaj et al. 2016), so any steps that might succeed in addressing these are well worth pursuing (Gupta and Basu 2016; Duffy and Kelly 2019c).

Finally, while there are hints about a possible right to healthcare in the RPWDA (Sections 2(h), 2(x) and 25), there is less clarity about a prohibition against deprivation of healthcare, as required by the CRPD. Section 92 of the RPWDA makes 'voluntarily or knowingly' denying food or fluids to a person with disability an offence, but this does not fully meet the CRPD requirement to 'prevent discriminatory denial of health care or health services or food and fluids on the basis of disability'.

### *8.2.22 Article 26: Habilitation and Rehabilitation*

Sections of the RPWDA and the MHCA that relate to Article 26 of the CRPD are summarized in Table 8.22. Rehabilitation is defined in Section 2(za) of the RPWDA, and the right is discussed in Section 27. In the MHCA, Section 2(o) defines mental healthcare as including rehabilitation, and there is further detail in Section 18(4). Rehabilitation is to be provided locally but there is no explicit requirement for early commencement or multidisciplinary assessment, as suggested by the CRPD.

The RPWDA emphasizes rehabilitation through the appointments it makes: the Central Government will nominate five experts in the field of disability and rehabilitation to the Central Advisory Board on Disability (Section 60(2)(r)(i)), and the Chief (Section 74(3)) and State Commissioners (Section 79(2)) for Persons with Disabilities must have 'special knowledge or practical experience in respect of matters relating to rehabilitation'.

While the word habilitation does not appear in the MHCA and appears only once in the RPWDA (in relation to 'research and development'; Section 28), many of the components of habilitation are present in both Acts. The Preamble of the RPWDA affirms 'individual autonomy including the freedom to make one's own choices, and independence of persons' (a), and 'full and effective participation and inclusion in society' (c). Across both Acts, education, vocational training, family life, capacity and expression are considered (see above) and, occupation, political and social life are also addressed (see below).

Section 27 of the RPWDA, which requires governments to develop rehabilitation policies and services, comes with the caveat that they must do so only 'within their economic capacity and development'. This greatly reduces the onus on governments, as 'economic capacity' is a decidedly vague concept; a proportion of budget to be spent on rehabilitation would be a much stronger provision. In India, only 5–10% of people have access to basic rehabilitation services (Mishra 2003). Much of the funding for this relies on non-governmental organizations, and the distribution of programmes is heterogeneous (National Disability Network and National Committee on the Rights of Persons with Disabilities 2017). Early intervention, in particular, is often absent (Kothari and Raturi 2014).

**Table 8.22** Incorporation of Article 26 of the Convention on the Rights of Persons with Disabilities ('Habilitation and rehabilitation') into Indian law through the Rights of Persons with Disabilities Act, 2016 and the Mental Healthcare Act, 2017

| Article of the CRPD | Abridged description of CRPD article and sub-articles | Key sections in the RPWDA | Key sections in the MHCA | Notes |
|---|---|---|---|---|
| 26 | Habilitation and rehabilitation | Preamble, 2(za), 7(1)(c) 27, 60(2)(r)(i), 74(3), 79(2) | 2(o), 18(4)(c, d) | – |
| 26.1.a | Habilitation and rehabilitation services to begin at the earliest possible stage, and to be based on multidisciplinary assessment | 38 | – | Very vague |
| 26.1.b | Habitation and rehabilitation services should be local, community-based and voluntary | 25(1)(a) | 17(e), 18(5)(c), 18(5)(d) | Provided for under the assumption that rehabilitation is part of healthcare |
| 26.2 | Promote the development of initial and continuing training for professionals and staff working in habilitation and rehabilitation | 27, 28, 47(1), 47(3) | 2(o), 31 | – |
| 26.3 | Promote the availability, knowledge and use of assistive devices and technologies, designed for persons with disabilities, as they relate to habilitation and rehabilitation | 28, 29(g), 30(3)(c), 40 | – | – |

*Notes*
*CRPD* Convention on the Rights of Persons with Disabilities
*RPWDA* Rights of Persons with Disabilities Act, 2016
*MHCA* Mental Healthcare Act, 2017

### 8.2.23 Article 27: Work and Employment

Sections of the RPWDA and the MHCA that relate to Article 27 of the CRPD are summarized in Table 8.23. The right to work and employment for people with disabilities is addressed predominantly in Chapter IV of the RPWDA ('Self-development and employment'). These Sections (19–23) make extensive use of the term 'establishment' which includes both government and private establishments (Section 2(i)). A private establishment is 'a company, firm, cooperative or other society, associations, trust, agency, institution, organisation, union, factory or such other establishment as the appropriate Government may, by notification, specify' (Section 2(v)). A government establishment is 'a corporation established by or under a Central Act or State Act or an authority or a body owned or controlled or aided by the Government or a local authority or a Government company as defined in Section 2 of the Companies Act, 2013 and includes a Department of the Government' (Section 2(k)).

The right to work is affirmed in general terms in government establishments, but while it is prohibited to discriminate against any person with disability in any matter relating to employment, an establishment may be exempt from this requirement depending on the type of work it carries out (Section 20(1)). In addition, while Article 27 of the CRPD requires specific prohibitions on discrimination relating to 'conditions of recruitment, hiring and employment, continuance of employment, career advancement and safe and healthy working conditions', most of these are not comprehensively addressed in the Indian legislation, with the exception of career advancement (Section 20(3) of the RPWDA).

The provisions for the private sector are more limited, although it is required to have an equal opportunity policy (Section 21). Incentives for the private sector are suggested in order to help ensure that at least 5% of their workforce is made up of persons with benchmark disabilities (Section 35).

The duty of the state to protect the rights of persons with disabilities to 'just and favourable conditions of work', required by the CRPD, receives no specific mention in the RPWDA. There are general protections relating to 'discrimination' (Section 2(h)), 'equality and non-discrimination' (Section 3), and weak provisions in Sections 20 and 35 (above), but these general protections are significantly undermined by Section 3(3) which permits discrimination on the grounds of disability if 'it is shown that the impugned act or omission is a proportionate means of achieving a legitimate aim'. In addition, there is no explicit mention of 'equal opportunities and equal remuneration for work of equal value, safe and healthy working conditions, including protection from harassment', as suggested in the CRPD. The RPWDA does make provisions for redressing grievances in government establishments (Section 23), but there is no specific mention of 'labour and trade union rights' (also required by the CRPD).

The RPWDA makes provision for technical and vocational guidance programmes, placement services, training and education for people with disabilities (Sections 18 and 19). Section 19, in particular, outlines practical steps to empower people with disabilities to become self-employed and gain work experience. These provisions,

**Table 8.23** Incorporation of Article 27 of the Convention on the Rights of Persons with Disabilities ('Work and employment') into Indian law through the Rights of Persons with Disabilities Act, 2016 and the Mental Healthcare Act, 2017

| Article of the CRPD | Abridged description of CRPD article and sub-articles | Key sections in the RPWDA | Key sections in the MHCA | Notes |
|---|---|---|---|---|
| 27 | Work and employment | 19, 20 | – | – |
| 27.1.a | States Parties shall prohibit discrimination on the basis of disability with regard to all matters concerning employment | 20, 35 | – | Public sector primarily |
| 27.1.b | States Parties shall protect the rights of persons with disabilities to just and favourable conditions of work | 2(h), 3, 20, 35 | – | Weakly protected, and Section 3(3) undermines it, although there are some protections for people with benchmark disabilities |
| 27.1.c | States Parties shall ensure that persons with disabilities are able to exercise their labour and trade union rights | | – | Absent from the legislation |
| 27.1.d | States Parties shall enable persons with disabilities to have access to technical and vocational guidance programmes, placement services and training | 18, 19, 39(d) | – | – |

(continued)

**Table 8.23** (continued)

| Article of the CRPD | Abridged description of CRPD article and sub-articles | Key sections in the RPWDA | Key sections in the MHCA | Notes |
|---|---|---|---|---|
| 27.1.e | States Parties shall promote employment opportunities and career advancement for persons with disabilities | 18, 19, 21 | – | – |
| 27.1.f | States Parties shall promote opportunities for self-employment, entrepreneurship, the development of cooperatives and starting one's own business | 19 | – | – |
| 27.1.g | States Parties shall employ persons with disabilities in the public sector | 20, 33, 34(1) | – | – |
| 27.1.h | States Parties shall promote the employment of persons with disabilities in the private sector through appropriate policies and measures | 35 | – | Persons with benchmark disabilities only |
| 27.1.i | States Parties shall ensure that reasonable accommodation is provided in the workplace | 2(h), 2(y), 3(5), 20(2), 65(2)(e), 71(2)(e) | – | – |
| 27.1.j | States Parties shall promote access to work experience | 19 | – | – |

(continued)

**Table 8.23** (continued)

| Article of the CRPD | Abridged description of CRPD article and sub-articles | Key sections in the RPWDA | Key sections in the MHCA | Notes |
|---|---|---|---|---|
| 27.1.k | States Parties shall promote vocational and professional rehabilitation, job retention and return-to-work programmes | 20(4) | – | – |
| 27.2 | States Parties shall ensure that persons with disabilities are not held in slavery or in servitude, and are protected, on an equal basis with others, from forced or compulsory labour | 7 | 20(2)(f) | More explicit legislation needed |

*Notes*
*CRPD* Convention on the Rights of Persons with Disabilities
*RPWDA* Rights of Persons with Disabilities Act, 2016
*MHCA* Mental Healthcare Act, 2017

combined with the RPWDA's equal opportunity measures (Section 21), enhance employment opportunities and career advancement for persons with disabilities. There are also provisions to promote the employment of people with benchmark disabilities in both the public (Sections 33 and 34(1)) and private (Section 35) sectors. Provisions are made for reasonable accommodation in government establishments (Section 20(2)) and protection of people who acquire a disability while working in government establishments (Section 20(4)).

The CRPD requirement for explicit protection from forced labour or slavery is very limited in the RPWDA. It could be argued that this is addressed through general protection from discrimination (Preamble (b)), the RPWDA's expansive definition of 'discrimination' (Section 2(h)) and the Act's general 'protection from abuse, violence and exploitation' (Section 7), combined with the prohibition of 'forced labour' in the Constitution of India (Article 23(1)). However, in light of the fact that India ranked 53rd out of 167 countries for the estimated prevalence of modern slavery (Walk Free Foundation 2018), and the vulnerable nature of some people with disabilities, specific legislation is required. The MHCA has a provision that deals with forced labour while an inpatient in a mental health establishment (Section 20(2)(f)) but does not expand on this in other contexts.

As is the case in other countries, low rates of employment are seen among people with disabilities in India, especially people with psychosocial disabilities whose rate of employment can be as low as 15% (National Disability Network and National Committee on the Rights of Persons with Disabilities 2017). Clearly, there is urgent need for robust legal provision in this area. Moreover, it is likely that, in the future, increasing levels of informal employment in India would necessitate additional protections over time.

### 8.2.24 Article 28: Adequate Standard of Living and Social Protection

Sections of the RPWDA and the MHCA that relate to Article 28 of the CRPD are summarized in Table 8.24. The right to an adequate standard of living and social protection is addressed in Section 24 of the RPWDA. The provision of good living conditions, sanitation, access to drinking water, financial support, disability pension and access to insurance schemes are all considered (Section 24(3)). Specific consideration is given to 'diversity of disability, gender, age, and socio-economic status' (Section 24(2)), and women (Section 24(3)(d)), as suggested in the CRPD. Section 24 also provides for community centres and facilities (Section 24(3)(a)), but not accommodation or homes, although people with benchmark disabilities have a 5% reservation in housing schemes and land allotment (Section 37). People with disabilities also get free local healthcare (as discussed above). The RPWDA provisions for social security are, however, accompanied by the caveat that each government must provide the specified supports 'within the limit of its economic capacity and development' (Section 24(1)). In addition, the RPWDA does not meet the CRPD specifications in terms of respite care, food and clothing.

Section 20 of the MHCA delivers some more clearly defined rights. When providing a right to protection from cruel, inhuman and degrading treatment, it also states that people 'have a right to live with dignity' (Section 20(1)), while in a mental health establishment, all people with mental illness have rights to, *inter alia*, a safe and hygienic environment, proper clothing, adequate provision for wholesome food, facilities for leisure, recreation, education and religious practices, and provision for preparing for living in the community (Section 20(2)). People with mental illness are also to be provided with halfway homes, sheltered accommodation and supported accommodation (Section 18(4)(b)).

Housing issues for people with disabilities are poorly addressed in India in general (National CRPD Coalition-India 2019). The Indira Gandhi Disability Pension is insufficient to cover food for a month, and over 95% of people with disabilities are ineligible or do not receive it (National Disability Network and National Committee on the Rights of Persons with Disabilities 2017). The age limit for social protection

**Table 8.24** Incorporation of Article 28 of the Convention on the Rights of Persons with Disabilities ('Adequate standard of living and social protection') into Indian law through the Rights of Persons with Disabilities Act, 2016 and the Mental Healthcare Act, 2017

| Article of the CRPD | Abridged description of CRPD article and sub-articles | Key sections in the RPWDA | Key sections in the MHCA | Notes |
|---|---|---|---|---|
| 28 | Adequate standard of living and social protection | 24 | 18–20 | – |
| 28.1 | The right of persons with disabilities to an adequate standard of living for themselves and their families, including adequate food, clothing and housing | 24, 37 | 18(11), 19(2), 20 | Food and clothing not mentioned in the RPWDA |
| 28.2.a | States Parties to ensure equal access by persons with disabilities to clean water services and other assistance for disability-related needs | 5(2)(b), 24(3)(e), 40, 46, 65(2)(e), 71(2)(e) | 18, 19, 20, 21 | – |
| 28.2.b | States Parties to ensure access to social protection programmes and poverty reduction programmes, in particular for women and girls with disabilities and older persons with disabilities | 17(g), 24(1), 24(3)(d, f, g), 37(b) | 18 | – |

(continued)

**Table 8.24** (continued)

| Article of the CRPD | Abridged description of CRPD article and sub-articles | Key sections in the RPWDA | Key sections in the MHCA | Notes |
|---|---|---|---|---|
| 28.2.c | States Parties to ensure access by persons with disabilities and their families living in poverty to assistance with disability-related expenses, including adequate training, counselling, financial assistance and respite care | 24(1), 24(3)(d, f, g), 25(1)(a), 31, 37(b) | 18 | No mention of respite |
| 28.2.d | States Parties to ensure access by persons with disabilities to public housing programmes | 37 | – | For benchmark disabilities |
| 28.2.e | States Parties ensure equal access by persons with disabilities to retirement benefits and programmes | 24(3)(g) | – | – |

*Notes*
*CRPD* Convention on the Rights of Persons with Disabilities
*RPWDA* Rights of Persons with Disabilities Act, 2016
*MHCA* Mental Healthcare Act, 2017

schemes needs to be removed; financial provisions should cover the cost of living as well as disability-related costs; and sanitation and water systems need to be given particular consideration for people with disabilities.

### 8.2.25 Article 29: Participation in Political and Public Life

Sections of the RPWDA and the MHCA that relate to Article 29 of the CRPD are summarized in Table 8.25. The two Acts contain limited consideration of the right to participate in political and public life, although some general protections could be inferred from the RPWDA's broad definitions of 'barrier' (Section 2(c)) and 'discrimination' (Section 2(h)). The RPWDA also states that 'the Election Commission of India and the State Election Commissions shall ensure that all polling stations are accessible to persons with disabilities and all materials related to the electoral process are easily understandable by and accessible to them' (Section 11). Provision is made for privacy and assistance by the Election Commission of India (2018), but neither the RPWDA nor MHCA articulate a right to vote for people with disabilities or mental illness.

This paucity of protection of political rights is of particular concern as people with disabilities have significantly reduced political participation which has proven resistant to legislative remedies in, for example, the US (Matsubayashi and Ueda 2014). The level of support available to people with disabilities, their residence type and their level of need all impact on voter participation (Friedman and Rizzolo 2017). Consequently, it is important that these factors would be considered in the RPWDA and MHCA.

Reduced participation of people with disability and mental illness in political life is an issue in many countries (Kelly 2014b; Bhugra et al. 2016; Kelly and Nash 2019), and, while neither the RPWDA nor the MHCA met the CRPD requirement to promote participation in public life, both include people with disabilities and mental illness on various decision-making boards, which is a good start. However, the exclusion of people of 'unsound mind' from the Central Advisory Board on Disability (Section 62(1)(b) of the RPWDA) and State Advisory Boards (Section 68(1)(b)) contrasts starkly with the CRPD. It is, however, encouraging that the protections offered by the Election Commission of India (2018) specifically apply to people with 'mental illness (psychosocial disabilities)'.

Other Indian legislation presents cause for concern too. The Representation of the People Act, 1950 disqualifies people who have been judged to be of 'unsound mind' from voting (Sections 16(1)(b) and 16(2)); some state laws bar persons of 'unsound mind' or who are 'deaf-mute' from running in elections (National CRPD Coalition-India 2019); and the Constitution of India cites 'unsoundness of mind' as possible grounds for disenfranchisement (Article 326). All need reform.

**Table 8.25** Incorporation of Article 29 of the Convention on the Rights of Persons with Disabilities ('Participation in political and public life') into Indian law through the Rights of Persons with Disabilities Act, 2016 and the Mental Healthcare Act, 2017

| Article of the CRPD | Abridged description of CRPD article and sub-articles | Key sections in the RPWDA | Key sections in the MHCA | Notes |
|---|---|---|---|---|
| 29 | Participation in political and public life | 2(c, h), 3(3), 11 | – | Representation of the People Act, 1950, Sections 16(1)(b) and 16(2) |
| 29.a.i | Ensuring that voting procedures, facilities and materials are appropriate, accessible and easy to understand and use | 11 | – | – |
| 29.a.ii | Protecting the right of persons with disabilities to vote by secret ballot, to stand for elections, to effectively hold office and perform all public functions | 2(c, h), 13(5), 20, 62(1)(b), 68(1)(b) | 3(3) | Limited cover of these rights; discrimination against people of 'unsound mind' |
| 29.a.iii | Guaranteeing free expression of the will of persons with disabilities as electors | 11, 14 | | Not clearly protected |
| 29.b.i | Encourage persons with disabilities to participate in non-governmental organizations and associations concerned with public and political life | 29(d) | 3(3) | Limited |
| 29.b.ii | Support the forming and joining of organizations of persons with disabilities to represent persons with disabilities at international, national, regional and local levels | 29(d) | 3(3) | Limited; contradicted by Sections 62(1)(b) and 68(1)(b) of the RPWDA |

*Notes*
*CRPD* Convention on the Rights of Persons with Disabilities
*RPWDA* Rights of Persons with Disabilities Act, 2016
*MHCA* Mental Healthcare Act, 2017

### 8.2.26 *Article 30: Participation in Cultural Life, Recreation, Leisure and Sport*

Sections of the RPWDA and the MHCA that relate to Article 30 of the CRPD are summarized in Table 8.26. Rights to participate in cultural life, recreation, leisure and sport are moderately well protected in the RPWDA. Access to cultural materials, media and locations is, arguably, dealt with in the Act's general non-discrimination provisions (Sections 2(h) and 3(3)). The legislation also defines a 'public building', which much be accessible (Section 45(1)), quite broadly, as 'a Government or private building, used or accessed by the public at large, including a building used for...public utilities, religious, cultural, leisure or recreational activities' (Section 2(w)); this essentially covers the activities described in this article of the CRPD. Leisure, recreational and cultural services are also considered as 'public facilities and services' in the RPWDA (Section 2(x)).

In addition to these general provisions, the RPWDA also addresses directly the rights of people with disabilities to participate in culture, recreation (Section 29) and sport (Section 30), and these provisions will hopefully be underpinned by Section 40, which promotes 'accessibility' more generally.

The RPWDA gives no consideration to the potential role of 'laws protecting intellectual property rights' as barriers to accessing cultural materials (as required by the CRPD), but this is addressed in the Copyright Act, 1957 (Section 31(B)), as amended by the Copyright (Amendment) Act, 2012 (Section 18) ('Compulsory licence for benefit of disabled'). Access to tourism is not explicitly considered in the RPWDA but is likely included under 'Culture and recreation' (Section 29).

**Table 8.26** Incorporation of Article 30 of the Convention on the Rights of Persons with Disabilities ('Participation in cultural life, recreation, leisure and sport') into Indian law through the Rights of Persons with Disabilities Act, 2016 and the Mental Healthcare Act, 2017

| Article of the CRPD | Abridged description of CRPD article and sub-articles | Key sections in the RPWDA | Key sections in the MHCA | Notes |
|---|---|---|---|---|
| 30 | Participation in cultural life, recreation, leisure and sport | 2(c, h, w, x), 3(3), 45 29, 30 | – | General provisions |
| 30.1.a | The state to ensure that persons with disabilities enjoy access to cultural materials in accessible formats | 2(c, h), 29(c, f), 42, 44, 45 | – | General provisions, mostly concerning accessibility |

(continued)

**Table 8.26** (continued)

| Article of the CRPD | Abridged description of CRPD article and sub-articles | Key sections in the RPWDA | Key sections in the MHCA | Notes |
|---|---|---|---|---|
| 30.1.b | The state to ensure that persons with disabilities have appropriate access to television programmes, films, theatre and other cultural activities | 29(a, c, f, g, h), 42(i, ii) | – | Only television explicitly mentioned |
| 30.1.c | The state to ensure that persons with disabilities have access to places for cultural performances or services, monuments and sites of national importance | 29, 30 | – | – |
| 30.2 | Persons with disabilities should have the opportunity to develop and utilize their creative, artistic and intellectual potential | 16–18, 29(a, c, d, e, f, g) | – | – |
| 30.3 | Laws protecting intellectual property rights must not constitute an unreasonable or discriminatory barrier to access by persons with disabilities to cultural materials | – | – | Copyright Act, 1957 (Section 31(B)) |

(continued)

**Table 8.26** (continued)

| Article of the CRPD | Abridged description of CRPD article and sub-articles | Key sections in the RPWDA | Key sections in the MHCA | Notes |
|---|---|---|---|---|
| 30.4 | Recognition and support of specific cultural and linguistic identity, including sign languages and deaf culture | 2(f), 17(c), 29(b, f), | – | – |
| 30.5.a | Encourage and promote the participation of persons with disabilities in mainstream sporting activities | 16(i), 30, 47(1)(e) | – | – |
| 30.5.b | Organize, develop and participate in disability-specific sporting and recreational activities | 30(3)(f) | – | – |
| 30.5.c | Access to sporting, recreational and tourism venues | 29(c, d, e, f, g), 41 | – | No mention of tourism |
| 30.5.d | Children with disabilities have access to participation in play, recreation and leisure and sporting activities including those activities in the school system | 16(I, ii), 30, 47(1)(e) | – | – |
| 30.5.e | Access to services from those involved in the organization of recreational, tourism, leisure and sporting activities | 29(c, d, e, f, g), 30, 44, 45(1) | – | – |

*Notes*
*CRPD* Convention on the Rights of Persons with Disabilities
*RPWDA* Rights of Persons with Disabilities Act, 2016
*MHCA* Mental Healthcare Act, 2017

## 8.3 Overall Assessment

The RPWDA and the MHCA have taken substantial steps to incorporate many elements of the CRPD. They have avoided the complexity of directly incorporating the entire CRPD as a whole, but have still addressed the great majority of its requirements. Certain areas could be improved, especially in the areas of political rights, liberty of movement and nationality. More consideration could be given to the practical implementation of many legal provisions, although this might better occur at policy level rather than in legislation. Careful monitoring of the realization of the RPWDA and MHCA will also be important, both for India and for other countries seeking to bring their legislation in line with the CRPD. Globally, India has taken the strongest steps to date towards legislating for social rights in this way, including, in particular, rights to free healthcare and rehabilitation.

As other countries seek to develop CRPD-concordant legislation, the RPWDA and MHCA provide a carefully considered example of what is possible. India has demonstrated that passing such legislation is feasible for a middle-income country. The use of legislation to promote social rights in this way is increasingly acknowledged as an important and often over-looked step (WHO 2017). However, legislation alone is rarely sufficient to realize social rights, especially in a context of limited resources, as is the case in India (National CRPD Coalition-India 2019; National Disability Network and National Committee on the Rights of Persons with Disabilities 2017). While it remains to be seen how the RPWDA and MHCA will be realized in practice, their very existence undoubtedly promotes the rights of people with disabilities and mental illnesses, and will play an important role in societal development over the years ahead.

Mental health legislation, such as the MHCA, always presents particular challenges in practice, especially in relation to mental capacity and involuntary treatment. Psychiatrists are well placed to promote the adoption and realization of such new legislation given their familiarity with utilizing legislation and navigating complex ethical issues (Duffy and Kelly 2017a). Probably, the most contentious Article in the CRPD in terms of mental health legislation is Article 12 which relates to 'Equal recognition before the law' (Freeman et al. 2015; Appelbaum 2019; Byrne et al. 2018). This will be considered in some detail next, in Chap. 9.

## References

Alagappan, V., Hefferan, A., & Parivallal, A. (2018). Exploring accessibility issues of a public building for the mobility impaired. Case study: Interstate bus terminal (ISBT), Vijayawada, India. *Disability and Rehabilitation. Assistive Technology, 13*(3), 271–279.

Amaddeo, F., & Tansella, M. (2012). Mental health, natural and human-made disasters: Lessons learnt and future needs. *Epidemiology and Psychiatric Sciences, 21*(1), 1–5.

Appelbaum, P. S. (2019). Saving the UN Convention on the Rights of Persons with Disabilities—From itself. *World Psychiatry, 18*(1), 1–2.

Awasthi, A., Pandey, C. M., Dubey, M., & Rastogi, S. (2017). Trends, prospects and deprivation index of disability in India: Evidences from census 2001 and 2011. *Disability and Health Journal, 10*(2), 247–256.

Batra, R., & Reio, T. G. (2016). Gender inequality issues in India. *Advances in Developing Human Resources, 18*(1), 88–101.

Bauer, I. (2018). When travel is a challenge: Travel medicine and the 'dis-abled' traveller. *Travel Medicine and Infectious Diseases, 22,* 66–72.

Bhugra, D., Pathare, S., Gosavi, C., Ventriglio, A., Torales, J., Castaldelli-Maia, J., et al. (2016). Mental illness and the right to vote: A review of legislation across the world. *International Review of Psychiatry, 28*(4), 395–399.

Brownridge, D. A. (2006). Partner violence against women with disabilities: Prevalence, risk, and explanations. *Violence Against Women, 12*(9), 805–822.

Byrne, M., White, B., & McDonald, F. (2018). A new tool to assess compliance of mental health laws with the Convention on the Rights of Persons with Disabilities. *International Journal of Law Psychiatry, 58,* 122–142.

Chang, C. K., Hayes, R. D., Perera, G., Broadbent, M. T., Fernandes, A. C., Lee, W. E., et al. (2011). Life expectancy at birth for people with serious mental illness and other major disorders from a secondary mental health care case register in London. *PLoS ONE, 6*(5), e19590.

Cherian, R., Davar, B., Gupta, S., Balasubramanian, M., Rajan, R., Valliappan, R., et al. (2013). *Legal capacity in national laws.* New Delhi: National Centre for Promotion of Employment for Disabled People and Inclusive Planet.

Dawn, R. (2014). 'Our lives, our identity': Women with disabilities in India. *Disability and Rehabilitation, 36*(21), 1768–1773.

Dean, L., Tolhurst, R., Khanna, R., & Jehan, K. (2017). 'You're disabled, why did you have sex in the first place?' An intersectional analysis of experiences of disabled women with regard to their sexual and reproductive health and rights in Gujarat State, India. *Global Health Action, 10*(suppl.2), 1290316.

Delhi Commission for Protection of Child Rights. (2010). *Report received in response to RTI enquiry vide letter no. 40/RTI/2/DD(FAS)/DSW/2008/8084 dated 10/08/08* and *A Report on the Visit (1.02.2010) of Asha Kiran Complex, Government of NCT of Delhi.* New Delhi: Delhi Commission for Protection of Child Rights.

Disability Rights India Foundation, National Centre for Promotion of Employment for Disabled People & National Committee on the Rights of Persons with Disabilities. (2018). *Two years of the RPWD Act 2016: Status of implementation in states and UTs of India.* New Delhi: Disability Rights India Foundation, National Centre for Promotion of Employment for Disabled People & National Committee on the Rights of Persons with Disabilities. Retrieved July 25, 2019, from http://www.ncpedp.org/sites/all/themes/marinelli/documents/Report_of_Status_of_RPWD_Act_Final.pdf.

Duffy, R. M., & Kelly, B. D. (2017a). Can psychiatry lead the way in legislating for health and wellbeing? *Irish Medical Journal, 110*(6), 591.

Duffy, R. M., & Kelly, B. D. (2017b). Rights, laws and tensions: A comparative analysis of the Convention on the Rights of Persons with Disabilities and the WHO Resource Book on Mental Health, Human Rights and Legislation. *International Journal of Law and Psychiatry, 54,* 26–35.

Duffy, R. M., & Kelly, B. D. (2017c). Concordance of the Indian Mental Healthcare Act, 2017 with the World Health Organization's Checklist on Mental Health Legislation. *International Journal of Mental Health Systems, 11,* 48.

Duffy, R. M., & Kelly, B. D. (2017d). Privacy, confidentiality and carers: India's harmonization of national guidelines and international mental health law. *Ethics, Medicine and Public Health, 3*(1), 98–106.

Duffy, R. M., & Kelly, B. D. (2019a). India's Mental Healthcare Act, 2017: Content, context, controversy. *International Journal of Law and Psychiatry, 62,* 169–178.

Duffy, R. M., & Kelly, B. D. (2019b). Global mental health. *Lancet, 394*(10193), 118–119.

Duffy, R. M., & Kelly, B. D. (2019c). The right to mental healthcare: India moves forward. *British Journal of Psychiatry, 214*(2), 59–60.

Duffy, R. M., Narayan, C. L., Goyal, N., & Kelly, B. D. (2018). New legislation, new frontiers: Indian psychiatrists' perspective of the mental healthcare act 2017 prior to implementation. *Indian Journal of Psychiatry, 60*(3), 351–354.

Duffy, R. M., Gulati, G., Paralikar, V., Kasar, N., Goyal, N., Desousa, A., et al. (2019). A focus group study of Indian psychiatrists' views on electroconvulsive therapy under India's Mental Healthcare Act 2017: 'the ground reality is different'. *Indian Journal of Psychological Medicine, 41,* 507–515.

Election Commission of India. (2018). *FAQs for voters with disabilities.* New Delhi: Election Commission of India. Retrieved July 25, 2019, from https://eci.gov.in/pwd/pwd-articles/faqs-for-voters-with-disabilities/faqs-for-voters-with-disabilities-r6/.

European Union. (2000). Charter of fundamental rights of the European Union. *Official Journal of the European Communities*, C364, 01. Retrieved July 28, 2019, from https://www.europarl.europa.eu/charter/pdf/text_en.pdf.

Freeman, M. C., Kolappa, K., de Almeida, J. M., Kleinman, A., Makhashvili, N., Phakathi, S., et al. (2015). Reversing hard won victories in the name of human rights: A critique of the General Comment on Article 12 of the UN Convention on the Rights of Persons with Disabilities. *Lancet Psychiatry, 2*(9), 844–850.

Friedman, C., & Rizzolo, M. C. (2017). Correlates of voting participation of people with intellectual and developmental disabilities. *Journal of Social Work in Disability and Rehabilitation, 16*(3–4), 347–360.

Goyal, S. K., Singh, P., Gargi, P. D., Goyal, S., & Garg, A. (2011). Psychiatric morbidity in prisoners. *Indian Journal of Psychiatry, 53*(3), 253–257.

Gudlavalleti, M. V., John, N., Allagh, K., Sagar, J., Kamalakannan, S., Ramachandra, S. S., et al. (2014). Access to health care and employment status of people with disabilities in South India, the SIDE (South India Disability Evidence) study. *BMC Public Health, 14,* 1125.

Gupta, N., & Basu D. (2016). The Mental Healthcare Bill 2016: Exotic in nature, quixotic in scope …but let's take the plunge, shall we? *National Medical Journal of India, 29*(6), 317–320.

Gururaj, G., Varghese, M., Benegal, V., Rao, G. N., Pathak, K., Singh, L. K., et al. (2016). *National Mental Health Survey of India, 2015–16: Prevalence, patterns and outcomes (NIMHANS publication no. 129).* Bengaluru: National Institute of Mental Health and Neuro Sciences. Retrieved August 7, 2019, from http://www.nimhans.ac.in/sites/default/files/u197/NMHS%20Report%20%28Prevalence%20patterns%20and%20outcomes%29%201.pdf.

Harpur, P. (2012). Embracing the new disability rights paradigm: The importance of the Convention on the Rights of Persons with Disabilities. *Disability & Society, 27*(1), 1–14.

Hughes, K., Bellis, M. A., Jones, L., Wood, S., Bates, G., Eckley, et al. (2012). Prevalence and risk of violence against adults with disabilities: Asystematic review and meta-analysis of observational studies. *Lancet, 379*(9826), 1621–1629.

Human Rights Watch. (2014). *'Treated worse than animals': Abuses against women and girls with psychosocial or intellectual disabilities in institutions in India.* New York: Human Rights Watch. Retrieved July 25, 2019, from https://www.hrw.org/report/2014/12/03/treated-worse-animals/abuses-against-women-and-girls-psychosocial-or-intellectual.

Independent Review of the Mental Health Act 1983. (2018). *Modernising the Mental Health Act: Increasing choice, reducing compulsion.* London: Gov.uk. Retrieved July 27, 2019, from https://assets.publishing.service.gov.uk/government/uploads/system/uploads/attachment_data/file/778897/Modernising_the_Mental_Health_Act_-_increasing_choice__reducing_compulsion.pdf.

Jefferds, A. N., Beyene, N. M., Upadhyay, N., Shoker, P., Pearlman, J. L., Cooper, R. A., et al. (2010). Current state of mobility technology provision in less-resourced countries. *Physical Medicine and Rehabilitation Clinics of North America, 21*(1), 221–242.

Kallivayalil, R. A., Trivedi, J. K., & Tripathi, A. (2009). Social factors and forensic psychiatry in India. *Current Opinion in Psychiatry, 22*(5), 482–487.

Kelly, B. D. (2014a). An end to psychiatric detention? Implications of the United Nations' Convention on the Rights of Persons with Disabilities. *British Journal of Psychiatry, 204*(3), 174–175.

Kelly, B. D. (2014b). Voting and mental illness: The silent constituency. *Irish Journal of Psychological Medicine, 31*(4), 225–227.

Kelly, B. D., & Nash, M. (2019). Voter participation among people attending mental health services in Ireland. *Irish Journal of Medical Science, 188*(3), 925–929.

Kett, M., & van Ommeren, M. (2009). Disability, conflict, and emergencies. *Lancet, 374*(9704), 1801–1803.

Kothari, J., & Raturi, R. (Eds.). (2014). *The right to health of persons with disabilities in India: Access to and non-discrimination in health care for persons with disabilities.* New Delhi: Human Rights Law Network. Retrieved July 25, 2019, from https://hrln.org/reporting_publications/the-right-to-health-of-persons-with-disabilities-in-india-access-to-and-non-discrimination-in-health-care-for-persons-with-disabilities/.

Kumar, S. G., Roy, G., & Kar, S. S. (2012). Disability and rehabilitation services in India: Issues and challenges. *Journal of Family Medicine and Primary Care, 1*(1), 69–73.

Mace, S. E., & Doyle, C. J. (2017). Patients with access and functional needs in a disaster. *Southern Medical Journal, 110*(8), 509–515.

Mathias, K., Pant, H., Marella, M., Singh, L., Murthy, G., & Grills, N. (2018). Multiple barriers to participation for people with psychosocial disability in Dehradun district, North India: A cross-sectional study. *British Medical Journal Open, 8*(2), e019443.

Matsubayashi, T., & Ueda, M. (2014). Disability and voting. *Disability and Health Journal, 7*(3), 285–291.

Matter, R., Harniss, M., Oderud, T., Borg, J., & Eide, A. H. (2017). Assistive technology in resource-limited environments: A scoping review. *Disability and Rehabilitation. Assistive Technology, 12*(2), 105–114.

Ministry of Health and Family Welfare. (2017). *Mental healthcare rules.* New Delhi: Ministry of Health and Family Welfare.

Mishra, S. (2003). Occupational therapy in community-based rehabilitation. *Indian Journal of Occupational Therapy, 35*(1), 13–16.

Mullan, G. (2012). Incorporation of the European Convention on Human Rights in Irish law. In B. Moriarty & E. Massa (Eds.), *Human rights law* (4th ed., pp. 80–96). Oxford: Oxford University Press and Law Society of Ireland.

Murthy, P., Isaac, M., & Dabholkar, H. (2017). Mental Hospitals in India in the 21st century: Transformation and relevance. *Epidemiology and Psychiatric Sciences, 26*(1), 10–15.

National CRPD Coalition-India. (2019). *CRPD alternate report for India.* Hyderabad: National CRPD Coalition-India. Retrieved July 25, 2019, from http://accessability.co.in/wp-content/uploads/2019/02/CRPD-Alternate-Report-for-India-1.pdf.

National Disability Network & National Committee on the Rights of Persons with Disabilities. (2017). *Parallel report of India on the Convention on the Rights of Persons with Disabilities.* New Delhi: National Committee on the Rights of Persons with Disabilities. Retrieved July 25, 2019, from https://www.ncpedp.org/sites/all/themes/marinelli/documents/DRAFT%20CRPD%20India%20Parallel%20Report%20(31st%20March%202017).pdf.

National Informatics Centre. (2018). *Guidelines for Indian government websites (revised edition, includes apps)* (2nd ed.). New Delhi: National Informatics Centre.

Office of the Registrar General and Census Commissioner, India. (2019). *Table C 20: Disabled population by type of disability, age and sex (Census 2011).* New Delhi: Ministry of Home Affairs, Government of India. Retrieved July 25, 2019, from http://www.censusindia.gov.in/2011census/C-series/c-20.html.

Parry, B., & Ghoshal, R. (2018). Regulation of surrogacy in India: Whenceforth now? *BMJ Global Health, 3*(5), e000986.

Patel, V., Xiao, S., Chen, H., Hanna, F., Jotheeswaran, A. T., Luo, D., et al. (2016). The magnitude of and health system responses to the mental health treatment gap in adults in India and China. *Lancet, 388*(10063), 3074–3084.

Poreddi, V., Ramachandra, Thimmaiah, R., & Math, S. B. (2015). Human rights violations among economically disadvantaged women with mental illness: An Indian perspective. *Indian Journal of Psychiatry, 57*(2), 174–180.

Sagar, R., Pattanayak, R. D., Chandrasekaran, R., Chaudhury, P. K., Deswal, B. S., Lenin Singh, R. K., et al. (2017). Twelve-month prevalence and treatment gap for common mental disorders: Findings from a large-scale epidemiological survey in India. *Indian Journal of Psychiatry, 59*(1), 46–55.

Schulze, M. (2010). *Understanding the UN Convention on the Rights of Persons with Disabilities* (3rd ed.). New York: Handicap International.

Sharan, P., & Kumar, S. (2016). Bridging the mental health gap in India: Issues and perspectives. In S. Malhotra & P. Santosh (Eds.), *Child and adolescent psychiatry: Asian perspectives* (pp. 463–478). New Delhi: Springer India.

Sharma, E., & Kommu, J. V. S. (2019). Mental Healthcare Act 2017, India: Child and adolescent perspectives. *Indian Journal of Psychiatry, 61*(10), S756–S762.

Siddeswara, B. L., Kattimani, S., & Seshadri, S. (2018). Mental health care act (MHCA) 2017: What child mental health professionals need to know? *Journal of Indian Association for Child and Adolescent Mental Health, 14*(3), 91–97.

Szmukler, G., & Bach, M. (2015). Mental health disabilities and human rights protections. *Global Mental Health, 2,* e20.

Tangcharoensathien, V., Witthayapipopsakul, W., Viriyathorn, S., & Patcharanarumol, W. (2018). Improving access to assistive technologies: Challenges and solutions in low- and middle-income countries. *WHO South-East Asia Journal of Public Health, 7*(2), 84–89.

Thomas, R., & Barnes, M. (2010). Life expectancy for people with disabilities. *NeuroRehabilitation, 27*(2), 201–209.

United Nations. (2006). *Convention on the rights of persons with disabilities.* New York: United Nations. Retrieved June 1, 2019, from https://www.un.org/development/desa/disabilities/convention-on-the-rights-of-persons-with-disabilities/convention-on-the-rights-of-persons-with-disabilities-2.html.

United Nations Committee on the Rights of Persons with Disabilities. (2014). *General comment No. 1: Article 12: Equal recognition before the law.* New York: United Nations. Retrieved July 25, 2019, from http://www.ohchr.org/EN/HRBodies/CRPD/Pages/GC.aspx.

United Nations High Commissioner for Human Rights. (2009). *Annual report of the United Nations High Commissioner for Human Rights and reports of the Office of the High Commissioner and the Secretary-General: Thematic Study by the Office of the United Nations High Commissioner for Human Rights on enhancing awareness and understanding of the Convention on the Rights of Persons with Disabilities (A/HRD/10/48).* New York: United Nations General Assembly. Retrieved July 25, 2019, from https://www2.ohchr.org/english/bodies/hrcouncil/docs/10session/A.HRC.10.48.pdf.

Walk Free Foundation. (2018). *The global slavery Index 2018.* Nedlands: Minderoo Foundation. Retrieved July 25, 2019, from https://www.globalslaveryindex.org/resources/downloads/.

Walker, E. R., McGee, R. E., & Druss, B. G. (2015). Mortality in mental disorders and global disease burden implications: A systematic review and meta-analysis. *JAMA Psychiatry, 72*(4), 334–341.

World Economic Forum. (2018). *The global gender gap report 2018.* Geneva: World Economic Forum.

World Health Organization. (2005). *WHO resource book on mental health, human rights and legislation.* Geneva: World Health Organization.

World Health Organization. (2017). *Advancing the right to health: The vital role of law.* Geneva: World Health Organization. Retrieved June 1, 2019, from https://www.who.int/gender-equity-rights/knowledge/advancing-the-right-to-health/en/.

# Chapter 9
# Compliance of India's Mental Healthcare Act, 2017 with the United Nations' Convention on the Rights of Persons with Disabilities

## 9.1 Introduction

India's Mental Healthcare Act, 2017 (MHCA) is a pioneering piece of mental health legislation owing to the fact that it was written with an explicit desire to bring India's mental health law into compliance with the United Nations' (UN) Convention on the Rights of Persons with Disabilities (CRPD) (UN 2006). Prior to the MHCA, Szmukler and Bach (2015) argued that no mental health legislation was fully compliant with the CRPD, suggesting that the two key issues limiting compliance related to capacity and involuntary treatment.

Assessment of compliance with the CRPD is complex. Some of the articles of the CRPD appear inconsistent with each other, and there are internal conflicts within the Convention that seem to require a balancing or weighing up of different rights (Duffy and Kelly 2017). As described in Chap. 8 of this book, the MHCA was highly influenced by the CRPD and addresses many of its articles directly. This chapter examines articles of the CRPD with which the MHCA is potentially non-compliant. These articles were identified in the 'black-letter analysis' presented in Chap. 8 and relate to capacity, involuntary treatment and various other areas of potentially significant non-compliance.

## 9.2 Capacity

Legal and mental capacity have been two of the most intensely debated topics in relation to the CRPD (Appelbaum 2019; Freeman et al. 2015; Szmukler 2019). They are of particular importance in relation to mental health where there is a greater propensity for a person's decision-making capacity to fluctuate within a relatively short time frame owing to an episode of illness. Historically, mental health legislation in many jurisdictions has provided for involuntary treatment and substitute decision-making under specific circumstances. The CRPD leads mental health legislation away from



R. M. Duffy and B. D. Kelly, *India's Mental Healthcare Act, 2017*,
https://doi.org/10.1007/978-981-15-5009-6_9

this paradigm towards a supported decision-making framework, especially through the provisions of Article 12 which protects equal recognition before the law. Article 12.2 requires that 'States Parties shall recognize that persons with disabilities enjoy legal capacity on an equal basis with others in all aspects of life'. Article 12 also shifts the response to impaired capacity from substitute decision-making to supported decision-making and replaces the underpinning principle of 'best interests' with an onus to 'respect the rights, will and preferences of the person' (Article 12(4)).

The CRPD was strongly influenced by national and international human rights organizations who were deeply opposed to any form of involuntary treatment (Byrnes 2014; Melish 2014). During the drafting of the CRPD, there was a move to create exceptions to this provision in extreme cases, to allow for involuntary treatment, but no agreement could be reached and the CRPD was finalized in its current form (MacQuarrie and Laurin-Bowie 2014). The omission of these exceptions has been cemented by the UN Committee on the Rights of Persons with Disabilities (2014), which stated that 'states parties must abolish policies and legislative provisions that allow or perpetrate forced treatment, as it is an ongoing violation found in mental health laws across the globe' (Paragraph 42). The Committee also stated that people should have 'the right to be free from involuntary detention in a mental health facility and not to be forced to undergo mental health treatment' (Paragraph 31).

The Committee's views have led some countries, including England and Wales, to formally and openly ignore their guidance (Independent Review of the Mental Health Act 1983 2018) and have placed them at significant odds with other UN organizations (Szmukler 2019). Dawson (2015) argues that such a dogmatic interpretation of the CRPD is unrealistic and suggests less radical reforms.

The Committee's 'General Comment' also differentiates between mental and legal capacity. They see mental capacity as a highly subjective medical construct with limited validity, and legal capacity as an integral, non-derogable right that is unaffected by a person's level of cognition or mental state (Paragraph 14). No explicit distinction is made between mental and legal capacity in India's MHCA, even though both the MHCA and the Rights of Persons with Disabilities Act, 2016 (RPWDA 2016) discuss capacity, as laid out in Table 9.1.

Despite these issues, both the MHCA and RPWDA present a number of mechanisms that aim to promote compliance with the CRPD. These key constructs are discussed in the remainder of this chapter. In many ways, these provisions all hinge on the concept of capacity. This is one of the most controversial areas of the CRPD, and it is generally poorly described in the MHCA. While the legislation proposes the provision of additional guidance outside the Act, and the *Mental Healthcare (State Mental Health Authority) Rules, 2018* (Ministry of Health and Family Welfare 2018) also make reference to an expert group, there is, at present, no additional guidance in relation to capacity, which is regrettable.

A true realization of Articles 12–17 of the CRPD may require a complete shift away from mental health law, which can be discriminatory. With mental health law, questions of mental capacity and the evaluation of decision-making ability are applied to people with mental illness, while people without mental illness are free to make autonomous decisions without their capacity being called into question. In contrast,

**Table 9.1** References to capacity in the Mental Healthcare Act, 2017 and the Rights of Persons with Disabilities Act, 2016

| Section of Indian legislation referring to capacity | Meaning of legislation | Type of capacity discussed | Notes |
|---|---|---|---|
| Mental Healthcare Act, 2017, Section 4(1) | Affirmation of universal capacity provided the person can understand, appreciate and communicate information | Mental capacity | There is a typographical error in the current legislation where it states that a person must understand *or* appreciate *or* communicate. This should read understand *and* appreciate *and* communicate |
| Mental Healthcare Act, 2017, Section 4(3) | Decisions regarding mental healthcare perceived by others as inappropriate or wrong shall not mean the decision-maker lacks capacity | Mental capacity | Strong affirmation of will and preference over best interests |
| Mental Healthcare Act, 2017, Section 5(3) | Advance directives come into force when a person ceases to have capacity | Mental capacity | In contravention of the interpretation of the UN Committee on the Rights of Persons with Disabilities |
| Mental Healthcare Act, 2017, Section 5(4) | Decisions made by a person with capacity to make mental healthcare decisions shall over-ride any advance directive | Mental capacity | Implies that people without decision-making capacity cannot over-ride advance directives, but this is not explicitly stated |
| Mental Healthcare Act, 2017, Section 11(2)(d) | Capacity required to make advance directive but only evaluated when the advance directive comes into force | Mental capacity | It is very difficult to establish retrospective capacity in a person currently suffering from a major mental illness |
| Mental Healthcare Act, 2017, Section 14 (8) | The appointment of a nominated representative does not mean a person lacks capacity | Legal capacity | – |

(continued)

**Table 9.1** (continued)

| Section of Indian legislation referring to capacity | Meaning of legislation | Type of capacity discussed | Notes |
|---|---|---|---|
| Mental Healthcare Act, 2017, Section 14(9) | Affirmation of universal capacity with an acknowledgement of the need for varying levels of support | Legal capacity | – |
| Mental Healthcare Act, 2017, Section 81 | Central Authority to prepare a guidance document for professionals, containing procedures for assessing capacity | Mental capacity | – |
| Mental Healthcare Act, 2017, Sections 85(1) and 86(2)(c) | Capacity with minimal support needed to be an independent patient | Mental capacity | This requires people who require moderate or high supports in making decisions to be supported patients even when they are assenting to admission |
| Mental Healthcare Act, 2017, Sections 89(7&8) and 90(12&13) | Regular review of capacity for people with such high support needs that their nominated representative is giving proxy consent | Mental capacity | Additional guidance will be needed to clarify level of support needed and level of capacity present |
| Rights of Persons with Disabilities Act, 2016, Section 13(2) | Persons with disabilities enjoy legal capacity on an equal basis with others and have the right to equal recognition before the law | Legal capacity | – |
| Rights of Persons with Disabilities Act, 2016, Section 15 | The government to support persons with disabilities in exercising their legal capacity | Legal capacity | – |

a generic or 'fusion' law for decision-making in health and social care that evaluated mental or physical health in all people making such decisions could, in theory, be applied equally across the population (Dawson and Szmukler 2006). Such a law is being attempted in Northern Ireland (Szmukler and Bach 2015). This may be one of the most significant areas where the MHCA deviates from comprehensive realization of the CRPD, as the MHCA does not adhere to a 'fusion' model.

Not all parties agree, however, that removal of mental illness as a justification for the restriction of liberty would be a good thing (Freeman et al. 2015; Appelbaum 2019). Such a step might well result in the criminalization of people who break the law as a consequence of mental illness. It might also persevere autonomy at the expensive of dignity or protect liberty at the expensive of health. There are many finely balanced tensions that are currently held within psychiatric systems, and specific mental health legislation might still be needed to clarify and navigate these nuanced circumstances (Duffy and Kelly 2017).

### 9.2.1 Advance Directives

Advance directives (ADs) have emerged from the field of end-of-life care, an area in which they are now well established (Philip et al. 2019). Owing to this evolutionary path, they sometimes appear poorly designed to meet fluctuating, unpredictable mental health needs. The CRPD, however, appears to require developments in this area, and many countries are rising to the challenge (Davidson et al. 2016; Morrissey 2012).

Sections 5–13 of India's MHCA outline the workings of ADs. Under Indian law, everyone who is aged 18 years or over has the right to make an AD (Section 5(1)). This AD describes how they wish 'to be cared for and treated for a mental illness' (Section 5(1)(a)); how they wish 'not to be cared for and treated' (Section 5(1)(b)); and 'the individual or individuals, in order of precedence' whom they wish to appoint as their nominated representative (NR) (Section 5(1)(c)). An AD only applies when a 'person ceases to have capacity to make mental healthcare or treatment decisions' (Section 5(3)), and it remains in force until they regain such capacity. This is left somewhat ambiguous, as an AD 'may be revoked, amended or cancelled by the person who made it at any time'. No qualifier regarding capacity is made here. ADs do not apply in the emergency setting (Section 9), but in all other circumstances mental health professionals have a duty to follow them (Section 10).

Relatives, carers or mental health professionals can apply to Mental Health Review Boards to have an AD reviewed, altered, modified or cancelled (Section 11). Challenges can occur on the following five grounds: if the AD was coerced; if the AD was not intended to apply in the current circumstances; if the person was insufficiently informed to make an AD; if they lacked capacity at the time of making an AD; or if an AD is illegal or unconstitutional. The application of these criteria will strongly influence the impact of ADs as they are highly subjective and require a knowledge of the thought process of the person at a time when they made the AD.

Every Mental Health Review Board is directed to maintain an online register of ADs (Section 7). In addition, 'a medical practitioner or a mental health professional shall not be held liable for any unforeseen consequences on following a valid AD' (Section 13(1)) and 'shall not be held liable for not following a valid AD' if they have not been given a copy (Section 13(2)). Regulations for making ADs are laid out by the Central Authority (Section 6) in the Mental Healthcare (State Mental Health Authority) Rules, 2018 (Ministry of Health and Family Welfare 2018). ADs must be made in writing and signed by two witnesses; if an NR is named, they should sign the AD too and a copy is given to them. ADs should be registered with the local Mental Health Review Board and can be altered at any time. This process is free of charge. This approach is designed to limit the legal barriers to creating ADs (Rolnick et al. 2017) and open up supported decision-making to all who may require it.

The UN Committee on the Rights of Persons with Disabilities (2014) has shown support for advance directives, stating that 'all persons with disabilities have the right to engage in advance planning and should be given the opportunity to do so on an equal basis with others' (Paragraph 17). However, they explicitly state that 'the point at which an advance directive enters into force (and ceases to have effect) should be decided by the person and included in the text of the directive; it should not be based on an assessment that the person lacks mental capacity'. In this respect, the MHCA fails to comply with the Committee's interpretation of the CRPD.

### 9.2.2 *Nominated Representative*

The second key construct in the MHCA that is intended to maximize the capacity of people with mental illness is the nominated representative (NR). As described above, nominating an NR is one of the provisions of an AD in India. Overall, however, the role of NR is poorly defined in the medical literature; their involvement can be highly variable across different jurisdictions; and they may have a wide variety of roles in different contexts (Davidson et al. 2016). Sections 14–17 of the MHCA define the role of the NRs in an Indian context.

Under Indian law, everyone who is aged 18 years or over has the right to appoint an NR (Section 14(1)). This application is made in writing. The NR must also be aged 18 years or over, must consent to undertake the role, and must be competent to discharge their duties (Section 14(3)). If no NR is appointed and a person is found to lack capacity, then the MHCA provides guidance for choosing an NR, starting with family and carers. A person can alter the appointment of an NR and, if deemed to be in the interests of the person, a Mental Health Review Board can revoke an NR.

As a general rule, the MHCA protects the person's right to make mental health-care decisions themselves but acknowledges that people may require varying levels of support from their NR (Section 14(9)). A relative concerned by the decisions of an NR may apply to the Mental Health Review Board to have their role revoked or modified (Section 16). Section 17 of the MHCA describes the roles and responsibilities of the NR, and these include supporting the person in making treatment decisions, with acknowledgement of their background and preferences; receiving information; seeking admission and discharge; being involved in discharge planning; and supporting the rights of the person represented.

Despite the positive aspects of some of these provisions, the mechanism by which an NR may come to take up their role is inconsistent with the UN Committee on the Rights of Persons with Disabilities' (2014) lack of enthusiasm for the use of capacity as a reason for putting an AD into force. However, the NR does conform to the Committee's suggestion that countries 'review the laws allowing for guardianship and trusteeship, and take action to develop laws and policies to replace regimes of substitute decision-making by supported decision-making, which respects the person's autonomy, will and preferences' (Paragraph 26).

Much debate has taken place as to how socially acceptable ADs and NRs are in an Indian context; how prepared people are to use them (Tekkalaki et al. 2018); the extent to which their utilization will impact treatment (Pathare et al. 2015); and the effect they will have on families (Duffy et al. 2018). This is an ongoing issue that is likely to be clarified only during implementation of the new legislation.

### *9.2.3 Supported Decision-Making and Individual Will and Preference*

The CRPD is very clear, even outside of the interpretations of the UN Committee on the Rights of Persons with Disabilities (2014), that there should be a shift from substitute decision-making to supported decision-making. Again, this protection is primarily contained in Article 12. A natural outcome of this is a shift from substitute decisions being made in a person's 'best interests' to supported decisions being made in line with a person's rights, will and preferences (Craigie et al. 2019). Table 9.2 demonstrates how this shift is reflected in the MHCA by examining the relevant ethical principles concerning decision-making.

In the case of minors, 'best interests' remains the guiding principle but, in the case of adults, their will and preference are to be the key factors, although Section 17 of the MHCA ('Duties of nominated representative') also includes 'best interests' as a consideration. In any place where there is substitute decision-making, this is framed in the context of Section 17 which instructs an NR to consider 'the current and past wishes, the life history, values, cultural background and the best interests of the person with mental illness'. An interesting view is taken on research with patients who are unable to give informed consent in Section 99(3)(b), where research can proceed with relevant checks and balances if it 'is necessary to promote the mental health of the population represented by the person'.

**Table 9.2** Key references to the ethical principles underpinning decision-making in the Mental Healthcare Act, 2017 and the Rights of Persons with Disabilities Act, 2016

| Sections of the Act relevant to decision-making | Meaning of the legislation | Ethical principles underpinning the decision-making process |
|---|---|---|
| Mental Healthcare Act, 2017, Section 4 | Affirmation of universal capacity, provided people can understand, appreciate and communicate information | Individual will and preference |
| Mental Healthcare Act, 2017, Section 14(9) | Affirmation of universal capacity with an acknowledgement of the need for varying levels of support | Individual will and preference, with support from nominated representatives |
| Mental Healthcare Act, 2017, Section 15(2) | Best interests the underpinning principle for nominated representatives of minors | Best interests |
| Mental Healthcare Act, 2017, Section 17 | Current and past wishes, life history, values, cultural background and best interests to inform the decisions of nominated representatives | Individual will, preference, and best interests, with support from nominated representatives |
| Mental Healthcare Act, 2017, Section 87(3)(b) | Admissions of minors have to be in their best interests | Best interests |
| Mental Healthcare Act, 2017, Sections 89(7) and 90(12) | Substitute decision-making where a very high level of support is needed during a supported admission | Substitute decision-making framed by Section 17, justified by the risk of harm to self or others, intentionally or unintentionally |
| Mental Healthcare Act, 2017, Section 94 | Proxy consent by nominated representative permitted in emergency contexts for medical and psychiatric treatment, with a 72-h limit. Possible treatment without consent if nominated representative unavailable | Substitute decision-making framed by Section 17, justified by the risk of harm to self or others or harm to property |
| Mental Healthcare Act, 2017, Section 99(3) | Research in people without capacity to consent | Individual assent; the benefit of the mental health of the population represented by the person; substitute decision-making framed by Section 17 |
| Rights of Persons with Disabilities Act, 2016, Section 9(1) | Best interests of a minor can be grounds for the separation of a child from its parents | Best interests |
| Rights of Persons with Disabilities Act, 2016, Section 12(2) | Suitable support measures for persons with disabilities in exercising legal rights | Legal rights |

## 9.3 Involuntary Treatment

Provisions for involuntary treatment are greatly limited in the MHCA compared to both earlier Indian legislation and current legislation in many other jurisdictions. The word 'involuntary' does not appear in the MHCA. The voluntary admissions of India's Mental Health Act, 1987 have been replaced by 'independent admissions' (Sections 85 and 86) and admissions 'under special circumstances' have been replaced by admissions 'of persons with mental illness, with high support needs' (Sections 89 and 90) (Duffy and Kelly 2019). Some of these changes might appear semantic, but they represent an important shift towards rights-based mental health law. Even so, there are still contexts in which a person can be treated without consent (see below), and these provisions might well shift the paradigm back again to one driven by best interests rather than rights, will and preference (Feiring and Ugstad 2014). The MHCA makes no provision for community treatment orders.

### *9.3.1 Supported Admissions*

Supported admissions are described in Sections 89 and 90 of the MHCA, and relate to 'persons with mental illness, with high support needs'. Section 89 applies to the first 30 days, and Section 90 comes into force subsequent to that, or if a person has been discharged from a Section 89 admission within the previous seven days. While a Section 89 order can last up to 30 days, the supported admission should be terminated if the person regains capacity or no longer poses a risk to themselves or others (Section 89(3)). Both admission and treatment must take account of ADs and the person's consent, with the support of their NR.

The Mental Health Review Board must be notified when a supported admission occurs (Section 89(9)). The supported admission can be challenged to the Mental Health Review Board by the person admitted, their NR or a representative of a registered non-governmental organization with the consent of the admitted person (Section 89(10)). With a Section 90 admission (i.e. beyond 30 days), there are some additional protections: the Mental Health Review Board must consider if care can be provided in a less restrictive setting (Section 90(5)(b)) and may require a plan for community-based treatment to be drawn up (Section 90(6)).

Section 85(1) states that an independent patient must have 'the capacity to make mental healthcare and treatment decisions or requires minimal support in making decisions'. Consequently, people who lack capacity or require moderate support must be admitted as supported admissions.

A person who has a 'supported admission' must have a mental illness and present a risk (Sections 89(1) and 90(2)). There is no provision for 'supported admission' based on illness alone or the need for treatment, as there is in some countries (Zhang et al. 2015). This is problematic from a clinical perspective because psychiatrists are much better equipped to predict the course of illness than they are to predict risk (Mulder et al. 2016). The concept of risk under the MHCA is also very broad: it includes a risk of harm to the person themselves or to other people, and a risk of harm through self-neglect. The inclusion of self-neglect as a justification for admission could be an indirect route to involuntary admission on the grounds of illness alone. There is, however, no need for evidence that treatment will benefit the person.

The wording of the MHCA may be problematic for people with moderate support needs who do not present an active risk. Such people will not qualify for 'supported admission', and so their right to health and healthcare may be limited. They cannot be an 'independent patient' owing to their lack of capacity and their need for support, but they can only be a 'supported patient' if there is sufficient risk identified.

### *9.3.2 Treatment During a 'Supported Admission'*

During a 'supported admission', treatment will generally take place under Sections 89(6) and 90(11) of the MHCA, which describe a supported decision-making framework that takes into account the patient's AD and their informed consent, with the support of their NR. Sections 89(7) and 90(12) acknowledge that some people who require 'supported admissions' will require 'nearly hundred per cent support' in making treatment decisions. In these instances, 'the nominated representative may temporarily consent to the treatment plan of such person on his behalf'. If this is the case, the responsible medical professional must regularly review the person's capacity to give consent (Sections 89(8) and 90(13)).

While these arrangements constitute a form of substitute decision-making, they are framed by the Section 17 of the MHCA which puts an onus on the NR to consider the wishes of the individual. Therefore, adults cannot receive treatment without some consideration being given to their preferences and significant steps being taken to maximize their decision-making capacity. At the same time, the MHCA does not deprive people with impaired ability to give informed consent from receiving effective treatments. In this respect, the MHCA attempts to balance the CRPD's rights to 'life' (Article 10) and 'health' (Article 25) with its rights to 'equal recognition before the law' (Article 12), 'liberty and security of person' (Article 14), 'integrity of the person' (Article 17) and 'freedom from torture or cruel, inhuman or degrading treatment or punishment' (Article 15).

### *9.3.3 Emergency Treatment*

Emergency treatment is described in Section 94 of the MHCA. This section permits the provision of 'any medical treatment, including treatment for mental illness' by a medical practitioner to a person with mental illness at a 'health establishment or in the community' in an emergency. If an NR is available, they can give proxy consent. No direction is contained in the text about a situation in which the NR is *not* present, although the Act seems to imply that treatment can proceed without consent in such a circumstance. An emergency situation is defined as one in which there is an immediate risk of '(a) death or irreversible harm to the health of the person; or (b) the person inflicting serious harm to himself or to others; or (c) the person causing serious damage to property belonging to himself or to others where such behaviour is believed to flow directly from the person's mental illness' (Section 94(1)).

This final clause, relating to property (Section 94(1)(c)), is one of the most significant ways in which the MHCA deviates from the CRPD. Damage to property only applies as a criterion for treatment without consent in the context of emergencies; it is not grounds for 'supported admission' (Sections 89 and 90). During emergency treatment, the person may have extremely limited input into their treatment options. Should an NR be unavailable, it appears that treatment can be given on an involuntary basis in an emergency; this is, therefore, the most coercive area of the MHCA. In other parts of the MHCA, where free and informed consent are not obtained for treatment, the justifications are risk to life or health. Those non-emergency provisions, therefore, reflect a careful balancing of the right to life and health with Articles 12–17 of the CRPD.

In an emergency situation, however, some of the rights outlined in Articles 12–17 are limited in order to protect *property*. This appears disproportionate. Admittedly, the MHCA provides the protection that emergency treatment is limited to 'seventy-two hours or till the person with mental illness has been assessed at a mental health establishment' (Section 94(4)), and it prohibits both 'medical treatment which is not directly related to the emergency' (Section 94(2)) and electroconvulsive therapy (ECT) (Section 94(3)) during this period. In addition, it is just about arguable that the provisions of Section 94(1)(c) might actually *protect* rights, because an inability to intervene when a person is damaging property due to mental illness could increase the stigmatization and criminalization of people with mental illness (Freeman et al. 2015).

In addition, the 'right to life' is affirmed by Article 10 of the CRPD. This has particular relevance to psychiatry because people with mental illness have significantly reduced life expectancy, and suicidality is part of many psychiatric conditions. Even in high-income countries, people with major mental illness have life expectancies that are approximately ten years shorter than those of people without mental illness (Walker et al. 2015). In light of this, the provision of care without consent in emergency situations might do much to protect the 'right to life' in certain cases, especially in the setting of acute suicidality.

Even so, however, this provision of the MHCA to provide emergency care without consent on the basis of damage to *property* appears especially inconsistent with the CRPD, which the MHCA purports to uphold (and, to be fair, generally does).

### *9.3.4 Restraint and Seclusion*

Seclusion is prohibited under the MHCA (Section 97(1)). While seclusion is a highly contentious practice, it is still widely used internationally (Al-Maraira and Hayajneh 2019; Steinert et al. 2010) and its prohibition in the MHCA is a highly progressive step. Seclusion potentially breaches Articles 14 ('Liberty and security of person'), 15 ('Freedom from torture or cruel, inhuman or degrading treatment or punishment'), 16 ('Freedom from exploitation, violence and abuse') and 17 ('Protecting the integrity of the person') of the CRPD.

Physical restraint is permitted under the MHCA. It is, however, only allowed to prevent imminent and immediate harm to the person concerned or others (Section 97(1)). It can only be used when absolutely necessary (Section 97(2)); it cannot be used as a form of punishment (Section 97(4)); its use must be carefully documented and justified (Section 97(3)); and the NR (Section 97(5)) and Mental Health Review Board (Section 97(7)) must be informed. This is an example of the MHCA striking a balance between CRPD rights to health (Article 25) and life (Article 10) on the one hand, and Articles 14 through 17 on the other hand. Interestingly, this balance also considers the right to health and life of other people in addition to the person requiring treatment.

While multiple CRPD rights are plainly limited by the use of restraint, these limitations are described in law in partial compliance with Article 14(1)(b) of the CRPD which requires that 'any deprivation of liberty is in conformity with the law, and that the existence of a disability shall in no case justify a deprivation of liberty'. The description in law is clearly in line with the first part of this requirement, but the inclusion of restraint in the first place is clearly a breach of the second.

## 9.4 Other Areas of Non-concordance with the CRPD

### *9.4.1 Research*

The MHCA permits research involving people who are unable to give free and informed consent but do not resist participation (Section 99(2)). In this case, consent can be obtained from the NR, and the State Mental Health Authority must be satisfied that five conditions are met: (a) that the research cannot be performed on persons who are capable of giving consent; (b) that the research promotes the mental health of the population represented by the person; (c) that the research aims to obtain knowledge relevant to the mental health needs of persons with mental illness; (d) that there are no conflict of interests; and (e) that the research follows all relevant national and international guidelines and regulations (Section 99(3)).

The second condition is very interesting because it describes a utilitarian ethical principle whereby the research is occurring for the good of society at large. This is a significant departure from the individualistic principles of the CRPD and is more in keeping with the more family-centric principles of Indian society (Ademosu 2018). The final condition may prove problematic, however, as it could be argued that the CRPD is an 'international guideline' that states that 'no one shall be subjected without his or her free consent to medical or scientific experimentation' (Article 15(1)).

### 9.4.2 Privacy and Confidentiality

The CRPD does not, for the most part, devote substantial attention to confidentiality in explicit terms (Article 31(1)(a)), but it's description of 'privacy' also covers confidentiality, stating that 'States Parties shall protect the privacy of personal, health and rehabilitation information of persons with disabilities on an equal basis with others' (Article 22(2)).

Under the MHCA, people admitted to mental healthcare establishments have a right to privacy (Section 20(2)(d)). This is the only mention of privacy in the MHCA. Sections 23 and 24 address confidentiality. Section 23(1) articulates a right to confidentiality in respect of mental health, mental healthcare, treatment and physical healthcare. Section 24 extends this protection to photographs of people undergoing treatment at mental health establishments and to digital and electronic data. Section 23(2) outlines five conditions under which confidentiality may be breached; these are summarized in Table 9.3. Where information has to be released to protect the safety of others, the MHCA is clear that only information that is necessary to prevent harm should be released.

By including provisions for breaching confidentiality in mental health legislation rather than general health legislation, it would appear that personal health and rehabilitation information is not protected on an equal basis in people with mental illness compared to those without. Four of the five justifications for breaching confidentiality could have been included in general health legislation and if this had been the case the MHCA would have been concordant with the CRPD in relation to privacy; as matters stand, it is not.

### 9.4.3 Electroconvulsive Therapy

ECT has proved to be one of the most controversial areas of the MHCA (Duffy et al. 2018, 2019). Psychiatrists are strongly divided regarding the limitations placed on its use by the MHCA, which totally prohibits the use of unmodified ECT (i.e. ECT without anaesthetic) (Section 95(1)(a)), bans its use in the emergency setting (Section 94(3)) and creates substantial barriers to its use in minors (Sections 95(1)(b) and 95(2)). These provisions are in line with the *WHO Resource Book on Mental Health, Human Rights and Legislation* (WHO 2005). The key issue in relation to the CRPD is whether ECT amounts to cruel and inhumane treatment, as this would be a violation of Article 15.

**Table 9.3** Justifications for breaching confidentiality in India's Mental Healthcare Act, 2017

| Reason for breach of right to privacy or confidentiality | Section of the Mental Healthcare Act, 2017 permitting the breach | Principles justifying the area of non-concordance with the United Nations' Convention on the Rights of Persons with Disabilities |
|---|---|---|
| To the nominated representative to enable him to fulfil his duties under the Act | 22(2) and 23(2)(a) | To facilitate supported decision-making |
| To other health professionals to enable them to provide care and treatment | 23(2)(b) | To protect the right to health |
| If it is necessary to protect any other person from harm or violence | 23(2)(c) | To protect the right to life, health and freedom from violence for other people |
| Upon an order by the concerned Mental Health Review Board or the Central Authority or High Court or Supreme Court or any other competent statutory authority | 23(2)(f) | Judicial authority |
| In the interests of public safety and security. | 23(2)(g) | To protect the right to life, health and freedom from violence for other people |

Portrayals of ECT in the media are often highly negative and may lead people to believe that such treatment is inhumane (Sienaert 2016). In practice, a substantial evidence base supports the treatment (van Diermen et al. 2018; Mutz et al. 2019) and many Indian psychiatrists are strong advocates of it (Antony 2015; Thippeswamy et al. 2012). However, many people who have received ECT are much less convinced of its safety (Read et al. 2019), and many more are afraid of it (Morrison 2009). Weitz (2013) argues that ECT is a form of assault, especially when administered without informed consent.

A strong case could be made that unmodified ECT is torture and that India's prohibition of this is in line with international standards (WHO 2005). In light of the available evidence, voluntary, modified ECT (i.e. with anaesthetic) appears to be an important treatment, although critics argue that side effects have been minimized, possibly making informed consent invalid (Seniuk 2018). Consequently, psychiatrists need to conduct high-quality research on side effects and carefully communicate their findings to people who may receive ECT if they are to be concordant with the CRPD.

The most contentious area relates to supported patients, who need a moderate or high level of support to make treatment decisions and consequently could receive ECT without having given their own free and informed consent. Banning ECT in this cohort would deprive them of an effective treatment that is available to people who are able to give informed consent. In this instance, the protection of the person's rights relies heavily on the NR, and on a difficult balancing of CRPD rights to 'life' (Article 10) and 'health' (Article 25) with the right to freedom from treatments to which the person has not consented.

## 9.5 Conclusions

Despite the limitations discussed in this chapter, both the MHCA and the RPWDA have done much to realize the principles of the CRPD in Indian law. Where practices might appear to contravene the CRPD, multiple protections have been put in place, chiefly mediated by Mental Health Review Boards. Areas of non-concordance are generally the product of efforts to balance competing CRPD rights with each other, and this balancing act is often directly reflected in the text of the MHCA. The two most significant areas of potential non-concordance with the CRPD relate to the role of capacity in the MHCA and the lack of sufficient protection during emergency treatment. These limitations may reflect pragmatic compromises in a setting of limited resources, especially as some of the other provisions described in the MHCA might already prove too ambitious to be implemented in the first place. Overall, while India's MHCA might not be entirely in line with the interpretations of the UN Committee on the Rights of Persons with Disabilities (2014), the vast majority of its provisions are compatible with the CRPD itself.

## References


Ademosu, T. (2018). Here and there. *Lancet Psychiatry, 5*(12), 970–972.

Al-Maraira, O. A., & Hayajneh, F. A. (2019). Use of restraint and seclusion in psychiatric settings: A literature review. *Journal of Psychosocial Nursing and Mental Health Services, 57*(4), 32–39.

Antony, J. T. (2015). The ban on unmodified ECT and psychiatrists craving for a new identity. *Kerala Journal of Psychiatry, 28,* 11–15.

Appelbaum, P. S. (2019). Saving the UN Convention on the Rights of Persons with Disabilities—From itself. *World Psychiatry, 18*(1), 1–2.

Byrnes, A. (2014). The role of national human rights institutions. In M. Sabatello & M. Schulze (Eds.), *Human rights and disability advocacy* (pp. 222–238). Philadelphia: University of Pennsylvania Press.

Craigie, J., Bach, M., Gurbai, S., Kanter, A., Kim, S. Y. H., Lewis, O., et al. (2019). Legal capacity, mental capacity and supported decision-making: Report from a panel event. *International Journal of Law and Psychiatry, 62,* 160–168.

Davidson, G., Brophy, L., Campbell, J., Farrell, S. J., Gooding, P., & O'Brien, A. M. (2016). An international comparison of legal frameworks for supported and substitute decision-making in mental health services. *International Journal of Law and Psychiatry, 44,* 30–40.

Dawson, J. (2015). A realistic approach to assessing mental health laws' compliance with the UNCRPD. *International Journal of Law and Psychiatry, 40,* 70–79.

Dawson, J., & Szmukler, G. (2006). Fusion of mental health and incapacity legislation. *British Journal of Psychiatry, 188,* 504–509.

Duffy, R. M., & Kelly, B. D. (2017). Rights, laws and tensions: A comparative analysis of the Convention on the Rights of Persons with Disabilities and the WHO Resource Book on Mental Health, Human Rights and Legislation. *International Journal of Law and Psychiatry, 54,* 26–35.

Duffy, R. M., & Kelly, B. D. (2019). India's Mental Healthcare Act, 2017: Content, context, controversy. *International Journal of Law and Psychiatry, 62,* 169–178.

Duffy, R. M., Narayan, C. L., Goyal, N., & Kelly, B. D. (2018). New legislation, new frontiers: Indian psychiatrists' perspective of the mental healthcare act 2017 prior to implementation. *Indian Journal of Psychiatry, 60*(3), 351–354.

Duffy, R. M., Gulati, G., Paralikar, V., Kasar, N., Goyal, N., Desousa, A., et al. (2019). A focus group study of Indian psychiatrists' views on electroconvulsive therapy under India's Mental Healthcare Act 2017: 'the ground reality is different'. *Indian Journal of Psychological Medicine, 41,* 507–515.

Feiring, E., & Ugstad, K. N. (2014). Interpretations of legal criteria for involuntary psychiatric admission: A qualitative analysis. *BMC Health Services Research, 14,* 500.

Freeman, M. C., Kolappa, K., de Almeida, J. M., Kleinman, A., Makhashvili, N., Phakathi, S., et al. (2015). Reversing hard won victories in the name of human rights: A critique of the General Comment on Article 12 of the UN Convention on the Rights of Persons with Disabilities. *Lancet Psychiatry, 2*(9), 844–850.

Independent Review of the Mental Health Act 1983. (2018). *Modernising the Mental Health Act: Increasing choice, reducing compulsion.* London: Gov.uk. Retrieved July 27, 2019, from https://assets.publishing.service.gov.uk/government/uploads/system/uploads/attachment_data/file/778897/Modernising_the_Mental_Health_Act_-_increasing_choice__reducing_compulsion.pdf.

MacQuarrie, A., & Laurin-Bowie, C. (2014). Our lives, our voices: People with intellectual disabilities and their families. In M. Sabatello & M. Schulze (Eds.), *Human rights and disability advocacy* (pp. 25–44). Philadelphia: University of Pennsylvania Press.

Melish, T. J. (2014). An eye towards effective enforcement: Technical-comparative approach to the negotiations. In M. Sabatello & M. Schulze (Eds.), *Human rights and disability advocacy* (pp. 70–96). Philadelphia: University of Pennsylvania Press.

Ministry of Health and Family Welfare. (2018). *Mental Healthcare (State Mental Health Authority) Rules, 2018.* New Delhi: Ministry of Health and Family Welfare. Retrieved August 27, 2019, from https://mohfw.gov.in/sites/default/files/Mental%20Healthcare%20SMHA%20Rules_0.pdf.

Morrison, L. (2009). ECT: Shocked beyond belief. *Australasian Psychiatry, 17*(2), 164–167.

Morrissey, F. (2012). The United Nations Convention on the Rights of Persons with Disabilities: A new approach to decision-making in mental health law. *European Journal of Health Law, 19,* 423–440.

Mulder, R., Newton-Howes, G., & Coid, J. W. (2016). The futility of risk prediction in psychiatry. *British Journal of Psychiatry, 209*(4), 271–272.

Mutz, J., Vipulananthan, V., Carter, B., Hurlemann, R., Fu, C. H. Y., & Young, A. H. (2019). Comparative efficacy and acceptability of non-surgical brain stimulation for the acute treatment of major depressive episodes in adults: Systematic review and network meta-analysis. *British Medical Journal, 364,* 1079.

Pathare, S., Shields, L., Nardodkar, R., Narasimhan, L., & Bunders, J. (2015). What do service users want? A content analysis of what users may write in psychiatric advance directives in India. *Asian Journal of Psychiatry, 14,* 52–56.

Philip, S., Rangarajan, S. K., Moirangthem, S., Kumar, C. N., Gowda, M. R., Gowda, G. S., et al. (2019). Advance directives and nominated representatives: A critique. *Indian Journal of Psychiatry, 61*(Suppl 4), S680–S685.

Read, J., Cunliffe, S., Jauhar, S., & McLoughlin, D. M. (2019). Should we stop using electroconvulsive therapy? *British Medical Journal, 364,* k5233.

Rolnick, J. A., Asch, D. A., & Halpern, S. D. (2017). Delegalizing advance directives—Facilitating advance care planning. *New England Journal of Medicine, 376*(22), 2105–2107.

Seniuk, P. (2018). I'm shocked: Informed consent in ECT and the phenomenological-self. *Life Science Society and Policy, 14*(1), 5.

Sienaert, P. (2016). Based on a true story? The portrayal of ECT in international movies and television programs. *Brain Stimulation, 9*(6), 882–891.

Steinert, T., Lepping, P., Bernhardsgrütter, R., Conca, A., Hatling, T., Janssen, W., et al. (2010). Incidence of seclusion and restraint in psychiatric hospitals: A literature review and survey of international trends. *Social Psychiatry and Psychiatric Epidemiology, 45*(9), 889–897.

Szmukler, G. (2019). "Capacity", "best interests", "will and preferences" and the UN Convention on the Rights of Persons with Disabilities. *World Psychiatry, 18,* 34–41.

Szmukler, G., & Bach, M. (2015). Mental health disabilities and human rights protections. *Global Mental Health, 2,* e20.

Tekkalaki, B., Patil, V. Y., Patil, S., Chate, S. S., Dhabale, R., & Patil, N. M. (2018). How do our patients respond to the concept of psychiatric advance directives? An exploratory study from India. *Indian Journal of Psychological Medicine, 40*(6), 588–589.

Thippeswamy, H., Goswami, K., & Chaturvedi, S. (2012). Ethical aspects of public health legislation: The Mental Health Care Bill, 2011. *Indian Journal of Medical Ethics, 9*(1), 46–49.

United Nations. (2006). *Convention on the rights of persons with disabilities.* New York: United Nations. Retrieved June 1, 2019, from https://www.un.org/development/desa/disabilities/convention-on-the-rights-of-persons-with-disabilities/convention-on-the-rights-of-persons-with-disabilities-2.html.

United Nations Committee on the Rights of Persons with Disabilities. (2014). *General comment No. 1: Article 12: Equal recognition before the law.* New York: United Nations. Retrieved July 25, 2019, from http://www.ohchr.org/EN/HRBodies/CRPD/Pages/GC.aspx.

Van Diermen, L., van den Ameele, S., Kamperman, A. M., Sabbe, B. C. G., Vermeulen, T., Schrijvers, D., et al. (2018). Prediction of electroconvulsive therapy response and remission in major depression: Meta-analysis. *British Journal of Psychiatry, 212*(2), 71–80.

Walker, E. R., McGee, R. E., & Druss, B. G. (2015). Mortality in mental disorders and global disease burden implications: a systematic review and meta-analysis. *JAMA Psychiatry, 72*(4), 334–341.

Weitz, D. Electroshock: torture as "treatment". (2013). In: B. A. Lefrancois, R. Menzies, & G. Reaume (Eds.), *Mad matters: A critical reader in Canadian mad studies* (pp. 158–169). Toronto: Canadian Scholar's press.

World Health Organization. (2005). *WHO resource book on mental health, human rights and legislation.* Geneva: World Health Organization.

Zhang, S., Mellsop, G., Brink, J., & Wang, X. (2015). Involuntary admission and treatment of patients with mental disorder. *Neuroscience Bulletin, 31*(1), 99–112.

# Chapter 10
# Adhering to Conventions: Intentional Grey Areas or Shirking Responsibility?

## 10.1 Introduction

Mental health legislation is going through a welcome transformation. The most recent iterations depart from a traditional model focused on the treatment of severe illness and involuntary care, and are beginning to deliver rights-based legislation that provides mental healthcare while also protecting the rights of people with mental illness. Much of this change has been driven by international guidelines and conventions, including the World Health Organization's (WHO) Resource Book on Mental Health, Human Rights and Legislation (WHO RB) (WHO 2005) and the United Nations' (UN) Principles for the Protection of Persons with Mental Illness and the Improvement of Mental Health Care (UN 1991). Since 2006, the primary document driving this change has been the highly influential UN Convention on the Rights of Persons with Disabilities (CRPD) (UN 2006; Harpur 2012).

India has taken one of the most proactive approaches to incorporating the CRPD into mental health legislation with explicit references to the Convention in the preambles of both the Mental Healthcare Act, 2017 (MHCA) and the Rights of Persons with Disabilities Act, 2016 (RPWDA). This attempted alignment with the CRPD takes the form of pragmatic legislation that strives to avoid the postulated pitfalls of CRPD-concordant legislation such as possible criminalization of the mentally ill, stigmatization and a widening of the mental health treatment gap (Appelbaum 2019; Freeman et al. 2015). The MHCA has proven controversial: many Indian psychiatrists feel that they were not included in its drafting, that the rights articulated do not reflect the priorities of Indian culture, and that the legislation will not receive sufficient funding (Duffy et al. 2018; Pavitra et al. 2019; Math et al. 2019).

The treatment of mental illness often requires a balancing of rights. This is often highly complex, with multiple competing rights, preferences and interests at play. Clearly, many tensions have to be held in balance in the practice of psychiatry (Duffy and Kelly 2017a). These present challenges and paradoxes that become particularly apparent when national legislation, written to work on the ground, is compared with



R. M. Duffy and B. D. Kelly, *India's Mental Healthcare Act, 2017*,
https://doi.org/10.1007/978-981-15-5009-6_10

international standards, shaped by theoretical principles. In this chapter, we examine how the MHCA and RPWDA have attempted to strike this balance. Both Acts have areas that appear non-concordant with the WHO RB and CRPD. This chapter explores whether these divergences represent necessary and appropriate flexibility to facilitate person-centred care, or, on the other hand, a failure by legislators to deliver CRPD-concordant provisions.

## 10.2 The Role of International Bodies in Reforming Mental Health Law

Legislation is increasingly recognized as a key tool for enhancing population health (WHO 2017). Psychiatry is well placed to harness the potential of law owing to psychiatry's well-established use of legal processes for various reasons (Duffy and Kelly 2017b). Other health-related areas governed by legislation in many jurisdictions include public smoking, speeding, drink driving and even the use of traffic lights. Such legislation tends to be most effective when it is part of a broader process of societal change—one piece of a larger puzzle. The same is true in psychiatry.

As a result, laws can act as a catalyst for change but in isolation they can rarely realize this change in and of themselves. The role of legislation in promoting health care needs to be supported by funding and political will. In this context, what role do international conventions and guidelines have? Are they purely rhetorical or can they truly drive change?

International guidelines can certainly help to bring a topic into political consciousness, raise general awareness or even stimulate research. In the context of female genital mutilation, for example, Khosla et al. (2017) show how the statements of international bodies interact with research to influence political debate. International conventions have these benefits too, but they also carry added legal weight which can lead to the adoption of legislation and influence judicial rulings. For example, the European Convention on Human Rights has done much to promote progressive legislation in relation to transgender rights within its jurisdiction (D'Amico and Nardocci 2016). The magnitude of the impact varies depending on how a jurisdiction has chosen to incorporate a given document or convention. In the two examples we have taken, the WHO RB and the CRPD, the latter has had significantly more impact due to the legal obligations it places on its signatories.

It is worth questioning, however, if the impact of the CRPD might be limited as a result of its dogmatic interpretation by the UN Committee on the Rights of Persons with Disabilities (2014; Appelbaum 2019). Its interpretation of the CRPD as presenting a total ban on coercive treatments is proving highly controversial. England and Wales have already indicated that they will not adhere to its position (Independent Review of the Mental Health Act 1983 2018). Freeman et al. (2015) and Szmukler (2019) also highlight many of the potential negative unintended consequences of making Article 12 ('Equal recognition before the law') non-derogable. Such an approach could potentially limit liberty through the criminalization of people who break the law while unwell or limit access to treatment for people with acute illness who lack insight.

The cultural sensitivity and generalizability of international standards and conventions must also be examined. Historically, psychiatry has been defined by Eurocentric ideologies which continue to have negative impacts (Ademosu 2018). It would be naïve to assume that modern WHO and UN publications have removed all forms of bias. Davar (2014) has gone a step further, suggesting that the impact of international bodies on Indian mental health law and practice represents a form of neo-colonialism. The emphasis on autonomy, equality, individualism and privacy seen in western societies is not a readily embraced in all societies. For example, Indian psychiatrists have expressed concerns that the revised and limited CRPD-informed role of the family in the MHCA is at odds with Indian culture (Duffy et al. 2018; Pavitra et al. 2019). Similarly, the imposition of a WHO RB-concordant prohibition on unmodified ECT has been seen as limiting the availability of the only effective treatment to some of India's most vulnerable people (Andrade et al. 2012; Duffy et al. 2019).

## 10.3 An Ethical Analysis of India's Mental Healthcare Act, 2017's Deviations from the World Health Organization's *Resource Book on Mental Health, Human Rights and Legislation*

The concordance of the RPWDA and the MHCA with the WHO RB is examined in Chaps. 5, 6 and 7 of this book. As discussed, India has exceeded the levels of concordance seen in other countries owing to their extensive inclusion of social rights and attempts to limit coercive measures (Kelly 2011; Duffy and Kelly 2017a). Many of the omissions in the Indian legislation are either intentional or related to issues that can be addressed in policy or guidelines. In the following sections, we examine some of the key ethical issues that arise as India's legislation is viewed through the lens of the WHO RB.

### *10.3.1 Medical Ethics in Resource-Scarce Environments*

The need to ration in medicine is unavoidable (Scheunemann and White 2011). This presents one of the key ethical issues raised by the MHCA: justice and equity in the distribution of resources. Healthcare has an almost infinite capacity to absorb funding, so difficult decisions to limit services must be made on a regular basis. The Indian legislation attempts to implement many new practices that will place additional burdens on already stretched services. There are already major financial restraints on the Indian healthcare system, with less than 1% of the Indian health budget allocated to mental healthcare (Patel et al. 2018). Human resource limitations may present an even greater challenge than financial limitations in the longer term (Jiloha 2015).

The authors of the MHCA do, however, show an awareness of the need for rationing and resource limitations. This is an area with which many medical professionals feel uncomfortable (Strech et al. 2009), but it is one that policymakers cannot shy away from. Rationing is complex and specific to its context, as a rationing decision that is justifiable in one health system might not be justifiable in another (Scheunemann and White 2011). Rationing is particularly important in state-sponsored healthcare where macro-allocation is necessary. Some of the areas of deviation from the WHO RB in the MHCA are examples of *explicit* rationing which is inherently more just than *implicit* rationing. Given the population size and diversity of India, however, it is likely that there will be a high level of implicit rationing of services at both a macro- and a micro-level. The State Mental Health Authorities might partly facilitate an explicit rationing process (Section 55(1)(b)) but it would be preferable for *all* rationing to be explicit.

In many areas, the MHCA has refused to ration access *rights* even in situations where it is unclear if there will be sufficient mental health professionals to deliver the required standard of care. Examples are found throughout the Act, including, *inter alia*, the right to access mental health care and treatment (Section 18(1)), the right to access review by a Mental Health Review Board (Section 28(1)) and the right not to be subjected to unmodified electroconvulsive therapy (ECT) (Section 95(1)(a)). The last of these three examples is especially relevant in relation to resource rationing (Duffy et al. 2019).

Narayan and Shekhar (2013) argue that banning unmodified ECT will deprive certain people of a life-saving treatment. The authors of the MHCA were, however, either unconvinced by the evidence for this (Ray 2016; Andrade et al. 2012; Shah et al. 2010) or decided that unmodified ECT is cruel and inhumane treatment, tantamount to torture. The retention of unmodified ECT has been argued on the ethical grounds of beneficence (Rajkumar 2014), but the right to healthcare is a positive right (i.e. an entitlement to receive something), while the right to freedom from torture is a negative right (i.e. a right not to be exposed to something)—and negative rights are usually treated as the more valid claim. This is reinforced in the WHO's view that protection from cruel inhumane or degrading treatment or punishment is a non-derogable right (UN Economic and Social Council 1985).

The WHO RB recommends that the qualification and skill level required to make a diagnosis of mental disorder are clearly laid out, but the MHCA provides no direction on this issue. Despite this, the MHCA is keenly aware of the importance of diagnosis and goes to great lengths to avoid secondary or malicious motives (Section 3). This is an example of resource rationing; while in an ideal situation a suitably qualified professional would diagnose, such professionals are sparse in India and a less robust diagnosis might be an acceptable compromise if it facilitates more people receiving timely treatment.

The MHCA and the RPWDA are worryingly vague when it comes to funding. The RPWDA in particular has incorporated multiple steps to try to speed social change and promote the role of people with disabilities in society. It will be important that these educational and legal provisions are acted upon—and this will require funding. The attitudinal change that these measures might produce could potentially increase the social appetite to better fund disability services, but this will take some time.

### *10.3.2 Beneficence and Definitions*

Diagnoses and definitions are essential for the provision of good healthcare and are an integral element of sustainable treatment, prognosis and service planning. They are particularly important in psychiatry owing to the level of subjectivity in diagnosis. In an attempt to increase robustness, in the face of revelations like Rosenhan's (1973) work 'on being sane in insane places' (Rogler 1997; Cahalan 2019), psychiatry might now have over-corrected and sought an unrealistic degree of diagnostic certainty, as reflected in an over-reliance on diagnostic manuals (Fuchs 2010).

In addition, the increasing momentum behind human rights in psychiatry is shifting mental health legislation from a so-called 'medical model' towards a more 'social model' (Oliver 2013; Duffy and Kelly 2017a). This shift might explain the less precise definitions in the MHCA where personality disorder is not mentioned (but appears to fall within the remit of the Act) and substance misuse is defined only in broad terms. This approach mirrors that of the CRPD which was intentionally ambiguous in its definitions in order to increase inclusivity (Kanter 2011). Peterson and Keeley (2014) highlight how rigid definitions in the area of disability contribute to exclusion. However, while a broad, inclusive definition may be of benefit to people looking to access services, it makes service planning challenging and introduces uncertainty about to whom the law applies (Schulze 2010). Providing a justiciable right to mental health care is challenging enough without introducing ambiguity about to whom the right applies. Ultimately, this situation might also disproportionately limit the rights of people with personality and substance misuse disorders.

A helpful example of flexibility in the MHCA (resulting in a deviation from the WHO RB) is that it allows minors to receive ECT in extreme circumstances. This might reflect a welcome movement away from a strict, dichotomous age cut-off. It also has face validity, because it does not logically follow that it would be unethical to give ECT to a 17-year old with severe treatment-resistant psychosis but ethical if they were aged 18. This non-concordance with the WHO RB may reflect the evolution of broader, more flexible definitions in an attempt to realize the best health outcomes and promote beneficence.

### *10.3.3 Autonomy and Capacity*

The MHCA does much to maximize the capacity of people with mental illness through advance directives and nominated representatives, thus promoting autonomy.

Capacity is, however, a highly contentious topic and one of the areas where the WHO RB and CRPD are most at odds (Duffy and Kelly 2017a). Article 12 of the CRPD and its subsequent commentary, which affirm the legal capacity of all people at all times (UN Committee on the Rights of Persons with Disabilities 2014), have brought this topic to the fore in mental health law, although there is also growing recognition that over-literal interpretation of the CRPD might well hinder the realization of rights of people with mental illness (Freeman et al. 2015).

In light of India's legal obligation to adhere to the CRPD, much is done in the legislation to enhance the capacity of people with mental illness. First, 'supported' patients are not automatically seen as lacking capacity; their status as supported patients does not make them unable to consent for other treatments; and it is acknowledged that they might not need support in making other decisions. Second, the appreciation of capacity as time- and decision-specific is incorporated into the Indian legislation. This is an important deviation from the WHO RB and reflects the high level of decision-making capacity that has been identified in involuntary patients (Mandarelli et al. 2018).

Family plays a very central role in Indian life, and the WHO RB promotes the involvement of family throughout the delivery of mental healthcare. But while the WHO RB does much to support the rights of family, the CRPD is virtually silent on the matter (Duffy and Kelly 2017a). India's MHCA, interestingly, provides the family with an advantaged position, but also affirms the individual's capacity to seek treatment separately from them, allowing them to protect their privacy should they so desire—consistent with the principle of autonomy.

Historically, the principles of beneficence and non-maleficence have tended to dominate medical ethics, and the application of these principles in mental health has often kindled paternalism at the disproportionate expense of autonomy and liberty. The increasingly prominent position of justice and rights as an ethical principle is doing much to reverse this paternalism and protect the rights of the individual. This has, however, potential drawbacks including the marginalization of families and possible non-treatment of people who are unwell enough to warrant a supported admission but retain capacity to refuse treatment: balancing beneficence and autonomy will always prove challenging in these situations. The CRPD has, however, made autonomy its guiding principle and has installed it as *the* unquestionable right (Del Villar 2015). This 'autonomy dogma' might, in time, result in substantial limitations of other rights.

### *10.3.4 Ethics and the Evidence Base*

The process of creating, evaluating and operationalising evidence in medicine is not a solely scientific process; it is equally influenced by context, culture and ethics. This is apparent in the MHCA's interesting positions on a range of issues including compulsory community treatment orders, unmodified ECT and ECT in minors.

Provisions for involuntary treatment in the community setting were included in the WHO RB because the community can be seen as a less restrictive setting in which to receive treatment, and therefore preferable to involuntary admission. Multiple arguments have been made supporting the ethics of involuntary treatment in the community (Munetz et al. 2003). However, a meta-analysis of community treatment orders shows them to be ineffective in terms of readmission, social functioning and symptomology (Kisely and Hall 2014), although there is some evidence that they may make individuals less likely to be victims of crime.

Munetz et al. (2003) suggest communitarianism as a justification for community treatment orders; this is an ethical principle that promotes communal good and cooperation and is often at odds with the liberal principle of neutrality (i.e. tolerance of a plurality of world views). Communitarianism may be a more accurate reflection of Indian society and the place of the family in India (Rao et al. 2016). The CRPD is underpinned by liberal ethics rooted firmly in autonomy, individualism and beneficence. Community treatment orders have yet to demonstrate substantial benefit in these terms. To truly evaluate the potential role of community treatment orders and enhance their evidence base, they would need to be evaluated in an Indian context using outcome variables informed by Indian culture and values, even though this could conflict with the values embedded in the CRPD.

Turning to ECT, Indian psychiatrists have argued for the use of unmodified ECT and ECT in minors, pointing to an apparent evidence base for these practices (Ray 2016; Andrade et al. 2012; Shah et al. 2010). While this research has its limitations, the MHCA permits ECT in minors in very limited circumstances but prohibits unmodified ECT. This might well deprive some people of ECT in situations where no other effective treatment is available (Duffy et al. 2019). In this context, it is important to consider whether preconceived political agendas, rather than medical evidence, drove legislation.

The areas of the MHCA that do not concord with the WHO RB are a canvas for the complex interactions between different ethical principles and various political and economic considerations. While classifying each item in the WHO RB as either satisfactorily or unsatisfactorily addressed in the MHCA (as in this book) provides some information, a deeper exploration of the ethical principles at play provides a more nuanced understanding of the Act in its ethical, medical, political and cultural contexts.

## 10.4 An Ethical Analysis of India's Mental Healthcare Act, 2017's Deviations from the United Nations Convention on the Rights of Persons with Disabilities

The MHCA and the RPWDA set out explicitly to accord with the CRPD and, as described in Chap. 8, they comprehensively address many of the relevant areas. Where legislative provision is less than thorough, this can, at times, be attributed to both financial and infrastructural limitations. However, there are three notable and intentional deviations from the CRPD and the ethics underpinning these merit further analysis.

### *10.4.1 Capacity and Limited Guardianship*

The RPWDA and MHCA could be seen as sidestepping controversial issues linked with capacity and limited guardianship. In relation to both of these topics, the legislation points to external guidelines (MHCA, Section 81(1); RPWDA, Section 14(1)). This could represent an attempt to move the potentially non-concordant elements outside of the Indian legislation and into policy. Alternatively, this might represent incremental application of the new legislation, with provisions in policy being easier to revise than those in legislation. This approach might also allow states with varying resource levels to realize the legislation in a graded, contextualized and possibly more successful manner.

This flexibility might well prove especially important as the debate about capacity, and its place in mental health law continues (Szmukler 2019; Flynn 2019). It appears that the initial assessments of capacity will be based on assessments of decision-making ability (MHCA, Section 4(1)), but this might evolve in time, to place increasing weight on individual will and preference through the roles of advance directives and nominated representatives. Should advance directives become commonly employed in Indian psychiatry, a modification of the legislation might well allow them to come into force without an assessment of capacity, as suggested by Flynn (2019).

In any case, data will need to be collected on the utilization of advance directives, limited guardianship and assessments of capacity in order to ensure that the new provisions minimize coercion and promote meaningful change.

### *10.4.2 Coercive Treatments*

Some of the areas of non-concordance between the MHCA and the CRPD appear to be an intentional attempt to continue to permit coercive treatments in situations of severe mental illness. This aligns with the legislation of other jurisdictions such as Queensland, Australia (Del Villar 2015) and England and Wales (Independent Review of the Mental Health Act, 1983 2018) . It intentionally disregards the UN Committee on the Rights of Persons with Disabilities' (2014) interpretation of the CRPD and, in particular, its interpretation of Article 12 ('Equal recognition before the law').

Under the MHCA, coercive treatments can occur on the basis of risk, which can be intentional or unintentional, and can be directed at the person themselves, others or (in some instances) property. As discussed in Chap. 9, risk can be highly subjective. 'Illness criteria' would better align with the skills psychiatrists have. The UN Committee on the Rights of Persons with Disabilities (2014) has been clear that they see no place for coercive treatments at all, but Freeman et al. (2015) correctly highlight how this could lead to deprivation of treatment, criminalization and stigmatization, and it might also infringe on the rights of others (through risk). Nonetheless, the impact of *potential* coercion on people in mental health services and, more broadly, all people with disabilities is difficult to quantify and should not be underestimated (Molodynski et al. 2010; Burns et al. 2011).

Taking all of this into account, it could be argued that the strong family ties and paternalistic practice of medicine in India (Rao et al. 2016) might mean that apparently coercive measures could help *realize* rights, including autonomy, through provision of care. Similarly, the removal of all formal coercion could lead to a significant increase in informal coercion, without appropriate oversight or review.

### *10.4.3 Migration, Citizenship and Nationality*

CRPD rights concerning migration are the most striking omission from the MHCA. This is especially noteworthy given that the legislation emerged from what was clearly a very carefully considered legislative process. The RPWDA and MHCA appear to address almost every other area of the CRPD, generally in a comprehensive manner, but this topic is given no consideration. This is possibly because there is limited medical research on this topic, although it will require greater consideration in the future: international migration is on the increase and will continue to rise in future decades, driven by climate change and economic inequality (UN Department of Economic and Social Affairs Population Division 2017). With many countries seeking to limit immigration, it is important that protections are in place to ensure that disability is not used as a basis for exclusion.

This issue is not limited to mental health. People with leprosy, HIV and other infectious diseases often fear or experience problems when entering other countries, and while this has greatly lessened in recent years, it has not disappeared (Nielsen et al. 2014; Qureshi 1995). The UN Human Rights Council (2008) has been trying assertively to eliminate the discrimination that people with leprosy face, and travel restriction is one of the key areas they have identified. Similar attention is needed in the area of mental health.

## 10.5 Balancing Idealism with Pragmatism

As we have already discussed, the ideals of the CRPD are not universally accepted as necessarily representing the best course of action. The interpretation of the CRPD by the UN Committee on the Rights of Persons with Disabilities (2014) might have led to the articulation of rights that were not intended by all parties involved in the creation of the CRPD. The Committee's interpretations that 'state parties must abolish policies or legislative provisions that allow or perpetuate forced treatment' (p. 11) and that individuals must 'be free from involuntary detention in a mental health facility and not be forced to undergo mental health treatment' (p. 8) were not universally held perspectives among those who drafted the CRPD (Byrnes 2014; Degener and Begg 2017). The Committee's position has also been rejected by England and Wales (Independent Review of the Mental Health Act 1983 2018).

India has opted for a pragmatic rather than idealistic approach to realizing the CRPD. Indian legislation permits a degree of treatment without consent, makes provision for lost capacity, but—most simply of all—it is, clearly and explicitly, *mental health* legislation. Some commentators argue that *any* mental health legislation is, in and of itself, discriminatory (Richardson 2012) and that the ideal approach would be a fusion law based on the absence of decision-making capacity rather than the presence of mental illness.

But many tensions need to be held in balance in psychiatry, and these often require the partial limiting of certain individual rights in order to more completely realize others. This balance can require a deviation from the ideal in order to operate pragmatic systems of care in the real world. We have previously discussed six specific tensions in this context (Duffy and Kelly 2017a), and we now examine these further here, in the particular context of the MHCA.

### 10.5.1 Autonomy in Tension with Dignity

During episodes of acute mental illness or late in a progressive neurodegenerative illness, a person's autonomy is sometimes limited in order to protect their dignity. For example, a disinhibited person having a manic episode might be prevented from going to their place of work to confront their boss in an aggressive, inappropriate and damaging way.

For these situations, the MHCA does much to affirm the principles of both autonomy and dignity, but it enshrines autonomy as the more important principle of the two. Section 4(3) states that as long as a person has 'capacity to make mental healthcare or treatment decisions' they can make decisions 'perceived by others as inappropriate or wrong'. The MHCA also affirms the right of every person with mental illness (not just those in mental health establishments) to 'live with dignity' (Section 20(1)).

Autonomy has its limits in the MHCA, most notably when a person loses capacity to make mental healthcare or treatment decisions, following which, as discussed in Chap. 9, there are multiple circumstances in which a person can be treated without consent. These judgments are based primarily on risk criteria, rather than illness criteria, further supporting the principle of autonomy.

Overall, the MHCA and the RPWDA both do much to enhance the quality of life and social participation of people with mental illness, generally with their consent. The legislation's nuanced protections of both autonomy and dignity, while acknowledging limitations and potential deviations from each, highlights how the two principles are intertwined rather than existing in simple opposition (Randers and Mattiasson 2004).

### *10.5.2 Restriction in Tension with Ineffectual Treatment*

Many mental health professionals have managed the cases of people who have decided not to take any effective treatment. On occasion, some of these people become unwell enough that treatment is administered without their consent. This common situation represents the balance between restriction and ineffective treatment. Subtler forms of this tension often play out during other contacts with mental health services and, regrettably, delivery of effective treatment is not the only motivation for restrictive measures (Johansson et al. 2006).

The MHCA permits coercive treatments but makes provisions for a person to make an advanced directive. These should be followed even where mental health professionals believe there are better treatments available. The MHCA even protects psychiatrists from legal action based on negative outcomes as a result of following advance directives (Section 13(1)). The default position in the MHCA is to follow them even when a person is receiving emergency treatment or is a 'supported' patient.

Despite this, there are still occasions when a Mental Health Review Board can decide to over-ride an advance directive or change a nominated representative. In extreme circumstances, with multiple checks and balances, treatments can be delivered to patients in contravention of their will. Again, the fact that coercive treatments generally occur under the MHCA on the grounds of risk rather than illness emphasizes the priority given to avoiding restrictive treatments.

### *10.5.3 Universal in Tension with Personalized Treatment Options*

There is often a tension in psychiatry between providing someone with personalized treatment and following general policy, treatment protocols or guidelines. For example, a person with depression may have a preference for a non-standard first-line treatment that is poorly supported by evidence. Under the MHCA, the balance has shifted greatly towards personalized treatments. The inclusion of advance directives and a supported decision-making framework accords enhanced priority to personal choice and tailored treatments.

Resource limitation, especially in the areas of funding and staffing, may, however, result in an inability of Indian mental health professionals to personalize treatment to the extent that the MHCA envisages (Shields et al. 2013). The banning of direct ECT, in line with the WHO RB and Article 15 of the CRPD, may deprive some people of treatments that they would have freely chosen (Antony 2015; Thippeswamy et al. 2012; Duffy et al. 2019). In a similar manner, the emphasis on outpatient treatment, while greatly to be welcomed overall, might also inadvertently deprive some people of their preferred (inpatient) treatment option.

### *10.5.4 Ideal Treatment in Tension with Pragmatic Treatment*

All areas of medicine hold a tension between ideal and pragmatic treatments, often driven by limitations on funding and resources. In the field of mental health, ethical principles may also impact on this balance. England and Wales, for example, have decided that the total prohibition on coercive treatment proposed by the UN Committee on the Rights of Persons with Disabilities (2014) is unjustified, unworkable and possibly counter-productive (Independent Review of the Mental Health Act, 1983 2018). Rather than create idealistic legislation, they have opted for a pragmatic interpretation of the CRPD. India has, in many ways, taken a similar approach. Their legislation is highly informed by the CRPD but departs from the Committee's interpretation of the Convention, at least to the extent that the Indian legislation permits coercive treatments and, on occasion, substitute decision-making.

However, India is also striving for the ideal, in many ways. The MHCA makes multiple references to community-based services and rehabilitation centres, and—most of all—provides an extensive, justiciable right to mental healthcare (Duffy and Kelly 2019). The new legislation has laid out a vision on mental healthcare that will be highly challenging to realize and will require a substantial increase in funding. Should this project receive insufficient support, however, there is a real danger that people with mental illness in India will be left with an 'ideal' but largely ignored piece of legislation. This would be a real pity.

Another area where India has opted for the ideal standard, despite many objections, relates to unmodified ECT (Andrade et al. 2012). This has been one of the most contentious areas of the MHCA to date (Duffy et al. 2018, 2019). Many Indian psychiatrists argue in favour of retaining unmodified ECT and highlight how unmodified ECT can be the *only* treatment available in certain circumstances, owing to cost or the non-availability of anaesthetic support (Andrade et al. 2012; Ray 2016; Shah et al. 2010). Despite these concerns, a total prohibition of unmodified ECT was included in the legislation (Section 95(1)(a)).

In many areas, then, India's MHCA strives to be a piece of idealistic legislation, but it also seeks to be practical. Generally, it succeeds in striking a reasonable balance between the two positions.

### 10.5.5 The Individual in Tension with Society

At times, the rights of society need to be balanced against the rights of individuals with mental illness. For example, a person who poses a risk to other people due to a delusion might be detained under mental health legislation. In recent decades, there has been much more of a drive to emphasize the rights of the person with the illness, rather than the rights of others, but the protection of society still features in multiple places in the MHCA.

The MHCA's endorsement of the CRPD does much to ensure that the interests of the patient are at the centre of the legislation. Personal autonomy is protected and preserved in many ways; the will and preferences of people with mental illness are supported; and there is a right to mental healthcare (Duffy and Kelly 2019). Provided they have capacity, people have the freedom to make choices 'perceived by others as inappropriate or wrong' (Section 4(3)).

The inclusion of risk-based criteria for emergency treatment and 'supported' admission, however, means that, in extreme circumstances, the MHCA takes steps to protect society over the individual. A 'supported' admission can occur if the person 'has recently behaved or is behaving violently towards another person or has caused or is causing another person to fear bodily harm from him' (Section 89(1)(a)(ii)), and this can be extended where a person 'has consistently over time behaved violently towards another person or has consistently over time caused another person to fear bodily harm from him' (Section 90(2)(a)(ii)). Interestingly, for emergency treatment, causing harm to property can be enough to incur a deprivation of liberty for up to 72 h (Section 94(1)(c)). The RPWDA, on the other hand, is solely focused on benefiting the person with the disability and, consequently, gives little consideration to broader societal impacts.

### 10.5.6 Involvement in Tension with Privacy

The important role of confidentiality and its limitations often arise in the area of mental healthcare and can present highly challenging ethical situations.

The MHCA appears to favour privacy over the involvement of other individuals (Section 20(2)(d)), and psychiatrists have expressed certain concerns about this (Duffy et al. 2018). In many ways, families could potentially be marginalized by the legislation and replaced by nominated representatives. Pathare and colleagues (2015), however, highlight that 80% of people choose to involve their families in care and where an individual has not made an advance directive, a family member automatically is offered the role (Section 14(4)).

Relatives are commonly deeply involved in the treatment of mental health conditions in India, often to the great benefit to the person (Avasthi 2010). Protections are nonetheless needed to prevent the family members enforcing their will. The role of the nominated representative provides this protection but also comes with checks and balances (Duffy and Kelly 2017c).

Overall, both the MHCA and RPWDA take many steps to protect the privacy of people with disabilities, but they remove some of the automatic privileges that families previously received. Further examination is needed, over future years, to see if this possible imposition of the western concept of 'individualism' in an Indian culture with strong family ties is, in fact, a form of neo-colonialism (Davar 2014). It is, however, noteworthy that family still retains many special rights under the MHCA. Section 19(2) clearly conceptualizes the family home as the primary residence of people with mental illness, and families are entitled to involvement in discharge planning (Section 98(1)). In the case of a person 'with mental illness who is homeless or found wandering in the community', confidentiality can be breached and the police have a duty to find and inform the family (Section 100(7)). Relatives are also one of the special groups that can apply to have an advance directive overturned under the MHCA (Section 11(1)).

Under the RPWDA, it remains to be seen how the limited guardianship role will be utilized before its impact on privacy can be assessed. Finally, Section 23 of the MHCA lays out the contexts in which confidentiality can be breached. In addition to the sharing of information with a nominated representative and health care providers, there are grounds for breaching confidentiality if there is thought to be a risk to another person (Section 23(2)(c)).

## 10.6 Conclusions

Discussing sociology and political models, Chomsky (2013) points out that nobody can actually design a society, but reasonable principles on which to build a society are quite clear. In a similar fashion, it might be difficult to design just, rights-based mental health legislation from scratch, but the CRPD and the WHO RB lay out reasonable principles for the development of such legislation over time. India has taken up these principles with vigour and is now—essentially—conducting the world's largest ever experiment in rights-based mental health law.

Chomsky (2013) also points out that, in the eighteenth century, it was very difficult to find a working model of a political democracy, but that didn't prove that such a thing could not exist. By the following century, it did exist. Therefore, unless we argue that human history is over (which it clearly is not), then it is not a valid argument to say that something, such as a perfect mental health law, *cannot* exist simply because it does not exist *yet*. It is entirely possible that such a law could be created and that India has come closer to achieving this goal than any other country has.

As we have discussed throughout this book, many commentators highlight the potential drawbacks of CRPD-concordant legislation, the practical problems with implementation, and the time and resource demands it will place on services. Some have questioned if such legislation is workable in the first place, and many jurisdictions are simply ignoring the challenge created by the CRPD. This is an error.

India's new legislation is a bold experiment that will hopefully prove an important step on the way to reframing mental health legislation internationally for the twenty-first century, both embracing the CRPD and maintaining an awareness of practical challenges on the ground.

With both the MHCA and RPWDA, India has taken bold, important steps to align with the CRPD and address many areas of the WHO RB. Key additional elements of this legislation will appear in guidelines or other legislation, and these will need to be carefully evaluated in due course.

In some areas, questionable concordance with the CRPD in the Indian legislation reflects a progressive desire to provide high-quality mental healthcare (e.g. in relation to research and the role of families). In addition, some of the omissions from the legislation have moved certain controversial topics outside the RPWDA and the MHCA (e.g. limited guardianship and the finer details of assessing mental capacity). While some of these changes might appear primarily semantic, they form part of a much larger and necessarily incremental process of change to the network of laws and regulations governing these areas. For example, 'supported' admissions are not so far removed from more traditional 'involuntary' admissions in many ways, but the tone taken in the MHCA is an important and progressive change.

Overall, India has not shirked its responsibility in relation to the CRPD and has made a bold attempt at pragmatically realizing the Convention in national mental health legislation. It falls short of the interpretation of the UN Committee on the Rights of Persons with Disabilities (2014) but all mental health legislation will, by very definition, fail to concord with that Committee's perspective.

India has also left a few areas intentionally obscure, in relation to capacity, the role of family and emergency treatments. But even these provisions include many checks and balances, which will hopefully facilitate a degree of flexibility in implementation so as to better meet the complex needs of people with mental health problems.

In addition, the MHCA and RPWDA will hopefully help shape new laws in other jurisdictions too. Importantly, they demonstrate that it is possible for a lower middle-income country to develop modern rights-based legislation. These Acts may even help shape future interpretations of the CRPD and inform the existing interpretations with some much-needed pragmatism. Hopefully, implementation of the MHCA will continue to be studied closely, in order to help refine its idealistic principles with quantitative and qualitative evidence, and optimize learning for all stakeholders involved in this extraordinary initiative.

## 10.7 Directions for Future Research

There are extensive unmet research needs in relation to ethics, human rights and mental health law. Addressing these deficits may be part of the experimentation needed to design effective mental health legislation as part of a just society. Multiple meta-questions arise, including the role of legislation in realizing human rights and the importance to be accorded to competing for ethical principles. Looking more specifically at the issue of coercive care, two key issues emerge: understanding coercion itself and developing ways of avoiding and reducing it.

### 10.7.1 Understanding Coercion

There is a clear and ongoing need for greater research about the experiences and views of people with mental illness in relation to coercion, and about the prevalence, degree and legal basis of such coercion in the first place. Szmukler (2019) has highlighted how the perspective of the UN Committee on the Rights of Persons with Disabilities (2014) might not reflect the views of significant groups of people with mental illness. Surveys of people who have been involuntarily detained demonstrate that many feel future detention and treatment could be justified (O'Donoghue et al. 2010; Tekkalaki et al. 2018). Greater understanding of these perspectives would help better inform discussions relating to the CRPD in the context of mental health legislation.

The UN Committee on the Rights of Persons with Disabilities (2014) makes the unreferenced statement that involuntary treatment occurs despite 'empirical evidence indicating its lack of effectiveness' (p. 11). While it is unclear what research this statement is based on, and there is evidence to suggest the contrary (Steinert et al. 2014), this is certainly an area that requires additional research, with consideration given to a broad spectrum of outcomes over a sustained period of time. Research in this area is complicated by the need to recruit participants who might not have the capacity to provide free and informed consent. This must be addressed through revised, adapted ethical paradigms and more novel, inclusive approaches by research ethics committees. It is important that political drives do not supplant the need for a clear evidence base for care, as the imposition of well-intentioned principles without careful consideration might well have unintended consequences (Freeman et al. 2015).

In many ways, Article 12 of the CRPD is the key sticking point when it comes to mental health legislation. Adherence with Article 12 cannot occur through a minor revision of legislation (as many countries have attempted) but requires a complete overhaul of existing legislation (Del Villar 2015). Byrne and colleagues (2018) have proposed a tool for evaluating concordance of legislation with Article 12. It would be highly informative to see countries use this tool, although the assumption that full adherence is desired or even possible remains unproven in medical research, unpopular with legislators (Independent Review of the Mental Health Act, 1983 2018) and not fully supported by other elements within the UN (Szmukler 2019). In a similar fashion, the development of an updated, CRPD-informed checklist to replace the WHO RB (WHO 2005) would be of great assistance to legislators evaluating and drafting new mental health law.

### *10.7.2 Reducing Coercion*

When seeking to reduce coercion in mental healthcare, it is important that both *formal* and *experienced* coercion are addressed. For example, many of the protections required for 'substitute decision-making' frameworks are also required for 'supported decision-making' frameworks. The UN Committee on the Rights of Persons with Disabilities (2014) highlights the 'deep pain and trauma as a result of forced treatment' (p. 11), and this will remain a problem even in contexts where people receive treatment in a highly supported decision-making paradigm, such as that in India. As a result, research is needed to identify precisely how admission and treatment can occur in the least traumatic and stressful manner possible in *any* decision-making paradigm. There is also a real need to develop alternatives to coercive treatments; a robust evidence base to support such alternatives would greatly hasten their adoption (Szmukler 2019).

It will also be increasingly important in future years to identify the positive and negative impacts of supported decision-making involving family members. While substitute decisions made by medical professionals have many limitations, even more conflicts of interest can arise when family members are making the decisions, especially if they lack an understanding of mental illness. On the opposite side of this argument is the fact that the MHCA does not protect rights of families to the degree suggested in the WHO RB, presumably because to do so would be inconsistent with the CRPD.

Despite this tension, and despite the provisions of the MHCA, there is still a general expectation of family involvement in Indian psychiatry (Duffy et al. 2018; Pavitra et al. 2019). As a result, it would be highly informative to study the impact of the new legislation on the wider families of people with mental illness, how satisfied patients are with family involvement and how families feel about the MHCA as implementation continues over the coming years.

## References

Ademosu, T. (2018). Here and there. *Lancet Psychiatry, 5*(12), 970–972.

Andrade, C., Shah, N., Tharyan, P., Reddy, M. S., Thirunavukarasu, M., Kallivayalil, R. A., et al. (2012). Position statement and guidelines on unmodified electroconvulsive therapy. *Indian Journal of Psychiatry, 54*(2), 119–133.

Antony, J. T. (2015). The ban on unmodified ECT and psychiatrists craving for a new identity. *Kerala Journal of Psychiatry, 28,* 11–15.

Appelbaum, P. S. (2019). Saving the UN Convention on the Rights of Persons with Disabilities—From itself. *World Psychiatry, 18*(1), 1–2.

Avasthi, A. (2010). Preserve and strengthen family to promote mental health. *Indian Journal of Psychiatry, 52*(2), 113–126.

Burns, T., Yeeles, K., Molodynski, A., Nightingale, H., Vazquez-Montes, M., Sheehan, K., et al. (2011). Pressures to adhere to treatment ('leverage') in English mental healthcare. *British Journal of Psychiatry, 199*(2), 145–150.

Byrne, M., White, B., & McDonald, F. (2018). A new tool to assess compliance of mental health laws with the Convention on the Rights of Persons with Disabilities. *International Journal of Law Psychiatry, 58,* 122–142.

Byrnes, A. (2014). The role of national human rights institutions. In M. Sabatello & M. Schulze (Eds.), *Human rights and disability advocacy* (pp. 222–238). Philadelphia: University of Pennsylvania Press.

Cahalan, S. (2019). *The great pretender: The undercover mission that changed our understanding of madness*. New York and Boston: Grand Central Publishing.

Chomsky, N. (2013). *On anarchism*. London: Penguin.

D'Amico, M., & Nardocci, C. (2016). LGBT rights and the way forward: The evolution of the case law of the ECtHR in relation to transgender individuals' identity. *ERA Forum, 17,* 191.

Davar, B. V. (2014). Globalizing psychiatry and the case of 'vanishing' alternatives in a neo-colonial state. *Disability and the Global South, 1*(2), 266–284.

Degener, T., & Begg, A. (2017). From invisible citizens to agents of change: A short history of the struggle for the recognition of the rights of persons with disabilities at the United Nations. In V. D. Fina, R. Cera, & G. Palmisano (Eds.), *The United Nations Convention on the Rights of Persons with Disabilities: A commentary* (pp. 1–40). Cham: Springer.

Del Villar, K. (2015). Should supported decision-making replace substituted decision-making? The Convention on the Rights of Persons with Disabilities and coercive treatment under Queensland's Mental Health Act, 2000. *Laws, 4,* 173–200.

Duffy, R. M., & Kelly, B. D. (2017a). Rights, laws and tensions: a comparative analysis of the Convention on the Rights of Persons with Disabilities and the WHO Resource Book on Mental Health, Human Rights and Legislation. *International Journal of Law and Psychiatry, 54,* 26–35.

Duffy, R. M., & Kelly, B. D. (2017b). Can psychiatry lead the way in legislating for health and wellbeing? *Irish Medical Journal, 110*(6), 591.

Duffy, R. M., & Kelly, B. D. (2017c). Privacy, confidentiality and carers: India's harmonization of national guidelines and international mental health law. *Ethics, Medicine and Public Health, 3*(1), 98–106.

Duffy, R. M., & Kelly, B. D. (2019). The right to mental healthcare: India moves forward. *British Journal of Psychiatry, 214*(2), 59–60.

Duffy, R. M., Narayan, C. L., Goyal, N., & Kelly, B. D. (2018). New legislation, new frontiers: Indian psychiatrists' perspective of the mental healthcare act 2017 prior to implementation. *Indian Journal of Psychiatry, 60*(3), 351–354.

Duffy, R. M., Gulati, G., Paralikar, V., Kasar, N., Goyal, N., Desousa, A., et al. (2019). A focus group study of Indian psychiatrists' views on electroconvulsive therapy under India's Mental Healthcare Act 2017: 'the ground reality is different'. *Indian Journal of Psychological Medicine, 41,* 507–515.

Flynn, E. (2019). The rejection of capacity assessments in favor of respect for will and preferences: The radical promise of the UN Convention on the Rights of Persons with Disabilities. *World Psychiatry, 18*(1), 50–51.

Freeman, M. C., Kolappa, K., de Almeida, J. M., Kleinman, A., Makhashvili, N., Phakathi, S., et al. (2015). Reversing hard won victories in the name of human rights: A critique of the General Comment on Article 12 of the UN Convention on the Rights of Persons with Disabilities. *Lancet Psychiatry, 2*(9), 844–850.

Fuchs, T. (2010). Subjectivity and intersubjectivity in psychiatric diagnosis. *Psychopathology, 43*(4), 268–274.

Harpur, P. (2012). Embracing the new disability rights paradigm: The importance of the Convention on the Rights of Persons with Disabilities. *Disability & Society, 27*(1), 1–14.

Independent Review of the Mental Health Act 1983. (2018). *Modernising the Mental Health Act: Increasing choice, reducing compulsion.* London: Gov.uk. Retrieved September 23, 2019, from https://assets.publishing.service.gov.uk/government/uploads/system/uploads/attachment_data/file/778897/Modernising_the_Mental_Health_Act_-_increasing_choice__reducing_compulsion.pdf.

Jiloha, R. C. (2015). The Mental Health Act of India. In S. Malhotra & S. Chakrabarti (Eds.), *Developments in psychiatry in India: Clinical, research and policy perspectives* (pp. 611–622). New Delhi: Springer.

Johansson, I. M., Skärsäter, I., & Danielson, E. (2006). The health-care environment on a locked psychiatric ward: An ethnographic study. *International Journal of Mental Health Nursing, 15*(4), 242–250.

Kanter, A. S. (2011). The law: What's disability studies got to do with it or an introduction to disability legal studies. *Columbia Human Rights Law Review, 42*(2), 403–479.

Kelly, B. D. (2011). Mental health legislation and human rights in England, Wales and the Republic of Ireland. *International Journal of Law and Psychiatry, 34*(6), 439–454.

Khosla, R., Banerjee, J., Chou, D., Say, L., & Fried, S. T. (2017). Gender equality and human rights approaches to female genital mutilation: A review of international human rights norms and standards. *Reproductive Health, 14*(1), 59.

Kisely, S., & Hall, K. (2014). An updated meta-analysis of randomized controlled evidence for the effectiveness of community treatment orders. *Canadian Journal of Psychiatry. Revue Canadienne de Psychiatrie, 59*(10), 561–564.

Mandarelli, G., Carabellese, F., Parmigiani, G., Bernardini, F., Pauselli, L., Quartesan, R., et al. (2018). Treatment decision-making capacity in non-consensual psychiatric treatment: A multicentre study. *Epidemiology and Psychiatric Sciences, 27*(5), 492–499.

Math, S. B., Gowda, G. S., Basavaraju, V., Manjunatha, N., Kumar, C. N., Enara, A., et al. (2019). Cost estimation for the implementation of the Mental Healthcare Act 2017. *Indian Journal of Psychiatry, 61*(10), S650–S659.

Molodynski, A., Rugkåsa, J., & Burns, T. (2010). Coercion and compulsion in community mental health care. *British Medical Bulletin, 95,* 105–119.

Munetz, M. R., Galon, P. A., & Frese, F. J., 3rd. (2003). The ethics of mandatory community treatment. *Journal of the American Academy of Psychiatry and the Law, 31*(2), 173–183.

Narayan, C. L., & Shekhar, S. (2013). The Mental Health Care Bill 2013: A critical appraisal. *Indian Journal of Psychiatry, 37*(2), 215–219.

Nielsen, U. S., Jensen-Fangel, S., Pedersen, G., Lohse, N., Pedersen, C., Kronborg, G., et al. (2014). Travelling with HIV: A cross sectional analysis of Danish HIV-infected patients. *Travel Medicine and Infectious Disease, 12*(1), 72–78.

O'Donoghue, B., Lyne, J., Hill, M., O'Rourke, L., Daly, S., & Feeney, L. (2010). Patient attitudes towards compulsory community treatment orders and advance directives. *Irish Journal of Psychological Medicine, 27*(2), 66–71.

Oliver, M. (2013). The social model of disability: Thirty years on. *Disability & Society, 28*(7), 1024–1026.

Patel, V., Saxena, S., Lund, C., Thornicroft, G., Baingana, F., Bolton, P., et al. (2018). The Lancet Commission on global mental health and sustainable development. *Lancet, 392*(10157), 1553–1598.

Pathare, S., Shields, L., Nardodkar, R., Narasimhan, L., & Bunders, J. (2015). What do service users want? A content analysis of what users may write in psychiatric advance directives in India. *Asian Journal of Psychiatry, 14,* 52–56.

Pavitra, K. S., Kalmane, S., Kumar, A., & Gowda, M. (2019). Family matters! The caregivers' perspective of Mental Healthcare Act 2017. *Indian Journal of Psychiatry, 61*(10), S832–S837.

Peterson, D., & Keeley, J. (2014). Definition of mental disorder. *Encyclopedia of Clinical Psychology*, 1–6.

Qureshi, S. N. (1995). Global ostracism of HIV-positive aliens: International restrictions barring HIV-positive aliens. *Maryland Journal of International Law and Trade, 19*(1), 81–120.

Rajkumar, R. P. (2014). Unmodified electroconvulsive therapy: A false dilemma. *Indian Journal of Medical Ethics, 11*(2), 89–93.

Randers, I., & Mattiasson, A. C. (2004). Autonomy and integrity: Upholding older adult patients' dignity. *Journal of Advanced Nursing, 45*(1), 63–71.

Rao, G. P., Math, S. B., Raju, M. S., Saha, G., Jagiwala, M., Sagar, R., et al. (2016). Mental Health Care Bill, 2016: A boon or bane? *Indian journal of Psychiatry, 58*(3), 244–249.
Ray, A. K. (2016). How bad was unmodified electroconvulsive therapy? A retrospective study. *Indian Journal of Psychiatry, 58*(2), 212–215.
Richardson, G. (2012). Mental disabilities and the law: from substitute to supported decision-making? *Current Legal Problems, 65*(1), 333–354.
Rogler, L. H. (1997). Making sense of historical changes in the Diagnostic and Statistical Manual of Mental Disorders: Five propositions. *Journal of Health and Social Behavior, 38*(1), 9–20.
Rosenhan, D. L. (1973). On being sane in insane places. *Science, 179*(4070), 250–258.
Scheunemann, L. P., & White, D. B. (2011). The ethics and reality of rationing in medicine. *Chest, 140*(6), 1625–1632.
Schulze, M. (2010). *Understanding the UN Convention on the Rights of Persons with Disabilities* (3rd ed.). New York: Handicap International.
Shah, N., Mahadeshwar, S., Bhakta, S., Bhirud, M., Fernandes, P., & Andrade, C. (2010). The safety and efficacy of benzodiazepine-modified treatments as a special form of unmodified ECT. *Journal of ECT, 26*(1), 23–29.
Shields, L. S., Pathare, S., van Zelst, S. D., Dijkkamp, S., Narasimhan, L., & Bunders, J. G. (2013). Unpacking the psychiatric advance directive in low-resource settings: An exploratory qualitative study in Tamil Nadu, India. *International Journal of Mental Health Systems, 7*(1), 29.
Steinert, T., Noorthoorn, E. O., & Mulder, C. L. (2014). The use of coercive interventions in mental health care in Germany and the Netherlands. A comparison of the developments in two neighboring countries. *Frontiers in Public Health, 2*, 141.
Strech, D., Persad, G., Marckmann, G., & Danis, M. (2009). Are physicians willing to ration health care? Conflicting findings in a systematic review of survey research. *Health Policy, 90*(2–3), 113–124.
Szmukler, G. (2019). "Capacity", "best interests", "will and preferences" and the UN Convention on the Rights of Persons with Disabilities. *World Psychiatry, 18*(1), 34–41.
Tekkalaki, B., Patil, V. Y., Patil, S., Chate, S. S., Dhabale, R., & Patil, N. M. (2018). How do our patients respond to the concept of psychiatric advance directives? An exploratory study from India. *Indian Journal of Psychological Medicine, 40*(4), 305–309.
Thippeswamy, H., Goswami, K., & Chaturvedi, S. (2012). Ethical aspects of public health legislation: The Mental Health Care Bill, 2011. *Indian Journal of Medical Ethics, 9*(1), 46–49.
United Nations. (1991). *Principles for the protection of persons with mental illness and the improvement of mental health care.* New York: United Nations, Secretariat Centre For Human Rights. Retrieved September 23, 2019, from https://www.who.int/mental_health/policy/en/UN_Resolution_on_protection_of_persons_with_mental_illness.pdf.
United Nations. (2006). *Convention on the rights of persons with disabilities.* New York: United Nations. Retrieved September 23, 2019, from https://www.un.org/development/desa/disabilities/convention-on-the-rights-of-persons-with-disabilities/convention-on-the-rights-of-persons-with-disabilities-2.html.
United Nations Committee on the Rights of Persons with Disabilities. (2014). *General comment No. 1: Article 12: Equal recognition before the law.* New York: United Nations. Retrieved September 23, 2019, from http://www.ohchr.org/EN/HRBodies/CRPD/Pages/GC.aspx.
United Nations Department of Economic and Social Affairs Population Division. (2017). *International migration report 2017: highlights.* New York: United Nations. Retrieved September 23, 2019, from http://www.un.org/en/development/desa/population/migration/publications/migrationreport/docs/MigrationReport2017_Highlights.pdf.
United Nations Economic and Social Council. (1985). *Siracusa principles on the limitation and Derogation Provisions in the International Covenant on Civil and Political Rights.* Geneva: United Nations.
United Nations Human Rights Council. (2008). *Elimination of discrimination against persons affected by leprosy and their family members. Resolution A/HRC/8/L.18, 2008.* Geneva: United

Nations. Retrieved September 23, 2019, from https://documents-dds-ny.un.org/doc/UNDOC/LTD/G08/143/76/PDF/G0814376.pdf?OpenElement.

World Health Organization. (2005). *WHO resource book on mental health, human rights and legislation*. Geneva: World Health Organization.

World Health Organization. (2017). *Advancing the right to health: The vital role of law*. Geneva: World Health Organization. Retrieved September 23, 2019, from https://www.who.int/gender-equity-rights/knowledge/advancing-the-right-to-health/en/.

# Part IV
# Where Now?—Contribution by Dr Soumitra Pathare and Arjun Kapoor

# Chapter 11
# Implementation Update on Mental Healthcare Act, 2017

**Soumitra Pathare and Arjun Kapoor**

## 11.1 Introduction

The promise of India's Mental Healthcare Act, 2017 (MHCA), as outlined in the previous chapters of this book, will remain just that—a promise—without effective implementation of the legislation. Readers who are not familiar with India will be more than a little surprised by the idea of a law existing on statute but not being implemented. However, India has a history of enacting progressive social sector legislation which remains unimplemented and 'customary practices' continue unhindered. For example, the previous Mental Health Act, 1987 was enacted by Parliament in 1987 but only brought into force six years later in 1993—a significant delay. As late as 2013, many state governments had not established a State Mental Health Authority as required under the 1987 Act. Glaringly, there continue to be anecdotal examples, frequently reported by popular media, of magistrates issuing Reception Orders under the Indian Lunacy Act, 1912, which was repealed by the 1987 Act!

In this chapter, we discuss key developments regarding the implementation of the MHCA since its enactment as a law. We also discuss key challenges in the implementation of the MHCA based on our interactions with service users, family caregivers, government officials, mental health professionals, judicial officers and other stakeholders. Finally, we highlight priority areas, obligations of duty-bearers, and make recommendations for implementing the MHCA in its letter and spirit.

## 11.2 Progress Under the Mental Healthcare Act, 2017

The MHCA was enacted after receiving presidential assent on 7 April 2017. The Central Government was mandated to enforce the Act within a period of nine months from this date. This window period was expected to provide the Central Government and State Governments sufficient time to draft the Central and State rules and initiate preliminary steps for implementation at the ground level. Among other measures,

 
R. M. Duffy and B. D. Kelly, *India's Mental Healthcare Act, 2017*,
https://doi.org/10.1007/978-981-15-5009-6_11

this included establishment of the State Mental Health Authorities and the Mental Health Review Boards and developing any transitional schemes for persons with mental illness governed under the erstwhile Mental Health Act, 1987. However, for reasons unknown, the MHCA was brought into force only eleven months later, on 29 May 2018.

It has been more than one and a half years since then, however, and implementation of the MHCA has progressed at a very slow pace (as of time of writing, December 2019). While the Central Government has notified the Central Rules, no State Government has notified the State Rules for implementation of the MHCA. So far, out of 37 States and Union Territories, only 19 States have established a State Mental Health Authority, while only four States have notified Mental Health Review Boards. None of the notified Mental Health Review Boards has begun functioning and monitoring implementation of the MHCA. The Mental Health Review Boards play a crucial role in implementation as they are mandated to register advance directives, monitor supported admissions (involuntary admissions), adjudicate complaints of rights violations, inspect mental health establishments and address issues of non-compliance by duty-bearers. Therefore, in the absence of the Mental Health Review Boards, implementation of the MHCA is not possible. Further, none of the State Mental Health Authorities has notified regulations and/or minimum standards for registering mental health establishments. As a result, despite the enforcement of the MHCA, mental health establishments continue to function as per norms under the previous Mental Health Act, 1987. According to the Ministry of Health and Family Welfare, Government of India, no State has submitted proposals to the Ministry of Health and Family Welfare for reimbursement of funds meant for progress at field level under various mental health schemes.

However, a significant development has been the Insurance Regulatory and Development Authority of India (2018) issuing a notification to all insurance companies to provide medical insurance cover to all persons with mental illness on a par with persons with physical illness in accordance with the Section 21(4) of the MHCA. The Insurance Regulatory and Development Authority of India has also in its guidelines on standardisation of exclusions in health insurance contracts, disallowed the exclusion of treatment of mental illness, stress and psychological disorders from health insurance contracts.

## 11.3 Judiciary

The MHCA has been subject to judicial scrutiny by the Supreme Court of India and High Courts in matters of public interest. The judiciary's engagement with the MHCA has primarily been twofold: (i) reliance on the MHCA's provisions to adjudicate important questions of constitutional law and fundamental rights; and (ii) monitoring and holding duty-bearers accountable for implementation of the MHCA at the central and state levels.

With respect to the former, the Supreme Court of India has relied extensively on the MHCA's provisions in two landmark cases involving interpretations of fundamental rights under the Constitution. In the historic case of Navtej Singh Johar v. Union of Indian Thr. Secretary Ministry of Law and Justice,[1] the Supreme Court read down Section 377 of the Indian Penal Code, 1860 which criminalized consensual sexual acts between adults of the same sex. The Supreme Court decisively ruled that Section 377 in so far as it criminalized consensual sexual acts between adults was unconstitutional. The Court held that Section 377 discriminated against homosexual persons based on their sexual orientation and violated their fundamental rights under the Constitution of India. The Court while explaining its decision relied extensively on the anti-discrimination provisions of the MHCA. The Court cited Sections 18 and 21 of the MHCA which prohibit discrimination on various grounds including a person's sexual orientation while receiving mental healthcare and treatment. The Court extended this principle of the MHCA to hold that discrimination on grounds of sexual orientation under Section 377 was unconstitutional. Further, the Court relied on the definition of 'mental illness' under Sections 2(1)(s) and 3 of the MHCA regarding determination of mental illness in accordance with internationally or nationally accepted medical standards to hold that homosexuality is not a mental disorder. Finally, the Court recognized that the existence of anti-discriminatory provisions prohibiting discrimination based on sexual orientation in the MHCA was a strong legal ground to test the constitutionality of Section 377 and its discriminatory effects on homosexual persons.

In the second case, Common Cause (A Regd. Society) v. Union of India, the Supreme Court was confronted with the constitutionality of passive euthanasia.[2] The Court ruled that a decision to withdraw life-saving treatment for a patient suffering from terminally ill disease with no possibility of recovery is legal and permissible. Further, the Court also held that in cases where such a person does not have mental capacity to take an informed decision but has written a valid medical advance directive directing withdrawal of life-supporting treatment, then such advance directive must be executed. The Court thereon laid down principles for a valid advance directive and the procedure for executing the same. While recognizing the right of a person to prepare an advance directive, the Court relied on the MHCA's provisions which provide for advance directives in the case of mental healthcare and treatment. Thus, the Supreme Court recognized the importance of the MHCA as an authoritative precedent to legally recognize and permit the use of advance directives in the case of passive euthanasia.

The Supreme Court and High Courts have also been proactive in monitoring the implementation of the MHCA at the central and state levels. In an ongoing case of Gaurav Kumar Bansal v. Union of India, the petitioner filed a public interest litigation to challenge the chaining of persons with mental illness in a faith-based centre in

[1]Navtej Singh Johar v. Union of Indian Thr. Secretary Ministry of Law and Justice. Writ Petition (Criminal) No. 76 of 2016. https://indiankanoon.org/doc/168671544/. Accessed 12 December 2019.

[2]Common Cause (A Regd. Society) v. Union of India. Writ Petition (Civil) No. 215 of 2005 https://indiankanoon.org/doc/184449972/. Accessed 12 December 2019.

District Badaun of the State of Uttar Pradesh. The Supreme Court, while taking cognizance of the same as in contravention of the MHCA, issued a notice to all State Governments to provide a status report on the measures taken for implementation of the MHCA and further directed them to set up a State Mental Health Authority and a fund for implementing the MHCA (Anonymous 2019).

In another ongoing case of Gaurav Kumar Bansal v. Dinesh Kumar & Ors., the Supreme Court issued directions to all State Governments to submit data to the Secretary, Ministry of Health and Family Welfare, Government of India on the status of compliance and facilities for rehabilitation of deinstitutionalized persons who have been treated for mental illnesses.[3] The State Governments were also directed to provide a road map for setting up halfway homes within each of the States. Both cases continue to be monitored by the Supreme Court on a regular basis.

In another case, Accused X versus State of Maharashtra, of a review petition of a person sentenced to death penalty, the Supreme Court ruled that 'in line with Section 23 (1) of the Mental Healthcare Act, 2017, (Act 10 of 2017) and the right to privacy of the accused herein, while taking further action on this judgment, we direct the Registry to not disclose the actual name of the accused and other pertinent information which could lead to his identification as it concerns confidential information. In this context we shall address the accused herein as "accused x".[4]

Recently, the Delhi High Court (Sharma 2019), Karnataka High Court (Special Correspondent 2019) and Uttarakhand High Court[5] have issued notice and asked for a status update on the implementation of the MHCA from the respective State Governments. Further, in the case of Dr. Sangamitra Acharya & Anr. v. State (NCT of Delhi) & Ors,[6] the Delhi High Court has issued directions to the Delhi Police to develop a manual detailing how to deal with cases under the MHCA in consultation with experts in mental healthcare. The Delhi High Court has also issued directions to the State Mental Health Authority and the Delhi Judicial Academy to hold programmes on a periodic basis with different stakeholders to sensitize them about the various compliances under the MHCA.

## 11.4 Other Developments

The Centre for Mental Health Law and Policy, Indian Law Society, Pune, where both authors of this chapter work, has been at the forefront of providing technical support to various stakeholders for driving the implementation of the MHCA. The

[3]Gaurav Kumar Bansal v. Mr. Dinesh Kumar. Conmt. Pet. (C) No. 1653/2018 in W.P. (C) No. 412/2016. https://indiankanoon.org/doc/46614748/. Accessed 12 December 2019.

[4]Accused X v. State of Maharashtra. Review Petition (Criminal) No. 301 of 2008 in Criminal Appeal No. 680 of 2007. https://indiankanoon.org/doc/155869274/. Accessed 12 December 2019.

[5]Dr. Vijay Verma v. Union of India and Others. Writ Petition (PIL) No. 17 of 2018. https://indiankanoon.org/doc/80173720/. Accessed 12 December 2019.

[6]Dr. Sangamitra Acharya & Anr. v. State (NCT of Delhi) & Ors. W.P. (CRL.) 1804/2017 & CM No. 9963/2017. https://indiankanoon.org/doc/149583932/. Accessed 12 December 2019.

Centre has signed three Memoranda of Understanding with the State Governments of Maharashtra, Chhattisgarh and Gujarat for capacity building of duty-bearers under the MHCA. During these processes, the Centre has engaged with government officials of the public health departments, district judges, District Mental Health Programme professionals, law enforcement officials, service users and caregivers. Through these interactions and anecdotal experiences, we discuss below some key challenges to the effective and speedy implementation of the MHCA since its enforcement.

### *11.4.1 Resistance of Mental Health Professionals*

The MHCA has been subject to considerable resistance and criticism from the psychiatric profession. It has been criticized as being an impractical legislation on the ground that the law has an overwhelming mandate which cannot be implemented in a resource-strapped country like India. The legislation has also been accused of being a western import and at complete odds with India's cultural context on the grounds that the concept of nominated representative threatens the family structure by reducing the role of the 'family' (Math et al. 2019a). The provisions on advance directives have also been criticized as being impractical while giving too much autonomy to persons with mental illness to take decisions about their mental healthcare and treatment (Math et al. 2019a). Psychiatrists feel that advance directives can be used by patients to reject treatment to the detriment of their best interests (Antony 2016).

Many of these criticisms are unfounded and go against the spirit of the United Nations (UN) Convention on Rights of Persons with Disabilities (CRPD). The criticism of the concept of 'nominated representatives' is unfounded as, in India, family members are still considered as the primary caregivers across different contexts. Further, this criticism fails to recognize the family as a site of violence and triggers for mental health problems (Patel 2003). This provision for nominated representatives actually gives a respite to many persons with mental illness, especially women and lesbian, gay, bisexual, transgender, queer and intersex persons who face immense violence within their families or are often abandoned by family members on account of their choices (Patel 2003; Chakravarty 2019). Further, the psychiatric community fails to take into consideration the evidence of advance directive as an effective tool for supported decision-making and exercising legal capacity as recognized by the CRPD (UN Committee on the Rights of Persons with Disabilities 2014) and now by the Supreme Court of India.[7]

Psychiatrists' resistance to the MHCA has taken a legal flavour as well. The Indian Psychiatric Society has filed a writ petition in the Bombay High Court challenging the MHCA as unconstitutional and violative of fundamental rights. The Indian Psychiatric Society's petition makes several claims without offering any cogent evidence or arguments in its support. The first claim is that the definition of 'mental illness'

[7]Common Cause (A Regd. Society) v. Union of India. Writ Petition (Civil) No. 215 of 2005 https://indiankanoon.org/doc/184449972/. Accessed 12 December 2019.

in the MHCA is arbitrary as it excludes a whole class of persons with mental illness from receiving treatment, even though Section 3(1) of the MHCA makes it clear that the determination of mental illness must be in accordance with nationally or internationally accepted medical standards. The petition also challenges the provisions on modified electroconvulsive therapy (ECT) on grounds that it denies mental healthcare and treatment to persons who require the same in contexts where anaesthesia and muscle relaxants are not available. This petition has not yet been admitted by the Bombay High Court.

Furthermore, the MHCA has done away with 'reception orders' as used to be issued by magistrates to authorize admissions in hospitals under the erstwhile Mental Health Act, 1987. In the case of homeless and wandering persons, the MHCA, under Section 100, mandates police authorities to take them into protection and present them before a public health establishment within 24 h for assessment. The magistrates only have powers to issue orders for assessment in the case of persons with mental illness who have been neglected or ill-treated in their private residences. However, it has been noticed that hospitals are deferring admissions (especially of homeless and wandering persons) until magistrates authorize reception orders.

In the State of Maharashtra, the Department of Health Services has issued a circular to magistrates to comply with the Mental Health Act, 1987 and issue reception orders until further instructions. In many jurisdictions, magistrates are either continuing to authorize reception orders, and, in cases where they refuse to do so, hospitals are refusing admissions in the absence of reception orders, leading to an impasse for persons with mental illness. Many psychiatric hospitals continue to follow this practice even though it is completely in contravention of the MHCA. The challenge has been to convince both psychiatrists and the magistrates to change their practice in compliance with the new law.

### *11.4.2 Bureaucracy*

India is a quasi-federal state with a three-tiered governance system at the central, state and district levels. According to India's Constitution, 'health' is a State subject. Thus, State Governments have the primary responsibility for implementing health legislations and policies. However, mental healthcare and treatment is a concurrent subject which implies that the Central Government also has powers to legislate on the same. Further, given the existing system of taxation, the Central Government often exercises greater power in the formulation and implementation of health policies (Sahoo 2016).

At the apex level, the Ministry of Health and Family Welfare, Government of India is the nodal ministry for implementing the MHCA through the Department of Health and Family Welfare (which oversees implementation of national health programmes) and Directorate General of Health Services (which, as the technical wing, oversees medical services, medical education and training). At the State level, the Department of Health and Family Welfare is the nodal agency for implementation of the MHCA with support from other sub-departments such as the Directorate of Health Services and the Department of Medical Education. In respect of financial disbursements, the National Health Mission (under the Central Ministry) is the central body which oversees implementation and financial allocations for the National Mental Health Programme and District Mental Health Programme (Ministry of Health and Family Welfare 2019a). The National Health Mission disburses a fixed ratio of funds to State Governments for implementation of the National Mental Health Programme and District Mental Health Programme (Ministry of Health and Family Welfare 2019b). State Governments are expected to utilize these funds based on action plans approved by the Central Ministry, as well as allocate a limited ratio of funds from the State budgets for the same. In our experience, it has been observed that the disbursement of funds is often subject to bureaucratic delay and underutilization by State Governments, or is insufficient to fill the deficits in infrastructure and human resources.

Furthermore, States in India do not have a uniform administrative structure for health governance. In fact, there are wide variations in decision-making processes, duty-bearers and last-mile delivery of health services across different States. This is further complicated by the fact that mental health is an inter-sectoral issue which requires coordination with several other ministries and departments. This is of significance since the MHCA has very clear prescriptions for ensuring community living, rehabilitation services and role of law enforcement agencies (police officers and magistrates) in ensuring mental healthcare and treatment.

For example, at the Central and State levels, rehabilitation of persons with disabilities falls under the purview of the Ministry of Social Justice and Empowerment. The rehabilitation of women and children is largely addressed by the Ministry of Women and Child Development. Similarly, the Ministry of Labour, Ministry of Agriculture, Ministry of Home Affairs, Ministry of Law and Ministry of Youth Affairs all play a crucial role in addressing specific needs of persons with mental illness. Lack of coordination between these departments is often responsible for poor planning, inefficient resource utilization and significant delays in implementation.

For example, many States in India do not have adequate community-based rehabilitation facilities and infrastructure such as halfway homes, long-stay homes or rehabilitation services. The MHCA mandates the right to community living for persons with mental illness with institutionalization as the last resort. Since the provision of rehabilitation services falls under the purview of Ministry of Social Justice and Empowerment, the Department of Health and Family Welfare is expected to coordinate with the former to ensure that community-based rehabilitation facilities are available to ensure that persons admitted in hospitals are able to live in the community once their treatment is over. However, in the absence of these facilities and with poor inter-sectoral coordination, hospitals are encountering severe challenges in discharging patients who do not require institutionalization but need community-based rehabilitation and care.

Similarly, psychiatric hospitals are often faced with the challenge of addressing the safety and wellbeing of homeless and wandering persons who have been abandoned by their families. In many cases, such persons have nowhere to go and instead are admitted to psychiatric hospitals (even if they do not have a mental illness) in the absence of government shelter homes. Addressing these concerns requires inter-sectoral coordination and planning between different departments of the Government. However, the fragmented nature of the governance system is likely to hinder implementation of the MHCA in the absence of efficient coordination, streamlined processes and clear demarcation of duties.

### *11.4.3 Political Will*

A significant barrier to the MHCA's implementation is the reluctance of government stakeholders to treat mental health as a priority on the governance agenda. There exists at multiple levels a lack of political commitment to address mental health as a legitimate health concern on a par with physical health. To illustrate, budgetary spending for mental health is estimated approximately at a meagre 1% of the total health budget (Gururaj et al. 2016). Most States do not allocate separate budgets for mental health as the same is subsumed under the larger rubric of non-communicable diseases. As mentioned previously, most State governments have not submitted budgets for implementation of the MHCA even after one and a half years since its enforcement.

Furthermore, there exists a huge deficit in the provision of mental health services with between 70 and 92% of persons with mental illness having no access to mental healthcare (Gururaj et al. 2016). This is an outcome of several years of governmental apathy which has led to the current crisis of mental healthcare in India. While one can attribute this crisis (in part) to India's overall poor performance in addressing health challenges (Gupta and Pushkar 2017), this situation also indicates a prevailing perception among government stakeholders that mental health is not as significant a 'health' concern as compared to physical health conditions. This is compounded by the fact that mental health is often seen as an amorphous or invisible phenomenon with no clear and verifiable diagnostic parameters (Kapoor and Pathare 2018). Thus, the apparent 'invisibility' of mental illness serves as an underlying premise for governments underestimating the crisis of mental health in India. Furthermore, lack of awareness, stigma and misinformation about mental illnesses continue to play a primary role in contributing to these widely held perceptions among different stakeholders.

At the same time, it is crucial to note that the lack of 'political will' is not a challenge limited to the implementation of mental health law and policy alone. Over the past decade and a half, India has developed an impressive record of enacting rights-based legislations. Some of these legislations which have been the outcome of decades long social movements led by civil society include the Right to Information Act, 2005, National Rural Employment Guarantee Act, 2005, the Forest Rights Act, 2006, the Right to Education Act, 2009 and the National Food Security Act, 2013. However, the implementation of these legislations has been riddled with various challenges such as slow pace of implementation, infrastructural deficits, lack of financial resources, poor inter-sectoral coordination and lack of awareness among rights-holders about the provisions of these laws (Nandy 2019; Anonymous 2017; Bose et al. 2017; Oxfam India 2018).

Equally significant has been the lack of political commitment across different stakeholders ranging from the political class, bureaucrats and front-line workers to deliver commitments under these legislations. While there are no measurable indicators for assessing lack of political commitment, the same may be associated with situations involving a conflict of power interests between the bureaucracy and rights-holders (as seen through experiences of the Forest Rights Act, 2006), lack of incentives, low motivation among duty-bearers, high burden of already existing responsibilities or lack of conviction in rights-based approaches (Gupta and Pushkar 2017; Chopra 2015).

### *11.4.4 Human Resources*

The implementation of the MHCA relies on the availability of a qualified and trained mental health workforce that spans across multiple cadres. These cadres include psychiatrists, medical practitioners, psychiatric nurses, clinical psychologists, psychiatric social workers, para-medicals and other non-specialized health professionals such as caregivers, community health workers and rehabilitation professionals. However, with an estimated demand of at least 150 million persons who have some sort of mental health problem, India faces a severe deficit in the availability of a mental health workforce that is qualified and trained to address the needs of this population (Gururaj et al. 2016).

According to the World Mental Health Atlas in 2014, India had 0.3 psychiatrists, 0.07 clinical psychologists, 0.12 psychiatric nurses and 0.07 social workers per 100,000 of the population (Gururaj et al. 2016). However, other estimates suggest that India currently has 9,000 psychiatrists, 2,000 psychiatric nurses, 1,000 clinical psychologists and 1,000 social workers (Math et al. 2019b). Further, according to estimates, India requires a median of three mental health professionals (psychiatrists, psychologists, nurses and social workers) per one lakh (100,000) population (Garg et al. 2019). Section 31(3) of the MHCA mandates the Central and State Governments to ensure that appropriate steps are taken to meet internationally recognized standards for the number of mental health professionals by 2028. However, given the current deficit and resource constraints, it is unlikely that India will be able to meet these targets.

Currently, the District Mental Health Programme is active in 655 districts of India (National Human Rights Commission 2019). The District Mental Health Programme is expected to have one psychiatrist, medical practitioner, clinical psychologist, psychiatric nurse and social worker in each district to provide mental healthcare treatment and support. However, many States in India (especially lesser developed states) do not have enough qualified psychiatrists to cover all districts in the State. In fact, many States such as Chhattisgarh and Jharkhand are offering significantly high salaries to psychiatrists and psychologists to work in more challenged districts. However, most of these positions are currently unfilled as there is very little interest among psychiatrists to work in these areas.

This situation begets several questions: How can the mental health system bridge the existing deficit of mental health professionals? Is increasing the number of specialized mental health professionals the only solution to ensuring access to mental healthcare and treatment? Further, is it desirable to focus on expanding a specialized workforce that focuses more on curative services rather than preventive services? In our opinion, some of these questions can be addressed through three different approaches:

1. The first approach is to broaden the ambit of preventive care through services which are available in the community. This involves leveraging existing social capital in the community for providing basic mental healthcare and support, especially in cases which do not require specialized mental health professionals. This essentially involves training community volunteers as front-line mental health service providers to provide lay counselling services and psychosocial support to persons experiencing distress. Additionally, they should be trained to identify mental health problems which require specialized support and make referrals to the formal healthcare system. A sustainable model for recruiting volunteers would involve leveraging self-help groups, cooperative societies, farmers groups and other youth groups who have a certain standing and outreach in the community. An example of such an approach is the Atmiyata programme being implemented by the Centre for Mental Health Law and Policy, Indian Law Society (Shields-Zeeman et al. 2017). This programme is currently being scaled up in over 500 villages in Mehsana District, State of Gujarat. The programme involves training community volunteers as lay counsellors to provide lay counselling to persons in distress. The community volunteers are also trained to provide support to facilitate access to social benefits. The volunteers are trained over a period of one month in different aspects of counselling such as identifying mental health problems, active listening, behavioural activation, problem-solving and making referrals. The programme has been implemented as a step-wedged randomized control trial and has shown positive results.
2. The second approach is to leverage the public healthcare system which consists of a cadre of over 900,000 community health workers also known as ASHA workers (accredited social health activists) across India (Ministry of Health and Family Welfare 2017). ASHA workers are usually women between the ages of 25 and 45 years and have completed 10th grade schooling (Ministry of Health and Family Welfare 2019c). They act as the interface or first point of contact between the community and public health system and are trained to provide basic health diagnostic services, facilitating immunizations, pre- and post-natal services, and family planning counselling. ASHA workers can be trained in identifying mental health problems, providing psychosocial support and making referrals (Ministry of Health and Family Welfare 2019c). An example of this approach is the ESSENCE (Enabling Translation of Science to Service to Enhance Depression

Care) hub which is testing the effectiveness and cost-effectiveness of digital compared with face-to-face training interventions on the competence of ASHA workers to deliver a brief psychological treatment for depression in primary care (National Institute of Mental Health 2019). However, it is important to point out that ASHA workers are extremely burdened with multiple responsibilities within existing healthcare schemes and programmes. While it may be beneficial to train them in providing preventive services, it is crucial that they are adequately incentivized and not burdened with high targets.

3. The third crucial approach is to train existing healthcare practitioners such as medical practitioners to provide psychiatric treatment and support. This training may be provided either face-to-face or by distance learning through certificate or diploma programmes. The National Institute of Mental Health and Neuro-Sciences (NIMHANS) Digital ECHO programme has proven quite effective in training medical practitioners and other health professionals through blended learning modules (face-to-face and digital) especially in lesser developed states such as Bihar and Chhattisgarh (Mehrotra et al. 2018; Sagi et al. 2018). This must be pursued in parallel with efforts to increase the number of post-graduate courses in psychiatry, psychiatric nursing and social work within the higher education system to train a larger number of mental health professionals each year. Currently, there are 761 post-graduate seats and 84 diploma seats for psychiatry in India which need to be increased in the coming years to meet the deficit of mental health professionals (National Human Rights Commission 2019).

The implementation of the MHCA is incumbent on the availability of a well-trained and qualified workforce that provides preventive, curative and rehabilitative care through rights-based approaches. It will take several years to bridge the deficit in India's mental health system and reach internationally accepted standards as mandated by the MHCA. Meanwhile, the human resource challenge has to be addressed through creative and strategic means given existing resource constraints and systemic gaps. In our opinion, it is crucial to leverage social capital in the community and develop alternative models of peer support which can reduce the burden on the formal healthcare system and at the same time increase access to mental healthcare services and support in the community itself (Pathare et al. 2018).

## 11.5 Reflections and Conclusions

India's diversity poses significant challenges in drafting legislation that is appropriate for the entire country. Regional differences in development and the resulting human resource and health system challenges are not easy to factor in when drafting legislation. For example, Bihar in North East India (population 124 million) has social development indices closer to the least developed countries such as Sudan, while

Kerala (population 35 million) in South India has social development indices better than a few European Union member states.[8]

The National Mental Health Survey analysed the health and mental health systems of nine Indian States (Gururaj et al. 2016). Table 11.1 shows data comparing two states of Jharkhand (which neighbours Bihar and has similar social development indices) with Kerala, both with similar size of population (33 million versus 35 million). Given the wide disparities in development and availability of mental health human resources, particular provisions of mental health legislation (e.g. a person being admitted as a supported admission to a mental health facility should be examined by at least one and preferably two psychiatrists, and should have access to review by a Mental Health Review Board) can pose significant challenges to implementation, especially in resource-poor States.

There are equally huge social disparities such as caste, gender and poverty in India's mental health system. These disparities create a skewed power dynamic

**Table 11.1** Disparities in the mental health systems of two states in India

| Metric | Jharkhand state | Kerala state |
|---|---|---|
| Population (2016) | 32. 98 million | 33.40 million |
| General health workers/100,000 population | 193.87 | 994.96 |
| Districts covered by District Mental Health programme (%) | 16.67 | 100 |
| Mental Hospitals | 3 | 3 |
| Medical Colleges with psychiatry department | 1 | 7 |
| General hospitals with psychiatry department | 2 | 18 |
| Day-care centres | 4 | 43 |
| Long-stay homes | 2 | 146 |
| Sheltered workshops | 2 | 6 |
| Psychiatrists | 103 | 400 |
| Medical doctors with training in psychiatry | – | 917 |
| Clinical Psychologists | 19 | 211 |
| Nurses trained in mental health | – | 818 |
| Psychiatric social workers | 8 | 15 |
| Rehabilitation workers | 18 | 3,429 |
| Professional and paraprofessional psychosocial counsellors | 39 | 931 |

*Note*
*Table data source* Gururaj and colleagues (2016)

[8]https://www.mapmania.org/map/83384/hdi_of_indian_states_compared_to_other_countries. Accessed 12 December 2019; https://commons.wikimedia.org/wiki/File:2012_Poverty_distribution_map_in_India_by_its_states_and_union_territories.svg. Accessed 12 December 2019.

between service providers and service users and any progressive mental health legislation has to take these social disparities into account when drafting provisions of the legislation.

The CRPD provisions, while recognizing the power differentials between mental health professionals and service users, are devoid of the social, cultural and economic context in which country legislation has to necessarily operate.

There is a risk that such wide disparities could result in mental health legislation pandering to the lowest common denominator. This is highly undesirable from a human rights and clinical perspective and also represents a lost opportunity for change. It is also important to keep in mind that legislation is usually drafted not just for the present but also for a significant future duration, as frequent changes to legislation are uncommon not just in India but across the world. There was a 30-year gap between the previous Mental Health Act, 1987 and the MHCA. Legislation therefore has to presume that development and social change will reduce these social, health system and power disparities over time.

The drafters of India's new mental health legislation had the difficult task of finding a middle ground between two extremes: enacting legislation which is totally grounded in existing reality and thus codifying existing inequalities and power imbalances versus being aspirational and using the law to promote social and health system change.

Finding this balance is not easy, and it is no one's claim that the MHCA strikes the right balance between these two disparate positions, while simultaneously fulfilling India's international obligations under the CRPD. Depending on their own professional or personal perspective, commentators on the Act have criticized it either for being too conservative, rooted in existing inequalities and not meeting the CRPD obligations (Davar 2015) or, alternatively, being too aspirational, driven by CRPD compliance and therefore difficult to implement in the current circumstances across the country (Kala 2013; Rao et al. 2016).

In our opinion, many implementation challenges outlined earlier in this chapter arise not only out from an expected resistance to change customary practices but also due to reluctance to 'share' power. For example, provisions of the MHCA such as nominated representatives and advance directives challenge the power of families and mental health professionals, respectively, to unilaterally make decisions for those with mental illness. There is a need to guard against attempts to do lip service to such transformative provisions without addressing these power equations while implementing the MHCA.

It is thus incumbent upon civil society to assume a proactive role in advocating mental health as priority on the national agenda to address the systemic gaps, infrastructural deficits and human resource challenges in improving access to mental healthcare and treatment. Given these practical realities, the MHCA's mandate is mammoth and far-reaching in terms of the obligations on the Central and State Governments to ensure the right to access mental healthcare and treatment. The success of this mandate will depend entirely on how all mental health stakeholders can be motivated to actualize commitments made under this law, and, further, how proactive civil society is in compelling Governments to fulfil this mandate.

## References


Anonymous. (2017). National Food Security Act not implemented as it should be: supreme court. Economic Times. Retrieved December 12, 2019, from https://economictimes.indiatimes.com/news/politics-and-nation/national-food-security-act-not-implemented-as-it-should-be-supreme-court/articleshow/59702676.cms?from=mdr.

Anonymous. (2019). Chaining mentally ill atrocious and inhuman, says SC. Press Trust of India. Retrieved December 12, 2019, from http://www.ptinews.com/news/10286304_Chaining-mentally-ill-atrocious—inhuman–says-SC.html.

Antony, J. T. (2016). Mental health legislation: A journey back to 'madhouses era?'. *Indian Journal of Psychiatry, 58*(2), 114–118.

Bose, S., Ghosh, P., & Sardana, A. (2017). *Resource requirements for right to education (RTE): Normative and the real (No. 201)*. New Delhi: National Institute of Public Finance and Policy.

Chakravarty, S. (2019). Nominated representative and queer lives. Mariwala Health Initiative. Retrieved December 12, 2019, from http://mhi.org.in/voice/details/nominatedrep/.

Chopra, D. (2015). *Political commitment in India's social policy implementation: Shaping the performance of MGNREGA*. Manchester: Effective States and Inclusive Development Research Centre.

Davar, B. V. (2015). Legal frameworks for and against people with psychosocial disabilities. *Economic and Political Weekly, 47*, 7–8.

Garg, K., Kumar, C. N., & Chandra, P. S. (2019). Number of psychiatrists in India: Baby steps forward, but a long way to go. *Indian Journal of Psychiatry, 61*(1), 104–105.

Gupta, M., & Pushkar. (2017). Where will the political will to improve healthcare come from? The Wire. Retrieved December 12, 2019, from https://thewire.in/government/political-will-to-improve-india-healthcare.

Gururaj, G., Varghese, M., Benegal, V., Rao, G. N., Pathak, K., Singh, L. K., et al. (2016). *National Mental Health Survey of India, 2015–16: Prevalence, patterns and outcomes (NIMHANS publication no. 129)*. Bengaluru: National Institute of Mental Health and Neuro Sciences.

Insurance Regulatory and Development Authority of India. (2018). The Mental Healthcare Act, 2017 (IRDA/HLT/MISC/CIR/128/08/2018). Insurance Regulatory and Development Authority of India. Retrieved December 12, 2019, from https://www.irdai.gov.in/ADMINCMS/cms/Circulars_Layout.aspx?page=PageNo3555&flag=1.

Kala, A. (2013). Time to face new realities: Mental Healthcare Bill 2013. *Indian Journal of Psychiatry, 55*(3), 216–219.

Kapoor, A., & Pathare, S. (2018). Radicalising public mental healthcare in India. Seminar. Retrieved December 12, 2019, from http://www.india-seminar.com/2019/714/714_arjun_soumitra.htm.

Math, S. B., Basavaraju, V., Harihara, S. N., Gowda, G. S., Manjunatha, N., Kumar, C. N., et al. (2019a). Mental Healthcare Act 2017—Aspiration to action. *Indian Journal of Psychiatry, 61*(10), 660–666.

Math, S. B., Gowda, G. S., Basavaraju, V., Manjunatha, N., Kumar, C. N., Enara, A., et al. (2019b). Cost estimation for the implementation of the Mental Healthcare Act 2017. *Indian Journal of Psychiatry, 61*(10), S650–S659.

Mehrotra, K., Chand, P., Bandawar, M., Rao Sagi, M., Kaur, S., Aurobind, G., et al. (2018). Effectiveness of NIMHANS ECHO blended tele-mentoring model on integrated mental health and addiction for counsellors in rural and underserved districts of Chhattisgarh, India. *Asian Journal of Psychiatry, 36*, 123–127.

Ministry of Health and Family Welfare. (2017). Update on ASHA Programme. National Health Mission. Retrieved December 12, 2019, from http://nhsrcindia.org/sites/default/files/UpdateonASHAProgramme-January-2017.pdf.

Ministry of Health and Family Welfare. (2019a). National Health Mission. Government of India. Retrieved December 12, 2019, from https://nhm.gov.in/images/pdf/NHM/NHM_more_information.pdf.

Ministry of Health and Family Welfare. (2019b). National Health Mission. Government of India. Retrieved December 12, 2019, from https://nhm.gov.in/index4.php?lang=1&level=0&linkid=445&lid=38.

Ministry of Health and Family Welfare. (2019c). National Health Mission. About Accredited Social Health Activist (ASHA). Retrieved December 12, 2019, from https://nhm.gov.in/index1.php?lang=1&level=1&sublinkid=150&lid=226.

Nandy, D. (2019). Underfunding, misleading claims: the story of MGNREGA in New India. Down To Earth. Retrieved December 12, 2019, from https://www.downtoearth.org.in/blog/economy/underfunding-misleading-claims-the-story-of-mgnrega-in-new-india-65627.

National Human Rights Commission. (2019). *Minutes of National Level Review Meeting on Mental Health*. Delhi: National Human Rights Commission.

National Institute of Mental Health. (2019). Enabling translation of science to service to enhance depression care (ESSENCE). National Institute of Mental Health. Retrieved December 12, 2019, from https://www.nimh.nih.gov/about/organization/cgmhr/scaleuphubs/enabling-translation-of-science-to-service-to-enhance-depression-care-essence.shtml.

Oxfam India. (2018). Four reasons why the Forest Rights Act fails to empower forest-dwelling communities. Oxfam India. Retrieved December 12, 2019, from https://www.oxfamindia.org/blog/forest-rights-act.

Patel, V. (2003). Domestic violence, mental health of women and medical ethics. *Indian Journal of Medical Ethics, 11*, 13–14.

Pathare, S., Kalha, J., & Krishnamoorthy, S. (2018). Peer support for mental illness in India: An underutilised resource. *Epidemiology and Psychiatric Sciences, 27*(5), 415–419.

Rao, G. P., Math, S. B., Raju, M. S., Saha, G., Jagiwala, M., Sagar, R., et al. (2016). Mental Health Care Bill, 2016: A boon or bane? *Indian journal of Psychiatry, 58*(3), 244–249.

Sagi, M. R., Aurobind, G., Chand, P., Ashfak, A., Karthick, C., Kubenthiran, N., et al. (2018). Innovative telementoring for addiction management for remote primary care physicians: A feasibility study. *Indian Journal of Psychiatry, 60*(4), 461–466.

Sahoo, N. (2016). An examination of India's federal system and its impact on healthcare. Observer Research Foundation. Retrieved December 12, 2019, from https://www.orfonline.org/research/indias-federal-impact-on-healthcare/.

Sharma, P. (2019). Delhi HC issues notice to AAP government on enforcement of mental healthcare law. Live Mint. Retrieved December 12, 2019, from https://www.livemint.com/news/india/delhi-hc-issues-notice-to-aap-government-on-enforcement-of-mental-healthcare-law-1561981283071.html.

Shields-Zeeman, L., Pathare, S., Walters, B. H., Kapadia-Kundu, N., & Joag, K. (2017). Promoting wellbeing and improving access to mental health care through community champions in rural India: The *Atmiyata* intervention approach. *International Journal of Mental Health Systems, 11*, 6.

Special Correspondent. (2019). HC seeks status report on mental health care law. The Hindu. Retrieved December 12, 2019, from https://www.thehindu.com/news/cities/bangalore/hc-seeks-status-report-on-mental-health-care-law/article26749067.ece.

United Nations Committee on the Rights of Persons with Disabilities. (2014). *General comment No. 1: Article 12: Equal recognition before the law*. New York: United Nations. Retrieved July 25, 2019, from http://www.ohchr.org/EN/HRBodies/CRPD/Pages/GC.aspx.

# Index




R. M. Duffy and B. D. Kelly, *India's Mental Healthcare Act, 2017*,
https://doi.org/10.1007/978-981-15-5009-6

The manufacturer's authorised representative in the EU is Springer Nature Customer Service Centre GmbH, Europaplatz 3, 69115 Heidelberg, Germany. If you have any concerns regarding our products, please contact ProductSafety@springernature.com

Printed and bound by CPI Group (UK) Ltd, Croydon, CR0 4YY

05/10/2026

02228121-0015